THE SYMBOLISM
OF EVIL

PAUL RICOEUR

Translated from the French by
Emerson Buchanan

BEACON PRESS : BOSTON

PUBLISHER'S NOTE

This Beacon paperback edition reprints Volume XVII
of the Religious Perspectives Series
which is planned and edited by Ruth Nanda Anshen
Dr. Anshen's Epilogue to this reprint appears on page 358

Contents

PART I

PART II

THE "MYTHS" OF THE BEGINNING AND OF THE END

CONTENTS

Part One

The Primary Symbols:
Defilement, Sin, Guilt

Introduction:
Phenomenology
of "Confession"

1. Speculation, Myth, and Symbol

HOW SHALL WE MAKE the transition from the possibility of evil in man to its reality, from fallibility to fault?*

We will try to surprise the transition in the act by "re-enacting" in ourselves the confession that the religious consciousness makes of it.

Of course, this sympathetic re-enactment in imagination cannot take the place of a philosophy of fault. It will still remain to be seen what the philosopher makes of it—that is to say, how he incorporates it into the discourse on man begun in the first volume of this work under the influence of the dialectic of the finite and the infinite. This final development will occupy the third volume. We cannot yet anticipate the direction it will take, since we do not yet know the new situation from which philosophy will have to take its bearings.[1]

But if the "re-enactment" of the confession of the evil in man by the religious consciousness does not take the place of philosophy,

* The present volume is the second in the author's *Finitude and Guilt.* The first volume has been translated under the title: *Fallible Man* (H. Regnery, 1966).—TR.

[1] See the concluding chapter, "The Symbol Gives Rise to Thought."

3

nevertheless that confession lies within the sphere of interest of philosophy, for it is an utterance, an utterance of man about himself; and every utterance can and must be taken up into the element of philosophic discourse. We shall indicate presently the philosophic locus, so to speak, of this "re-enactment," which is no longer religious experience and which is not yet philosophy. But let us indicate first what is *said* in the utterance that we have called the confession of the evil in man by the religious consciousness.

It seems tempting, at first, to begin with the most elaborate, the most rationalized expressions of that confession, in the hope that those expressions will be closest to the language of philosophy in virtue of their "explanatory" character. Thus, one will be inclined to think that it is against the late constructions of the Augustinian epoch concerning *original sin* that philosophy is challenged to measure itself. Many philosophies, classical and modern, take this supposed concept as a religious and theological datum and reduce the philosophical problem of fault to a critique of the idea of original sin.

Nothing is less amenable to a direct confrontation with philosophy than the concept of original sin, for nothing is more deceptive than its appearance of rationality. On the contrary, it is to the least elaborate, the most inarticulate expressions of the confession of evil that philosophic reason must listen. Therefore we must proceed regressively and revert from the "speculative" expressions to the "spontaneous" ones. In particular, it is essential to be convinced from the start that the concept of original sin is not at the beginning but at the end of a cycle of living experience, the Christian experience of sin. Moreover, the interpretation that it gives of this experience is only one of the possible rationalizations of the root of evil according to Christianity. Finally and above all, this rationalization, which is embalmed by tradition and has become the cornerstone of Christian anthropology, belongs to a period of thought marked by gnostic pretensions to "know" the mysteries of God and human destiny. Not that original sin is a gnostic concept; on the contrary, it is an anti-gnostic concept. But it belongs to the age of gnosis in the sense that it tries to rationalize the Christian experience of radical evil in the same way as gnosis set up as "knowledge" its pseudo-philosophic interpretation of primordial dualism, of the fall of Sophia, and of every other entity prior to man. It is this contamination by pseudo-philosophy that, in the last resort, forbids us to start with the most rationalized notions of confession.

To what does speculation refer us? To living experience? Not yet. Behind speculation, and beneath gnosis and anti-gnostic constructions, we find *myths*. Myth will here be taken to mean what the history of religions now finds in it: not a false explanation by means of images and fables, but a traditional narration which relates to events that happened at the beginning of time and which has the purpose of providing grounds for the ritual actions of men of today and, in a general manner, establishing all the forms of action and thought by which man understands himself in his world. For us, moderns, a myth is *only* a myth because we can no longer connect that time with the time of history as we write it, employing the critical method, nor can we connect mythical places with our geographical space. This is why the myth can no longer be an explanation; to exclude its etiological intention is the theme of all necessary demythologization. But in losing its explanatory pretensions the myth reveals its exploratory significance and its contribution to understanding, which we shall later call its symbolic function—that is to say, its power of discovering and revealing the bond between man and what he considers sacred. Paradoxical as it may seem, the myth, when it is thus demythologized through contact with scientific history and elevated to the dignity of a symbol, is a dimension of modern thought.

But what is it that is thus explored, discovered, revealed? We shall not pretend to give in this book a total theory of myths; our contribution to the problem will be strictly limited to the myths that speak of the beginning and the end of evil. We hope that this limitation of our investigation will be repaid by a more rigorous understanding of the function of myths in relation to what we have just called, in terms intentionally vague, the bond between man and what he considers sacred. Evil—defilement or sin—is the sensitive point and, as it were, the "crisis" of this bond which myth makes explicit in its own way. By limiting ourselves to myths concerning the origin and the end, we have a chance of attaining an intensive rather than an extensive understanding of myth. It is, in fact, because evil is supremely the crucial experience of the sacred that the threat of the dissolution of the bond between man and the sacred makes us most intensely aware of man's dependence on the powers of the sacred. Therefore the myth of "crisis" is at the same time the myth of "totality": in recounting how these things began and how they will end, the myth places the experience of man in a whole that receives orientation and meaning from the narration. Thus, an understanding of human reality as a whole operates through the myth by means of a reminiscence and an expectation.[2]

Shall we begin, then, with an interpretation of the myths about the origin and the end of evil? Not yet. The stratum of myths, to which we are referred by pseudo-rational speculation, refers us in its turn back to an experience lying at a lower level than any narration or any gnosis. Thus, the account of the fall in the Bible, even if it comes from traditions older than the preaching of the prophets of Israel, gets its meaning only from an experience of sin which is itself an attainment of Jewish piety. It is the "confession of sins" in the cult and the prophetic appeal for "justice and righteousness" that furnish the myth with a substructure of meaning.

Thus, speculation on original sin sends us back to the myth of the fall, and this, in its turn, sends us back to the confession of sins. The myth of the fall is so far from being the cornerstone of the Judeo-Christian conception of sin that the figure of Adam, placed by the myth at the origin of the history of human evil, remained a mute figure for practically all of the writers of the Old Testament. Abraham, the father of believers, the founder-ancestor of the elect people, and Noah, the father of post-diluvian humanity, produced more of an echo in the Biblical theology of history than the figure of Adam, which remained in a state of suspended animation, so to speak, until St. Paul revived it by making it parallel to the second Adam, Jesus Christ. At the same time, the "event" of the Christ transformed the fall of Adam retroactively into a similar "event"; the historicity of the second Adam, by reflection, conferred upon the first Adam a comparable historicity and an individuality cor-

[2] For the theory of myths, see the Introduction to Part II.

responding to the Christ's. The demythologization of the story of the fall was made more urgent by this retroactive action of Paulinian Christology on the Adamic symbol.

Now this dimension of the symbol can only be recovered by the "re-enactment" of the experience made explicit by the myth. It is, then, to this experience that we must try to penetrate.

But is this re-enactment possible? Does not the mediative role that we have granted to speculation and myth condemn in advance the attempt to restore the pre-mythical and pre-speculative foundation? The venture would be hopeless if, lower than gnosis and myth, there were no longer any language. But this is not the case; there is the language of *confession,* which in the languages of myth and speculation is raised to the second and third degrees.

This language of confession is the counterpart of the triple character of the experience it brings to light: blindness, equivocalness, scandalousness.

The experience of which the penitent makes confession is a blind experience, still embedded in the matrix of emotion, fear, anguish. It is this emotional note that gives rise to objectification in discourse; the confession expresses, pushes to the outside, the emotion which without it would be shut up in itself, as an impression in the soul. Language is the light of the emotions. Through confession the consciousness of fault is brought into the light of speech; through confession man remains speech, even in the experience of his own absurdity, suffering, and anguish.

Moreover, this experience is complex. Instead of the simple experience that one might expect, the confession of sins reveals several layers of experience. "Guilt," in the precise sense of a feeling of the unworthiness at the core of one's personal being, is only the advanced point of a radically individualized and interiorized experience. This feeling of guilt points to a more fundamental experience, the experience of "sin," which includes *all* men and indicates the *real* situation of man before God, whether man knows it or not. It is this sin of which the myth of the fall recounts the entry into the world and which speculation on original sin attempts to erect into a doctrine. But sin, in its turn, is a correction and even a revolution with respect to a more archaic conception of fault—

the notion of "defilement" conceived in the guise of a strain or blemish that infects from without. Guilt, sin, and defilement thus constitute a primitive diversity in experience. Hence, the feeling involved is not only blind in virtue of being emotional; it is also equivocal, laden with a multiplicity of meanings. This is why language is needed a second time to elucidate the subterranean crises of the consciousness of fault.

Finally, the experience of which the believer makes avowal in the confession of sins creates a language for itself by its very strangeness; the experience of being oneself but alienated from oneself gets transcribed immediately on the plane of language in the mode of interrogation. Sin, as alienation from oneself, is an experience even more astonishing, disconcerting, and scandalous, perhaps, than the spectacle of nature, and for this reason it is the richest source of interrogative thought. In the oldest Babylonian psalters the believer asks: "How long, O Lord? What god have I sinned against? What sin have I committed?" Sin makes me incomprehensible to myself: God is hidden; the course of things no longer has meaning. It is in line with this questioning and for the purpose of warding off the threat of meaninglessness that the myth relates "how that began," and that gnosis elaborates the famous question: πόθεν τὰ κακά?—Whence come evils?—and mobilizes all its resources for explanation. Sin is perhaps the most important of the occasions for questioning, but also for reasoning incorrectly by giving premature answers. But just as the transcendental illusion, according to Kant, testifies by its very perplexities that reason is the faculty of the unconditioned, so the unseasonable answers of gnosis and of the etiological myths testify that man's most moving experience, that of being lost as a sinner, communicates with the need to understand and excites attention by its very character as a scandal.

By this threefold route man's living experience of fault gives itself a language: a language that expresses it in spite of its blind character; a language that makes explicit its contradictions and its internal revolutions; a language, finally, that reveals the experience of alienation as astonishing.

Now, the Hebraic and Hellenic literatures give evidence of a linguistic inventiveness that marks the existential eruptions of this consciousness of fault. It is by discovering the motivations of those linguistic inventions that we re-enact the passage from defilement to sin and guilt. Thus, the Hebrew and Greek words that express the consciousness of fault have a sort of wisdom of their own which we must make explicit and take as our guide in the labyrinth of living experience. We are not, therefore, reduced to the ineffable when we try to dig beneath the myths of evil; we still come up with a language.

Moreover, the merely semantic understanding that we can acquire from the vocabulary of fault is an exercise preparatory to the hermeneutics of myths. Indeed, it is itself already a hermeneutics, for *the most primitive and least mythical language is already a symbolic language:* defilement is spoken of under the symbol of a stain or blemish, sin under the symbol of missing the mark, of a tortuous road, of trespass, etc. In short, the preferred language of fault appears to be indirect and based on imagery. There is something quite astonishing in this: the consciousness of self seems to constitute itself at its lowest level by means of symbolism and to work out an abstract language only subsequently, by means of a spontaneous hermeneutics of its primary symbols. We shall see later the extensive implications of this assertion. For the moment it is enough to have established that the "re-enactment" in sympathetic imagination always moves in the element of language as reflection reverts from gnosis to myth and from myth to the primary symbolic expressions brought into play in the confession of fault. This reversion to the primary symbols permits us henceforth to consider myths and gnosis as secondary and tertiary symbols, the interpretation of which rests on the interpretation of the primary symbols.

We must therefore take as a whole the elementary language of confession, the developed language of myths, and the elaborated language of gnosis and counter-gnosis. Speculation is not autonomous and myths themselves are secondary; but neither is there any immediate consciousness of fault that can do without the secondary and tertiary elaborations. It is the whole circle, made up of confession, myth, and speculation, that we must understand.

If, then, we begin with the interpretation of living experience, we must not lose sight of the fact that that experience is abstract, in spite of its lifelike appearance; it is abstract because it is separated from the totality of meaning from which we detach it for didactic purposes. We must not forget, either, that this experience is never immediate; it can be expressed only by means of the primary symbolisms that prepare the way for its treatment in myths and speculation.[3]

2. CRITERIOLOGY OF SYMBOLS

Confession, we have said, always manifests itself in the element of language. Now, that language is essentially symbolic. Hence a philosophy that is concerned to integrate confession with the consciousness of self cannot escape the task of elaborating, at least in outline, a criteriology of symbols.

Before proceeding to a direct intentional analysis of symbolism, we must determine the extent and the variety of its zones of emergence. One cannot, in fact, understand the reflective use of symbolism—as one sees, for example, in the examination of conscience of the penitent of Babylonia or Israel—without reverting to its naïve forms, where the prerogatives of reflective consciousness are subordinated to the cosmic aspect of hierophanies, to the nocturnal aspect of dream productions, or finally to the creativity of the poetic word. These three dimensions of symbolism—cosmic, oneiric, and poetic—are present in every authentic symbol. The reflective aspect of symbols, which we shall examine further on (defilement, deviation, straying, exile, weight of fault, etc.), is intelligible only if it is connected with these three functions of symbols.

Man first reads the sacred *on* the world, *on* some elements or aspects of the world, on the heavens, on the sun and moon, on the waters and vegetation. Spoken symbolism thus refers back to manifestations of the sacred, to hierophanies, where the sacred is shown

[3] This second volume does not push reflection beyond myths; the elaboration of speculative symbols will be the object of the third volume. It appears, in fact, that the immediate debate of gnosis is with philosophy, and so it is in the framework of a *philosophy* of fault that gnosis must be examined.

in a fragment of the cosmos, which, in return, loses its concrete limits, gets charged with innumerable meanings, integrates and unifies the greatest possible number of the sectors of anthropocosmic experience.[4] First of all, then, it is the sun, the moon, the waters—that is to say, cosmic realities—that are symbols. Shall we say, therefore, that symbols, in their cosmic aspect, are anterior to language, or even foreign to it? Not at all. For these realities to be a symbol is to gather together at one point a mass of significations which, before giving rise to thought, give rise to speech. The symbolic *manifestation* as a *thing* is a matrix of symbolic meanings as words. We have never ceased to find meanings in the sky (to take the first example on which Eliade practices his comparative phenomenology). It is the same thing to say that the sky *manifests* the sacred and to say that it *signifies* the most high, the elevated and the immense, the powerful and the orderly, the clairvoyant and the wise, the sovereign, the immutable. The manifestation through the thing is like the condensation of an infinite discourse; manifestation and meaning are strictly contemporaneous and reciprocal; the concretion in the thing is the counterpart of the surcharge of inexhaustible meaning which has ramifications in the cosmic, in the ethical, and in the political. Thus, the symbol-thing is the potentiality of innumerable spoken symbols which, on the other hand, are knotted together in a single cosmic manifestation.

Hence, although we shall deal only with spoken symbols and, indeed, only symbols of the self, we must never forget that these symbols, which will appear to us as primary in comparison with the elaborated and intellectualized formations of the consciousness of self, are already on the way to cutting themselves loose from the cosmic roots of symbolism. The movement that we shall follow from the symbolism of defilement to the symbolism of sin, and then to the symbolism of guilt properly so-called, is at the same time a progressive movement away from the cosmic ground of symbolism. The symbolism of defilement is still immersed in the cosmic; the subterranean equivalences and correspondences between the defiled, the consecrated, and the sacred are perhaps ineffaceable. It is the hierophanies, as a sphere of reality, that first engender the "onto-

[4] Eliade, *Traité d'Histoire des Religions* (Paris, 1949), p. 385.

logical regime"[5] characteristic of the defiled; the peril of the soul which defilement will later serve to symbolize is at first peril in the presence of *things* which are forbidden to profane experience and which cannot be approached without risk when one is not ritually prepared. Taboo is nothing else than this condition of objects, actions, or persons that are "isolated" or "forbidden" because of the danger involved in contact with them (*ibid.*). It is because the symbolism of defilement still clings by its manifold root hairs to the cosmic sacralizations, because defilement adheres to everything unusual, everything terrifying in the world, attractive and repellent at the same time, that this symbolism is ultimately inexhaustible and ineradicable. As we shall see, the more historical and less cosmic symbolism of sin and guilt makes up for the poverty and abstractness of its imagery only by a series of revivals and transpositions of the more archaic, but more highly surcharged, symbolism of defilement. The richness of the symbolism of defilement, even when this symbolism is fully interiorized, is the corollary of its cosmic roots.

These cosmic resonances, reaching even into reflective consciousness, are less surprising if the second dimension of symbolism is taken into consideration—the oneiric dimension. It is in dreams that one can catch sight of the most fundamental and stable symbolisms of humanity passing from the "cosmic" function to the "psychic" function. We should not be able to comprehend how symbols can signify the bond between the being of man and total being if we opposed to one another the hierophanies described by the phenomenology of religion and the dream productions described by Freudian and Jungian psychoanalysis (at least those which, by Freud's own admission, go beyond the projections of individual history and plunge beneath the private archeology of a subject into the common representations of a culture, or into the folklore of humanity as a whole). To manifest the "sacred" *on* the "cosmos" and to manifest it *in* the "psyche" are the same thing.

Perhaps we ought even to refuse to choose between the interpretation that makes these symbols the disguised expression of the

[5] Eliade, *op. cit.*, p. 27.

infantile and instinctual part of the psychism and the interpretation that finds in them the anticipation of our possibilities of evolution and maturation. Later we shall have to explore an interpretation according to which "regression" is a roundabout way of "progression" and of the exploration of our potentialities.[6] For that we shall have to penetrate beyond the Freudian metapsychology of levels (ego, id, super-ego) and the Jungian metapsychology (energism and archetypes) and let ourselves be instructed directly by Freudian therapeutics and Jungian therapeutics, which, no doubt, are addressed to different types of patients. Re-immersion in *our* archaism is no doubt the roundabout way by which we immerse ourselves in the archaism of humanity, and this double "regression" is possibly, in its turn, the way to a discovery, a prospection, and a prophecy concerning ourselves.

It is this function of symbols as surveyor's staff and guide for "becoming oneself" that must be united with and not opposed to the "cosmic" function of symbols as it is expressed in the hierophanies described by the phenomenology of religion. Cosmos and Psyche are the two poles of the same "expressivity"; I express myself in expressing the world; I explore my own sacrality in deciphering that of the world.

Now, this double "expressivity"—cosmic and psychic—has its complement in a third modality of symbols: poetic imagination. But, to understand it properly, it is necessary firmly to distinguish imagination from image, if by image is understood a function of absence, the annulment of the real in an imaginary unreal. This image-representation, conceived on the model of a portrait of the absent, is still too dependent on the thing that it makes unreal; it remains a process for *making present* to oneself the things of the world. A poetic image is much closer to a word than to a portrait. As M. Bachelard excellently says, it "puts us at the origin of the speaking being"; "it becomes a new being of our language, it expresses us in making us that which it expresses." Unlike the two other modalities of symbols, hierophanic and oneiric, the poetic

---

[6] Heinz Hartmann, *Ego Psychology and the Problem of Adaptation* (1939), in David Rapaport, *Organization and Pathology of Thought* (Columbia University Press, 1951).

symbol shows us expressivity in its nascent state. In poetry the symbol is caught at the moment when it is a welling up of language, "when it puts language in a state of emergence,"[7] instead of being regarded in its hieratic stability under the protection of rites and myths, as in the history of religions, or instead of being deciphered through the resurgences of a suppressed infancy.

It should be understood that there are not three unconnected forms of symbols. The structure of the poetic image is also the structure of the dream when the latter extracts from the fragments of our past a prophecy of our future, and the structure of the hierophanies that make the sacred manifest in the sky and in the waters, in vegetation and in stones.

Can we arrive at this one structure by a direct eidetic analysis, which would account for this remarkable convergence of religious symbolism, oneiric symbolism, and poetic symbolism? It is possible, up to a certain point, to reveal the unifying principle of the preceding enumeration by an intentional analysis. But, like all eidetic reflection, this intentional analysis consists solely in *distinguishing* a symbol from what is not a symbol, and thus directing attention to the more or less intuitive grasp of an identical nucleus of meaning.

We will proceed, then, by a series of increasingly close approximations to the essence of a symbol.

1. That symbols are signs is certain: they are expressions that communicate a meaning; this meaning is declared in an intention of signifying which has speech as its vehicle. Even when the symbols are elements of the universe (sky, water, moon) or things (tree, stone set up), it is still in the universe of discourse that these realities take on a symbolic dimension (words of consecration or invocation, mythical utterances). As Dumézil very well says: "It is under the sign of *logos* and not under that of *mana* that research [in the history of religions] takes its stand today."[8]

Similarly, dreams, although they are nocturnal spectacles, are originally close to words, since they can be told, communicated.

[7] G. Bachelard, *La Poétique de l'Espace* (Paris, 1957).
[8] Preface to Eliade, *Traité d'Histoire des Religions*.

Finally, it has been seen that poetic images themselves are essentially words.

2. But to say that the symbol is a sign is to draw too large a circle, which must now be made smaller. Every sign aims at something beyond itself and stands for that something; but not every sign is a symbol. We shall say that the symbol conceals in its aim a double intentionality. Take the "defiled," the "impure." This significant expression presents a first or literal intentionality that, like every significant expression, supposes the triumph of the conventional sign over the natural sign. Thus, the literal meaning of "defilement" is "stain," but this literal meaning is already a conventional sign; the words "stain," "unclean," etc., do not resemble the thing signified. But upon this first intentionality there is erected a second intentionality which, through the physically "unclean," points to a certain situation of man in the sacred which is precisely that of being defiled, impure. The literal and manifest sense, then, points beyond itself to something that is *like* a stain or spot. Thus, contrary to perfectly transparent technical signs, which say only what they want to say in positing that which they signify, symbolic signs are opaque, because the first, literal, obvious meaning itself points analogically to a second meaning which is not given otherwise than in it (we shall return to this point in order to distinguish symbol from allegory). This opacity constitutes the depth of the symbol, which, it will be said, is inexhaustible.

3. But let us correctly understand the analogical bond between the literal meaning and the symbolic meaning. While analogy is inconclusive reasoning that proceeds by fourth proportional—A is to B as C is to D—in the symbol, I cannot objectify the analogical relation that connects the second meaning with the first. It is by living in the first meaning that I am led by it beyond itself; the symbolic meaning is constituted in and by the literal meaning which effects the analogy in giving the analogue. Maurice Blondel said: "Analogies are based less on notional resemblances (*similitudines*) than on an interior stimulation, on an assimilative solicitation (*intentio ad assimilationem*)."[9] In fact, unlike a comparison that

---

[9] Maurice Blondel, *L'Être et les Êtres,* pp. 225–26, quoted in Lalande, *Vocabulaire philosophique,* art. "Analogie."

we *consider* from outside, the symbol is the movement of the primary meaning which makes us participate in the latent meaning and thus assimilates us to that which is symbolized without our being able to master the similitude intellectually. It is in this sense that the symbol is donative; it is donative because it is a primary intentionality that gives the second meaning analogically.

4. The distinction between symbol and allegory is an extension of our remarks on the analogy effected by the literal meaning itself. M. Pepin[10] has elucidated this problem very well: in an allegory what is primarily signified—that is to say, the literal meaning—is contingent, and what is signified secondarily, the symbolic meaning itself, is external enough to be directly accessible. Hence, there is a relation of translation between the two meanings; once the translation is made, the henceforth useless allegory can be dropped. Now the specific character of the symbol as opposed to the allegory has been brought to light slowly and with difficulty. Historically, allegory has been less a literary and rhetorical procedure of artificial construction of pseudo-symbols than a mode of treating myths as allegories. Such is the case with the Stoic interpretation of the myths of Homer and Hesiod, which consists in treating the myths as a disguised philosophy. To interpret is then to penetrate the disguise and thereby to render it useless. In other words, allegory has been a modality of hermeneutics much more than a spontaneous creation of signs. It would be better, therefore, to speak of allegorizing interpretation rather than of allegory. Symbol and allegory, then, are not on the same footing: symbols precede hermeneutics; allegories are already hermeneutic. This is so because the symbol presents its meaning transparently in an entirely different way than by translation. One would say rather that it evokes its meaning or suggests it, in the sense of the Greek αἰνίττεσθαι (from which the word "enigma" comes). It presents its meaning in the opaque transparency of an enigma and not by translation. Hence, I oppose the *donation of meaning in trans-parency* in symbols to the interpretation by *trans-lation* of allegories.

5. Is it necessary to say that the sort of symbol which will be in

[10] *Mythe et allégorie* (Paris, 1958).

question here has nothing to do with that which symbolic logic calls by the same name? Indeed, it is the inverse of it. But it is not enough to say so; one must know why. For symbolic logic, symbolism is the acme of formalism. Formal logic, in the theory of the syllogism, had already replaced "terms" by signs standing for anything whatever; but the relations—for example, the expressions "all," "some," "is," "implies"—had not been cut loose from the ordinary linguistic expressions. In symbolic logic these expressions are themselves replaced by letters, or written signs, which need no longer be spoken and by means of which it is possible to calculate without asking oneself how they are incorporated in a deontology of reasoning.[11] These, then, are no longer abbreviations of familiar verbal expressions, but "characters" in the Leibnizian sense of the word— that is to say, elements of a calculus. It is clear that the kind of symbol with which we are concerned here is the contrary of a character. Not only does it belong to a kind of thinking that is bound to its contents, and therefore not formalized, but the intimate bond between its first and second intentions and the impossibility of presenting the symbolic meaning to oneself otherwise than by the actual operation of analogy make of the symbolic language a language essentially *bound,* bound to its content and, through its primary content, to its secondary content. In this sense, it is the absolute inverse of an absolute formalism. One might be astonished that the symbol has two such rigorously inverse uses. Perhaps the reason should be sought in the structure of signification, which is at once a function of absence and a function of presence: a function of absence because to signify is to signify "vacuously," it is to say things without the things, in substituted signs; a function of presence because to signify is to signify "something" and finally the world.[12] Signification, by its very structure, makes possible at the same time both total formalization—that is to say, the reduction of signs to

[11] R. Blanché, *Introduction à la logique contemporaine* (Paris, 1957); D. Dubarle, *Initiation à la Logique* (Paris, 1957).

[12] On the relation, within signification, between a designation, void of meaning, and reference to an object about which one says something, cf. Husserl, *Logische Untersuchungen,* II, First Investigation, "Expression and Signification," §§ 12–14.

"characters" and finally to elements of a calculus—*and* the restoration of a full language, heavy with implicit intentionalities and analogical references to something else, which it presents enigmatically.

6. Last criterion: how to distinguish myth and symbol? It is relatively easy to contrast myth and allegory, but much less easy to distinguish clearly between myth and symbol. Sometimes it seems that symbols are a manner of taking myths in a non-allegorical way. Thus, symbol and allegory would be intentional attitudes or dispositions of hermeneutics; and the symbolic and allegorical interpretations would then be two directions of interpretation bearing on the same mythical content. Contrarily to this interpretation, I shall always understand by symbol, in a much more primitive sense, analogical meanings which are spontaneously formed and immediately significant, such as defilement, analogue of stain; sin, analogue of deviation; guilt, analogue of accusation. These symbols are on the same level as, for example, the meaning of water as threat and as renewal in the flood and in baptism, and finally on the same level as the most primitive hierophanies. In this sense, symbols are more radical than myths. I shall regard myths as a species of symbols, as symbols developed in the form of narrations and articulated in a time and a space that cannot be co-ordinated with the time and space of history and geography according to the critical method. For example, exile is a primary symbol of human alienation, but the history of the expulsion of Adam and Eve from Paradise is a mythical narration of the second degree, bringing into play fabulous personages, places, times, and episodes. Exile is a primary symbol and not a myth, because it is a historical event made to signify human alienation analogically; but the same alienation creates for itself a fanciful history, the exile from Eden, which, as history that happened *in illo tempore,* is myth. It will be seen that this thickness of the narrative is essential to myth, without counting the attempt at explanation which, in etiological myths, accentuates their secondary character. I will return to this problem at the beginning of the second part of this study of the symbolism of evil.

3. The Philosophical "Re-enactment" of Confession

This re-enactment of confession, carried out at all its levels of symbolization,—what is it for philosophy? To resume the question left hanging, what is its philosophical locus?

What we are now seeking is not yet the philosophy of fault; it can only be a propaedeutic. Myth is already logos, but it has still to be taken up into *philosophic* discourse. This propaedeutic remains at the level of a purely descriptive phenomenology that permits the believing soul to speak. The philosopher adopts provisionally the motivations and intentions of the believing soul. He does not "feel" them in their first naïveté; he "re-feels" them in a neutralized mode, in the mode of "as if." It is in this sense that phenomenology is a re-enactment in sympathetic imagination. But this phenomenology falls short of reflection in the full sense, such as we pursued in the first part up to the concept of fallibility. The problem remains: how to integrate this re-enactment in sympathetic imagination into reflection? How give reflection a new start by means of a symbolics of liberty in bondage?

We are not in a position to answer this question, which will find its solution in the course of the third part of this work. Nevertheless, we shall set forth the principle of this solution at the end of this volume under the heading of an excellent maxim: *symbols give rise to thought.* We shall say then why it is necessary to renounce the chimera of a philosophy without presuppositions and begin from a *full* language. But we can say now, in a spirit of truthfulness, what constitutes our principal methodological bondage.

By beginning with a symbolism already there we give ourselves something to think about; but at the same time we introduce a radical contingency into our discourse. First *there are* symbols; I encounter them, I find them; they are like the innate ideas of the old philosophy. Why are they such? Why are they? This is cultural contingency, introduced into discourse. Moreover, I do not know them all; my field of investigation is oriented, and because it is oriented it is limited. By what is it oriented? Not only by my own situation in the universe of symbols, but, paradoxically, by the historical, geographical, cultural origin of the philosophical question itself.

Our philosophy is Greek by birth. Its intention and its pretension of universality are "situated." The philosopher does not speak from nowhere, but from the depths of his Greek memory, from which rises the question: τί τὸ ὄν? what is being? This question, which sounds the Greek note at the outset, embraces all later questions, including those of existence and reason, and consequently those of finitude and fault. The fact that the Greek question is situated at the beginning orients the human space of religions which is open to philosophical investigation.

Not that any culture is excluded in principle; but in this area oriented by the originally Greek question, there are relations of "proximity" and "distance" that belong inescapably to the structure of our cultural memory. Hence the privilege of "proximity" of the Greek and Jewish cultures; these two cultures, which would contain nothing exceptional for an eye not situated anywhere in particular, constitute the first stratum of our philosophical memory. More precisely, the *encounter* of the Jewish source with the Greek origin is the fundamental intersection that founds our culture. The Jewish source is the first "other" of philosophy, its "nearest" other; the abstractly contingent fact of that encounter is the very fate of our occidental existence. Since our existence begins with it, this encounter has become necessary, in the sense that it is the presupposition of our undeniable reality. This is why the history of the consciousness of fault in Greece and in Israel will constantly be our central point of reference; it is our "nearest" origin, in this spiritual economy of distance.

The rest follows from this double privilege of Athens and Jerusalem: everything that, step by step, has contributed to our spiritual genesis belongs to our investigation, but along the lines of motivation that are expressed by "near" and "far."

What, then, does "step by step" mean? Various sorts of relations of orientation: relations in "depth," "lateral" relations, "retroactive" relations.

"Relations in depth" first. There are themes of the religious consciousness that appear to us today, as it were, in the "thickness" and the transparency of our present motivations. The conception of fault as defilement is the best example of this; it shows through all our Greek and Hebrew documents. It is impossible to overestimate the importance of this stratified structure for the consciousness of fault. Psychoanalysis, it will be seen, tries to make a logical archaism coincide with this cultural "distance." It is to elucidate this sedimentation of our cultural memory that we can appeal to documents bearing on civilizations which do not belong to that memory—civilizations of Africa, Australia, Asia, etc.—and which are quite often contemporary civilizations. The objective likeness that ethnology discovers between them and our own past authorizes us to use knowledge about those civilizations to diagnose our own past, suppressed or buried in oblivion. It is solely in virtue of their diagnostic value in relation to our memory that we shall invoke the testimony of ethnology concerning modes of behavior and consciousness of fault.

But one cannot explicate these relations in "depth" in the bosom of our memory without bringing the "lateral" relations to light also. For example, it is impossible today to understand the Hebrew source without placing its beliefs and its institutions in the framework of the culture of the ancient Middle East, for it repeats some of the fundamental themes of that culture (by direct borrowing, by reference to common sources, or in virtue of the parallelism of material and cultural conditions), and above all it modifies some others profoundly. The understanding of those likenesses and unlikenesses pertains henceforth to the proper understanding of the Hebrew source of our memory, so that the culture of the ancient Middle East itself belongs marginally to our memory.

In their turn, these relations in "depth" and in "breadth" are reshaped by retroactive relations. Our cultural memory is unceasingly renewed retroactively by new discoveries, returns to the sources, reforms and renaissances that are much more than revivals of the past and constitute behind us what one might call a "neopast." Thus, our Hellenism is not exactly the Hellenism of the Alexandrians, or of the Church Fathers, or of Scholasticism, or of the Renaissance, or of the *Aufklärung;* think, for example, of the rediscovery of tragedy by the moderns. Thus, by retroaction from the successive "nows," our past never stops changing its meaning; the present appropriation of the past modifies that which motivates us from the depths of the past.

Two modalities of this neo-past deserve to be mentioned: restoration of lost intermediaries and later suppression of distance.

That such intermediaries have been lost is a part of the situation of our memory; but suddenly their restoration transforms the understanding that we had of ourselves on the basis of that past full of lacunae. Thus, the discovery of manuscripts in the desert of Judea restores an important transition in the Judeo-Christian past. Now, the ignorance of that transition was part of the motivations of our consciousness up to a recent date; the present discoveries reshape the established tradition, throw light on obscure motivations, and thus give us a new memory.

A second source of neo-formations in our memory comes from later modifications of the "distance" between the sources of our consciousness. The science of religion "brings together" cultures that have not encountered each other. But these "bringings together" remain arbitrary insofar as no bonds are formed such as engender great works of the sort that renew our patrimony, as was the case between the Hebrew and Greek cultures, which effectively encountered each other in a way that was decisive for the constitution of our memory. But there are cultures which have been brought together only in the mind of the scholar, but which have not yet encountered each other to the point of radically transforming our tradition; this is the case with the Far Eastern civilizations. This explains why a phenomenology *oriented* by the philosophical question of Greek origin cannot do justice to the great experiences of India and China. Here, not only the contingency but also the limits of our tradition become evident. There is a moment when the principle of orientation becomes a principle of limitation. It will be said, not without reason, that those civilizations are of equal value with the Greek and Jewish civilizations. But the point of view from which this equality of value can be seen does not yet exist, and it will exist eventually only when a universal human culture has brought all cultures together in a whole. In the meantime, neither the history of religions nor philosophy can be a concrete universal capable of embracing all human experience. On the one hand, the objectivity of science, without a point of view and without situation, does not equalize cultures except by neutralizing their value; it cannot think the positive reasons for their equal value. On the other hand, philosophy, as we have received it from the Greeks and perpetuated it in the West, will remain unequal to this concrete universal as long as no serious encounter and no mutual clarification have brought these civilizations into the field of our experience and at the same time removed its limitation. This encounter and this mutual clarification have not yet really taken place. They have taken place for some men and some groups and they have been the great concern of their lives; but they have remained episodic for our culture as a whole. This is why, up to the present, they have not had the significance of a foundation (as did the encounter of the Greek question with the Hebrew religion) and of a re-creation (as have the various renaissances and returns to sources in the bosom of Western culture). Their phenomenological character is precisely that they have remained episodic, and so the relation of our culture to the Far East remains a relation to something distant. No doubt we are drawing closer to the moment of a creative encounter and the reshaping of a memory based on the opposition of "near" and "far"; but we are not in a position to imagine what that will mean for the categories of our ontology and for our reading of the Pre-Socratics, Greek tragedy, and the Bible. But one thing is certain: we shall not enter into this great debate of each culture with all without our memory; the lessening of the distance between our civilization and those which today we still call "distant" will not suppress the structuration of our memory, but will complicate it. It will not cease to be true that we were born to philosophy by Greece and that as philosophers we have encountered the Jews before encountering the Hindus and the Chinese.

Shall we be astonished, shall we be scandalized by the contingent constitution of our memory? But contingency is not only the inescapable infirmity of the dialogue between philosophy and its "other"; it inhabits the history of philosophy itself; it breaks the sequence which that history forms with itself; the springing up of thinkers and their works is unforeseeable; it is always in the midst of contingency that rational sequences must be detected. Anyone who wished to escape this contingency of historical encounters and stand apart from the game in the name of a non-situated "objectivity" would at the most know everything, but would understand nothing. In truth, he would seek nothing, not being motivated by concern about any question.

I. Defilement

1. THE IMPURE

DREAD OF THE IMPURE and rites of purification are in the background of all our feelings and all our behavior relating to fault. What is there that the philosopher can understand about these feelings and these modes of behavior?

He would be tempted to reply: Nothing. Defilement itself is scarcely a representation, and what representation there is is immersed in a specific sort of fear that blocks reflection. With defilement we enter into the reign of Terror. Thereupon the philosopher recalls Spinoza's *nec spe nec metu:* hope for nothing in order to fear nothing; and he learns from the psychoanalyst that this fear is akin to an obsessional neurosis. The purifications, for their part, try to annul the evil of defilement by a specific action; but we can no longer co-ordinate this ritual action with any type of action for which we can construct a theory today: physical action, psychological influence, consciousness of ourselves. In short, even the representation of defilement, embedded in a specific fear and tied to ritual action, belongs to a mode of thought that we can no longer, it seems, "re-enact," even "in sympathetic imagination." What do we think of when with Pettazzoni we define defilement as "an act that evolves an evil, an impurity, a fluid, a mysterious and harmful something that acts dynamically—that is to say, magically"?[1]

What resists reflection is the idea of a quasi-material something that infects as a sort of filth, that harms by invisible properties, and

---

[1] Pettazzoni, *La confession des péchés* (Bologna, 1929–36, 3 vols.) ; French translation, Vol. I (1931), p. 184.

that nevertheless works in the manner of a force in the field of our undividedly psychic and corporeal existence. We no longer understand what the substance-force of evil, the efficacy of a something that makes purity itself an exemption from defilement and purification an annulment of defilement, could be.

Is it possible to "re-enact" this sense of defilement? Its irrational character permits only an oblique approach. In the first stage of our investigation we shall make use of ethnological science without being concerned to appropriate its content; defilement will then appear to us as a moment of consciousness that we have left behind. Thus we understand through contrast the feelings and the behavior that we have abandoned. But this frontier view of the world of defilement can prepare the way, in a second stage, for a less remote understanding of those aspects of defilement that made it ready to be left behind. It is here that we shall bring into the account the *symbolic richness* of this experience of fault; for it is in virtue of its unlimited potentiality for symbolization that we still cling to it. We shall have approached as close as possible to an experience which has not simply been left behind but has been retained, and which perhaps conceals something that cannot be left behind, by which it survives through a thousand mutations.

It is from a double point of view that defilement appears to us as a moment in the consciousness of fault that has been left behind: from an objective point of view and from a subjective point of view.

In the first place, our conscience no longer recognizes the repertory of defilement: what counts as defilement, for a conscience that lives under its regime, no longer coincides with what counts as evil for us. The variations in this inventory indicate a displacement of motivation. It is because we can no longer discern in impure actions of that sort any offense against an ethical god, any violation of the justice that we owe to other men, any lessening of our personal dignity, that they are excluded for us from the sphere of evil.

Thus the repertory of defilement appears to us sometimes too broad, sometimes too narrow, or unbalanced. We are astonished, for example, when we see involuntary or unconscious human actions, the actions of animals, and even simple material events called defilements—the frog that leaps into the fire, the hyena that leaves its excrements in the neighborhood of a tent. Why are we astonished? Because we do not find in these actions or events any point where we might insert a judgment of personal imputation, or even simply human imputation; we have to transport ourselves into a consciousness for which impurity is measured not by imputation to a responsible agent but by the objective violation of an interdict.

On the other hand, the inventory of defilement surprises us by its gaps. Not infrequently the same system of interdiction abounds in minute prescriptions in domains that for us are ethically neutral, but does not regard as defilements acts which the Semitic codes and Greek legislation have taught us to characterize as evil: theft, lying, sometimes even homicide. These actions become evil only in a system of reference other than that of infectious contact, in connection with the confession of divine holiness, respect for interhuman ties, and self-esteem.

Thus the inventory of faults under the regime of defilement is vaster on the side of happenings in the world in the degree to which it is narrower on the side of the intentions of the agent.

This breadth and this narrowness give evidence of a stage in which evil and misfortune have not been dissociated, in which the ethical order of doing ill has not been distinguished from the cosmobiological order of faring ill: suffering, sickness, death, failure. We shall see after a while how the anticipation of punishment, at the heart of the fear of the impure, strengthens this bond between evil and misfortune: punishment falls on man in the guise of misfortune and transforms all possible sufferings, all diseases, all death, all failure into a sign of defilement. Thus the world of defilement embraces in its order of the impure the consequences of impure actions or events; step by step, there is nothing that cannot be pure or impure. Hence, the division between the pure and the impure ignores any distinction between the physical and the ethical and follows a distribution of the sacred and the profane which has become irrational for us.

Finally, the archaic character of the inventory of faults, as something left behind, is revealed not only by changes in its *extension*, by the subtractions and additions in the list of evil things, but by variations in *intensity,* by changes that affect the *degree of gravity* of this or that violation of the Forbidden.

Thus one is struck by the importance and the gravity attached to the violation of interdictions of a sexual character in the economy of defilement. The prohibitions against incest, sodomy, abortion, relations at forbidden times—and sometimes places—are so fundamental that the inflation of the sexual is characteristic of the whole system of defilement, so that an indissoluble complicity between sexuality and defilement seems to have been formed from time immemorial. This preponderance of sexual interdictions becomes very strange when it is compared with the two other characteristics described above: the extension of interdiction to actions morally neutral and the silence of the same ritual codes with regard to lying, theft, and sometimes homicide. This convergence of traits reveals that the defilement of sexuality as such is a theme foreign to the ethics that proceeds from the confession of divine holiness, as well as to the ethics that is organized around the theme of justice or the integrity of the moral person. The defilement of sexuality is a belief that is pre-ethical in character; it can become ethical, as the defilement of the murderer can become ethical in becoming an offense against the reciprocity of the human bond, although it precedes any ethics of the second person and is immersed in the archaic belief in the maleficent virtues of shed blood. The comparison between sexuality and murder is supported by the same play of images: in both cases, impurity is connected with the presence of a material "something" that transmits itself by contact and contagion. We shall say presently what there is in the consciousness of defilement that resists a literal, realistic, even materialistic interpretation of impure contact. If, from the beginning, defilement were not a *symbolic* stain, it would be incomprehensible that the ideas of defilement and purity could be corrected and taken up into an interpersonal ethics that puts the accent on the acquisitive or oblative aspects of sexuality—in short, on the quality of the relation to another. Nevertheless, by many of its traits sexuality supports the ambiguity of a quasi-materiality of defilement. At the limit, the infant would be regarded as born impure, contaminated from the beginning by the paternal seed, by the impurity of the maternal genital region, and by the additional impurity of childbirth. It is not certain that such beliefs do not continue to prowl in the consciousness of modern man and that they have not played a decisive role in speculation on original sin. Indeed, not only does this notion remain dependent on the general imagery of contact and contagion, which it uses in speaking of the transmission of the primordial taint, but it is still magnetized by the theme of sexual defilement considered as pre-eminently the impure.[2]

This limiting interpretation, which pulls sexual defilement in the direction of a material impurity, is re-enforced by the spectacle of rites of purification which, here as everywhere else, have the negative significance of an exemption from defilement. Do not the marriage rites, among others, aim to remove the universal impurity of sexuality by marking out an enclosure within which sexuality ceases to be a defilement, but threatens to become so again if the rules concerning times, places, and sexual behavior are not observed? At the end of this line on which we have just encountered the theme of the primordial defilement of sexuality, there appears the identity of purity and virginity: virginity and spotlessness are as closely bound together as sexuality and contamination. This double assonance is in the background of all our ethics, where it constitutes the archaism that is most resistant to criticism. So true is this that it is not from meditation on sexuality that a refinement of the consciousness of fault will be able to proceed, but from the non-sexual sphere of existence: from the human relations created by work, appropriation, politics. It is there that an ethics of relations to others will be formed, an ethics of justice and love, capable of turning back toward sexuality, of re-evaluating and transvaluing it.

2. ETHICAL TERROR

We have been considering defilement up till now as an objective event; it is, we have said, a something that infects by contact. But this infectious contact is experienced subjectively in a specific feel-

---

[2] Pettazzoni, *op. cit.*, pp. 163–64, 169.

ing which is of the order of Dread. Man enters into the ethical world through fear and not through love.

By this second trait, again, the consciousness of impurity seems to be a moment inaccessible to any re-enactment in imagination and sympathy, a moment that has been abolished by the progress of moral consciousness itself. Nevertheless, that dread contains in germ all the later moments, because it conceals within itself the secret of its own passing; for it is already ethical dread and not merely physical fear, dread of a danger which is itself ethical and which, at a higher level of the consciousness of evil, will be the danger of not being able to love any more, the danger of being a dead man in the realm of ends.

This is why the primitive dread deserves to be interrogated as our oldest memory.

The origin of that dread is the primordial connection of vengeance with defilement. This "synthesis" is anterior to any justification; it is what is presupposed in any punishment conceived as revenge and expiation. It will be able to transform, transpose, spiritualize itself. It precedes itself in all its mutations and sublimations. At first, the Impure takes vengeance. It will be possible for this vengeance to be absorbed into the idea of Order and even into the idea of Salvation, by way of the "Passion" of a Suffering Just One. The initial intuition of the consciousness of defilement remains: suffering is the price for the violation of order; suffering is to "satisfy" the claim of purity for revenge.

Taken in its origin—that is to say, in its matrix of terror—this initial intuition is the intuition of primordial fatality. The invincible bond between Vengeance and defilement is anterior to any institution, any intention, any decree; it is so primitive that it is anterior even to the representation of an avenging god. The automatism in the sanction that the primitive consciousness dreads and adores expresses this *a priori* synthesis of avenging wrath, as if the fault wounded the potency of the interdict and as if that injury ineluctably triggered the response. Man confessed this ineluctability long before he recognized the regularity of the natural order. When he first wished to express the order in the world, he began by expressing it in the language of retribution. The famous fragment of

Anaximander is an example: "The origin from which beings proceed is also the end toward which their destruction proceeds according to necessity; for they offer satisfaction and expiation to one another for their injustice according to the order of time" (Diels, Fragment B 1).

This anonymous wrath, this faceless violence of Retribution, is inscribed in the human world in letters of suffering. Vengeance causes suffering. And thus, through the intermediary of retribution, the whole physical order is taken up into the ethical order; the evil of suffering is linked synthetically with the evil of fault; the very ambiguity of the word "evil" is a grounded ambiguity, grounded in the law of retribution as it is revealed with fear and trembling by the consciousness of defilement. Suffering evil clings to doing evil as punishment proceeds ineluctably from defilement.

Thus, for the second time, the world of defilement is a world anterior to the division between the ethical and the physical. Ethics is mingled with the physics of suffering, while suffering is surcharged with ethical meanings.

It is because vengeance for a violated interdict falls upon man as an evil of suffering that suffering can acquire the value and the role of a symptom: if a man is unfortunate in fishing or hunting, it is because his wife has adulterous relations. For the same reason, the prevention of defilement by rites of purification acquires the value of prevention of suffering: if you wish to avoid a painful or fatal confinement in childbirth, to protect yourself against a calamity (storm, eclipse, earthquake), to avoid failure in an extraordinary or dangerous undertaking (voyage, getting past an obstacle, hunting, or fishing), observe the practices for eliminating or exorcizing defilement.

This bond between defilement and suffering, experienced in fear and trembling, has been all the more tenacious because for a long time it furnished a scheme of rationalization, a first sketch of causality. If you suffer, if you are ill, if you fail, if you die, it is because you have sinned. The symptomatic and detective value of suffering with regard to defilement is reflected in the explanatory, etiological value of moral evil. Moreover, piety, and not only reason, will cling desperately to this explanation of suffering. If it is true that man suffers because he is impure, then God is innocent. Thus the world of ethical terror holds in reserve one of the most tenacious "rationalizations" of the evil of suffering. That is why it required nothing less than the calling in question of this first rationalization and the crisis of which the Babylonian Job and the Hebrew Job were the admirable witnesses to dissociate the ethical world of sin from the physical world of suffering. This dissociation has been one of the greatest sources of anguish for the human conscience, for suffering has had to become absurd and scandalous in order that sin might acquire its strictly spiritual meaning. At this terrible price, the fear that was attached to it could become fear of not loving enough and could be dissociated from the fear of suffering and failure; in short, the fear of spiritual death could be divorced from the fear of physical death. This conquest was a costly one. The price to be paid was the loss of a first rationalization, a first explanation of suffering. Suffering had to become inexplicable, a scandalous evil, in order that the evil of defilement might become the evil of fault.[3] The figure of the just man suffering, image and type of unjust suffering, constituted the stumbling block against which the premature rationalizations of misfortune were shattered. Henceforth, it will be impossible to co-ordinate doing evil and suffering evil in an immediate explanation.

Hence it is in the era before this crisis of the first rationalization, before the dissociation of misfortune (suffering, disease, death, failure) and fault that the dread of the impure deploys its anxieties: the prevention of defilement takes upon itself all fears and all sorrows; man, before any direct accusation, is already secretly accused of the misfortunes in the world; wrongly accused—thus does man appear to us at the origin of his ethical experience.

This confusion of suffering and punishment explains, in turn, certain characteristics of the interdict. Although interdiction precedes retribution, the latter is anticipated in the consciousness of the interdiction. An interdict is much more than a negative judgment of value, than a simple "this must not be," "this is not to be done"; it is more, too, than a "thou shalt not" where I feel myself pointed at by a threatening finger. Over the interdict there already stretches

[3] V. Jankélévitch, *Le Mal* (Paris, 1947).

the shadow of the vengeance which will be paid to it if it is violated. The "thou shalt not" gets its gravity, its weight, from "if not, thou shalt die." Thus, the interdict anticipates in itself the chastisement of suffering, and the moral constraint of the interdict bears in itself the emotion-laden effigy of the punishment. A taboo is nothing else: a punishment anticipated and forestalled emotionally in an interdiction. Thus the power of the interdict, in anticipatory fear, is a deadly power.

If one goes back still further, the shadow of punishment extends over the whole region and over the very source of the interdictions, and darkens the experience of the sacred. Seen from the point of view of the vengeance and the suffering anticipated in the interdiction, the sacred reveals itself as superhuman destruction of man; the death of man is inscribed in primordial purity. And so, in fearing defilement, man fears the negativity of the transcendent; the transcendent is that before which man cannot stand; no one can see God—at least the god of taboos and interdicts—without dying. It is from this, from this wrath and this terror, this deadly power of retribution, that the sacred gets its character of separateness. It cannot be touched; for if it is touched—that is to say, violated—its death-dealing power is unleashed.

3. THE SYMBOLISM OF STAIN

Such are the two archaic traits—objective and subjective—of defilement: a "something" that infects, a dread that anticipates the unleashing of the avenging wrath of the interdiction. These are the two traits that we no longer comprehend except as moments in the representation of evil that we have gone beyond.

What remains astonishing is that these two traits will never be simply abolished, but will also be retained and transformed in new moments. Among the Greeks, the tragic poets and the orators of Attica are the witnesses of a reviviscence of the representations and the cathartic practices related to defilement.[4] If it were simply a

[4] Kurt Latte, "Schuld und Sünde in der griechischen Religion," *Arch. f. Religionswissenschaft* 20 (1920–21), pp. 254–98; Moulinier, *Le pur et l'impur dans la pensée des Grecs, d'Homère à Aristote* (Paris, 1952);

question of a belated restoration of beliefs that life as a whole had gone beyond, there would be no real problem. But the world of defilement not only persists in the form of a survival; it furnishes the imaginative model on the basis of which the fundamental ideas of *philosophical purification* are constructed. How was such a "transposition" of ritual impurity possible in principle?

The Hebrew example is still more striking.[5] Indeed, it might be alleged that the Greeks never attained the feeling of sin in its peculiar quality and with the intensity of which only the people of Israel supply an example, and that that is why the Greeks had no other recourse than to "transpose philosophically" the schema of defilement. It must still be shown just why the theme of the pure and the impure could lend itself to such a transposition. The Hebrew experience makes the question even more urgent. It is not only ritual legislation that preserves the belief in defilement in Israel; even the experience of sin itself, the profound originality of which in comparison with the experience of defilement we shall show further on, is expressed in the old language of defilement. Thus, the prophet Isaiah, at the time of his vision in the Temple, cries: "Woe is me! I am undone. For I am a man of unclean lips . . . and mine eyes have seen the King, Yahweh Sabaoth." And after the seraph had touched his lips with the live coal from the altar: "Behold, this hath touched thy lips,—thy sin is taken away, —thine iniquity is expiated" (Is. 6:5, 7). Later, in the confession which is attributed after the event to David and which we shall cite further on in the framework not only of the consciousness of sin but of the feeling of guilt, the psalmist entreats: "Have mercy on me, O God, according to thy lovingkindness; according to the multitude of thy tender mercies blot out my sin. Wash me from all iniquity; cleanse me from my fault. . . . O God, create in me a pure heart" (Ps. 51). The theme of defilement must be very

---

E. R. Dodds, *The Greeks and the Irrational* (Univ. of California Press, 1951).

[5] Eichrodt, *Theologie des alten Testaments* (Leipzig, 1933–39), III, 23; Sven Herner, *Sühne und Vergebung in Israel* (Lund, 1942) ; G. von Rad, *Theologie des alten Testaments,* Vol. I (Munich, 1957), pp. 157–65, 249–79.

strong and very rich to have thus survived the magical and ritual conception that was its first vehicle.

How could the image of defilement have survived if, from the beginning, it had not had the power of a symbol?

In truth, defilement was never literally a stain; impurity was never literally filthiness, dirtiness. It is also true that impurity never attains the abstract level of unworthiness; otherwise the magic of contact and contagion would have disappeared. The representation of defilement dwells in the half-light of a quasi-physical infection that points toward a quasi-moral unworthiness. This ambiguity is not expressed conceptually but is experienced intentionally in the very quality of the half-physical, half-ethical fear that clings to the representation of the impure.

But if the symbolic structure of defilement is neither reflective nor representational, it is at least "acted out." One can catch sight of it in the acts of purification and go back from the act which suppresses to the "thing" suppressed. It is the rite that exhibits the symbolism of defilement;[6] and just as the rite suppresses symbolically, defilement infects symbolically.

In fact, even the ablution is never a simple washing; ablution is already a partial and fictive act. And it is because the ablution is already a symbolic washing that the suppression it signifies can be effected by a diversity of equivalent acts which mutually symbolize one another, at the same time as altogether they symbolize the same action, basically one; and as this exemption from defilement is not produced in any total and direct action, it is always signified in partial, substitutive, and abbreviated signs: burning, removing, chasing, throwing, spitting out, covering up, burying. Each of these acts marks out a ceremonial space, within which none of them exhausts its significance in immediate and, so to speak, literal usefulness. They are acts which stand for a total action addressed to the person taken as an undivided whole.

Hence, defilement, insofar as it is the "object" of this ritual suppression, is itself a *symbol* of evil. Defilement is to stain or spot

[6] J. Cazeneuve, *Les rites et la condition humaine* (Paris, 1958), pp. 37–154.

what lustration is to washing. Defilement is not a stain, but like a stain; it is a symbolic stain. Thus, it is the symbolism of the rites of suppression that reveals in practice the implicit symbolism contained in the representation of infection.

This is still not the most important thing. If the rite of suppression, by its symbolic acts, introduces the thing that it suppresses into the symbolic universe that it marks out, yet the rite, considered as act, or gesture, remains mute. Now, defilement enters into the universe of man through speech, or the word (*parole*); its anguish is communicated through speech; before being communicated, it is determined and defined through speech; the opposition of the pure and the impure is spoken; and the words which express it institute the opposition. A stain is a stain because it is there, mute; the impure is taught in the words that institute the taboo.

The case of the murderer is striking in this respect.[7] We have said above what basis shed blood provides for a literal interpretation of defilement. Nowhere else, unless in sexuality, does it appear more difficult to distinguish defilement from stain. Here, it seems, we have the model and, as it were, the limiting case of all impure contacts. Nevertheless, the defilement that comes from spilt blood is not something that can be removed by washing. Moreover, the maleficent power of which the murderer is the bearer is not a taint that exists absolutely without reference to a field of human presence, to words that express the defilement. A man is defiled in the sight of certain men, in the language of certain men. Only he is defiled who is regarded as defiled; a law is required to say it; the interdict is itself a defining utterance. It is necessary also to *say* what must be done in order that the impure may become pure; there is no rite without words that confer a meaning upon the action and consecrate its efficacy; the rite is never mute; and if no words accompany it, something said earlier provides the foundation for it.

This "education" of the feeling of impurity by the language which defines and legislates is of capital importance. Because of it, it is no longer only the action, the gesture, the rite which is symbolic; the pure and the impure themselves, as representations, create for themselves a *symbolic language* capable of transmitting

[7] Moulinier, *op. cit.*, pp. 176 ff.

the emotion aroused by the sacred. The formation of a vocabulary of the pure and the impure, which would exploit all the resources of the symbolism of stain, is thus the first linguistic and semantic foundation of the "feeling of guilt" and, first of all, of the "confession of sins."

As for us, men of the West, it is to classical Greece that we owe our vocabulary of the pure and the impure.[8] Now, it is remarkable that the formation of this language of defilement is in large part dependent on an *imaginary* experience connected with imaginary examples. It is a veritable cultural creation, relatively late, designed to reinterpret a fabled past and to give the Greek an ethical memory.

Indeed, it has been remarked that testimony relative to defilement and cathartic practices, rare before the fifth century, becomes suddenly abundant: the orators, with Demosthenes at their head, comment on the Draconian law regarding exile and public interdiction, which removes from contact with their fellow citizens those criminals who, by the same law, are nevertheless declared to be "involuntary" criminals and are distinguished from "voluntary" criminals. Thucydides, for his part, recounts the sacrilege—a murder in the holy place of the Acropolis—which rendered the members of the family of the Alcmaeonides ἐναγεῖς and made them bear the weight of Expiation. Finally, from the drama we learn that Orestes and Oedipus were defiled.

It is also the drama which, from the simply semantic point of view, plays the most important role in this formation of a symbolic language. It has been remarked that the words μίασμα, κηλίς, μύσος, and μαίνειν are very rare in prose when murder is spoken of; they are employed only to expound a doctrine or to relate a legend.[9] It was in imagining monstrous defilements in legendary criminals that the poets opened the way to a symbolics of impurity.

As for the word that dominates the whole vocabulary of defilement—καθαρός,—it expresses very well the ambiguity of *purity*, which oscillates between the physical and the ethical. Its central intention is to express *exemption* from the impure: non-inter-

[8] Moulinier, *op. cit.*, pp. 149 ff.
[9] *Ibid.*, p. 180.

mixture, non-dirtiness, non-obscurity, non-confusion; and this absence plays upon all the stops of the literal meaning and the
figurative meaning. Κάθαρσις itself can express physical cleansing,
and then, in the medical sense, evacuation, purgation of humors.
But this purgation in its turn can symbolize a ritual purification
and then a wholly moral purity. The group καθαρός-κάθαρσις thus
comes to express intellectual limpidity, clarity of style, orderli-
ness, absence of ambiguity in an oracle, and finally absence of
moral blemish or stigma. Thus the word lends itself to the change
in meaning by which it will come to express the essential purification, that of wisdom and philosophy. For this, it is true, there will
be required the intervention of a new myth which will make the
soul exiled in the body the paradigm of an originally pure being,
forced into "mixture"; but this Greek adventure of "purification"
presupposes that the experience of the pure and the impure was,
from the beginning, rich in all these harmonics and "ready for"
all these transpositions.

Hence, it makes little difference to us, since we are interested
only in the formation of symbolism, whether the defilements that the
classical authors ascribe to the legendary age of heroes were actually
known to the men of that archaic epoch. The pure historian has
serious reasons for doubting it. The silences of Homer on this subject seem to indicate that the old poet was a complete stranger to
the *guilt-culture* of the sixth and fifth centuries.[10] The heroes of
Homer, as Moulinier also notes, love cleanliness and bathe often;
their purifications are all material; it is dirtiness that repels them—
blood, dust, sweat, mud, and squalor—because dirtiness disfigures
(αἰσχύνειν). The Homeric hero who has slain someone is not defiled, and one does not find in the *Iliad* and the *Odyssey* "any of
the most typical cases of defilement of the classical era" (p. 30),
murder, birth, death, sacrilege. But, on the one hand, "the *Iliad*
and the *Odyssey* are not novels of manners and, if they imitate life,
they do it on a grand and ennobling scale" (p. 33). Thus, neither
the silences nor the assertions of Homer prove anything. On the

[10] E. R. Dodds, *op. cit.*, Chap. II, "From Shame-Culture to Guilt-
Culture."

other hand, the real beliefs of the men of the seventh century concern us less than the cultural event constituted by the literary expression of defilement among the orators, historians, and poets of
the classical era. The manner in which the Greeks represented their
own past to themselves and expressed their beliefs is the unique
contribution of Greece to the thematics of evil. It is here that the
theme of defilement has marked a literature from which we proceed
genealogically, and affected a *logos* which is our *logos*.

This is still not the most important thing. This Greek reading
of defilement not only educated feeling in giving it a literary expression, but it constitutes one of the non-philosophical sources of
philosophy. Greek philosophy was worked out in contact with myths
which are themselves interpretations, descriptive and explanatory
exegeses of beliefs and rites relative to defilement. Through those
myths, tragic and Orphic, which Greek philosophy contests or rejects, our philosophy is in debate not only with guilt, not only with
sin, but also with defilement. This bond, so fundamental for the
history of our culture, between defilement, purification, and philosophy obliges us to be attentive to the spiritual potential of this theme.
Because of its connection with philosophy, it cannot be a simple
survival or a simple loss, but a matrix of meaning.

The sense of the testimony of the historians, orators, and drama-
tists is, therefore, completely missed when one gives only a sociological interpretation of it and sees in it only the resistance of the
archaic rights of the family to the new law of the city. This interpretation is true in its place.[11] But it does not exclude another kind of
"understanding" which bears on the unlimited potentiality for
symbolization and transposition of the themes of defilement, purity,
and purification. It is precisely the connection of defilement with
words that define it which brings to light the primordially symbolic
character of the representation of the pure and the impure. Thus,
the "interdiction" which excludes the accused from all sacred places
and public places—sacred because public—signifies exclusion of
the defiled from a sacred space. After the judgment, the criminal

[11] Gustave Glotz, *La solidarité de la famille dans le droit criminel en
Grèce* (Paris, 1904).

is afflicted with even graver interdictions which annul, so to speak, him and his defilement. Exile and death are such annulments of the defiled and of defilement.

There is no question, of course, of denying the incompatibility of the two representations of the same murderer—the more *juridical* one which places him in the category of the "involuntary" and already belongs to the realm of guilt in the precise sense that we shall give to that word, and the more *religious* one which places him under the sign of the "impure"; but the contrast is somewhat attenuated if one considers the equivocal flexibility of the representation of defilement. The exile is not simply excluded from a material area of contact; he is chased out of a human environment measured off by the law. Henceforth the exile will no longer haunt the human space of the fatherland; where the fatherland ends, there his defilement also ceases. To kill a murderer in the territory of the Athenian fatherland is to purify it; to kill him outside of that territory is to kill an Athenian. New rites of asylum and welcome in another place, under other eyes, within the jurisdiction of another legislation will be able to give him a new purity.[12]

This relation to defining language and a human environment, which the Greek writings clearly show, can be discovered even in the most primitive forms of the prohibition of defilement studied by Frazer and Pettazzoni. The involuntary or unconscious actions, the material events, the accidents which provoke the emotion of impurity and require a process of purification, are not just any happenings; they always qualify a human environment. The fire into which the frog has jumped, the tent near which the hyena has left his excrements, belong to a space haunted by man, qualified by his presence and his acts.

Thus, it is always in the sight of other people who excite the feeling of shame and under the influence of the word which says what is pure and impure that a stain is defilement.

4. THE SUBLIMATION OF DREAD

At the same time as the "objective" representation of defilement

[12] Moulinier, *op. cit.,* pp. 81–85.

lends itself by its symbolic structure to all the transpositions which will make of it an enduring symbol of the evil of fault, the dread which is the "subjective" and affective counterpart of this notion of the pure and the impure is, no doubt from the beginning, also capable of an emotional transposition. Dread, as we shall see, is not abolished, but changes its meaning as it approaches the sphere of sin. The "experience" here follows the mutations of the "object."

Dread of the impure is, in fact, no more a physical fear than defilement is a stain or spot. Dread of the impure is like fear, but already it faces a threat which, beyond the threat of suffering and death, aims at a diminution of existence, a loss of the personal core of one's being.

Again, it is through the word that dread acquires its ethical quality. A little while ago we considered the word as an instrument for *defining* the pure and the impure. Now it insinuates itself into the experience itself as an instrument by which the defiled self becomes conscious of itself. Defilement enters into the universe of the word not only by way of the interdict, but by way of confession. Consciousness, crushed by the interdict and by fear of the interdict, opens itself to others and to itself; not only does it begin to communicate but it discovers the unlimited perspective of self-interrogation. Man asks himself: since I experience this failure, this sickness, this evil, what sin have I committed? Suspicion is born; the appearance of acts is called in question; a trial of veracity is begun; the project of a total confession, totally revealing the hidden meaning of one's acts, if not yet of one's intentions, appears at the heart of the humblest "confession of sins."

Of course, one cannot deny that the language of confession is still related to the magical procedures of elimination;[13] it is supposed to operate magically—that is to say, not by the communication to others, or to oneself, of an understood meaning, but by an efficacy comparable to that of lustration, of spitting out, of burying, of banishment. There is no dispute about that. But besides extending the symbolic side of those procedures, language adds a new

[13] In the same vein as Frazer, Pettazzoni writes: "Primitive confession is an enunciation of sin that aims at evoking it in order to eliminate its pernicious effects" (*op. cit.*, p. 183).

element in relation to the verbal ejection and expulsion of evil which is confession in the strict sense. It is a beginning of appropriation and, at the same time, of elucidation of dread in the element of language. Dread expressed in words is no longer simply a cry, but an avowal. In short, it is by being refracted in words that dread reveals an ethical rather than a physical aim.

This aim seems to me to comprise three successive degrees, three intentional references of increasing depth.

In the first place, fear of vengeance is not a simple passive fear; already it involves a *demand*, the demand for a just punishment. This demand finds its first expression and its provisional approximation in the law of retribution. As we said above, this law is felt at first as a crushing fatality; it is the loosing of an elementary wrath excited by the insolence of a violation. But this fatality to which one is subject involves a demand for legality, the legality of a Justice which makes just retribution. If a man *is* punished *because* he sins, he *ought* to be punished *as* he sins. This *ought to be,* seen through fear and trembling, is the principle of all our reflections on punishment.

This reflection at first went astray and came up against an impasse: the belief that all suffering is the actual realization of this retribution. Thus the demand for a just punishment found itself confused with the explanation of actual suffering. But this "etiological" usage of the demand for a just punishment was so far from exhausting the law of retribution that the latter survived the crisis of the religious consciousness that shook and ruined the explanation of suffering by sin. Not only did it survive, but, thanks to that crisis, it revealed itself as a demand, beyond any explanation. And conscience, not *finding* the manifestation of the law of retribution any longer in real suffering, *looked for* its satisfaction in other directions, whether at the end of history, in a Last Judgment, or in some exceptional event, such as the sacrifice of a victim offered for the sins of the world, or by means of penal laws elaborated by society with the intention of making the penalty proportionate to the crime, or by means of a wholly internal penalty, accepted as penance. We are not concerned here with the legitimacy and the compatibility of these multiple expressions of the law of retribution: Last Judgment, expiatory sacrifice, juridical penalty, internal penance. Their mere enumeration sufficiently attests that the demand implicit in the law of retribution is not exhausted in the archaic explanation of all human ills by the evil of fault.

But this appeal to a *just* punishment still does not express all that is implicit in primitive anxiety. To be punished, even justly, is still suffering; every punishment is a penalty; every penalty is afflictive, if not in the technical sense that it has received in our codes, at least in the affective sense of the word. Punishment afflicts; punishment is of the order of pain or sorrow. In *demanding* that a man suffer justly, we *expect* the pain to have not only a limit, but a direction—that is to say, an end. We said above that the Sacred is perceived, in the archaic stage of the religious consciousness, as that which does not permit a man to stand, that which makes him die. And yet this negation is not self-enclosed. The very idea of vengeance conceals something else; to avenge is not only to destroy, but by destroying to re-establish. Along with the dread of being stricken, annihilated, there is perception of the movement by which order—whatever order it may be—is restored. That which had been established and which has now been destroyed is re-established. By negation, order reaffirms itself.

Thus, in the negative moment of punishment, the sovereign affirmation of primordial integrity is anticipated; and, correlatively, the dread of avenging punishment is the negative envelope of a still more fundamental admiration, the admiration for order, for any order, even a provisional one, even one destined to be abolished. Perhaps there is no taboo in which there does not dwell some reverence, some veneration of order. It is the same confused, implicit feeling for order that already animates the *terror* of a consciousness bent under the fatality of avenging suffering.

Plato indicates the direction of this anticipation: true punishment is that which, in restoring order, produces happiness; true punishment results in happiness. This is the meaning of the famous paradoxes of the *Gorgias:* "the unjust man is not happy" (471*d*); "to escape punishment is worse than to suffer it" (474*b*); to suffer punishment and pay the penalty for our faults is the only way to be happy.

Punishment would then no longer be the death of a man in the presence of the sacred, but penance with a view to order and pain with a view to happiness.

This second anticipation, implicit in archaic dread, seems to me to predominate over the first; for why demand a penalty proportionate to the fault if it served no end, if it had no purpose? The degree of the penalty, without the purpose of the penalty, is meaningless. In other words, what is aimed at in vengeance is expiation —that is to say, the punishment that takes away defilement; but what is aimed at in this negative act of taking away is the act of reaffirming order. Now, order cannot be reaffirmed outside of the guilty person without being reaffirmed within him too. Hence, what is aimed at, through vengeance and expiation, is amendment —that is to say, the restoration of the personal worth of the guilty person through a just punishment.

This second intention, implicit in ethical anxiety, appears to me to conceal a third moment. If the *demand* for a just punishment involves the *expectation* of a punishment which has a meaning in relation to order, this expectation involves the *hope* that fear itself will disappear from the life of conscience, as a result of its sublimation.

The whole philosophy of Spinoza is an effort to eliminate the negative—fear and pain—from the regulation of one's life under the guidance of reason. The wise man does not act through fear of punishment, and he does not meditate on pain or sorrow. Wisdom is a pure affirmation of God, of nature, and of oneself. Before Spinoza, the Gospel preaches that "perfect love casts out fear."

But is a human existence entirely freed from negative feelings possible? The abolition of fear appears to me to be only the most distant goal of ethical consciousness. The change of rule which leads from fear of vengeance to love of order, the principal episode of which we shall consider presently with the Hebraic notion of the Covenant, does not simply abolish fear, but takes it over and remakes it in a new range of feeling.

It is not the *immediate* abolition but the *mediate* sublimation of fear, with a view to its *final* extenuation, which is the soul of all true education. Fear remains an indispensable element in all forms of education, familial, scholastic, civic, as well as in the protection of society against the infractions of citizens. The project of an education which would dispense with prohibition and punishment, and so with fear, is undoubtedly not only chimerical but harmful. Much is learned through fear and obedience—including the liberty which is inaccessible to fear. There are steps that cannot be dispensed with without harm. Certain forms of human relations, the relations that are properly speaking *civic,* cannot, perhaps, ever get beyond the stage of fear. One can imagine penalties that afflict less and less and amend more and more, but perhaps one cannot imagine a state which has no necessity to make law respected through the threat of sanctions and which can awaken consciences that are still unrefined to the notion of what is permitted and what prohibited without the threat of punishment. In short, it is possible that a whole part of human existence, the *public* part, cannot raise itself above the fear of punishment and that this fear is the indispensable means by which man advances toward a different order, hyperethical in a way, where fear would be entirely confounded with love.

Hence, the abolition of fear could only be the *horizon,* and, so to speak, the eschatological *future* of human morality. Before casting out fear, love transforms and transposes it. A conscience that is militant and not yet triumphant does not cease to discover ever sharper fears. The fear of not loving enough is the purest and worst of fears. It is the fear that the saints know, the fear that love itself begets. And because man never loves enough, it is not possible that the fear of not being loved enough in return should be abolished. Only *perfect* love casts out fear.

Such is the future of fear, of that archaic dread which anticipates vengeance in an interdiction. It is because that future belongs to it potentially that the "primitive" dread of the impure will not be an element that is simply abolished in the history of conscience, but will be able to be taken up in new forms of feeling that at first negate it.

If one should ask, then, what the *nucleus* is that remains constant through all the symbolizations of defilement, we should have to answer that it is only in the progress of conscience, as it advances beyond and at the same time retains the notion of defilement, that its meaning will be manifested. We shall try to show this when we have gone through the entire cycle of the primary symbols of evil. Let us content ourselves for the moment with Socrates' play on words in the *Cratylus* (404*e*–406*a*) : Apollo is the god "who washes" (ἀπολούων), but he is also the god who speaks the "simple" truth (ἁπλοῦν). If, then, sincerity can be a symbolic purification, every evil is symbolically a stain. The stain is the first "schema" of evil.

II. Sin

IT IS NECESSARY to have a just estimate of the divergence in meaning between defilement and sin. This divergence is "phenomenological" rather than "historical." In the societies studied by the history of religions, transitions from one form of fault to another are constantly observable. Among the Greeks, alliances of meaning are formed between καθαρός, in the sense of exempt from defilement, on the one hand, and, on the other hand, the imprecisely demarcated series of notions such as ἁγνός, consecrated, chaste, innocent,—ἅγιος, venerable, august, which already designates the majesty of the gods,—ὅσιος, pleasing to the gods, pious, in the sense of sacred justice, holy exactitude.[1] Thus one passes easily from the pure to the pious and the holy, and also to the just. The reference to the gods, essential to the idea of piety—one recalls Plato's *Euthyphro,*—insinuates itself, then, without any break in continuity, into the world of defilement. If one should descend lower in the archaic depths evoked in the introduction, one would always find at least tentative transitions from defilement to sin, with reference to something divine and more or less personalized; the fact that the impure could once be linked to the fear of demons, and so to fright in the presence of transcendent powers, at the risk of confounding the specific intentions of impurity and sin,[2] at least indicates that the confusion is inscribed in the very reality of the feelings and representations. From the point of view of phenomeno-

---

[1] See the index "Verborum et Rerum," in Moulinier, *op. cit.,* pp. 431 ff., which contains all the useful references concerning the Greek vocabulary of the Pure and the Impure.

[2] Cf. above, p. 29.

47

logical types, the most remarkable example of "transition" from
defilement to sin is furnished by the Babylonian confession of sins.[3]
The symbol of defilement is dominated by the symbol of "binding,"
which is still a symbol of externality, but which expresses seizure,
possession, enslavement, rather than contagion and contamination:
"May the evil that is in my body, in my muscles and tendons, depart
today," the penitent prays; but at the same time as the schema of
defilement is incorporated into that of possession, the notions of
transgression and iniquity are added: "Deliver me from the spell
that is upon me . . . for an evil spell and an impure disease and
transgression and iniquity and sin are in my body, and a wicked
spectre is attached to me." It is already the personal relation to a
god that determines the spiritual space where sin is distinguished
from defilement; the penitent experiences the assault of demons
as the counterpart of the absence of the god: "An evil curse has
cut the throat of this man as if he were a lamb; his god has gone
out of his body, his goddess has kept herself aloof." Polarly opposed to the god before whom he stands, the penitent becomes
conscious of his sin as a dimension of his existence, and no longer
only as a reality that haunts him; the examination of conscience
and the interrogative thinking that it gives rise to are already there:
from facts the penitent goes back to acts and their obscure background: "Has he afflicted a god, scorned a goddess? Can he have
scorned the name of his god in making an offering? Can he have
kept back what he might have consecrated?" The question makes
its way through the labyrinths of anguish and dereliction: "Call?
No one hears. And that crushes me. Cry out? No one answers. That
oppresses me." And the feeling of being abandoned gives a new
impulse to confession, which plunges into the depths of forgotten
or unknown sins, committed against an unknown god or goddess:
"The faults that I have committed I do not know. . . . The sins
that I have committed I do not know. . . . O god, known or un-

[3] Charles Fr. Jean, *Le péché chez les Babyloniens et les Mésopotamiens*
(Paris, 1925); Ed. Dhorme, *Les religions de Babylonie et d'Assyrie* (Paris,
1945), pp. 229–30, 239, 247, 250; and *La littérature babylonienne et
assyrienne* (Paris, 1937), Chap. VI, "La littérature lyrique," pp. 73–84.
The principal texts will be found in S. Langdon, *Babylonian Penitential
Psalms* (Oxford, 1927).

known, blot out my sins; goddess, known or unknown, blot out my sins." And the confession gives a new impulse to the question: "How long, O god, will you do this to me? I am treated as one who fears neither god nor goddess."

Without overestimating the subtle spirit of this confession, nor forgetting its place in a cultual and ritual context, nor neglecting its connection with fear, one can be sensible of all that forecasts the Jewish experience of sin and already exhibits it in a nascent state. The lamentation "for any god" already contains, in the manner of a litany, what is essential in Hebrew confession:

> Lord, my sins are many, my faults are heavy,
> My god! My sins are many, my faults are heavy,
> My goddess, my sins are many, my faults are heavy.
> God whom I know, whom I know not, my sins are many,
>   my faults are heavy;
> May thy heart, like the heart of the mother that
>   gave me birth, may it be appeased!
> Like the mother that bore me, like the father that
>   begot me, may it be appeased![4]

The school of Nippur even went very far in the direction of a theology of "natural" and "inherent" sin that S. Langdon sees in the background of all the penitential hymns and expiatory prayers of Babylonia and Assyria.[5] While it created a deeper consciousness of sin, this theology of sin made all suffering intelligible and delayed the crisis which Babylonian "wisdom" faced before Israel and which was to entwine itself around the theme of the suffering of the innocent.[6] The counterproof, moreover, is conclusive: the cultures that were most advanced in meditation upon sin as a religious dimension "before God"—and, above all, the Hebrew

---

[4] Ed. Dhorme, *op. cit.*, pp. 81–82. James B. Pritchard, ed., *Ancient Near Eastern Texts Relating to the Old Testament*, 2d ed. (Princeton, 1955), pp. 391–92.

[5] S. Langdon, *Babylonian Wisdom* (London, 1923), p. 19. Further on we shall see in what mythical context this confession is inserted (Part II, Chap. I).

[6] J. J. Stamm, *Das Leiden des Unschuldigen in Babylon und Israel* (Zürich, 1948). On this point, cf. below, Part II, Chap. V, 2, "The Reaffirmation of the Tragic."

culture—never broke with the representation of defilement. The
Levitical prescriptions, preserved in the Hebrew and Christian
canon of the Bible, are evidence enough. Even if, as we believe,
the intentions are different, and even opposed, they live together
and sometimes contaminate one another to the point of becoming
indistinguishable. We shall have to give an account of these contaminations at the end of this record of the religious consciousness
of fault. But we have every reason not to begin there. Just as we
have taken the idea of defilement without reference to demons or
gods—that is to say, powers in the presence of which the impure is
impure, we shall take sin in its purest formulation. Once again our
"re-enactment" is not of the historical order; it is a phenomenology,
philosophical in character, which works out "types" and consequently distinguishes before uniting.

1. The Category of "Before God": The Covenant

The category that dominates the notion of sin is the category of
"before" God.[7] But if this category determines all strict usage of
the notion of "sin," we must not restrict it unduly at the outset.

Before God does not mean before the Wholly Other, as the
Hegelian analysis of the unhappy consciousness began to make it
mean. That analysis is, strictly speaking, misleading; the initial
moment is not the separation of existence from its meaning, the
emptiness and the vanity of a human consciousness that has emptied
itself of its substance for the advantage of an absolute that has
become its vampire; the initial moment is not the nothingness of
man before the being and the all of God. The initial moment is
not the "unhappy consciousness," but the "Covenant," the *Berit*
of the Jews. It is in a preliminary dimension of encounter and
dialogue that there can appear such a thing as the absence and the
silence of God, corresponding to the vain and hollow existence of

---

[7] For the general relation between the idea of sin and the idea of
Covenant, see Eichrodt's magistral *Theologie des alten Testaments* (Leipzig,
1933–39, 3 vols.). I refer in particular to Vol. III, § 23, "Sünde und
Vergebung." See also the excellent synthesis in Ed. Jacob, *Les thèmes
essentiels d'une théologie de l'Ancien Testament* (Neuchâtel, 1955), pp.
75–82, 91–94, 170–77, and 226–40.

man. It is, then, the prior establishment of the bond of the Covenant that is important for the consciousness of sin; it is this that makes sin a violation of the Covenant.

Shall we say that sin presupposes a "theistic" perspective? This proposal is juster, but on two conditions: that we take the theistic thesis in a sense that includes both monotheistic and polytheistic representations, and that we take theism prior to the elaboration of any theology, as the fundamental situation of a man who finds himself implicated in the initiative taken by someone who, on his side, is essentially turned toward man; a god in the image of man, if you wish, but above all a god concerned about man; a god who is anthropotropic—before being anthropomorphic.

This initial situation, this disconcerting initiative that calls and elects, appears suddenly and becomes silent, is no less foreign to philosophical discourse—at least discourse instituted by a reason defined by universality and non-temporality—than defilement, interdict, and vengeance. But, just as defilement was related to philosophical meditation insofar as it had the character of language, or the word (*parole*)—the word of prohibition and rite, the word of confession,—so the Covenant as word penetrates into the same space of reflection. The *ruah* of Yahweh in the Old Testament, which we translate by Spirit for lack of a better term, designates the irrational aspect of the Covenant; but this *ruah* is also *davar,* word (*parole*).[8] It is no accident that the only suitable equivalent of the Hebrew *davar* was the Greek *logos*. This translation, even though only approximate and inexact, was itself an important cultural event. It expresses the conviction, first, that all languages are translatable into one another, and that all cultures belong to a *single* humanity; and then that we must seek the least bad equivalent for the calling of man by God in the *logos,* in which the Greeks recognized the unity of *ratio* and *oratio*. The projection of the Hebrew *davar* upon the Greek *logos,* a projection pregnant with equivocations in one sense, marked first of all the recognition of this fact: the initial situation of man as God's prey can enter into the universe of discourse because it is itself analyzable into an utterance of God and an utterance of man, into the reciprocity of

[8] A Néher, *L'Essence du prophétisme* (Paris, 1955), pp. 85–116.

a vocation and an invocation. Thus this initial situation, which plunges into the darkness of the power and violence of the Spirit, also emerges into the light of the Word.

It is in this exchange between vocation and invocation that the whole experience of sin is found.

Another way of limiting the scope of "before God" would be to reduce this Word prematurely to a moral commandment which would refer us to God or the gods as to a legislative and judicial power. A Law given by a Legislator and sanctioned by a Judge is much less than that total word into which the Covenant is transposed. The ethical character of the word of command is already a product of abstraction. The notion of law appears only when the word of command is on the point of detaching itself from the situation of calling, from the dialogal relation. Then it becomes a commandment that can be understood as an imperative, as a "Thou shalt" that no one has uttered and that can be ascribed only secondarily to an absolute Legislator. There is no question of ascribing the commandment to Someone after the fact, because there is in the first place no commandment which would have a meaning of its own after the fashion of a Value-Idea which would be valid and make demands by itself. What there is in the first place is not essence but presence; and the commandment is a modality of the presence, namely, the expression of a holy will. Thus sin is a religious dimension before being ethical; it is not the transgression of an abstract rule—of a value—but the violation of a personal bond. That is why the deepening of the sense of sin will be linked with the deepening of the meaning of the primordial relationship which is Spirit and Word. When the god is still one god among others, and when the bond with that god is still only an alliance for battle, in which god and people win or lose together, the violations of the bond between people and god have only as much weight as the god and the bond. Thus, from beginning to end sin is a religious dimension and not a moral one.

This subordination of the imperative to a word or utterance that includes it and confers upon it the dramatic accent of a summons, of an alliance, is reflected in the documents which the history of religions explores and which our phenomenology takes into account. The "codes" are not the only documents we have to be acquainted with, nor even the most important. The Jews, like the other Semitic peoples, elaborated ritual, penal, civil, and political codes to regulate conduct; but it is less in the letter of these codes than in their life and in the *direction of their transformations* that we must look for the Hebrew experience of sin. Now this life, this dynamism that produces the codes, is revealed in documents other than the codes—in "chronicles" that tell stories of sin and death, like the Chronicles of Saul and David; in the "hymns" in which distress, confession, and entreaty sing; in "oracles" in which the prophet accuses, warns, threatens; and finally in "sayings," in which the imperative of the code, the lament of the psalm, the thunder of the oracle are reflected in wisdom. Such is the rich palette of the "knowledge" of sin; it is in proportion to the vast utterance in which the Covenant is proclaimed.[9]

This utterance, this word, vaster than the imperative, is also vaster than "speculation." The knowledge of God and man, to speak as Calvin does at the beginning of the *Institutes,* is not "thought" in the sense of Greek philosophy, nor even in the sense of the rabbinical, Islamic, and Christian theologies, which presuppose philosophical speculation; nothing that resembles methodical study or a search for definitions. The prophet through whom this word is expressed (I here extend the notion of prophet to such personages as Abraham and Moses) does not "think" in the Hellenic sense of the word; he cries out, he threatens, he orders, he groans, he exults. His "oracle," which gives rise to chronicles, codes, hymns, and sayings, possesses the breadth and the depth of the primordial word that constitutes the dialogal situation at the heart of which sin breaks forth.

[9] A. Lods, in his *Histoire de la littérature hebraïque et juive* (Paris, 1950), follows a very valuable historical and literary guideline. G. von Rad, in his *Theologie des alten Testaments* (Vol. I, *Die Theologie der geschichtlichen Überlieferungen Israels,* Munich, 1957), is much farther away than Lods from Wellhausen's interpretation of the "sources" and refers to a much more remote past the *origin* of documents which the school of Wellhausen supposes to have been *edited* at a date later than propheticism. His study of theology in terms of documentary groups rather than in terms of guiding themes, which is Eichrodt's method, gives a considerable value to his monumental work.

A philosophical phenomenology that wishes to re-enact the "before God" which is essential to sin must re-enact the form of the "word" most foreign to the word of Greek speculation from which philosophy was born, namely, the prophetic "oracle"—a "word" foreign to the Greek *logos,* but a word, nevertheless, that came to the Gentiles in the Greek translation of *logos.*

2. THE INFINITE DEMAND AND THE FINITE COMMANDMENT

The prophet does not "reflect" *on* sin; he "prophesies" *against.*

The spoken oracle is not in itself a peculiarly Hebraic reality; other cults also have their seers and their soothsayers.[10] What is absolutely new and bewildering is not the prophetic form but the content of the oracle. Two traits principally concern the discovery of sin.

1. The prophet Amos, and after him Hosea and Isaiah, announces the *destruction* of his people by Yahweh. It is, then, under the sign of a total threat and in a sort of aggression of God against his people that man is revealed to himself. One must not weaken this disconcerting "announcement," but take it in its initial fury: you shall be destroyed, deported, ravaged. We can hardly imagine the sort of religious traumatism that this preaching must have caused. It is not an unknown and distant God who threatens man, but the God who made his people as a potter, who begot them as an ancestor; this is the God who reveals himself as the Enemy. To be a sinner is to find oneself subject to that wrath, involved in that enmity: "the day of Yahweh will be darkness and not light."

2. But this dreadful threat is tied to a kind of indignation and accusation which gives it its peculiarly ethical character:

> For three crimes of Damascus, and for four . . .
> For three crimes of Gaza, and for four . . .
> For three crimes of Tyre, and for four . . .

For a meditation on sin, prophecy is this mixture of threat and indignation, of imminent terror and ethical accusation. Thus, sin is made known in the union of Wrath and Indignation.

[10] A. Néher, *op. cit.,* pp. 17–85.

Following the didactic order adopted for the study of defilement, we shall go from the "objective" to the "subjective" pole. Consequently, we shall go straight to the ethical moment in sin that follows upon the representation of the impure; then we shall try to understand the new kind of dread, connected with sin, by the content of prophecy; and finally we shall attempt to disengage the symbolism peculiar to this specific moment in the experience of fault.

In what does the "ethical" moment of prophecy consist? We should grossly oversimplify and travesty the sense of this second moment in the religious consciousness of evil if we reduced it to the victory of *moral law* over *ritual law*. We should rather say, in Bergsonian language, that moral law is attained only because the prophetic demand aims further. Ethics is rather the slackening of an impulse that is fundamentally hyperethical. The prophetic moment in the consciousness of evil is the revelation in an infinite measure of the demand that God addresses to man. It is this infinite demand that creates an unfathomable distance and distress between God and man. But as this infinite demand does not declare itself in a sort of preceding void, but applies itself to a preceding matter, that of the old Semitic "codes,"[11] it inaugurates a tension character-

---

[11] The Bible preserves traces of a legislation not yet touched by the infinite demand. Before the prophets, Yahweh, God of battles, tribal God, is not yet the God of holiness who requires justice; the struggle against the Baals is a struggle for monolatry without any specifically moral accent; it is less purity of heart than the jealous exclusiveness of a cult that bears witness. That is why, according to A. Lods (*op. cit.*, § 3, "Le Droit"), the demands that serve to measure sins are not yet the radical demands of the prophets; thus the pre-decalogue of Exodus 34:14–26, sometimes called the "second decalogue," still places in the first rank respect for festivals, cultual obligations, and the wholly ritual interdiction of images made of precious metals. The "Book of the Covenant" (Exodus 20:24—23:19) is still more interesting; in all its cultual, criminal, civil, and moral prescriptions, that document resembles the other codes of the Ancient Near East. This kinship of all oriental law (A. Lods, pp. 210–11) is interesting for our purpose; it warns us that the specific character of the Biblical "message" is not to be sought in the direction of this elaboration of codes. Neither are the more humane aspects (prescriptions concerning the stranger, the widow, and the orphan, the restoration of pledges, equity, etc.) peculiar to the Bible: indeed, A. Lods remarks that on many points the "Book of the Covenant" represents a more archaic stage in the evolution of oriental legislations than, for example, the Babylonian code, although the latter is ten centuries older.

istic of all Hebrew ethics, the tension between an infinite demand and a finite commandment. It is this polarity that must be respected; it is this dialectic of unlimited indignation and detailed prescription that we must now understand without shattering it.

Amos—the shepherd Amos—was the first to elevate righteousness and justice (5:7; 5:21; 6:12) above the cult and its rites.[12] But there is no question of comparing these notions and all those which go with them—good, evil, life, iniquity—to those which the Sophists and Socrates tried to work out in their kind of pedagogical reflection. It is in the movement of indignation and accusation that Amos professes "righteousness and justice"; these words indicate the direction of a demand more radical than any enumeration of faults. The examples enumerated—cruelty of leaders in war, luxury among the great, traffic in slaves, harshness towards the lowly—are the scattered and convergent signs of one central evil that the prophet calls "iniquity." Thus the prophet aims at the wicked heart from which iniquity comes forth. Expressions such as "living" and "dying" designate this undivided root of the existence which is in question in justice and iniquity; the unlimited character of the demand reveals how deeply rooted human evil is. At the same time the prophet gives the man whom he calls to account a vis-à-vis, a neighbor, with whom he is never finished, contrary to the limited demand of the ritual codes. Thus, the demand is unlimited with respect to its transcendent origin, with respect to its existential root, with respect to others, with respect to those lowly ones in whom the appeal for "righteousness and justice" is incarnated. Such is the ethical distance that indignation creates in the very heart of the Covenant. Each accusation, in pointing to the seat of iniquity, is a summons to a conversion more complete than any partial correction: "Seek the Eternal and you shall live." To seek and to live—these two words indicate the radical level of the conversion—radical as the evil is radical.

In other words, the Biblical discovery of sin does not reside in the measuring of faults by a code. These views of Lods are complemented by the much less evolutionary interpretation of G. von Rad (*op. cit.*, pp. 192 ff.).

[12] For this contribution of the Scriptural prophets to the theme of sin, see A. Néher, *op. cit.*, pp. 213 ff., and A. Lods, *op. cit.*, Second Period.

Hosea, it is true, introduces into the consciousness of sin a note of tenderness that clings to his metaphor of the conjugal bond. For the ritual pact he substitutes the pact of affection, with its reciprocity and its abandon: "They did not understand that I brought them healing; I drew them with the bonds of kindness, with the chains of love. . . ." But this affection is no less demanding than the justice of Amos; the God of tenderness is a husband jealous of the lovers whom an adulterous wife prefers to him; and the prophet mimics, even in his own sexual behavior, the parable of adultery, accusation, and desertion. Thus adultery, criminal preference for another lover, becomes a metaphor for sin, at the same time as God reveals himself as the master who repudiates. This symbol of repudiation is frightening; it announces that man is abandoned by God's absenting himself. This absence of God, according to Hosea, is already the dereliction of the moderns, that is to say, an insecurity and an anguish worse than suffering. It is from the depths of this desolation of the repudiated spouse that Hosea tries to instigate the movement of return: "It is time . . . come back to me."

But Isaiah, in the lightning-like vision in the Temple (6:1–13), discovers another dimension of God, and so a new dimension of sin: after the God of justice, after the God of the conjugal bond betrayed, here is the God of sovereignty and majesty, the holy God. By his measure man appears "unclean in lips and heart." Henceforth sin is represented by the figure of violated suzerainty; sin is pride, arrogance, false greatness. Isaiah draws from it a policy that anticipates the defeatism of Jeremiah during the siege of Jerusalem; if sin is the false greatness of purely human domination, Judah should not seek support in its might or in its alliances; if Judah had abandoned itself to unarmed obedience, without any reliance on itself, without defense and without alliance, Judah would have been saved. This unarmed obedience, true contrary of sin, Isaiah, it seems, was the first to call faith. Thus, the consciousness of sin advances and becomes boundless as historical insecurity grows, as the sign of history as devastator replaces the sign of victory, and as the failure of might becomes the sacrament of holy majesty. He who threatens infinitely is he who demands infinitely.

Shall we say that this infinite measure, this immeasurability of perfection, this ethical immensity sets up an "impotence" of man, a "wretchedness" that alienates him before the face of an Other beyond reach? Does not sin make God the Wholly Other?

This question must be placed against the background of the Covenant, which is the all-embracing factor in the Biblical relation between God and man. Then it takes on a specific form: How does the bond of the Covenant embody the "ethical distance" between the holy God of the vision in the Temple and the man of unclean lips and heart? How does the Covenant involve this indignation and this distance? It is here that the dialectic of an unlimited demand and a limited imperative is disclosed.

We cannot understand Biblical sin if we consider only a conscience crushed beneath an imperative foreign to it; in this way one speaks facilely of the "morality of Sinai." We do not understand it any better if we purely and simply oppose the "morality of the prophets," as an open morality, to a closed morality, the ritualistic, legalistic, particularistic morality of the priests and the Levites. The dialectic of the code and the unlimited demand is the basic ethical structure of the Covenant.

We have already alluded to the codes which preceded the activity of the prophets of Israel and which relate Israel to its neighbors in the Near East. Prophetism introduces a tension between the immeasurability of perfection and the measure of the imperative. The consciousness of sin reflects this tension: on the one hand, it penetrates beyond faults towards a radical evil that affects the indivisible disposition of the "heart"; on the other hand, it is coined into multiple infractions denounced by particular commandments. Thus prophetism unceasingly leads up the slope from infractions to sin, while legalism unceasingly leads back down it from sin to infractions; but prophetism and legalism form an indivisible whole. The Decalogue of Exodus 20 is the central witness of this dialectic; even if we are less sure today than the preceding critical generation was that the Decalogue expresses the penetration of prophetic preaching into sacerdotal circles, it remains true that it expresses a tension that no doubt goes back to a time much before the scriptural prophets; for the old Semitic codes were revised and amended in a spirit akin to that of the prophets. The specific character of the Decalogue resides, then, less in the material content of its articles than in the sense of this elevation to a higher level undergone by the ancient codes. In spite of the negative character of its interdictions, the fragmentation that it introduces into the "will of God," the apparent indifference of its enunciations to intentions, nevertheless the rhythm of prophetism and legalism is visible in it. It is visible in the prohibition of "idols," inseparable from the prophetic preaching of the God of justice, of mercy, of fidelity, inseparable also from the reference to the "God who brought thee out of Egypt, out of the house of bondage"; so the code becomes the charter of a liberated people. This rhythm is visible also in the designation of "covetousness," in article 10, as an evil disposition more internal than the forbidden modes of behavior: "covetousness" recalls the endless demand that proceeds from divine holiness and that makes one's neighbor and all that belongs to him infinitely respectable.

There was a time when Biblical critics failed to recognize this rhythm of prophetism and legalism, essential to the Hebraic conception of sin. They also displayed an excessive contempt for legalism, which, they said, remained under the influence of the negative character of the ancient prohibitions, disregarded intentions, and finally fragmented, "atomized" the "will of God." This tension between the absolute, but formless, demand and the finite law, which breaks the demand into crumbs, is essential to the consciousness of sin: one cannot just feel oneself guilty in general; the law is a "pedagogue" which helps the penitent to determine how he is a sinner; he is a sinner through idolatry, filial disrespect, etc. It is true that he would fall back into moralism if he ceased to regard sin as something beyond the enumeration of his faults; but the breakthrough of prophetism would have remained futile if it had not carried forward an already ancient movement of revision of earlier codes and given a new impetus to the rhythm of the indeterminate demand and the determinate commandment. So far, then, is the law from being a concession of prophetic circles to the archaic religion of the priests that prophetism presupposes the law and refers to the law. The Covenant lives by this alternation of the prophet and the Levite. How could the prophet become indignant against injustice, if his indignation were not articulated in definite reproaches: exploitation of the poor, cruelty towards enemies, the insolence of luxury?

It may be granted without difficulty that this survival of the old codes was at the same time a snare and that the tension could be slackened in compromises. History confirms this fact: the reform of Josiah, connected with the more or less accidental "discovery" of the book which present criticism usually recognizes as Deuteronomy, again gave first place to the suppression of the high places, the concentration of worship at Jerusalem, the destruction of idols and baals. That reform in one sense extended the first commandment of the Decalogue; but at the same time it brought back religious scrupulousness alongside the rites.[13]

This displacement of accent in the Law has its counterpart in a new style of historiography. While the older chronicles of Saul and David, Ahab and Jehu were marked with the brand of the prophetic spirit and unfolded the stark tragedy born of the confrontation of the guilty king and the accusing prophet, the new history of the kings concentrates on the "sins" denounced by the reform of Josiah: worship on the high places apart from the Temple, religious syncretism with baals and other idols. Such are the sins designated by the books of Kings as "the sin of Ahab," "the sin of Jeroboam."[14]

Nevertheless, it is this same ritualistic and legalistic Deuteronomy[15] which, in its parenetic parts, contains the most vibrant

[13] A. Lods, op. cit., pp. 371-74. The author sees in Deuteronomy the birth of Judaism, in the precise sense of the term, founded on the authority of the written word: "Deuteronomy, moreover, was the first layer of the Torah in the Jewish sense, a written and definitive formula of the will of God. It was, at the same time (and thereby it has a still more extensive historical importance), the first nucleus of the Bible, conceived as the divine standard of life" (p. 374).

[14] A. Lods, op. cit., pp. 375 ff.

[15] G. von Rad, in his Deuteronomiumstudien (1948) and his Theologie des alten Testaments, pp. 218-30, using a method akin to that of the Formgeschichte school, has restated the problem of the structure of Deuteronomy and of the balance between exhortation, commandments, benediction, and malediction, seeking therein the unity of a liturgical development. The word Torah (we translate it by Law, for want of a better alternative),

pages on the unlimited demands of faith and love, and thereby internalizes sin in the most radical fashion. At the moment when Moses is supposed to promulgate the moral and cultual charter that will sanction the imminent establishment of the people in the promised land, it is to the inner obedience of the heart that he appeals (Deut. 6, 11, 29, 30). Thus Deuteronomy repeats the same balancing of infinite demand and determinate commandment at a new stage that anticipates Judaism and the religion of the Torah. It is not by chance that Jesus, who taught us at the same time to go beyond the Law and to retain it, took the *Summary of the Law* from Deuteronomy and not from a prophetic book: "Hear, O Israel, Yahweh our God is the only Yahweh. Thou shalt love Yahweh thy God with all thy heart, with all thy soul, and with all thy might. Let these words which I command thee this day be graven in thy heart" (Deut. 6:4–6). The "fear" of God, like the "covetousness" named in the Decalogue, proceeds from that fine point of existence that the prophets had sharpened by threats and indignation.

That the reform of Josiah had brought a false security into the consciousness of sin is sufficiently evidenced by the disconcerting, scandalous behavior of Jeremiah and Ezekiel. Those who had satisfied the cultual demands of the deuteronomic reform might nourish a legitimate confidence in the face of the storm that broke over Judah. But here is Jeremiah taking up the howling of Amos: "You shall be destroyed because of your sins." His non-resistance

---

which presides over the theological unity of the book, covers, then, all Yahweh's interventions and tends to raise to a "didactic" level what first appears as a liturgical unity. It is within this whole that one must place the exhortations (Chaps. 6–11) and the body of laws (Chaps. 12 ff.), which, moreover, sound homiletic rather than juridical, in the style of preaching. The legalistic and cultual aspect then gets a new meaning, polemical and militant, directed against the Canaanitish nature-religion. Finally, one must never lose sight of the fact that all these imperatives are motivated by the recognition of the gratuitous and merciful election of Israel by its God, who loved it first. Even the situation in which Deuteronomy is supposed to be proclaimed by Moses is full of symbolic meaning: *between* Egypt and Canaan, *between* the going out and the coming in, *between* the promise and the fulfillment—that spiritual "moment" is the moment of the Torah.

rises up accusingly against the false confidence spread by legalistic piety; his prophecy thus makes contact, over the reform of Josiah, with the accusation of the first prophets. It is within the horizon of the already declared wrath of history that he shatters any assurance that the pious man might draw from his observance of the commandments; the catastrophe must be consummated even to the end, Israel must have neither soil, nor temple, nor king (there were two kings, one protected, the other deported, but Jeremiah and Ezekiel worked unremittingly to destroy their influence). In short, there must be nothing left of Israel from a human point of view, no room for political hopes, in order that the song of hope of the second Isaiah might be heard.

This political "nihilism" is essential to the Hebraic consciousness of sin; it is, in fact, the expression of a pedagogy of historical failure that aims at placing the ethical demand beyond any assignable historical end, beyond any finite observance, beyond any self-justification. The deuteronomic spirit, then, is only an episode between the terrible preaching of Justice by Amos and the defeatism in which Jeremiah and Ezekiel mask their unlimited demand for self-abandonment to the absolute of Yahweh.

Thus, from Amos to Ezekiel the ethical tension essential to the Covenant was never broken, even if it was stretched in one direction or another:[16] on one side, an unconditional but formless demand that finds the root of evil in the "heart"; on the other, a finite law that determines, makes explicit, and breaks up sinfulness into enumerable "transgressions," subjects for a future casuistry. If this dialectic is broken, the God of the infinite demand withdraws into the distance and the absence of the Wholly Other; or the legislator of the commandments becomes indistinguishable from the finite moral consciousness and is confounded with the witness that the Just One bears to himself. In this double manner the paradox of distance and presence which constitutes the "before God" is abolished at the heart of the consciousness of sin.

---

[16] It is true that "post-exilic" Judaism is an undisputed historical dimension; but the moment that we have wished to grasp is thereafter outdistanced. We shall discover the contribution of the Judaism of the second Temple in the framework of a reflection on *Scrupulousness* (below, Chap. III, § 3).

3. THE "WRATH OF GOD"

Shifting our gaze from the "objective" to the "subjective" pole of the consciousness of sin, we are now led back to the threat and the fear that we provisionally placed within brackets in order to consider the ethical content of the indignation of the prophet, namely, the balance between the infinite demand and the finite commandment. As was said above, it is not possible, in Hebrew prophecy, to separate Wrath from Indignation, Terror from Accusation.

It is necessary, therefore, to look this enigma in the face: in rising from the consciousness of defilement to the consciousness of sin, fear and anguish did not disappear; rather, they changed their quality. It is this new quality of anguish that constitutes what we call the "subjective" pole of the consciousness of sin. Perhaps we can understand the sense of this specific sort of anguish if we place it in relation with the two characteristics of sin studied above— the "before God" and "the infinite demand"—or, in other words, if we place it within the Covenant, and if we see therein a dramatization of the dialogal relation that is constitutive of the Covenant.

How is this new modality of dread expressed?

It stamps all the relations of man with God; the religion of Israel is imbued with this conviction that man cannot see God without dying; Moses at Horeb, Isaiah in the Temple, Ezekiel face to face with the glory of God, are terror-stricken; they experience in the name of the whole people the incompatibility of God and man.[17] This terror expresses the situation of sinful man before God. It is the truth of a relation without truth. So the veridical representation of God that corresponds to it is "Wrath": not that God is wicked, but that Wrath is the countenance of Holiness for sinful man.

This symbol of the Wrath of God, of the Day of Yahweh, directly

[17] A. M. Dubarle, *Le péché originel dans l'Écriture* (Paris, 1950), Chap. 1, "La condition humaine dans l'Ancien Testament"; especially, "L'incompatibilité de Dieu et de l'homme," pp. 22–25. On the wrath of God, see Ed. Jacob, *op. cit.*, pp. 91–94.

concerns the political fate of the community of Israel. This point
is of capital importance and dominates to a great extent the distinction between sin and guilt that will be introduced later on.
Guilt represents an internalization and a personalization of the
consciousness of sin. This double operation will encounter the resistance of the historical and communal interpretation of sin which
found in the theme of the Wrath of God and the Day of Yahweh
its most powerful symbol. In fact, it is as a people that Israel feels
itself threatened through the mouth of the prophet; it is by the
roundabout way of a theology of history, of an oracle concerning
the future of the community, that the people feels itself condemned.
Historical failure is thus erected into a symbol of condemnation.

> For three crimes of Damascus, and for four,
> I have decided irrevocably!
> . . . I will send a fire into the house of Hazael . . .
>>   Amos 1:3–4

> For three crimes of Gaza, and for four,
> I have decided irrevocably!
> . . . I will send a fire against the walls of Gaza . . .
>>   Amos 1:6–7

> For three crimes of Israel, and for four,
> I have decided irrevocably!
> . . . I will nail you to the ground.
>>   Amos 2:6, 13

> Thus saith Yahweh.
> For three crimes of the children of Ammon, and for four,
> I have decided irrevocably!
> Because they have ripped up the women with child of Gilead,
> that they might enlarge their border.
> I will kindle a fire in the wall of Rabbah,
> and it shall devour the palaces thereof,
> with shouting in the day of battle,
> with a tempest in the day of the whirlwind:
> And their king shall go into captivity,
> he and his princes together,
> saith Yahweh.
>>   Amos 1:13–15

And again:

> Woe unto them that desire the day of Yahweh!
> What will it be for you, the day of Yahweh?
> It will be darkness, and not light.
> As if a man did flee from a lion,
> and a bear met him!
> As if he went into the house, and leaned his hand on the wall,
> and a serpent bit him!
> Shall not the day of Yahweh be darkness, and not light?
> It will be dark, without any brightness.

Amos 5:18–20

Hosea, the tender Hosea, the terrible Hosea, roars with similar violence:

> For I will be unto Ephraim as a lion,
> and as a lion's cub to the house of Judah:
> I, I, will tear and go away;
> I will take away my prey, and none shall rescue him.

Hos. 5:14

Isaiah, the prophet of divine Majesty and Holiness, who recognized in sin the same arrogance that the Greeks called *hybris,* sees in his turn, in the day of Yahweh, the day when all pride is reduced to nought:

> Human pride will lower its eyes,
> the arrogance of men will be humbled.
> Yahweh alone will be exalted
> in that day.
> Yea, that will be the day of Yahweh Sabaoth
> against all pride and all arrogance,
> against all greatness, to bring it low,
> against all the cedars of Lebanon . . .
> and all the oaks of Bashan,
> against all the high mountains
> and all the elevated hills,
> against all the high towers
> and all the steep ramparts,
> against all the ships of Tarshish
> and all precious objects . . .

> Human pride will be humbled,
> the arrogance of men will be made low.
> Yahweh alone will be exalted
> in that day,
> and all the idols will be thrown down.
> Go into the holes of the rocks
> and into the caves of the earth,
> for fear of Yahweh
> and the brightness of his majesty,
> when he rises up
> to make the earth tremble.
>
> Is. 2:11–19

Jeremiah has no doubt that the true prophet is a prophet of misfortune. When the prophet Hananiah prophesies the end of servitude and snatches away the yoke that the prophet Jeremiah carries on his neck for a mimed parable and breaks it, Jeremiah attacks him in these terms: "Hear now, Hananiah! Yahweh has not sent you, and you have made this people trust in a lie. Therefore thus says Yahweh: Behold I will cast you off from the face of the earth; this year you shall die, because you have preached rebellion against Yahweh" (Jer. 28:15–16).

Ezekiel and Jeremiah even go to the extent of co-operating actively with disaster by political defeatism. This defeatism and, in truth, this treason have a profound religious significance; they have a share in the deciphering of the Wrath of God in history; by defeatism and treason the prophet fulfills the enmity of God against his people. No commentary can reconstitute the emotional violence of that *aggression* against the security of man, for no people has ever been called to judgment with such brutality.

And yet it is within the horizon of the Covenant that we must consider what we have called, from the beginning of this study of sin, a traumatism of the religious consciousness.

The bond of the Covenant is not broken, but stretched, and thus deepened.

It is first of all its breadth, its universal scope that is perceived. By the cipher of defeat, the prophet manifests the movement of history as a whole; the tribal god becomes more distant; Yahweh is no longer the guarantor of the historical success of his people; the consciousness of sin, through the symbol of the Day of Yahweh and an inimical history, reveals its other pole: the Lord of History. This transcendence and this breadth are the correlatives of the ethical Holiness that is manifested in another way through the infinite demand. The threat places the Lord at a greater distance from history and shatters his historical complicity with the chosen people in the same way as the infinite demand introduced into the codes increases the ethical distance between God and man.

At the same time, it appears that this Wrath is no longer the vindication of taboos, nor the resurgence of a primordial chaos, as old as the oldest gods, but the Wrath of Holiness itself. Without doubt, there is still a long way to go in order to understand or guess that the Wrath of God is only the sadness of love. This Wrath will have to be converted and become the sorrow of the "Servant of Yahweh" and the lowliness of the "Son of Man". . . .

Nevertheless, the symbol of the "Wrath of God" owes to its closeness to the symbol of Holiness certain traits that anticipate its future absorption into another group of symbols generated by the theology of Love.

It is, in the first place, quite remarkable that the threat of the "Day of Yahweh," terrible as it is, remains a threat internal to history; no trace of a "hell" or "eternal punishments," outside historical time and geographical space; no "time" without recourse, no "place" without return. Thus, the final seal is never placed on the foretold catastrophe;[18] prophecy remains within the limits of a penal interpretation of real history (it must not be forgotten that the deportations and the other disasters foretold actually happened). Prophecy, then, consists in deciphering future history by giving it in advance a meaning relative to the ethical life of the people. This remark is far-reaching, for the calamity designated by the expression "Day of Yahweh" does not exactly consist in the

---

[18] Hell, it seems, is a product of the Apocalypses. As the Son of Man comes "on the clouds of Heaven" in Daniel, Enoch, and the Gospels, so the day of judgment and the place of eternal punishments are separated from our history and the place of our abode. It is true that the "abode of the dead" or Sheol belongs to the oldest representations of Hebrew thought, but it is not the absolute place of catastrophe, it is not at all "hell."

occurrence of defeat and destruction. As something that happened, the occurrence was irrevocable, and the prophet anticipated it as happening and as irrevocable. The calamity consists rather in the *meaning* attached to the occurrence, in the *penal* interpretation of the event prophesied. That is why the Day of Yahweh is not only in history; it is in an interpretation of history.

If, then, history is revealed as chastisement only through the ministration of the prophecy that interprets it in this way, the bare occurrence can be prophesied as irrevocable and its meaning as revocable.

This is what happened in fact: the same prophet who announces the imminent catastrophe joins promise to threat.[19] The mother-cell of prophecy is, then, no longer the prediction of a calamity, but the double imminence of catastrophe and salvation. This double oracle keeps up the temporal tension characteristic of the Covenant. Of course, this "dialectic" is not "thought"; it never rises to the level of "speculation" and a "logic of being"; it is a dialectic in imagination and experience. It is modeled after the symbolism of the Covenant familiar to every prophet. With Amos, salvation is a discreet "perhaps" that gives a touch of hope to the inexorable itself: "You shall surely die . . . perhaps God will have mercy." With Hosea, an interval of nothingness separates the two successive events of death and life. With Isaiah, the salvation of a "remnant" is contemporary with the destruction of the Temple, as the survival of the stump is contemporary with the fall of the tree; while with the Second Isaiah the new day is born in sorrow.

Sometimes it even happens that this dialectic of destruction and salvation admits a sort of respite, in which the inexorable appears to be subject to human choice: "If you do justice, perhaps God will have mercy" (Amos 5:15). In a more urgent tone, even the prophet of the Day of Yahweh cries out in the name of God: "I have set life and death before you; choose life and you shall live" (Deut. 30:19).

This appeal, considered by itself, would seem to declare the ambiguity of history, held in suspense by the ethical choice of man;

[19] On the twofold oracle, cf. Néher, *L'Essence du prophétisme,* pp. 213–47.

the Day of Yahweh, considered by itself, would make history fate. The paradox is that the inexorable is modified by an appeal to right choice, but the choice does not, in its turn, annex either the Wrath of God or his pardon to the arbitrament of man.

Thus, the threat is inseparable from the "nevertheless" of a reconciliation that is always possible and is promised in the end; and the fury of the Jealous One also is inscribed in the drama of a love that is at the same time broken and always carried beyond the point of rupture. Thus the distance that anguish discloses does not make God simply the Wholly Other; anguish dramatizes the Covenant without ever reaching the point of rupture where absolute otherness would be absence of relation. Just as jealousy is an affliction of love, so anguish is a moment that dialectizes the dialogue, but does not annul it.

The rhythm of distance and presence, which remains hidden in the preaching of the "Day of Yahweh," is made manifest through the poetic structure of the psalm. It is, in fact, in the psalm that the "unhappy consciousness" of the sinner discovers that its separation from God is still a relation.[20] It is to David, the David who was shown by the oldest chronicles in the situation of one accused, face to face with the prophet Nathan, that the tradition attributes the famous Psalm 51, which is called a penitential psalm. The suppliant confesses that he has sinned *against* God; but the "against" God is disclosed only in the movement of invocation that manifests the dialogal relation: O God, I have sinned against thee. "Out of the depths I cry unto thee, Yahweh"—thus begins Psalm 130. "Return, Yahweh, deliver my soul," is the cry of Psalm 6. The vocative —O God—which expresses the invocation of the petitioner, puts the moment of rupture back within the bond of participation; if God were the Wholly Other, he would no longer be invoked. And if the sinner were only the object of the prophetic accusation, he would no longer be invoking. In the movement of invocation the sinner becomes fully the subject of sin, at the same time as the terrible God of destruction becomes the supreme Thou.

[20] For a study of the penitential psalms, cf. Sven Herner, *Sühne und Vergebung in Israel,* pp. 92–109 (especially the study of Psalms 51, 130, 32, 6). We shall return to this subject in Chap. III.

Thus the psalms reveal the tenderness hidden in the heart of the prophetic accusation and proclaim that the Wrath which has already shown itself as the Wrath of Holiness might be only the Wrath of Love, if one dare say so.

4. THE SYMBOLISM OF SIN: (1) SIN AS "NOTHINGNESS"

We have tried to view the new experience of fault in as close proximity as possible to the drama of the Covenant in which it gets meaning. But this experience is not mute; the summons of the prophet, the confession of the sinner issue forth in the element of language. Moreover, we could not omit this impact of the experience of sin on discourse when we examined the diverse modalities of prophetic accusation: injustice according to Amos, adultery according to Hosea, arrogance according to Isaiah, lack of faith according to Jeremiah, etc.

The moment has come to consider in a more systematic manner the linguistic creations that correspond to this new cycle of experience. We shall take for reference the *symbolism* of defilement worked out at the preceding stage of the consciousness of fault. It was, we remember, the representation of a something, of a positive power, that infects and contaminates by contact; even if those representations are not to be taken literally, but symbolically, nevertheless the secondary intention that runs through the literal sense of stain indicates the positive character of defilement and the negative character of purity. This is why the symbolism of defilement was necessarily shattered under the pressure of a new experience and gave way little by little to a new symbolism. If sin is primarily the rupture of a relation, it becomes difficult to express it in terms of defilement. We shall look for the trail of this conversion from positive to negative in the vocabulary of sin.

Under this first aspect, the symbolism of sin breaks with that of defilement. But sin is not only the rupture of a relation; it is also the experience of a power that lays hold of man. In this respect, the symbolism of sin rediscovers the major intention of the symbolism of defilement; sin, too, is a "something," a "reality." Thus, we have to give an account at the same time of the preferment of a new symbolism and of the survival of the old under the direction of the new.

The break with the symbolism of defilement and its reaffirmation on a new level become still more striking when the symbolism of sin is complemented by the symbolism of redemption; indeed, it is not possible to understand the one without the other. It was no more possible to speak of defilement without speaking of purification. With stronger reason, the establishment, the negation, and the reaffirmation of the Covenant form a coherent symbolic whole. Although, in an investigation dedicated to the symbolics of evil, the principal emphasis must fall on the symbolism of sin as such, this symbolism itself is not complete unless it is considered retrospectively from the point of view of the faith in redemption. For this reason we will mark each of the stages of the symbolics of sin by a parallel symbolics of redemption.

Let us, then, consider, first of all, in the pair sin-redemption, that which is most opposed to the symbolism of defilement. The Covenant being the symbol of a quasi-personalistic relation, the fundamental symbolism of sin expresses the loss of a bond, of a root, of an ontological ground. To this there corresponds, from the side of redemption, the fundamental symbolism of "return."

It is remarkable that the Hebrew Bible does not have any abstract word to express sin, but a bundle of concrete expressions, each of which, in its own way, is the beginning in a figurative manner of a possible line of interpretation and announces what might be called a "theologoumenon."[21] Moreover, it will not be without interest, as we enumerate the Hebraic images and roots, to note the corresponding images and roots of the Greek language which, in their turn, were able to furnish equivalents to the Hebraic schemata when the Bible was translated into Greek. Furthermore, this translation is an important cultural event; it united the destinies of the two languages and gave rise to a Helleno-Hebraic

---

[21] *Theologisches Wörterbuch zum N. T.* (Kittel), art. "ἁμαρτάνω, ἁμάρτημα, ἁμαρτία," I, 267 f.; Ludwig Köhler, *Theologie des alten Testaments* (Tübingen, 1936); Ed. Jacob, *op. cit.,* p. 226; Eichrodt, *op. cit.,* Vol. III, § 23.

schematization and conceptualization, beyond which it is no longer possible to return.

We have a first root (*chattat*) which means missing the target, to which we can relate a second symbol, that of a tortuous road (*'awon*). These two roots, joined to one another, forecast the concept of the a-nomalous, a purely formal concept in which divergence from order, deviation from the straight road, are considered without regard to the motive of the act and the inner quality of the agent. The Greek ἁμάρτημα, which furnished the abstract concept of sin through the Latin *peccatum*, is akin to the first Hebrew root. On the other hand, the symbolism of the "way" or "road" is well known from Pythagoreanism; besides, it is almost universal. The symbolism of a journey is akin to it and furnishes the controlling schema for the Prelude of the *Poem* of Parmenides: "The horses which draw me carry me along, answering to the ardor of my desire. For in guiding me, they have led me along the famous route—of the Goddess who conducts men possessing the light of knowledge through all cities." It is true that among the Greeks the symbol of the "way" did not produce as distinctly as among the Hebrews the symbol of a circuitous, curving, tortuous way. The symbol of error or going astray, more adapted to the problem of truth than to that of ethical obedience, takes its place. On the other hand, we shall presently discover something like a symbol of going astray among the Hebrews.

A third root denotes rebellion (*pesha'*), revolt, stiff-neckedness. It is the evil intention itself that is here designated and not the objective deviation from the will of God. Here the rupture is thematized as initiative; and as the framework of schematization is that of a personalistic relation between God and man, it is the opposition of the human will to the holy will that furnishes the nucleus of the image: sin is "against" God, as existence is "before" God. The intersubjective, social symbol of revolt thus becomes the least formal and most existential symbol of sin. To this cycle belong the words and images that speak of infidelity, adultery, refusal to listen and to hear, hardness of hearing, and stiffness of neck. Every time the Greeks oriented themselves toward a relation of a personalistic character between man and the gods, they approached this theme of pride and arrogance and saw human evil in it; but the tragic and even pre-tragic *hybris,* which seems so close to the pride and arrogance denounced by Isaiah and Deuteronomy, is much more closely related to the "jealousy" of the gods with regard to men inclined to transgress the limits of their finitude than to the idea of a pact broken, a dialogue interrupted. Hence, the closeness of the images should not be overestimated, even though the symbol of the "Wrath of God" and that of the "jealousy" of Yahweh towards false gods creates a certain room for comparison between Biblical pride and Greek hybris.

Finally, another symbol (*shagah*), with apparently less emotional resonance, designates precisely the situation of having gone astray, of being lost, in which the sinner finds himself. But if the image of revolt is more forceful, the image of having gone astray is more radical, for it directly envisages a total situation, the state of being astray and lost. Thus, it forecasts the more modern symbols of alienation and dereliction; the interruption of the dialogue, having become a situation, makes man a being alien to his ontological place. The silence of God, the absence of God, are in a way a correlative symbol to the symbol of having gone astray, of being lost; for the being who has strayed is "abandoned" by God. As one sees, the "error" of the *Poem* of Parmenides is not without analogy, at least on the figurative level: "I put you on guard against that other way of investigation on which mortals without knowledge wander in every direction, monsters with two heads. For in them impotence guides their unsteady minds in their breasts. They are pushed this way and that, deaf as well as blind, thrown into a stupor, a mob without judgment—for whom being and not being appear the same and not the same, and for whom the path of all things turns back upon its steps." But the problematics of Truth and Opinion separates "error" according to Parmenides from "straying" according to the Prophets of Israel no less than the tragic problem of the "jealousy" of the gods just now separated Greek hybris from Hebrew pride. The structural relationship of the symbols nevertheless permits exchanges, even on the level of meanings. If it is true that error is more than intellectual error and is already moral fault, and if, on the other hand, there is no fault without some change in "opinion," in the representation of the "apparent" good, it is intelligible that the two symbols of "having gone astray" and "error" could cross their fires and exchange their intentions on a more speculative level of reflection on evil. But the sense of this development will not appear until later.

Thus, in various ways, a first conceptualization of sin radically different from that of defilement is outlined on the symbolic level: missing the mark, deviation, rebellion, straying from the path do not so much signify a harmful substance as a violated relation. This change in the intentionality of the symbol, arising from the new experience of evil, is reached through an upheaval on the level of the basic images themselves: for relations of contact in space, relations of orientation are substituted; the way, the straight line, straying, like the metaphor of a journey, are analogies of the movement of existence considered as a whole. At the same time, the symbol passes over from space to time; the "way" is the spatial projection of a movement that is the evolution of a destiny. Thus the revolution in the images prepares the way for the revolution in the meanings themselves.

The symbolism of sin, then, suggests the idea of a relation broken off. But the negativity of sin remains implicit in it; and we shall be able presently to survey these same key images from the point of view of the "power" of sin and also to extract from them an allusion to the positivity of human evil. This is why it is not without interest to join to this first bundle of symbols some other expressions that make the negative moment explicit and point toward the idea of a "nothingness" of sinful man. Of course, a culture that has not worked out the idea of being does not have a concept of nothingness either; but it may have a symbolism of negativity—through failure, deviation, rebellion, going astray. The sinner has "gone away from" God; he has "forgotten" God; he is "foolish," "without understanding." But there are more striking expressions of this negativity that can be classed with the "breath of air" that passes and is not retained or with the "idol" that deceives because it is not the true God.[22] The former schema is more concrete and corre-

---

[22] *Theologisches Wörterbuch zum N. T.* (Kittel), art. "μάταιος" (Nich-

sponds to a less advanced stage of conceptualization; but it furnishes the most powerful emotional analogue of nothingness. Starting from the impression of the light, the empty, the unsubstantial, the futile, which is connected with the material image of exhalation, breath, dust, it apprehends in a single glance the total character of human existence as "abandoned"; "man is like a breath of air; his days are as the shadow that passes away" (Ps. 144:4). "The sons of Adam are only a breath of air, the sons of man a lie; if they were placed in the balance together, they would be less than a breath of air" (Ps. 62:9). To this image of a breath of air we can relate the image of a desert and its empty desolation: "All nations are as nothing before him; they are counted to him as nothing and vanity" (Is. 40:17). The place accorded to this image of "vanity" by the Kohelet is well known. In that book it almost reaches the abstraction of nothingness. But if the word has lost its concrete sense and tends toward the non-being of error or, better, errancy that the Greeks worked out systematically, if it is almost equivalent to the "*doxa* of mortals" of Parmenides' *Poem,* it never breaks completely with the original image of "mist" or "breath": "Behold, all is vanity and pursuit of the wind" (1:14).

This existential image of "vanity" gets blended with the image of "idols," which comes from a more elaborate theological reflection on false gods. It is fed not by the spectacle of unsubstantial things— vapor, exhalation, mist, wind, dust—but by the spectacle of false sacredness. From this vanity receives its transcendent meaning: "For all the gods of the nations are idols, but the Lord made the heavens" (Ps. 96:5). (The Bible of Jerusalem translates: "All the gods of the nations are nothing.") To the false gods Yahweh declares through the mouth of the Second Isaiah: "You are nothing and your works are nought; to choose you is abominable" (41:24). Hence, priests and oracles of the false gods share in their nothingness: "All of them together are nothing. Their works are nothing; their statues are wind and void" (41:29). Here the meaning of the "jealousy" of Yahweh is made manifest: the "nothingness" of the idols is the symbol of that Other which is Nothing and of which,

tig); Köhler, *op. cit.,* art. on Elil (gods=nothing), Hebel (exhalation, vapor, dust=vanity=idols of nothingness), Aven (vanity, nothing, nought).

nevertheless, Yahweh is "jealous." But if the idol is Nothing in the eyes of Yahweh, it is real non-being for man. This is why Yahweh is jealous of that which is Nothing for him, but which is a Pseudo-Something for man. Amos had already forged the image of a choice between "good" and "evil" which is the equivalent of a radical choice between "God" and "Nothing."[23] For all the prophets, an idol is more than a "graven image"; it is a model of nothingness. Hence, the man who takes pleasure in it is nothing; the vision or the prophecy that is not sent by the Lord is nothing; sin itself, already symbolized by adultery, is now symbolized by idolatry. Finally, the two images of breath and idol transpose their significations and blend their meanings: the vanity of breath becomes the vanity of the idol, "by pursuing vanity they have become vanity" (Jer. 2:5); for man becomes that which he adores: "Like unto their idols shall be they that made them, whoever puts his trust in them" (Ps. 115:8).

This schema of the "nothingness" of idols and idolatry is the correlative, from the side of man, of the schema of the "Wrath of God" which we grasped directly in the oracle of the Day of Yahweh: man abandoned is the manifestation of God as the one who abandons; man's forgetfulness of God is reflected in God's forgetfulness of man. Thus, God is no longer the "Yes" of the word "who speaks and it is so"; he is the "No" who puts down the wicked, his idols, and all his vanity:

[23] Néher very judiciously compares the ethical choice of Amos 5:14–15 ("Seek good and not evil . . . hate the evil and love the good") with the ontological alternative set up in 5:5: "Seek not Beth-El, nor enter into Gilgal, and pass not to Beer-sheba [these are sanctuaries, high places; Beth-El, more particularly, means "house of God"]; for Gilgal shall surely go into captivity and Beth-El shall be Aven [=vanity, nothing, nought]." "The good," Néher writes (*Amos*, p. 112), "is God; evil is non-God, the idol, or, in the terminology of Amos, vanity, nought. Here the paronomasia from Beth-El to Beth-Aven gets all its force. . . . What is opposed to El, God, is Aven, nought, nothing." Deuteronomy repeats the same schema: on the one hand, the ethical choice, "See, I have set before thee this day life and good, and death and evil. . . . I have set before you life and death, blessing and cursing; therefore choose life" (30:15 and 19); on the other, the ontological alternative, "They have provoked me with non-God, they have angered me with their futile vanities; I will provoke them with non-people, I will anger them with a foolish nation" (32:21), quoted by Néher, *ibid.*, p. 113.

By thine anger we are consumed,
By thy wrath we are frightened.
Thou hast set our iniquities before thee,
Our secret sins in the light of thy countenance.
Under thy wrath our days decline,
We spend our years as a sigh.

Ps. 90:7–9

Perhaps even the "No" of the Interdiction, in the myth of the fall,[24] is a naïve projection, in the sphere of innocence, of a negation issuing from sin itself. Perhaps the order of creation is supported wholly by affirmation, even when it envelops dissonances, oppositions, and a primordial disproportion: "Let it be so." Even when this order signifies a limit for man, still this limit is constitutive of man; it protects his liberty and thus pertains simply to man's position in existence. Perhaps it is the nothingness of vanity, issuing from sin, which turns this very first creative limit into an Interdiction. Thus, step by step, vanity extends itself over everything and makes God himself appear as the "No" that forbids and destroys, as the Adversary whose will is summed up in the pursuit of death for the sinner. Then the man for whom God would no longer be anything but wrath and the willing of death, the man who would go to the end of this frightening possibility, would truly reach the bottom of the abyss and would be reduced to a cry, to this cry: "My God, my God, why hast thou forsaken me?" (Ps. 22:1). In this cry the agony of the Son of Man is consummated.

This symbolism of sin gets a new emphasis when sin is considered retrospectively from the standpoint of that which goes beyond it, namely, "pardon." At the end of this first part we shall stress the fact that the complete and concrete meaning of sin becomes apparent only in this retrospection.

Let us set aside for the moment the complex notion of "expiation" which we shall not be able to understand until we have explained the resumption of the symbolism of defilement in that of sin. Let us rather concern ourselves with the pair "pardon-return," which raises fewer difficulties of interpretation, and refrain from any

[24] Cf. below, Part II, Chap. III, "The Adamic Myth."

theological elaboration, any conceptual dialectics, any attempt at concordism or synergy between the initiative of God and the initiative of man. At the level where the concepts come to birth in images (or schemata) that have the potency of symbols, it is the whole, "pardon-return," that is full of meaning and that signifies as a whole the restoration of the Covenant.

Let us take as our point of departure the divine pole of "pardon." We shall soon find ourselves referred to the other pole, that of the "return" of man.[25]

The theme of "pardon" is itself a very rich symbol, of the same nature as that of the wrath of God, and its meaning is elaborated in connection with the latter. Pardon is, as it were, the forgetting or the renouncing of the wrath of holiness; it often takes the figurative form of a "repentance of God" (Ex. 32:14), as if God changed his own course, his own plan with regard to men. This imagined change in God is full of meaning; it means that the new direction imprinted on the relation of man to God has its origin in God, is divinely initiated. This origin, this initiative is represented as an event occurring in the divine sphere; instead of condemning man, God raises him up. Sometimes wrath and pardon are superimposed, the one on the other: when the name of the Eternal is proclaimed (Ex. 34), the Eternal is called God of mercy, slow to anger, abounding in grace and fidelity, who keeps his grace for thousands, tolerates faults, transgression, and sin, but leaves nothing unpunished and visits chastisement for the fault of the fathers upon the children and the grandchildren, even to the third and fourth generation (Ex. 34:6–7). The relation of "three generations" to "a thousand generations" anticipates the argument "how much more," which will be familiar to St. Paul, as will be said further on. More astonishingly, we read in Hosea:

[25] The most important study is E. K. Dietrich, *Die Umkehr im A. T. und in Judentum* (1936). For a study, book by book, of the ideas of "pardon" and "expiation," see Sven Herner, *Sühne und Vergebung in Israel.* Ed. Jacob gives an excellent synthetic view in *Les thèmes essentiels d'une théologie de l'Ancien Testament,* pp. 233 ff. H. W. Wolff examines the theological implications in "Das Thema 'Umkehr' in der alttestamentlichen Prophetie," *Zeitschrift f. Theol. u. Kirche* (1951). J. J. Stamm combines the exegetical and theological points of view in *Erlösen und Vergebung im A. T.* (Berne, 1940).

> I will not execute the fierceness of my wrath,
> I will not return to destroy Ephraim;
> For I am God, and not man,
> I am the Holy One in the midst of thee,
> and I do not love to destroy.

Hos. 11:9

The Biblical writers read this repenting of wrath into history itself, into the course of events which are interpreted as a divine pedagogy at work. Sometimes it is the postponement of a disaster, the end of a plague, a healing, which are immediately understood as "pardon." Thus the schema of pardon is taken up into a theology of history, like most of the Hebraic schemata. Sometimes, more subtly, pardon is discovered not in an actual and even physical deliverance, but in the punishment itself, which, although painful and even cruel, loses its aspect of irrevocable condemnation (it is thus in the dénouement of the crime of David, reported in II Samuel 12:13–14); pardon does not abolish suffering, but grants a respite which is interpreted as a horizon determined by divine patience. Another idea can then enter into this conception of pardon which is expressed by means of punishment: in addition to mitigation of the punishment, pardon appears as the transformation of an obstacle into a test; punishment becomes the instrument of awareness, the path of confession. Pardon is already fully evident in this restored capacity of knowing oneself in one's true situation in the bosom of the Covenant. Thus the penalty, felt as an affliction, is a part of punishment and of pardon at the same time. By the same token, "pardon" *is* "return"; for return, *a parte Dei,* is nothing else than the taking away of blame, the suppression of the charge of sin: "I have acknowledged my sin to thee, I have not concealed my iniquity. I said, I will confess my transgressions to the Eternal! And thou hast wiped out the penalty of my sin" (Ps. 32:5).

This schema of "return" (root *shub*), to which we are led by the schema of pardon, is at the origin of all our ideas concerning repentance (we shall see later the role of the Judaism of the second Temple in the elaboration of this concept, by means of the new term *teshubah,* which we shall translate by repentance[26]). The

[26] Erik Sjöberg, *Gott und die Sünder im palestinischen Judentum* (Stuttgart, 1939), pp. 125–84.

harmonics of this symbol of "return" are numerous. On the one hand, it belongs to the cycle of images of the "way." Just as sin is a "crooked way," the return is a turning from the evil way: "Let everyone turn from his evil way," says Jeremiah. This turning away anticipates the more abstract idea of renunciation. On the other hand, the return is a renewal of the primitive bond, a restoration. As such, it is often associated with images of tranquillity and repose, close to the rock of life: "By returning and being at rest you shall be saved" (Is. 30:15). Thus, the return is the equivalent of a re-instatement in stability; it is the end of the wandering of Cain, the possibility of "dwelling in the land" (Jer. 7:3–7; 25:5). The schema of return has something in common also with the conjugal metaphor; it is the end of adultery, of prostitution, in Hosea's sense. Jeremiah takes up this theme of love with a compelling pathos: "Return, unfaithful Israel! says the Eternal" (3:22). For the second Isaiah, "to return" is to "seek God"; the return becomes a quest for the living water, as in the Johannine Gospel.

Such is the symbolic richness of this pair, pardon-return: if we try to surprise it at the level of images, it immediately throws us into the very midst of a paradox which can perhaps not be ex-hausted by any systematic theology but only shattered. Thus the prophet does not hesitate to exhort the people to "return," as if it depended entirely on man, and to implore the "return," as if it depended wholly on God: "Make me return and I shall return," cries Jeremiah. Sometimes God's side alone is emphasized; then the "return" is the fruit of a free choice of the hidden majesty, the effect of a love, of a *hesed* beyond all reasons (Deut. 7:5 ff.). This *hesed* is magnified and amplified by Jeremiah, for example, to the dimensions of a universal reconciliation, from which even untamed nature is not excluded. "Pardon" and "return" then coincide in the gift of a "heart of flesh," substituted for a "heart of stone" (a theme common to Jeremiah and Ezekiel). But it was, perhaps, the Second Isaiah who had the most acute sense of the gratuitousness of grace in comparison with the nothingness of creatures (for ex-ample, Isaiah 40:1 and ff.). And yet the pendulum always swings back: it is Jeremiah, again, who transmits these words: "But if that nation, against which I have spoken, turn from its wickedness,

I will repent of the evil that I thought to do to it" (Jer. 18:8).
This suspensive power of human choice, which seems to make pardon conditional, leads us back to the famous choice in Deuteronomy: "Behold, I set before you this day a blessing and a curse . . ."
(11:26); "Behold, I set before you this day life and good, death
and evil" (30:15).[27] Thus the symbolism of "return" and of "pardon," in the land of its birth, holds in suspense all the aporias of
theology concerning grace and free will, predestination and liberty.
But perhaps it also holds in reserve the hyperlogical reconciliation
of terms that speculation isolates and sets in opposition.

Let us leave this symbolism of redemption for the moment. We
shall take it up again at a new stage, corresponding to a new stage
in the symbolism of sin.

5. The Symbolism of Sin: (2) Sin as Positive

We have followed the slope of negativity in the symbols of sin
to its ultimate outcome: the violated pact makes God the Wholly
Other and man Nothing in the presence of the Lord. It is the
moment of the "unhappy consciousness."

And yet, the structure of the symbolism of sin cannot be enclosed
within this elementary opposition between the "nothingness" of
vanity and the "something" of defilement. Through other characteristics, which may be called realistic, sin is also positive, as
Kierkegaard will say. It is these characteristics which assure a certain continuity between the two systems of symbols and a resumption of the symbol of defilement in the new symbol of sin.

This "realism" of sin will not be fully understood until it is approached through the new factor in the consciousness of fault that
we shall call guilt. Strictly speaking, it is only with this new moment
that the *consciousness* of sin becomes the criterion and the measure

[27] André Néher, *Amos,* p. 108. All the exhortations of Deuteronomy are
based on the schema: *If* you keep the commandments, *then* you will be
blessed; or, Keep the commandments *in order that* you may be happy. But
the same exhortations say: *Remember* that you have been graciously
rescued from Egypt; the Eternal has chosen you not because you are great,
but because he loves you. The paradox is not elaborated speculatively; it
remains at the level of religious *praxis* and maintains the tension by means
of exhortation.

of fault. The feeling of guilt will coincide exactly with the consciousness that the guilty one has of himself and will be indistinguishable from the "for itself" of the fault.

It is not so with the "confession" of sin; "confession" is the frontier view of a *real* evil that has been revealed and denounced by the prophetic summons and that is not measured by the sinner's consciousness of it. This is why the "reality" of sin—one might even say the ontological dimension of sin—must be contrasted with the "subjectivity" of the consciousness of guilt. It is the "heart" of man that is evil—that is to say, his very existence, whatever his consciousness of it may be.

It is this realism of sin that allows the penitent to repent of forgotten sins, or sins committed unwittingly—in short, sins that *are,* because they characterize his true situation within the Covenant. This first trait is one of those that most obviously insure the continuity between the system of defilement and that of sin. We remain at the surface of things if we see in this structural relationship only a survival of the archaic conception of objective sacrilege. Of course, a great number of crimes—true crimes without guilt— can be explained thus,[28] as well as the precept: "If anyone sins and

---

[28] A murder of which the perpetrator is unknown spreads a curse that the priest must conjure away by a special technique of expiation, for protection against the vengeance of blood (Deut. 21:1–9). The anathema pronounced against Jericho at the moment of its destruction cannot be violated without sacrilege, even by an unknown person; the sacrilege calls for vengeance; the sacred lots will designate the "guilty one," who will be stoned and destroyed by fire—himself, his family, and his goods (Josh. 7). That is why the "consequences" of sin, as well as the "action" and the "heart" from which it springs, are part of the sin. The ambivalence, from the semantic point of view, of such expressions as the following has been noticed: "But if you do not so, you will sin against the Eternal; and be sure that your sin will find you out" (Num. 32:23); or "to bear the penalty of sin" (Num. 12:11), an expression that does not differ at all from "to bear the punishment" (Gen. 4:13). Intention, act, consequences, punishment—it is the whole process that is sin (G. von Rad, *op. cit.,* pp. 262–67). That is why sin is something that is "borne" as long as it is not forgiven; that is why also getting rid of sin can be symbolized by "transference" to a scapegoat, which "carries away all their iniquities" (Lev. 16:22) on the great day of atonement. As we shall see further on, this resurgence of a rite of elimination in a full-blown theology of sin is explained perfectly by the "realism" of sin and by the symbolic transposition of the ritual of purification to the plane of the remission of sins.

does unwittingly any of the things that are forbidden by the commandments of Yahweh, he shall be responsible and shall bear the
weight of his fault" (Lev. 5:17). But the explanation of these
examples by some survival of the system of taboo, sacrilege, and
ritual expiation must not conceal the more important fact that
makes this survival possible, namely, that the Law, as the ethico-
juridical expression of the Covenant, has been substituted for the
anonymous power of taboo and the automatism of its vengeance,
and establishes a hypersubjective reference for sin. It is finally the
"real" situation of man within the Covenant that is the measure
of sin and confers upon it a genuine transcendence in relation to the
consciousness of guilt.

A second trait confirms this realism of sin: because it cannot be
reduced to its subjective measure, neither can sin be reduced to its
individual dimension; it is at once and primordially personal *and*
communal.[29] The misdeeds of the theory of retribution erected on
this theme of collective imputation will receive sufficient attention
when we come to the question of etiological myths; but the constructions of second degree and the abortive rationalizations to
which the confession of the sin of the people gave license should
not hide from us the profound significance of this confession at the
level of living experience and of the primary symbols that express
it. Speculation on the transmission of a sin issuing from a first man
is a later rationalization that mixes ethical categories with biological
ones. Indeed, it was because the original significance of a sin that
is personal *and* communal had been lost that an attempt was made
to compensate for the individualism of guilt by a solidarity on the

[29] A. M. Dubarle, *Le péché originel dans l'Écriture,* pp. 25–38. The
author studies the solidarity between successive generations, within the
family and the nation; the solidarity between contemporaries, for example
between a prince and his people, punished because of his sins; and finally,
collective sins, such as the proud pretension of the builders of Babel or, still
better, the idolatry of an entire people. Those two examples are striking,
for they exclude determination of personal guilt: the confusion of tongues,
opposition of groups, forms of worship, are *anonymous* phenomena, on a
linguistic and institutional level, which at once reveal the communal scale
of human evil; the hindrance to communication and the seductive power
of idols represent a purely cultural alienation and corruption. We shall
return to this point in our third volume.

biological level, constructed on the model of heredity. But this confusion of categories in the pseudo-concept of hereditary sin reflects
intentionally a communal bond attested by the liturgical confession
of sins. We must try, then, to recapture, at a stage prior to any
speculation concerning the transmission of an individualized sin,
the confession of a specific *Us,* of "us poor sinners," in which the
hyperbiological and hyperhistorical unity of the "people" and even
of "humanity" is attested. The Adamic myth expresses this concrete universal, acknowledged in the confession of sins; it expresses
it, but does not create it; rather, it presupposes it and only presents
it by means of a fanciful explanation.

There is no question of denying that the personal imputation of
fault marks an advance over the scandalous collective responsibility
that permits someone other than the guilty person to be punished.
But it must be understood that the price of this advance is the loss
of the unity of the human species, gathered together "before God"
by the more than biological and more than historical bond of fault.
The pseudo-concept of original sin is only the rationalization at
the third degree, through the Adamic myth, of that enigmatic bond
which is acknowledged rather than understood in the "we" of the
confession of sins.

Third characteristic trait of the hypersubjective reality of sin:
my sin is within the absolute sight (*regard*) of God. God—and not
my consciousness—is the *"for itself"* of sin. Does this mean that the
person who confesses, ashamed of being seen, feels himself stripped
of his subjectivity by being thus seen, and reduced to the condition
of an object? That is not the dominant note that makes itself heard
in the believer's acknowledgment of being seen by God; wonder at
such seeing, which "searches out the reins and the heart," is sufficient to keep the "fear" of God within the region of respect and
sublimity (Ps. 139:1–6). It is still the dialogal relation of the
Covenant that rules all those affective modulations which color this
consciousness of being in the sight of God. The very act of invocation—O God, thine eye is upon me!—keeps the observed consciousness from falling to the rank of an object; the first person who invokes feels himself become second person for this perception that
sees right through him. Finally, if the principal emphasis is not

placed on the degrading character of the situation of being-seen-by
God, it is because the primordial significance of this seeing is to
constitute the *truth* of my situation, the justness and the justice of
the ethical judgment that can be passed on my existence. That is
why this seeing, far from preventing the birth of the Self, gives rise
to self-awareness; it enters into the field of subjectivity as the *task*
of knowing oneself better; this seeing, which *is,* lays the foundation
for the ought-to-be of self-awareness. The examination of conscience
is thus justified: my own observation of myself is the attempt of
self-awareness to approximate the absolute view; I desire to know
myself as I am known (Ps. 139:23–24). The preferred form of this
act of awareness is interrogation, the putting in question of the
meaning of acts and motives.[30] The absolute view separates the
appearance from the reality by the sharp edge of suspicion. Suspicion of myself is thus the taking up by myself of the absolute
viewpoint; it co-operates thus with the growth of interrogative
thought, which perhaps owes more to the problem of evil than to
the enigmas of meteorology.

The advanced point of this awareness aroused by the absolute
Seeing (*Regard*) is the "wisdom" that knows the "vanity" of man
as God knows it: "The Eternal knows the thoughts of man; he
knows that they are vain" (Ps. 94:11). As we see, to know that one
is "vain" is not to become an object; it is to penetrate into the
enclosure of salvation through the strait gate of truth.

This faith in the truth and justice of the Seeing (*Regard*) will
have to grow weaker before the believer feels himself become an
object. Consciousness congealed into an object arises from the
decomposition of the primordial relation of the absolute Seeing to
the Self. The book of Job is the witness of this crisis: Job feels the
absolute seeing as an inimical seeing that pursues him and finally
kills him. We shall say later how the problem of suffering affects
the problem of sin and how the destruction of the old theory of
retribution raised a doubt about this seeing, which suddenly reveals
itself as the seeing of the hidden God who delivers man up to unjust

[30] This interrogative structure of the examination of conscience among
penitents of the ancient East is particularly striking. Cf. Ch. F. Jean, *Le
péché chez les Babyloniens et les Mésopotamiens,* pp. 99–104.

suffering. Then the absolute Seeing is no longer the seeing that gives rise to self-awareness, but that of the Hunter who lets fly the arrow. And yet, even at this extreme point, close to the breach, the accusation against God remains enveloped in the invocation, under pain of losing the very object of its resentment; which means that the discovery of the hostile Seeing is always inscribed within a relation in which the absolute Seeing continues to be the foundation of truth for the view that I have of myself.

Because it is the possible truth of the knowledge of oneself, this Seeing preserves the reality of my existence beyond the consciousness that I have of it, and more particularly the reality of sin beyond the feeling of guilt.

The traits that we have just analyzed attest that this sin, "internal" to existence, contrary to the defilement that infects it from "without," is no less irreducible to consciousness of guilt; it is internal but objective. This first group of characteristics assures the phenomenological continuity between defilement and sin.

A second group of characteristics re-enforces this structural continuity. We have insisted above on the "negativity" of sin—vanity of a breath of air and vanity of idols—in comparison with the "positivity" of defilement. Nevertheless, that contrast is too simple; for "vanity," which deprives existence of its force, is also, in a way, a *potency*.

Here, again, it was easy to recognize a survival of the system of defilement and of the theme of *"possession"* that belongs to that system. The descriptive situation is more complex.

What assures the continuity from one type to the other is the consciousness of alteration, of alienation, which is common to the two types. This consciousness was first fixed in the representation of a maleficent substance, without that maleficent substance's being necessarily dramatized in the shape of demons or evil gods. On the other hand, the sacred texts of the ancient East illustrate a stage at which this consciousness of alienation is fixed in the superabundant representation of quasi-personal forces of a demonic character, which take the place of the god and literally take up their abode in the sinner. The tenacious confusion of sin and sickness gives added support to this representation of personalized forces that take possession of the sinner and bind him. Here we are at a stage prior to the distinction of sickness and fault, a distinction bound up with the realization of guilt, in the precise sense of imputation of fault. This disjunction implies a certain dualism which is not necessarily the dualism of soul and body, but the dualism of a moral agent, author of moral evil, and a course of events that brings sickness, suffering, and death. The confusion of sin and sickness has as its counterpart an interpretation of pardon as being a healing, an unbinding, and a deliverance, all in one. "May the evil that is in my body, in my muscles and my sinews, depart from me this day," the suppliant begs. "Deliver me from the spell that is upon me. . . . For an evil spell and an impure disease and transgression and iniquity and sin are in my body, and a wicked spectre is attached to me." "Where the wrath of the god is, to that place the [evil spirits] betake themselves in haste, they utter loud cries. If a god has departed from a man, they settle upon him and cover him like a garment."

In these texts one finds a mixture of the negative and the positive under the combined form of exile of the god (or of the good genius) and invasion by an evil demon: "An evil curse has cut the throat of this man as if he were a lamb; his god has gone out of his body, his goddess has kept herself aloof." And one demon after another is named carefully and distinctly in interminable litanies, in which demonic figures abound.[31]

It is remarkable that prophetic preaching, otherwise so sparing with regard to representations of gods, demons, spirits,—so de-mythologizing, one might say,—retains this experience of the power of sin that binds the sinner. What is remarkable is that this experience becomes most acute when it is freest of any demonic representations.[32] It is at the very heart of the evil disposition, which has been called separation, rebellion, going astray, that the Biblical writers discern a fascinating, binding, frenetic force. The power of

[31] Cited in Ch. F. Jean, *op. cit., passim.*

[32] We shall see in the next chapter how far the psychological myth of the fall contains a residue of the demonological myth under the figure of the Serpent.

a man is mysteriously taken possession of by an inclination to evil
that corrupts its very source: "A spirit of debauchery leads them
astray and they go awhoring, abandoning their God" (Hos.
4:12);[33] "wickedness burns as the fire that devours the briers and
thorns and kindles the thickets of the forest, from which columns
of smoke mount up" (Is. 9:18). Jeremiah, perhaps more than anyone else, felt with terror the evil inclination of the hardened heart
(3:17; 9:14; 16:12); he compares it to the savage instinct, to the
rut of beasts (Jer. 2:23–25;[34] also 8:6). This inclination is so
deeply anchored in the will that it is as indelible as the blackness
of skin of the Ethiopian or the spots of the leopard (13:23).
The theme of radical evil is expressly proclaimed by the prophet:
"The heart of man is deceitful above all things and incurably evil:
who can know it? . . . I, the Eternal, search the heart and try
the reins" (17:9–10). Ezekiel calls this hardness of an existence
inaccessible to the divine summons a "heart of stone." The Yahwist
who was responsible for the essential part of the pessimistic chapters
at the beginning of the book of Genesis sums up in one stroke this
theology of wickedness (Gen. 6:5[35] and 8:21): "Yahweh saw that
the wickedness of man was great on the earth and that his heart
formed only evil designs all the day long."

Here one sees the beginning of an anthropology which is not

---

[33] Hosea here continues the image of adultery which covers all sorts of
sins.

[34] Ezekiel adopts the same violent image: "[Jerusalem] lusted after those
lechers [the children of Babylon], whose carnal heat is like that of asses and
whose lewdness is like that of stallions" (23:20). "You shall be dealt with
so harshly because you have gone awhoring after the nations, because you
have defiled yourself with their idols" (23:30).

[35] Genesis 8:21 also says: "I will never again curse the earth because of
man, because the designs of the heart of man are evil from his youth." This
ieser, which we translate by "design"—in the double sense of imagination
and inclination,—will be the subject of further comments in connection
with the Pharisees and scrupulousness; the rabbinical literature used this
theme to initiate a theory of evil that could lead in a different direction
than the Adamic myth. The author of P, who is not interested in the
psychological aspect of sin, sees in evil the "corruption" and the "violence"
that fill the "earth" (Gen. 6:11, 13), thus giving to evil a cosmic dimension
in keeping with the flood which overwhelms "all flesh" to "destroy them
with the earth," and in keeping with the cosmic covenant signified to Noah
(Gen. 9).

only pessimistic—that is to say, one in which the worst is to be
feared—but which is strictly "tragic"—that is to say (as we shall
say in the chapter on the tragic in Part II), one in which the worst
is not only to be feared, but is strictly inevitable, because God and
man conspire to produce evil. There is no great difference in this
respect between the "hardness" of certain texts of the Old Testament and the "blindness" (*Até*) of the Homeric writings and the
Greek tragedians. The "hardness" is here depicted as a *state* indistinguishable from the very existence of the sinner and, it seems,
a state for which he is not responsible; not only does this hardness
define him entirely, but it is the work of the divinity in his wrath:
"I will harden the heart of Pharaoh." We will discuss this theology
of the "God who leads astray" at greater length in the framework
of myths of the beginning and the end. Let us say now that there
is only a trace of this theology in the Hebrew Bible, although it
shaped a complete world, that of Greek "tragedy." In the Hebrew
Bible it is held in check by a theology of holiness on the one hand,
of mercy on the other. Nevertheless, this abortive theology could
be conceived because it is the prolongation of one of the constitutive experiences of the consciousness of sin, the experience of a
passivity, of an alteration, of an alienation, paradoxically blended
with the experience of a voluntary deviation, and hence of an
activity, an evil initiative.

This experience of alienation is equally one of the components
of the later dogma of original sin.[36] We have already evoked it once
in connection with the universality of sin. If that universality,
which is originally the universality of a tie that is more than biological and more than historical—the "we" of a community of sinners,
—could lend itself to pseudo-biological rationalizations and project
itself in the representation of a hereditary transmission, it is through
the medium of the experience of alienation.

Indeed, a universal tie which is at the same time an experience
of passivity suggests an "explanation" through birth. Is not the
hardness, as it were, the "nature" of the sinner, and so "born with
him"? The fifty-first Psalm expresses this dogma in its nascent state
well enough: "Alas! I was born in iniquity and my mother con-

[36] A. M. Dubarle, *op. cit.,* pp. 14–18.

ceived me in sin."[37] That is not all; neither the confession of the universality of sin nor the avowal of its alienating character accounts
sufficiently for the complex motivation which lies at the origin of
the dogma. There was needed, in addition, a resumption of the affective categories of defilement in the system of sin. This resumption
does not surprise us: the double character of reality and power in
sin, relating it to defilement, makes possible the inclusion of the
system of defilement in that of sin. Historically this resumption was
manifested through the inclusion of the cultual religion of the
Israelites in the ethical religion preached by the Prophets; and so
ritual impurities were juxtaposed to "iniquities" such as violence,
treachery, cruelty, and the destinies of the two systems were mingled. As a result of these contaminations and exchanges, sin, in the
strong sense of sin against God, becomes charged with the emotion
of defilement, in the strong sense of unclean contact. That same
fifty-first Psalm, although it proceeds from an acute experience of
personal fault, of guilt in the precise sense, adopts the language of
defilement: "Wash me thoroughly from my iniquity and cleanse
me from my sin! . . . Cleanse me with hyssop and I shall be without spot; wash me, and I shall be whiter than snow." This assonance
between sin and defilement is not without danger; the experience
of sin is, as it were, dragged backward by the experience of defilement. As an example of this regressive tendency we can cite the
reactivation, so frequent in the confession of sins, of the ancient tie
between defilement and sexuality, the great affective complexity of
which we have shown above: the sexual act, like birth, giving a
physical basis to the symbol of unclean contact. It will be enough
that the fault confessed be itself of the sexual order—as is the case
in the confession of Psalm 51, in which King David repents the

[37] A. Feuillet, "Verset 7 du Miserere et le péché originel," in *Recherches
de Science Religieuse* (1944), pp. 5–26. That verse does not mean that the
sexual act as such is culpable; the author uses current ideas about the
ritual defilement attached to conception and childbirth for the purpose of
expressing the more profound idea that, before any personal act, man finds
himself already separated from God; the bond established between the
generations by birth becomes the symbol of that anteriority of evil. It should
be remarked further that the verse does not say that that state "in" which
we exist constitutes an *inclination* to evil, and neither does it say that that
state proceeds from an ancestral transgression. See Dubarle, *op. cit.*, p. 21.

rape of Bathsheba and the murder of Uriah—in order to reactivate, one after the other, all the associations between the universality and the alienation of sin on the one hand and the symbolism of unclean contact on the other, as well as the sexual echoes of the theme of defilement. Finally, the myth of a first sin, committed by a first man and transmitted to his descendants conceived "in his image," will place its seal upon all these associations in an "explanation" in terms of origin, the structure of which we shall study further on. But this reactivation of the ancient associations connected with the theme of defilement is only the counterpart of the taking up of the symbolism of defilement into the symbolism of sin.

This second cycle of symbols of sin, which insure the taking up of the symbolism of defilement into the symbolism of sin, finds its prolongation in a symbolism of redemption which completes the symbolism of pardon that we left hanging, and which guarantees, in its turn, that the symbolism of "purification" will be taken up into the symbolism of "pardon."

In fact it is necessary to add to the cycle of symbols of "return" a new cycle of symbols that gravitate around "buying back." The symbolism of "return" refers us to the idea of sin as a breaking of the bond of the Covenant; that of "buying back" refers us to the idea of a power which holds man captive, and for the suppression of which a ransom must be given in exchange.

Of the three roots which express the idea of deliverance, each develops one aspect of this exchange,[38] which evokes a similar idea in the *Phaedo,* where an "exchange" of passions for virtue is proposed. The root *gaal* preserves something of the notion of *goel,* of the avenger or protector who can and even must marry the widow of a near relation. This root furnishes a whole chain of symbols: protect, cover in the sense of hide, buy back, deliver. Like all symbols, it keeps something of the initial analogue, but immediately goes beyond it in the direction of an existential situation.

A neighboring symbol—root *padah*—is furnished by the custom of buying back the offering of the firstborn or slaves by a ransom.

[38] Ed. Jacob, *Les thèmes essentiels d'une théologie de l'Ancien Testament,* pp. 235–36.

It is well known that this image of ransom, of buying back, was sufficiently powerful to lend support to the conceptualization of redemption (which means buying back).

The root *kapar*, which has been compared to the Arabian "to cover," and to the Akkadian "to efface," furnishes a symbol related to the preceding ones: the *kopher* is the ransom by which one can be released from a severe penalty or save one's life. It is true that it is the man who offers the *kopher;* but the symbolization extends far enough to furnish the basic image of "expiation," which we shall leave aside for the time being, in order to remain in the cycle of "buying back."

This symbolism of "buying back" owes a part of its force to its being coupled with that of the Exodus, the departure from Egypt. That event is at the center of the *Urbekenntnis* of Israel;[39] re-interpreted by the theology of history of the Biblical writers, it stands for all deliverance. Now the Exodus did not display its power of ethical symbolization until it passed through the gate of the symbolism of "buying back"; the Exodus *is* a buying back; the two symbols of buying back and of going out or up re-enforce each other, to the point of making the Exodus the most significant cipher of the destiny of Israel: "You shall say to the children of Israel: I am Yahweh, and I will bring you out from under the burdens that the Egyptians impose upon you. I will free you from the bondage in which they keep you and I will deliver you by striking hard and chastising severely" (Ex. 6:6).

But the symbol, as one sees in many psalms, makes its way from one transposition to another. At the end of these transpositions, the theme of the "liberator" who "buys back" his people is almost

---

[39] G. von Rad, *op. cit.*, pp. 177–81, studies, from a *formgeschichtlich* point of view, the rich palette of the meanings deposited and sedimented in this historical confession, beginning with the simple story of a military miracle (Ex. 14) which already has the value of "deliverance," of "buying back" (v. 30; cf. the confession of Deuteronomy 26:5). The theme of the "threat of the waters" (Pss. 106:9; 114:3) gives a cosmic resonance to the historical event, while the theology of election, so forcibly expressed in Deuteronomy 7:6–8, makes it the sign and the promise of all "buying back," of all "redemption" (Second Isaiah, 43, 44 ff.). At this extreme point, the symbol of the Exodus is indistinguishable from the symbol of "return" (Is. 51:9–10).

completely freed from its origin in the theology of history and in the end designates any internal deliverance. But all these levels of meaning were already superimposed in the most historical celebrations of the Exodus. At the limit, the symbols of "buying back," of "pardon," and of "return" join their forces: "Return to me, for I have bought you back," we read in the second Isaiah (44:22). "Forgive, O Eternal One, thy people Israel, whom thou hast bought back" (Deut. 21:8).

At the same time, the whole problematics of sin is enriched retrospectively: Egypt itself becomes by contrast the cipher of captivity and even the most powerful symbol of the human condition under the influence of evil. The solemn exordium of the Decalogue speaks in these terms: "It is I, Yahweh, thy God, who have brought thee out of the land of Egypt, out of the house of bondage" (Ex. 20:2).

The captivity is literally a social, intersubjective situation. In becoming the symbol of sin, this cipher displayed the alienating character of sin; the sinner is "in" the sin as the Hebrew was "in" bondage, and sin is thus an evil "in which" man is caught. That is why it can be at the same time personal and communal, transcending consciousness, known to God alone in its reality and its truth; that, too, is why it is a power that binds man, hardens him, and holds him captive; and it is this experience of the impotence of captivity that makes possible a taking over of the theme of defilement. However "internal" to the heart of man the principle of this bondage may be, the bondage in fact constitutes an enveloping situation, like a snare in which man is caught; and so something of unclean contact is retained in this idea of the "captivity" of sin.

Henceforth the fundamental problem of existence will be less that of liberty, understood in the sense of a choice to be made in the face of a radical alternative, than that of liberation; the man held captive by sin is a man to be delivered. All our ideas of salvation, of redemption—that is to say, of buying back—proceed from this initial cipher.

This meditation on the second cycle of symbols of sin and deliverance prepares us to understand, as far as it is possible, how the symbolism of defilement and purification could be taken up, reaffirmed, and even amplified when it came into contact with the symbolism of sin conceived as possession and the symbolism of pardon conceived as buying back and deliverance. This effort of understanding is imperative in the presence of texts as troubling as those of Leviticus and, in general, of the P cycle (*Priester Codex,* or priestly document), in which there is fully displayed a sense of ceremonial expiation that is all the more baffling because the editing is post-exilic (which of course does not exclude the content's being ancient and even archaic[40]).

To understand, as far as it is possible. . . . It must be confessed that for *reflection* there remains something impermeable in the idea of ceremonial expiation, something that refuses even to be reduced to the richest symbolism of "pardon." What resists reductive reflection is the ritual *praxis* itself. This *praxis* is non-reflective by its essence; the sacrifice is performed thus and not otherwise; the ritual behavior is inherited from a succession of other cultual actions, of which the meaning and even, in most cases, the memory are lost to the celebrant and to the faithful. Modern criticism likewise always finds other rituals at the origin of any ritual, and is never present at the birth of ritual in general. That is why a catalogue of rites, such as that of Leviticus, remains in the end a mute and sealed work, even when, and especially when, it distinguishes species of sacrifice: the holocaust (sacrifice of animals consumed by the fire), the sacrifice of thanksgiving (holocaust of the fat of animals and sacred repast), the offering (of flour, oil, incense), the sacrifice of expiation "for sin" (*hattat*) (Lev. 4:1–5, 13, and 6:7–13), the sacrifice of expiation "for an offense" (*âšâm*) (5:14–19). It is unusual if any of the circumstances in which this or that sacrifice (fourth and fifth types) is to be offered are indicated: the case in which "one has transgressed through ignorance against one of the commandments of Yahweh," the case in which one has through ignorance kept back the dues owed to the sanctuary, or, through ignorance or false swearing, has appropriated a deposit, a pledge, an object found, stolen, or unjustly kept. But in

[40] R. Dussaud, *Les origines cananéennes du sacrifice israëlite* (Paris, 1921).

the end these circumstances are difficult to define.[41] In the ritual, the principal emphasis is not placed on these circumstances, but on the ceremonial *praxis*. As Von Rad says, "the theory of the sacral procedure," its "basic idea," remains hidden; moreover, the same ritual lends itself to shifts and substitutions of motives; the ritual is a sort of cultual receptacle *which is there,* which reflection *finds,* and which can receive various successive significations without being exhausted by any one of them. The fact is that the ritual ignores subjectivities and recognizes only the exactitude of the *praxis*.[42]

And yet ceremonial expiation, although it is irreducible to any purely subjective or internal operation, is not a foreign body in the concrete totality of the relations of Israel to God; for if the cult comes from further back than the prophets, than Moses, and even than the people of Israel itself, the faith of Israel remodels it internally and expresses the whole of itself therein.

For one thing, the idea of expiation developed after the exile corresponds to an idea of sin in which the "realistic" side and the "dangerous" aspect alone were emphasized. Sin, as we have seen, could always find a symbol for itself in defilement, which nevertheless it radically transforms. As early as Ezekiel one finds the expression "bear the punishment" of sin (14:10)—an expression later so frequent in Paul—to express the subjective weight and the objective maleficence of a sin that has not been forgiven. Without doubt, this disquieting note must also be placed in the general tonality of dread, of threat of death, of a "blow" or a "wound" that lurks in all the narratives and warnings of the priestly cycle (for example, Lev. 10:6; Num. 1:53; 17:12; 18:3). This anxiety concerning the always possible annihilation of man by God explains in part the emphasis on the rites of expiation which were always

[41] *Supplément au Dictionnaire de la Bible,* Vol. III, art. "Expiation," cols. 55–68. Ed. Jacob, *op. cit.,* pp. 236–38. Von Rad, *op. cit.,* pp. 249–74. Sven Herner, *Sühne und Vergebung in Israel* (Lund, 1942), pp. 77–92.

[42] The procedure of the various sacrifices takes place "in a domain beyond man and his inwardness . . . ; no matter how far one penetrates, even the most fully comprehensive interpretation of the ancient sacrifice is arrested at an absolute limit beyond which there is no further explanation. And the exegete is obliged to say to himself that it is precisely what is most essential in the sacrifice that lies beyond that limit" (Von Rad, *op. cit.,* pp. 252 and 259).

to accompany the cult of Israel. There is nothing astonishing, therefore, in the fact that sensitiveness to sin understood as a threat of death reanimated all the earlier representations of defilement. On the other hand, the old idea of defilement was raised to the level of the experience of sin according to the Prophets.[43]

As to sacrifice itself, on the other hand, its objective efficacy is not without relation to "pardon" understood, as we have tried to understand it, without any reference to sacrifice. The very word "expiation" (*kipper*[44]) is connected by its moral harmonics with the other symbols of buying back and ransom; the gesture of "covering," or more probably of "wiping out" by rubbing, has immediately a symbolic resonance and signifies pardon itself (inversely, the word pardon—*salach*—recalls the ritual gesture of sprinkling[45]). One might believe at first that pardon and expiation are contrasted as the action of God who delivers and the action of the man (the priest) who "makes expiation." But the expression "make expiation" does not prejudge any of the representations connected with this verb; it is equivalent to: perform the action defined as expiatory by the ritual. It is not said what happens every time the ritual proclaims: "thus shall the sacrificer make expiation for them and it shall be forgiven them" (Lev. 4:20, 26, 31, 35, and 5:10 and 13); it cannot be concluded therefrom that the priest and his performance have a magical hold over the divine. On the contrary, the only breakthrough that Leviticus proposes in the direction of a theology of sacrifice—all the more precious because of its character as an exception—gives a hint of a possible inclusion of the gestural symbolism of the expiatory rite in the altogether spiritual symbolism of pardon. The text is this:

If any man of the house of Israel or any stranger that sojourns among you shall eat any manner of blood, I will turn against him who has eaten this blood, and I will cut him off from among his people. For the life of the flesh is in the blood. This blood I have given you that you might

[43] Von Rad, *op. cit.*, pp. 267–68.
[44] *Supplément au Dictionnaire de la Bible,* art. "Expiation," cols. 48–55.
[45] Jacob, *op. cit.*, p. 235.

perform upon the altar the rite of expiation for your lives; for it is the
blood that atones for a life.

Lev. 17:10–11

This text gives an indication that the *symbolism of blood* constitutes the bond between the rite of expiation and the faith in
pardon (a faith which is itself connected with the confession of sins
and repentance). In fact, it is not only forbidden to eat blood
(Gen. 9:4) out of respect for the life which has its seat in the
blood ("for the soul of the flesh is in the blood" or, as another text
says, "the blood is the life," Deut. 12:23); the blood, withdrawn
from profane use, is reserved for expiation "for your souls." How?
Here the Seventy *interpreted* the instrumental particle (the blood
makes expiation *by means of* the soul, hence of the life of the
animal sacrificed) as being the equivalent of the substitutive prepo-
sition in Greek, and they have translated: τὸ γὰρ αἷμα αὐτοῦ ἀντὶ τῆς
ψυχῆς ἐξιλάσεται: "for its blood shall make expiation in place of
the soul." Thus the translator makes a choice: the symbol of blood
is that of a *gift;* the faithful man offers himself in the figure of the
sacrificed animal and attests his desire for union with God. The
symbolism of blood, then, only enriches the symbolism of a present,
an offering; it adds to it the lively sense of a living and vital continuity between his offering and himself, between himself and his
God. As one sees, in this interpretation the expiation is indeed
"made" by the man, but what he "makes" is a gift. And this gift
does not have any penal nuance, at least insofar as the rites of
sprinkling are considered by themselves without taking immolation
into account; there is, in fact, no idea of a punishment undergone
in the presentation of the blood poured out. Only the immolation
opens the door to a possible idea of penal substitution; in place of
his death the faithful man considers with a contrite heart the death
of the victim that represents him.

If the suggestions of the translation of the Seventy, favorable to
a Christological interpretation of the Jewish sacrifice, are rejected,
and if one sticks to: "it is by the soul that the blood makes expiation," which designates the vehicle of expiation without revealing
the secret of its operation, then the emphasis is still placed on giving,

but this time upon God's gift of the means of expiation: "I have given it to you upon the altar, in order that. . . ." This emphasis is perhaps more important than the theology of *satisfactio vicaria* indicated by the Septuagint, for it suggests that the priest who "makes expiation" is the performer of a mystery, the sense of which is "given" by God, through the symbolism of blood and of life, however the rite may operate. This gift of the means of expiation is closely related to pardon itself.[46]

Ceremonial expiation, then, is no longer foreign to the central theme of "return" and "pardon." This theme is, in a way, objectified in a mime. There are not two worlds: a world of ceremony and a world of contrition; the latter is represented in the former as in a gestural enigma. The ritual of the "day of expiation" (Lev. 16) shows this synthesis of the two symbolisms very well: the confession of sins is an indispensable condition, but the expiation occupies the central place with its multiple sprinklings; and finally, the rite of the goat driven into the desert to carry away the sins of Israel makes sensible to all eyes the complete remission of sins. Thus the rite of expulsion expresses more completely what has already been signified in the rite of renewal, which externalizes the reconciliation through pardon.[47] Finally, it is because the foreign vegetation of ceremonial expiation grew like an excrescence on the tree of "repentance" and "pardon" that the symbolism of expiation could, in return, enrich that of "pardon"; and so one sees God invoked in

[46] Ed. Jacob attaches the sacrificial ritual to the themes of "buying back" and of "ransom," and finds the common nucleus in the idea of *substitution*. He subordinates the symbolization of the death of the guilty one to the communication of divine life to the sinner: "thus the essence of the sacrifice is not the death of the victim, but the offering of his life" (*op. cit.*, p. 237). In a neighboring sense, von Rad quotes Öhler, *Theologie des alten Testaments:* "In the sacrifice no act of punitive justice is performed, and the altar can in no way be compared to a tribunal." Von Rad adds: "Expiation, then, is not a punitive act, but a method of salvation," *op. cit.*, p. 270.

[47] The Mishnah indicates the formula that the high priest pronounced on this occasion: "Ah! Yahweh, thy people, the house of Israel, has committed before thee iniquities, transgressions, and sins; ah! Yahweh, pardon the iniquities, the transgressions, and the sins that thy people, the house of Israel, has committed before thee, as it is written in the Torah of thy servant Moses" (Yoma 6:2, cited in *Supplément au Dictionnaire de la Bible,* art. "Expiation," col. 78).

the Psalms as the subject of expiation (78:38; 65:3; 79:9).[48] To say that God "expiates" is to say that he "pardons." The symbolism of expiation, then, gives back to the symbolism of pardon what the latter had lent it.

[48] Sven Herner, *op. cit.*, pp. 92 ff.

III. Guilt

GUILT IS NOT SYNONYMOUS with fault. All our reflections protest against this identification, which destroys the tensions essential to the consciousness of fault.

Two reasons determine our resistance to this reduction of fault to guilt. In the first place, guilt, considered by itself, leads in several directions: in the direction of an ethico-juridical reflection on the relation of *penalty* to *responsibility;* in the direction of an ethico-religious reflection on a delicate and scrupulous conscience; and finally, in the direction of a psycho-theological reflection on the hell of an accused and condemned conscience. Penal rationalization in the Greek manner, internalization and refinement of ethical awareness in the Judaic manner, consciousness of the wretchedness of man under the regime of the Law and of the works of the Law in the Paulinian manner—these are three divergent possibilities which the notion of guilt carries. Now, it is not possible to understand directly the intimate connection among these three aspects of guilt, which are in constant opposition, two by two: the *rationality* of the Greek against the religiosity of the Jew and the Christian; the *internality* of "piety" against the externality of the city or of salvation by grace; Paulinian *antilegalism* against the law of the tribunal and against Mosaic law. All the rest of this chapter will be entirely devoted to this splintering of the idea of guilt. But to be able to perceive this internal dialectic of guilt, one must set it in a vaster dialectic, that of the three moments of fault: defilement, sin, guilt.

Guilt is *understood* through a double movement, starting from the two other stages of fault: a movement of rupture and a movement of resumption. A movement of rupture that causes a new stage to emerge—the *guilty* man—and a movement of resumption by which this new experience is charged with the earlier symbolism of sin and even of defilement, in order to express the paradox toward which the idea of fault points—namely, the concept of a man who is responsible *and* captive, or rather a man who is responsible for being captive—in short, the concept of the *servile will*.

1. Birth of a New Stage

Let us consider this double movement by which guilt emancipates itself from defilement and sin, and inherits their primordial symbolism.

It can be said, in very general terms, that guilt designates the *subjective* moment in fault as sin is its *ontological* moment. Sin designates the real situation of man before God, whatever consciousness he may have of it. This situation must be discovered in the proper sense of the word: the Prophet is the man capable of announcing to the King that his power is weak and vain. Guilt is the awareness of this real situation, and, if one may say so, the "for itself" of this kind of "in itself."

This moment is at first a subordinate and enveloped one. It can already be dimly made out in the theme of defilement. We have seen that the dread which is characteristic of defilement was an anticipation and forestalling of punishment. The chastisement thus anticipated extends its shadow over the consciousness of the present, which feels the *weight* of this threat *weighing* upon it. What is essential in guilt is already contained in this consciousness of being "burdened," burdened by a "weight." Guiltiness is never anything else than the anticipated chastisement itself, internalized and already weighing upon consciousness; and as dread is from the beginning the way of internalization of defilement itself, in spite of the radical externality of the evil, guilt is a moment contemporaneous with defilement itself. But at this stage this moment remains a subordinate one: it is because man is ritually unclean that he is "burdened" with fault; he need not be the author of the evil to feel himself burdened by its weight and the weight of its consequences. To be guilty is only to be ready to undergo the chastisement and to make oneself the subject of the chastisement. It is in this sense, and this sense only, that guilt is already implied in defilement. No doubt we can say that this guilt is already responsibility, if we mean that being responsible is being capable of answering for the consequences of an act; but this consciousness of responsibility is only an appendage of the consciousness of being charged with the weight of punishment in anticipation; it does not proceed from a consciousness of being the *author of.* . . . The sociology of responsibility is very illuminating at this point; man had the consciousness of responsibility before having the consciousness of being cause, agent, author. It is his situation in relation to interdictions that first makes him responsible.

That is why the consciousness of guilt constitutes a veritable revolution in the experience of evil: that which is primary is no longer the reality of defilement, the objective violation of the Interdict, or the Vengeance let loose by that violation, but the evil use of liberty, felt as an internal diminution of the value of the self. This revolution is considerable: it reverses the relation between punishment and guilt. Whereas guilt had hitherto issued from the punishment engendered by Vengeance, it was now the diminution of the value of existence that would be the origin of punishment and would call for it as healing and amendment. Thus the guilt begotten in the first place by the consciousness of chastisement revolutionizes that consciousness of chastisement and wholly reverses its meaning. It is guilt which demands that the chastisement itself be converted from vengeful expiation to educative expiation—in short, to amendment.

This revolution introduced into punishment by guilt is therefore very evident if one directly contrasts guilt and impurity, leaping over the stage of sin. It is more difficult to locate the point of change of direction between sin and guilt.

The relation of the third to the second stage in the consciousness of fault is in fact much more complex. On the one hand, the continuity from the one to the other is not doubtful. Nevertheless something new appears which constitutes, if not an inversion of meaning in the feeling of sin, at least a "crisis" which it is important to measure, although the novelty and the crisis issue from the deepening of the feeling of sin. On the one hand, the feeling of sin *is* a feeling of guilt; guiltiness *is* the burden of sin: it is the loss of the bond with the origin, insofar as that loss is felt. In this sense guilt is the achieved internality of sin. This internalization is the fruit of the deepening of the demand that is addressed to man. That deepening, we remember, is double: in becoming ethical and no longer only ritual, the Interdiction raises up a subjective pole of responsibility that can no longer be only one who answers for the sanction, one who is responsible in the elementary sense of a subject of punishment, but a center of decision, an author of acts. That is not all: the Interdiction not only passes from the ritual to the ethical; it becomes unlimited as the demand for perfection which goes beyond any enumeration of duties or virtues. This call to "perfection" reveals, behind acts, the depths of *possible* existence. In fact, just as man is called to a unique perfection that surpasses the multiplicity of his obligations, he is revealed to himself as the author not only of his many acts, but of the motives of his acts and, beyond the motives, of the most radical possibilities which are suddenly reduced to the pure and simple alternative: God or Nothing. We have previously evoked the "Deuteronomic choice": "I have placed before you life and death; choose the good and you shall live." This call to a radical choice raises up, over against itself, a subjective pole, a respondent, no longer in the sense of a bearer of punishment, but in the sense of an existent capable of embracing his whole life and considering it as one undivided destiny, hanging upon a simple alternative. Thus the prophetic call transformed the Covenant from a simple juridical contract between Yahweh and his people into a personal accusation and adjuration. There is henceforth an "I," because there is a "thou" to whom the Prophet addresses himself in the name of God.

Finally, the confession of sins completes this movement of the internalization of sin in personal guilt: the "thou" that is summoned becomes the "I" that accuses itself. But at the same time there appears the shift of emphasis that makes the sense of sin turn toward the feeling of guilt; in place of emphasizing the "before

God," the "against thee, against thee alone," the feeling of guilt emphasizes the "it is I who. . . ." The penitential Psalms in Hebrew literature show well this duality of emphasis:

> For I know my sin,
> and my fault is always before me.
> Against thee, thee only, have I sinned;
> I have done that which is evil in thy sight.
>
> Ps. 51:3–4

Let the "I" be emphasized more than the "before thee," let the "before thee" be even *forgotten,* and the consciousness of fault becomes guilt and no longer sin at all; it is "conscience" that now becomes the *measure* of evil in a completely solitary experience. It is not by accident that in many languages the same word designates moral consciousness (*conscience morale*), and psychological and reflective consciousness; guilt expresses above all the promotion of "conscience" as supreme.

In the religious literature that we are examining here, the complete substitution of guilt for sin never appears; the confession of the psalmist, evoked above, still expresses the equilibrium of two tribunals and two measures: the absolute measure, represented by the sight of God, who sees the sins there are, and the subjective measure, represented by the tribunal of the conscience, which appraises any guilt that becomes apparent. But a process was begun, at the end of which the "realism" of sin, illustrated by the confession of forgotten or unrecognized sins, would be entirely replaced by the "phenomenalism" of guilt, with its play of illusions and masks. This end is attained only at the price of the liquidation of the religious sense of sin. Then man is guilty as he feels himself guilty; guilt in the pure state has become a modality of man the *measure.* It is this possibility of a complete cleavage between guilt and sin that is presented in the three modalities that we shall study: in the individualization of offenses in the penal sense, in the delicate conscience of the scrupulous man, and in the hell of condemnation above all.

The birth of a new "measure" of fault is a decisive event in the history of the notion of fault; and this event represents a double advance, from which it is not possible to turn back.

On the one hand, guilt implies what may be called a judgment of personal imputation of evil; this individualization of guilt breaks with the "we" of the confession of sins. The Jewish prophets of the Exile are witnesses to this change from communal sin to individual guilt, and the change corresponds to a definite historical situation. The preaching of sin had represented a mode of prophetic summons in which the whole people was exhorted to remember a collective deliverance, that of the Exodus, and to fear a collective threat, that of the Day of Yahweh. But now that the evil hour has arrived, now that the national state is destroyed and the people deported, the same preaching which had been able to appeal for a collective reform has become a cause for despair; it has lost all the force of a summons and become nihilistic in its import. From the moment when the preaching of communal sin no longer signifies that a choice is open, but that fate has closed the door on an entire people, it is the preaching of individual sin, of personal guilt, that has the value of hope. For if sin is individual, salvation can be equally so. Even if the Exodus from Egypt could not be repeated in an exodus from Babylon, even if the Return was to be indefinitely postponed, there would still be hope for each man.

If, in fact, an entire people is punished without respect of persons, then the generations are inseparably joined in the fault and in the sanction, and the children are punished for the fathers; then the captive of Babylon pays for a sin that he has not committed. It is then that Ezekiel proclaims: "What mean you, that you use this proverb concerning the land of Israel, saying, The fathers have eaten sour grapes, and the children's teeth are set on edge? As I live, saith the Lord Yahweh, you shall not have occasion anymore to use this proverb in Israel. Behold, all lives are mine. . . . He that has sinned, it is he that shall die" (Ezek. 18:2–4). Henceforth it is an individual that is summoned; "perversion" and "conversion" are decisions that make each individual a "just" man or a "wicked" man. That the emphasis is finally placed on mercy is beyond doubt: "If I say to the wicked, Thou shalt die, and he turns from his sins and practices righteousness and justice, if he returns the pledge, restores what he has stolen, observes the laws that give life, and ceases to do evil, he shall live, he shall not die" (Ezek. 33:14–15).

Even more strongly in Jeremiah, the proclamation of personal responsibility and retribution—in terms that anticipate those of
Ezekiel: "In those days they shall say no more, *The fathers have
eaten sour grapes and the children's teeth are set on edge,* but
everyone shall die for his own crime. Every man that eats sour
grapes, his own teeth shall be set on edge" (31:29–30)—is indissolubly linked with the announcement of a new Covenant, in
which the Law will dwell "in the depths of their being" and will
be "written in their hearts"; then "they shall all know me, from
the least of them to the greatest, saith Yahweh, because I will
pardon their crime and I will remember their sin no more" (31:
31–34). Thus are put in question jointly the collective imputation
that visits the iniquity of the fathers upon the children from
generation to generation and the old Terror, whose sway marks
both the regime of defilement and that of sin. It is possible to
free oneself from the chain of acts, as it is possible to break the
chain of generations; a *revocable time* is substituted for a suprahistorical fate.

The similarity to the criticism of hereditary defilement among
the Greeks of the fifth century is obvious. There also the curse that
chains the generations together gives way to a new time and new
gods; the Erinyes become the Eumenides, at the same time that
the age-old debt gives way to individual responsibility. This time
can be a time of radical condemnation or a time for mercy. It is,
then, a whole new temporal economy that is instituted: the law of
hereditary debt is broken; everyone pays for his own faults; everyone can at every instant begin again, "come back to the Eternal."
We shall see later how this discovery aggravated rather than resolved the crisis opened up in the doctrine of retribution. That every
man dies for his own crime is precisely what Job will dispute, and
a new idea of tragedy will be born from this discovery (cf. Pt. II,
Chap. V).

Thus the tension between the "realism" of sin and the "phenomenalism" of guilt has as its first corollary the individualization
of imputation. A new opposition arises in the consciousness of
fault: according to the schema of sin, evil is a situation "in which"
mankind is caught as a single collective; according to the schema

of guilt, evil is an act that each individual "begins." This pulveriza-
tion of fault into a multiplicity of subjective guilts puts in question
the "we" of the confession of sins and makes evident the loneliness
of the guilty conscience.

The second conquest, contemporary with the individualization
of fault, is the idea that guilt has *degrees*. Whereas sin is a qualitative situation—it is or it is not,—guilt designates an intensive
quantity, capable of more and less. Here is the law of all or nothing
in sin that St. Paul takes from the psalmist: "There is no one who
is just, no, not one; there is no one who understands, no one who
seeks God. They are all gone out of the way, they are together
become unprofitable; there is no one who does good, no, not one"
(Rom. 3:10 ff.). The guilty conscience, on the contrary, confesses
that its fault allows of more and less, that it has degrees of seriousness. Now, if guilt has degrees, it also has extremes that are designated by the two polar figures of the "wicked" and the "just."
And justice itself will be a relative justice, measured no longer in
comparison with an unlimited perfection beyond reach, but in
comparison with an optimal justice embodied in the figure of the
"just man." This figure of the "just man"—of the just man among
us—perhaps always accompanied paradoxically the preaching of
absolute justice. Thus the same chapter of Genesis juxtaposes these
two declarations: on the one hand, "Yahweh saw that the wickedness of man was great on the earth, and that his heart formed only
evil designs all the day long" (6:5); and on the other hand,
"Noah was a just man, upright among his contemporaries, and he
walked with God" (6:9). That one belongs to the Yahweh tradition and the other to the priestly tradition does not change the fact
that the final editor could juxtapose these two themes and respect
them in their divergence. That Noah was "the only just man in this
generation" (7:1) does not suppress the enigma constituted by the
exception itself. Moreover, the exception is not unique; Enoch also
"walked with God" (Gen. 5:24). And Job also was "a simple and
upright man, who feared God and kept himself from evil" (Job
1:1). The astonishing "apology" of Job, in Chapter 31, is the
description of the relative and finite justice, the optimal justice,

which, unlike total perfection, can be approached and even satisfied, and which in turn determines the degrees of relative injustice on which the delicate and scrupulous conscience of the "pious" man will be able to meditate.

We shall speak later of the greatness of the ethics of the just and the pious (sect. 3); we shall speak also of its illusion and its failure (sect. 4). But it would be impossible to go back and annul this moment of conscience that opposes to the *equalitarian* experience of sin the *graduated* experience of guilt; it is all the more impossible because it is this profession of degrees of guilt that is presupposed in other respects by every imputation not only moral, but juridical and penal. While a man is entirely and radically a sinner, he is more or less guilty; and with a scale of offenses a scale of penalties is possible. It is, then, not only the delicate conscience of the "pious" and the anguished conscience confined in the hell of its own justice, it is also the conscience of the legislator and the judge that is nourished by this profession of degress of guilt (sect. 2).

The significance of guilt, then, is the possibility of the primacy of "man the measure" over the "sight of God"; the division between individual fault and the sin of the people, the opposition between a graduated imputation and an all-inclusive accusation anticipate this reversal. By all these traits reflection has led us to the crossing of the three roads along which this new experience proceeds.

2. Guilt and Penal Imputation

The first direction in which the consciousness of guilt moves is, then, that of our *ethico-juridical* experience. The metaphor of the tribunal, we shall see, invades all registers of the consciousness of guilt. But before being a metaphor of the moral consciousness, the tribunal is a real institution of the city, and this institution was the channel by which the religious consciousness of sin was reformed. In what sense?

In this chapter, devoted like the preceding ones to the nascent conceptualization of fault through its most primitive symbols, we

shall not address ourselves to the modern forms of penal law and
the problems raised by the encounter of law and criminology; we
shall come to those questions later. We shall not have recourse,
either, to Roman penal law; the order that it introduces into its
concepts is already late in comparison to the themes of impurity,
impiety, and injustice, which we want to catch in their nascent
state. Much more revelatory of the "beginnings" of conscience is
the penal experience of the Greeks;[1] precisely because it never
attained the order and rigor of that of the Romans, it offers an
opportunity to observe penal conceptualization in its inchoate state.
Moreover, it is contemporaneous with the philosophical reflection—
of the Sophists, of Plato, of Aristotle—in which it is both reflected
and modified. Besides, its relations with tragedy keep it in proximity not only with philosophy but with antiphilosophy. Finally,
the elaboration of the Greek vocabulary of guilt in connection
with the determination of penalties is an immense cultural event:
the adventure of ὕβρις, ἁμάρτημα, ἀδικία is the adventure of our
own conscience, the conscience of men of the West; even the Bible
has influenced our culture through the Greek translation. Now,
the choice of Greek equivalents for Biblical sin and for all the
ethico-religious concepts of Hebrew origin is in itself a decision
about the meaning of our symbols; on this level we are indivisibly
Greeks and Jews. Thus, the elaboration of the concepts of guilt
through the juridical and penal experience of the Greeks is more
than the simple history of the penal institutions of classical Greece,
and belongs to that history of the ethico-religious consciousness, the
principal motivations of which we are here tracing.

The contribution of the Greeks to this third stage in the consciousness of fault differs profoundly from the contribution of the
Jews in virtue of the role played in it by the direct application of
reflection to the city, to its legislation, and to the organization of
penal law. Here it is not a Covenant, ethical monotheism, a per-

[1] Gernet, *Recherches sur le développement de la pensée juridique et
morale en Grèce* (Paris, 1917). Moulinier, *Le pur et l'impur dans la pensée
des Grecs d'Homère à Aristote* (Paris, 1952). Kurt Latte, "Schuld und
Sünde in der griechischen Religion," *Arch. f. Religionswissenschaft* 20
(1920–21).

sonalistic relation between God and man that raises the counterpole of an accused subjectivity; it is the ethics of a city of men that
constitutes the focus of a reasonable indictment. Of course, this
process still evolves on the fringes of religious consciousness; the
city remains a "holy" magnitude; its charge of sacredness in the
classical epoch remains such that injustice is still synonymous with
impiety.[2] Inversely, impiety and even impurity were never spoken
of in Greece without reference to injustice. Whichever one you
start with, the three factors of purity, holiness, and justice constantly encroach upon one another at the height of the classical
epoch. It must be said that the passage from one to the other was
never marked, in the Hellenic consciousness, by crises comparable
to the crisis produced in Israel by prophetic preaching; the taste
of the poets and, above all, of the tragedians for archaic situations,
the literary and theatrical revival of the old myths of defilement
and purification, make the interferences among the various notions
even more inextricable. It must be acknowledged that if we had
only the testimony of Greece, we could never reach even a slightly
coherent idea of the typological succession of defilement, sin, and
guilt.

Thus, the notion of ἀδικεῖν, often taken abstractly in the sense
of committing an injustice and also of being unjust, marks the
emergence of a purely moral notion of evil outside the sinister
operation of impurity. But injustice, like justice itself, thrusts its
roots down into the archaic consciousness of the impure and the
pure. It was δίκη which, in becoming rationalized, established
the rationality of the ἀδίκημα. This rationality consisted essentially in a division between Cosmos and City. The same justice, the
same injustice, the same expiation which, in the fragment of
Anaximander, were categories of the Whole of nature as the totality of being "according to the order of time," became crystallized into something solely human by settling down upon the civic

[2] The expression ἀσεβεῖν—to commit an impiety—connected with the
expression ἀδικεῖν—to commit an injustice—attests that injustice is always impiety with regard to the sacredness of the city. 'Αδικεῖν τὴν πόλιν
is an offense with regard to the ἱερὰ καὶ ὅσια (Gernet, op. cit., Part I, Chap.
1, on ἀδικεῖν).

and juridical. And this settling down consists essentially in the activity by which the city is defined. Demosthenes, commenting on the distinction between "voluntary" and "involuntary" murder, writes: "If a man kills another in a contest, the legislator determines [in the sense of defines] that he has not committed an injustice": ἄν τις ἐν ἄθλοις ἀποκτείνῃ τινά, τοῦτον ὥρισεν οὐκ ἀδικεῖν. Heraclitus well described this division in the whole produced by the decision-making action of the city: "For God all is good and beautiful and just; men hold (ὑπηλείφασι) certain things for just, others for unjust" (frag. 102). Gernet emphasizes that this action of delimitation could not develop except in those parts of the law where the sacredness of the city was less at stake. Whereas the public offenses of sacrilege (in the precise sense of an attack on the patrimony of the city or on its sanctuaries) and treason continue to awaken a sort of sacred horror, private offenses, which harm individuals and give them the privilege of prosecution, provide an opportunity to form a more objective notion of the wrong suffered and penalized by a defined and measured reparation.[3] As one can see, this action of definition and measurement by the human tribunal was exercised on the penalty itself, and it was by measuring the penalty and in order to measure it that the city measured the guilt itself. Thus the notion of *degree* of guilt, which among the Jews is rather a conquest of personal meditation in the midst of communal confession, is correlative among the Greeks with an evolution in punishment.

Gernet, by his critical study of some Greek words, has mapped out this conquest of measure in punishment. Κολάζειν, which denotes repression by society and so springs from social anger, came to denote, in classical Greece, corrective punishment, with its double meaning: one bearing on the nature of the punishment (κολάζειν denoting moderate punishment, such as that administered by the father of a family, from whipping to reproving), the other on the intention, amendment prevailing over vengeance.

---

[3] "It is by practice in judgment that social thought raises itself to the objective notion of offenses, and it was private offenses that imposed the idea and suggested the forms of judgment" (p. 94).

What Plato says about this in the *Protagoras* and the *Gorgias* is well known.[4] But it was especially τιμωρία which, in designating satisfaction for the victim rather than the anger of society, was destined to be the vehicle for the most important changes introduced into the juridical conscience by the concept of measure in punishments (οὐ δεῖ τὰς τιμωρίας ἀπεράντους εἶναι, says Demosthenes). Measure becomes so essential to punishment that the delinquent himself will be said to "get his punishment" (τυγχάνειν τιμωρίας). As to the law that "gives" the τιμωρίαι to the delinquent and grants the award to the victim, it is the δίκη of the city. Thus δίκη ceases to denote the cosmic order and becomes identified with the proceedings of the tribunal.

In becoming rationalized, punishment, in turn, caused a like differentiation with regard to guilt. In view of this regressive movement from punishment to guilt, we must persist in the assertion that the first coherent distinction between "voluntary" and "involuntary," such as we find in the legislation of Draco, was not a result of introspection, not a psychological modality of "know thyself." It was a discrimination *a priori*, imposed upon ancient ideas of violence and presumption, to make possible the institutional distinctions that found expression in the reorganization of tribunals: to the Areopagus, henceforth, went "voluntary" murders, vengeance for which was taken over by the city from the family; to the Palladion, certain debatable "involuntary" crimes, which might be excused or punished by exile; to the Delphinion, homicides that were clearly "involuntary," having occurred in games or in war. The tribunal goes before, psychology follows after. And the psychology itself is rarely direct; it takes the roundabout way of poetry—gnomic, elegiac, tragic—which, in various ways, evolved a γνώμη, a meditation on oneself and a subtle analysis of acts. In particular, the imaginative treatment of legendary crimes, which tragedy took over from the epic, provided an opportunity for reflection on the "voluntary" and "involuntary" that took the path of meditation on defilement and on blindness caused by the gods. Thus the aged Oedipus considers the problem

---

[4] *Prot.*, 324ab; *Gorg.*, 418a, 505b, 480cd; and *Laws*, VI, 762c, 777e; X, 854d, 867c; XII, 944d, 964bc.

of involuntary crime from every point of view, blaming and acquitting himself by turns, sometimes of incest and the crime that began his misfortunes, sometimes of the wrath that made him lay hands on his own body.[5] Of course, to this imaginative treatment of sacred crimes we must add the more modest work of the "exegetes" of Delphi, concerned to mete out a just penance to the devotees of the god.

From these convergent reflections on penal law, on legendary crimes, and on the penances meted out to initiates, there issued the fundamental concepts which the Plato of the *Laws* and especially the author of the *Nicomachean Ethics* later brought to a certain degree of rigor: (*a*) the intentional or voluntary pure and simple (ἐκούσιον) and its contrary, the involuntary product of compulsion (βία) or ignorance (ἄγνοια); (*b*) preferential choice (προαίρεσις), bearing on the means, and deliberation (βουλή, βούλευσις), which makes the choice a deliberative desire (βουλευτικὴ ὄρεξις); (*c*) the wish (βούλησις), bearing on ends. Before this reforming work of reflection, the distinction, purely penal, between the voluntary and the involuntary, remained imprecise; thus, the "voluntary" sometimes involved premeditation, sometimes simple volition, while the "involuntary" embraced absence of fault, negligence, imprudence, sometimes cases of being carried away, or simple accidents.

The elucidation of various limiting cases, such as faults incurred through imprudence or negligence, in games or in war, played a decisive role in what might be called a subtle psychology of guilt. Responsibility without premeditation constitutes, indeed, a sort of preliminary zone to the voluntary which is very favorable to the distinctions of jurisprudence: blows delivered in the heat of

[5] The repetition of the word ἀέκων (involuntary) in the *Oedipus at Colonus* is not fortuitous. Antigone first speaks of the "unpurposed actions" of her old father (239–40). The latter declares solemnly that he has "suffered" rather than "done" his acts (256–57); "I have burdened myself with an alien misfortune; yes, I am burdened with it in spite of myself (ἀέκων). Let the divinity be witness! nothing of all that was purposed (αὐθαίρετον)" (522–23). To Creon he replies: "Thy mouth reproaches me with murders, incests, evils that I have borne, unfortunate that I am, against my will (ἄκων)" (964). Involuntary (ἄκων) was the murder of his father (977), involuntary his union with his mother (987).

discussion, wounds inflicted in a state of intoxication, revenge for an outrage in the case of a flagrant act of adultery—all such acts a man repents when he returns to reason, as Lysias remarks (Moulinier, 190); so there is some fault and yet no προνοία, and even a certain conformity to the laws. It was more precisely accidents in games and mistakes in war that provoked the most rigorous reflection; and one can see why. In these two situations the social bond that underlies the holding of games and the conduct of war is a civic bond, which extends beyond and engulfs the two family groups of the plaintiff and the defendant set at variance by the murder. In such a case society becomes aware of its sympathy and indulgence for the murderer; in its turn this sympathy, which itself extends beyond and engulfs the anger of a wronged family, invents a juridical expression for itself by creating a suitable penal category.

In all these cases conceptual analysis comes second; the conceptual distinctions are regulated by the degrees of public indignation and reprobation, and the education of judgment is effected by the work of legal proceedings and by the disputes of lawyers. Thus it is always by the roundabout way of legislation, legal contests, and the sentences of judges that conceptual analysis advances.

But this analysis does not consist only in a work of differentiation carried on within the nebula of guilt. It leads to a recasting of the principal notions that bore the mark of the religious conceptions of defilement, sacrilege, or offense to the gods.

Two notions studied by Gernet and Moulinier are very instructive from this point of view: ἁμαρτία, which, in the tragic conception of existence, expresses the fatal error, the going astray, of the great crimes, and ὕβρις, which, in the same vision of the world, denotes the presumption that propels the hero beyond the limits of his station and of due measure.

In the first place, it is surprising to find ἁμαρτία, in a penal context and consequently in an ethics of responsible intention, with the much weakened sense of excusable fault.[6] This filiation from

[6] Moulinier also calls attention to the idea of ἁμάρτημα: "It seems

theological involuntariness, so to speak, to psychological involuntariness is most remarkable; for the ἁμαρτία that was the result of being blinded by the gods was imprinted, as if passively, upon the heart: "If anyone here has other prayers for the state," cries the leader of the chorus in *Agamemnon,* "let him reap the fruit of the crime of his heart" (φρενῶν ... ἁμαρτίαν; *Ag.,* 502). "Errors of my foolish wisdom" (ἰὼ φρενῶν δυσφρόνων ἁμαρτήματα), replies Creon to the chorus, which has just contrasted the misfortune that comes from another (ἀλλοτρίαν ἄτην) to one's own fault (αὐτὸς ἁμαρτών; *Antigone,* 1259–61). The history of the word reveals that it subsequently denoted the intentional moment in injustice, and then, within the "voluntary," that degree which Aristotle placed between an injustice that is clearly voluntary and an accident that is clearly involuntary, as in the *Rhetoric,* I, 12–13: "ἁμαρτήματα are faults committed after forethought, but without malice; while ἀδικήματα imply both forethought and malice, and ἀτυχήματα imply neither" (Moulinier, 188).

How shall we explain this evolution, which looks like an inversion of meaning? Perhaps we should say that the tragic myth itself furnishes the schema of irresponsibility, the principle of exculpation; if the hero is blinded by the god, then he is not guilty of his faults. One sees the contradiction and the hesitation about the meaning of ἁμαρτία in the tragedy of *Oedipus at Colonus,* which we have already cited. Those facts of which he bears the weight in spite of himself (ἄκων) continue to be called "faults" (τῶν πρὶν ἡμαρτημένων, 439). Oedipus can even say: "In me personally you would not find a fault [ἁμαρτίας] to reproach me with for having thus committed these crimes against myself and against my kin" (τάδ᾽ εἰς ἐμαυτόν τοὺς ἐμούς θ᾽ἡμάρτανον, 967–68). It is precisely Oedipus who is the symbol of monstrous crime *and* excusable fault, of divine infatuation (ἄτη) *and* human misfortune (συμφορά), as the chorus-leader says later (1014).

This evolution of ἁμαρτία in the direction of excusable fault did not prevent a development in a contrary direction, equally

---

to us difficult to understand, just because it seems to mix chance and guilt, innocence and responsibility" (p. 188).

inherent in the initial indignation aroused by crime. In the *Antigone* of Sophocles we came upon the contrast between the "misfortune that comes from another" (ἀλλοτρίαν ἄτην) and "one's own fault" (αὐτὸς ἁμαρτών, 1260). Ἁμάρτημα, then, could just as well lead to the notion of moral fault, in contrast to faults punished by the tribunals. The ἁμάρτημα of the Greek Bible, which denotes the ethico-religious dimension of fault, is an extension of this meaning. It is fundamentally the same meaning that was adumbrated in the *Antigone* of Sophocles.

This surcharge of meaning in ἁμάρτημα is found also in ἀτύχημα, which marks the limit of extenuation.[7] We referred above to Aristotle's effort to arrange "injustice," "excusable fault," and "accident" in order. But it must not be forgotten that τύχη, before being the limit of penal non-responsibility, and hence the inverse of the guilt of voluntary and premeditated crime, was the heir of μοῖρα; in the tragic view it is not the opposite of crime, but crime itself as allotted destiny. There is misfortune (ξυμφορά), luck in the form of bad luck, in the greatest crimes. In Demosthenes one sees exiled murderers, guilty of premeditated crimes, called ἀτυχοῦντες (Moulinier, 189). Thus the same words betray the crossing of several conceptual "series"—the series of "defilement" and the series of "injustice," the series of "misfortune" and the series of the "voluntary."

This reinterpretation of the religious, poetic, and tragic vocabulary in the juridical and penal perspective goes even further, since, as Gernet has shown, ὕβρις was able to supply penal thought with the individual principle of transgression—something like a deliberate will, distinct from being led astray by desire and from

---

[7] It is precisely as ἁμαρτία that an accident during physical training is treated in the second Tetralogy of Antiphon. Moulinier, who summarizes the discussion (*op. cit.,* pp. 188–89), shows that the defense and the accusation are in accord on the point that negligence or imprudence determines a ἁμαρτία, but the defense says: that does not make a murder, even an involuntary one, but only a misfortune (ξυμφορά), exempt from fault but not from defilement. According to the accusation, there was fault and murder and defilement and need for purification, because of culpable haste and negligence (the trainer had given the order to gather up the javelins when the accused threw his).

being carried away by anger—an intelligent will to evil for the sake of evil.

It is perhaps astonishing that the same notion could furnish both the support for a tragic vision of the world and the foundation for juridical incrimination; and it is perhaps even more astonishing because, in the case of ἁμαρτία, tragic blindness, transferred to psychology, supplied a reason for excusing and exonerating. If ὕβρις followed a different route, to the point of furnishing the very principle of incrimination, the basis for accusation, this is because ὕβρις was from the beginning more paradoxical than ἁμαρτία. Unlike the "error" inherent in going astray, ὕβρις is active transgression, and one cannot read divine blindness into human presumption without doing violence to the concept. Whereas ἁμαρτία naturally became secularized as excusable fault, the paradox of ὕβρις, in the process of dissociation, liberated its psychological component, the spirit of perdition interpreted non-theologically—in short, the evil root of wicked premeditation, or what Gernet calls "the guilty will in its pure state, so to speak" (394), or what one might venture to call, before Kant, radical evil, the general maxim of evil maxims. This psychological component is present from the beginning. A psychology of pride appears in its nascent state in the Homeric ὕβρις, which commits outrages and plunders; in the ὕβρις of Hesiod, which arms oblique judgments; in the ὕβρις of Solon, which, in association with κόρος, is insolence (τίκτει γὰρ κόρος ὕβριν), and which is attracted sometimes towards a desire for wealth τε (ὕβριν τίκτει πλοῦτος), sometimes towards a desire for domination: "Pride begets tyranny."

This astonishing relationship between tragic ὕβρις and penal ὕβρις has perhaps an even more subterranean source. Punishment, even when meted out by the city, needs to be faced with a mystery of iniquity. This mystery of iniquity is the vis-à-vis of the indignation of the judge; it justifies the judge and his judgment; the evil will of the delinquent confirms the good conscience of the tribunal. Thus the sacredness of the city reconstructs *in* the criminal, but beyond his acts, a will to evil for the sake of evil which is the analogue of the spirit of perdition that, according to tragedy, blows where it will; and in this will is crystallized the danger that threatens the sacredness of the city. Thus the city tends to re-establish, for its own benefit, the "jealousy" of the gods toward all overweening greatness; every criminal is to the city what "presumption" is to the divine Justice celebrated by the poets.

It was by this roundabout way that the penal thought of the Greeks worked out concepts comparable to the Jewish concepts of guilt. The sacred character of the city was what kept Greek penal thought within the field where it could be compared to the notions that Jewish piety worked out after the Exile.

3. SCRUPULOUSNESS

The second direction in which the consciousness of guilt breaks out is that of the delicate and scrupulous conscience. Adhering to our practice of capturing each of the most fundamental possibilities of experience in an especially clear example, we do not hesitate to seek in Pharisaism both the birthplace of this modality of consciousness and the summit of its perfection.

The Pharisees constitute the crux of that movement of thought which goes from Ezra (that is, from the return from the Exile) to the composition of the Talmud (that is to say, to the first six centuries of our era). It was they who gave to Judaism the character which it still has today; and it is to them that Christianity and Islam owe their existence (if only because Judaism offered to St. Paul the most perfect expression of that which he was to reject most forcefully).

We shall try to disengage whatever is paradigmatic in this pedagogical adventure for our history of types of guilt. The fact that it is specifically *Jewish* ought not to stop us, since it was for the benefit of all "nations"—that is to say, of all mankind—that the Pharisees thought of their people "as a kingdom of priests and a holy nation." The universalism of this experience must be sought for precisely in its particularism. What benefit, then, does Pharisaism offer to all men?

It is possible to approach the core of this experience by taking as our point of departure certain traits of the Biblical religion with which we are already familiar. Without in any way underestimating the novelty of the Judaism of the Second Temple in comparison with the Hebrew thought of the epoch of the Prophets, from Amos to Jeremiah, we must grant without hesitation that the Judaism "of the scribes and Pharisees" has deep roots in propheticism itself and, through it, in the strictly *Mosaic* aspects of the religious experience of pre-exilic and exilic Israel.[8] From the beginning and, no doubt, from Moses, whatever that legislator and leader of his people may have been, the unique adventure of Israel is tied to an ethics and, inversely, that ethics, virtually universal, is tied to an adventure that separates Israel from other peoples. We have already insisted on this double character. On the one hand, the monotheism of Israel is an *ethical* monotheism: the giving of the Law dominates the exodus from Egypt, the sojourn in the wilderness, the settlement in Canaan; the Prophets give an ethical meaning to the catastrophe that they see coming; all the historical experience of Israel is interpreted in ethical terms. But, on the other hand, the monotheism of Israel is a *historical* monotheism: the giving of the Law is not abstract and non-temporal; it is bound up, in the Hebrew consciousness, with the representation of an "event," the exodus from Egypt, the "going up" out of the "house of bondage." Consequently, the ethics itself is historical through and through; it is the ethics of a chosen people. That is why also the whole of the symbolism of sin and repentance is itself a "historical" symbol that draws its "types" from certain significant events (captivity-deliverance).

As a result of this bond between "ethics" and "history," the Law, for the Jew, could never be wholly rationalized and universalized, in a sort of non-temporal, moral deism; because it is bound up with events, the Law is itself a sort of event of conscience, a *factum;* the sign of the distinction of Israel among the peoples is that it has the Law, *this* Law. The Deuteronomist proclaims with pride: "What great nation is there that has just laws and ordinances like all this Law that I set before you this day?"

---

[8] S. W. Baron, *A Social and Religious History of the Jews*, 2d ed. (New York, 1952). The first two volumes of this monumental work in eight volumes are devoted to the period from the origins to the Talmud.

(Deut. 4:8). This Law cannot be reduced to a formal structure of the universal conscience; it clings to the historical figure, the cultural patron, interpreted by the theology of history of the Biblical writers; and so its structure is ineluctably contingent. Thus the specific ethical character that Judaism will have is foreshadowed at the beginning. As a great historian of Judaism says, from the initial historical monotheism proceeds "the distinction between the 613 laws regulating the behavior of the Jew and the 6 or 7 fundamental duties enjoined upon all the sons of Noah" (S. W. Baron, *A Social and Religious History of the Jews,* Vol. I, p. 12). The coherent and thoroughgoing heteronomy of the Pharisees is inscribed in the "historical" character of the monotheism that successive legislators placed under the authority of Moses and that Moses himelf no doubt founded.

The Prophets presuppose this ethical and historical monotheism. Their challenges and their fulminations are not directed against it essentially, but against its being forgotten in times of historical success, in consequence of social injustice as well as of concessions to the religious syncretism of the surrounding world. The great work of "casuistry," which was to be characteristic of the scribes of the Exile and the Return, must have begun before the Exile. In contrast to the conceptualization and the systematization of Roman law, the Jewish mind was already proceeding by way of "a large collection of typical cases from which judges and students could draw analogies" (S. W. Baron, *ibid.,* p. 80). Thus, what is called Jewish legalism, although it is rather a genius for jurisprudence, develops traits which were strongly adumbrated before the Exile. Before the Exile, also, the abortive reform of Josiah, to which we owe the Deuteronomic legislation, is the first coherent anticipation of the attempt of the Pharisees to make a whole people, corporately and individually, lead an actual and effectively practical existence under the Law and by the Law. But Deuteronomy still hovers at a distance from the real, like a utopia of daily life. The endeavor of the Pharisees and their scribes will be precisely to inscribe in reality this life under the Law and by the Law.

It was during the Exile and, consequently, at the time of the final blaze of prophecy, with Ezekiel and Jeremiah, that Israel conceived the project of an effectively practical existence in obedience; the Exile created a situation comparable to that of the Egyptian captivity and the sojourn in the desert, a situation that might be called essentially Mosaic. It was during the Exile that Israel came to understand itself as a weak and despised people according to the canons of historical and political success, but great and blessed by the Law; the Law would henceforth give to the individual Jew and to the Jewish people their definite profile.

It was because the way was prepared in the old Mosaic spirit[9] that Nehemiah could return to Jerusalem with a troop of exiles, revive the ruins of Israel, rebuild the Temple, and one day set the scribe Ezra to read "the book of the Law of Moses prescribed by the Eternal to Israel" (Neh. 8:1). The question may be debated whether the book which was read "from the morning until midday," and which even then learned men "explained" to the people to "make them understand" what had been read, was only Leviticus or the whole of the Pentateuch (or at least large sections of the Five Books of Moses). What is certain is that Ezra opened an historical epoch of conscience "as important as the rise of prophecy, and only less important than the work of Moses."[10] This epoch is that which is properly called the religion of the Torah. (We shall return later to this word and its Greek translation, *Nomos*, Law.) It is no longer the time of inspired and impulsive men preaching in the desert, but the time of colleges of students and exegetes of the Law; no longer the time of creation, but that of interpretation; nor of challenge, but of the reconstruction and direction of life. Neither is it the time of the unlimited demand, but that of minute and detailed practice, according to

---

[9] An important link between the Prophets and the Pharisees was, no doubt, the group or order of *Hassidim*, those "pious ones," those vigil-keepers, close to the Levites and the Prophets, who taught penitence, ritual as well as moral, and practiced the discipline of nocturnal prayer. They were already "separated ones," as the Pharisees were to be ("Pharisee"= separated). A. Néher, *Essence du prophétisme,* pp. 264–76, 294–95.

[10] R. Travers Herford, *The Pharisees* (New York, 1924), p. 18.

circumstances and cases.[11] It was this wedge of intransigence driven into the Persian Empire, and then the Seleucid Empire, and then the Roman, that guaranteed the survival of the Jewish people and the complete manifestation of the meaning of its task. But there was needed for this purpose a people that believed itself set apart, cut off from the nations by the Law, and at the same time internally united by the Law.[12]

As to the Pharisees themselves, it would be a great mistake to reduce their role to that of a sect opposed to the sect of the Sadducees (as such they hardly appear before the end of the second century B.C.) and involved in the trial of Jesus. They are the crucial factor in the whole spiritual history that unfolds from Ezra to the compilers of the Talmud, and the educators of the Jewish people even to this day. That is why a phenomenological study of the scrupulous conscience cannot neglect their testimony.

The Pharisees are first of all and essentially men of the Torah.[13] And immediately a preconceived idea comes into our minds: men of the Torah can mean only men of legalism, moral slavery, hardness of heart, literalism. If that judgment were true, the Pharisees could have no part in an elucidation of *typical* experiences, concepts, and symbols; they would belong only to moral teratology. If we rank their experience with the ethico-juridical conception of the Greeks and the ethico-theological conception of St. Paul, it is because we see in them the purest representatives of an irreducible *type* of moral experience, in whom every man can recognize one of the fundamental possibilities of his own humanity.

But to make contact with this type, we must traverse a forest of prejudices.

Legalism? But first we should have to understand the word

[11] "Thus legalistic accusation took the place of inspired denunciations" (Baron, *op. cit.*, I, p. 226).

[12] Throughout his work, S. W. Baron, in a perhaps equivocal manner, interprets this fundamental option as a choice in favor of the "artificial and contrary to nature" (I, p. 164).

[13] George Foot Moore, *Judaism in the First Centuries of the Christian Era* (Harvard University Press, 1927–30, 3 vols.); on revelation as Torah, see Vol. I, pp. 235–80. See also J. Bonsirven, *Le Judaïsme palestinien au temps de Jésus-Christ* (Paris, 1934, 2 vols.), Vol. I, pp. 247–307, and M. J. Lagrange, *Le Judaïsme avant Jésus-Christ* (Paris, 1931).

torah in the same way as the Pharisees themselves understood it. The Seventy translated it by νόμος; St. Paul also says νόμος; and νόμος gave *lex* and "law" in all the modern languages. But we come after Roman law and the great juridical systematizations that issued from the Latin mind, and for us law is abstract, universal, and written; we represent the scrupulous conscience to ourselves as following with its finger a set of rules built up by the systematic arrangement of general precepts. The *Torah* of the Pharisees is certainly a book, the Law of Moses, the Pentateuch; but what makes the Law law is that it is an instruction from the Lord. Torah means teaching, instruction, and not law. The law of the Torah is both *religious* and *ethical:* ethical because it demands, commands; religious because it is a transparent deliverance of the will of God with regard to men. The whole problem for the Pharisees was this: How will God be truly served in this world?

It is here that one encounters the classic accusation of moral servility. That the morality of the Pharisees is a heteronomy is beyond doubt; but it is a *thoroughgoing* heteronomy. In posing the problem, How to do the will of God?, the Pharisees were confronted with the failure of the great Prophets, with their powerlessness to change their people, with the fact of the Exile, which, according to the common opinion, was the chastisement of Israel. Hence, they wished to realize the ethics of the Prophets in an ethics of *detail*. The task this time is to give practical realization to the Torah in all sectors of existence, ritual and ethical, family and communal, penal and economic, and in the smallest circumstances. Pharisaism is this will to follow heteronomy all the way to the end, to stake daily existence without reserve on the "statutes of God." Such thoroughgoingness transforms heteronomy into an obedience accepted and willed unconditionally; the abdication of freedom of choice becomes the supreme assertion of the will. Psalms 19 and 119 are the most beautiful lyrical witnesses that we have of this joyous abandonment of the will to direction by the Law:

> I rejoice in following thy precepts,
> As if I possessed all treasures.
>
> 119:14

> I delight in thy commandments,
> I love them.
>
> 119:47
>
> Thy word is a lamp unto my feet
> and a light on my path.
>
> 119:105
>
> The law of Yahweh is perfect,
>   converting the soul;
> the testimony of Yahweh is sure,
>   making wise the simple.
>
> The precepts of Yahweh are right,
>   rejoicing the heart;
> the commandment of Yahweh is pure,
>   enlightening the eyes.
>
> The fear of the Lord is clean,
>   enduring forever;
> the judgments of Yahweh are true
>   and righteous altogether,
>
> more to be desired than gold,
>   yea, than the finest gold;
> his words are sweeter than honey
>   and the honeycomb.
>
> 19:7–10

This tenderness of devotion is surely not unrelated to the feeling for friendship and mutual, fraternal aid that one takes pleasure in recognizing in the Pharisees and that justifies one of their best interpreters in speaking of the "urbanity" of the Pharisees.[14] The

---

[14] Louis Finkelstein, *The Pharisees; the Sociological Background of Their Faith* (Philadelphia, 1940, 2 vols.): "It was this paradoxical combination of religious passion and intellectual objectivity which differentiated Pharisaic tolerance from that affected by some of the Sadducees" (I, p. 10). The Pharisees, according to him, show the reaction of the plebeians—more exactly, the urban plebeians—against the patricians, represented at that time by the Sadducees ("The Sadducean influence radiated from the Temple, the Pharisaic from the market place," *ibid.*, p. 81). This would explain likewise their relation to the Prophets, for the latter must have belonged to the same social levels ("The main thesis emerging out of this analysis is that the prophetic, Pharisaic and rabbinic traditions were the products of a persistent cultural battle, carried on in Palestine for fifteen

Pharisean movement represents one of the most significant victories
of lay understanding over the haughty and illiterate dogmatism
of the priests and the great ones of this world. This trait gives
them a singular resemblance to many of the "wise men" of Greece,
to the Pythagoreans, and also to some of the lesser Socratics,
Cynics and others.

These remarks make us ready to regard with some suspicion the
last and gravest accusation against the Pharisees, that of killing the
spirit by the letter. What the Pharisees, or certain Pharisees, were
is one thing; what they wished to be is another. Now, what they
tried to set up is exactly the opposite of a monument of literalism;
since the great thing, according to them, is to "fulfill" the Law
and the Prophets, it is not possible to cling to the Scriptures—that
is to say, to the written Torah—as a relic of the past. It was precisely on this point that they broke with the Sadducees. Against
the Sadducees, they aimed to raise the oral tradition to the rank
of Torah—which they called unwritten Torah—in order to make
use of it as a divine teaching, actual and living, able to serve as
guide and interpreter with respect to the written text of the
Pentateuch. This aim is the consequence of the major option of
Pharisaism: if the Torah is a teaching addressed here and now
to the Jewish man by God himself, and not an abstract system of

centuries, between the submerged, unlanded groups, and their oppressors,
the great landowners," *ibid.*, p. 2). The same sort of explanation can be
given for the co-operative spirit of the Pharisees, their patience, their
leniency in penal matters, and especially their passion for study ("This
devotion to intellectual pursuits is essentially urban . . . the dominant
characteristic of Pharisaism was study, that of Sadducism was contempt for
scholarship," *ibid.*, p. 97). Finkelstein attempts also—with less success, in
my opinion—to explain the content of some of the theses maintained by
the Pharisees about Providence and free will, angelology and the resurrection of the dead. More interesting is the application of his thesis to the
understanding of the Pharisees' battle on two fronts: on the one hand, the
battle for the oral tradition, in which Finkelstein discovers a "plebeian
interpretation of the Torah" (I, p. 74), against the conservatism of the
priests and patricians; on the other hand, the battle for a stricter observance
of the rules of Levitical purity by the whole people, which put them in
opposition to the "provincials," the *am ha-aretz,* who became in their eyes
not only peasants, but pagans. Like all sociological explanations, Finkelstein's accounts for the social *impact* of the doctrine, but not for its *origin,*
as far as its meaning is concerned.

morality, if religion consists in doing the will of God here and now, then the Torah must be living and actual. Now, life creates situations, circumstances, cases, on which the written Torah is mute; and so an interpretation is needed, faithful and creative at the same time, that can be considered as the disclosure of the Torah of Moses, although not written. That, quite precisely, is where the ethico-religious pedagogy of the scribes and Pharisees takes its stand: they "study" and "teach" the Torah. Starting with the conviction that there is no sector of life in which there is no occasion or obligation to do the will of God (*mitzvah*), they ask what is the right way in this particular case, what is the unwritten Torah for this particular case. The "wise men" do not invent it, they find it; and the solution does not become an official decision—*halachah*[15]—until after consultation among masters and ratification by a majority. Then the *halachah* is "fixed," although it can still be amended or suppressed by another *halachah*. The whole body of these *halachoth* constitutes the legislation that is binding upon the community of those who seek to live in accordance with the Torah. Thus the Torah became inexhaustible, plastic and not static; the Torah interpreted by means of exegesis and casuistry was a living source of instruction for each and for all. As soon as two points were granted—that there is a *halachah* for every circumstance, and that the oral ordinances that explicate the written Torah are the unwritten Torah,—the interpretation of the Torah became unlimited. According to the remark of a later rabbi: "Whatever an acute disciple shall hereafter teach in the presence of his Rabbi has already been said to Moses on Sinaï" (cited by Travers Herford, *op. cit.*, p. 85).

Let us attempt now to work out the "type" exemplified by the

---

[15] Bonsirven defines *halachah* thus: "Decision, rule having the force of law, considered in itself without any reference to Scripture . . . , the law in its juridical part" (*op. cit.*, p. 293). The author gives, on this occasion, a good exposition of the exegetic and hermeneutic rules of the scribes and rabbis (*ibid.*, pp. 295–303). Travers Herford stresses the opposition between the imperative character of the *halachah*, as a "specific declaration of the divine will applicable to a given case" (p. 73), and the free and non-constraining character of the *haggadah,* which denotes everything which is not of the order of precepts in the Torah.

experience of Pharisaism (and, in general, of Judaism) and to make manifest the dimension proper to this type of guilt.

We have said that the core of this type of experience is *scrupulousness;* and it is with scrupulousness also that we shall link the particular kind of guilt that seems to us to attach itself to this type. Scrupulousness can be characterized as a general regime of thoroughgoing and voluntary heteronomy. Judaism expresses this heteronomy by saying that the Torah is revelation and that the revelation is Torah. The Torah is revelation: in the language of Judaism, Moses knew all the Law that was communicated to him "from mouth to mouth" (Num. 12:6–8), "face to face" (Deut. 34:10), so that hermeneutics can only be the explication, by means of an ongoing history, of an instruction that itself has no history, or at least that has only one history, that of the absolute event of the "giving of the Law"; but that instruction took place in the past, it is complete and definitive; indeed, it can be called older than the world, if it is true that it is identical with the "Wisdom" celebrated in the books of wisdom; the oral law that explicates it, whether it be hallowed custom, or a product of Biblical exegesis, or the decrees of casuistry, is itself placed at the service of that primordial wisdom. But if the Torah is revelation, reciprocally the revelation is Torah: the heart of the God-man relation is an instruction concerning what is to be done; even if this instruction is more than law, it is inscribed in a voluntaristic context: God is ethical and the bond between man and God is a bond of obedience to instruction.

From these two reciprocal propositions—the Torah is revelation and the revelation is Torah—are derived all the traits of scrupulousness and of the consciousness of guilt that is characteristic of scrupulousness. For the scrupulous conscience the commandment is "holy, right, and good"; the commandment is the past absolute of such a conscience, the completed revelation of its meaning, although this revelation in the past is accessible only by means of custom, exegesis, and casuistry, intelligent and humble, which are the living present of scrupulousness. The fundamental option of the scrupulous conscience is thus exactly the reverse of that of a hazarded existence, in the sense of the "glorious liberty of the children of God" according to St. Paul, or the "love and do what you will" of St. Augustine. But its greatness is that it is heteronomous *right to the end,* that it is obedient to the divine teaching in all things, in spite of everything, and in every detail: in all things—that is to say, without reservation of any sector of existence; in spite of everything—that is to say, without taking into account adverse situations, the interdiction of a prince, the obstacles presented by foreign manners and customs, or, finally, persecution; in every detail—that is to say, giving as much importance to little things as to great ones. The scrupulous conscience, because it is heteronomous right to the end, is happy; it finds its happiness in doing without reserve that which is in its eyes the instruction of God here and now; it is dependent, but not alienated; for it is not "outside itself," but "within," since its heteronomy is consistent and willed.

What, now, is the peculiar contribution of scrupulousness to the consciousness of fault?

Everything attained by the scrupulous conscience lies within the dimension of "transgression";[16] and that, no doubt, is the reason for the subtle narrowing of the scrupulous conscience. But before speaking of its narrowness, we must recognize its depth; for its narrowness is the exact counterpart of its depth.

Scrupulousness is the advanced point of guilt, in the sense that it carries to the extreme the two traits that we started to analyze at the beginning of this chapter: the personal imputation of evil and the polarity of the just man and the wicked man. Accusation against the individual as the seat of guilt is, as we know, the fruit of the teaching of Jeremiah and Ezekiel; Pharisaism extends this preaching of the last great prophets. At the same time, its confession of sins comes to express itself in the great penitential poetry of the Psalms, which become, in the setting of the synagogue, the liturgy of the delicate conscience; and it is in them that scruple finds its preferred language, its particular happiness. The opposi-

---

[16] Moore, *Judaism,* Vol. I, pp. 443–552: *Man, Sin, Atonement.* In that study one will find all the necessary analyses concerning deliberate violations, transgressions through ignorance or inadvertence, and the corresponding types of expiation.

tion of the just and the wicked is not an invention of the Pharisees either, but the ultimate outcome of the idea of degrees in guilt; if there is a more and a less in "transgression," the just and the wicked mark the extremes on this scale of intensity of values. But the Pharisees further accentuated this sense of moral polarity to the extent that they made observance of the Law not only an ideal limit but a practical program for living; the impossible maximum of perfection is the background for the attainable optimum of justice; nothing is demanded of a man that he cannot *do*.

The language of guilt bears the stamp of this ethico-religious experience in the idea of *merit* (*zachuth*), which, says Travers Herford, is "constantly used in the Rabbinical literature, [although it] does not occur in the Old Testament" (*op. cit.*, p. 125). This author has perceived clearly the coherence of the idea of merit with the whole of Pharisaism: the God of Judaism is not beyond good and evil; he is the very foundation of the relation between religion and morality; to say that God is just is to profess this foundation; on the other hand, the distinction is not something to be contemplated, but "to be realized by man"; it is immediately "practical" and not speculative: "Be holy; for I, Yahweh, your God, am holy" (Lev. 19:2). Consequently there is an intrinsic difference between a man who *does* what is good and a man who *does* what is evil; the one is pleasing to God, the other is not. Now, this character of being pleasing to God does not remain external to a man, defined by his practical relation to the holiness of God; it adds something to his personality, to his inmost existence. This something is "merit." Merit is the imprint of the just act; it is, we might say, a modification of the good will; it is an increase in the worth of a man, issuing from the worth of his acts. A second idea is added, in the notion of merit, to the idea of an increase in personal worth, namely, its connection with the idea of "reward." This old idea of "reward" is found everywhere in the Old Testament, and the New Testament does not repudiate it (Mat. 6:4 and 12; 10:42). In the Old Testament it oscillates between temporal success, intimate enjoyment of the presence of God, here and now, and expectation of an eschatological fulfillment. None of these things is peculiarly Pharisean. What is peculiar to Pharisaism, it seems, is the connection of the idea of "reward" with the idea of "merit": to have merit is to merit something; it is to merit a reward; conversely, the reward is the reward of merit. In an ethical vision of the world like that of the Pharisees, where *to do* the will of God is greater than anything else, it is a blessing to have the Law and, with it, opportunities for obedience (*mitzvoth*) and the possibility of acquiring merit. This is another way of saying that the obedient man is "happy," that he has "found life," that he has obtained the "favor of God" (Prov. 8:34–35).

If, then, "merit" expresses the new conceptualization that Pharisaism developed in carrying on the two themes of personal imputation and the polarity of the just and the wicked, the explicit contribution of Pharisaism to the idea of guilt can be expected to be something like the contrary of merit. Objectively sin is transgression; subjectively guilt is the loss of a degree of worth; it is *perdition* itself. In the language of "reward" it can be said, with one of the "wise men" of Judaism: "The reward of a mitzvah is a mitzvah; and the reward of a sin is a sin" (quoted by T. Herford, *op. cit.*, p. 128). What is lost is what is subtracted from existence, as merit is an increase of life. Proverbs had already said: "For he who finds me finds life; he will obtain the favor of Yahweh. But he who offends me injures his own soul; whoever hates me cherishes death" (8:35–36).

Pharisaism (and, in general, the spirit of the scribes, the sages, and the rabbis) is not turned toward speculation, and so we must not look for any theoretical elaboration of all these notions. Nevertheless, what underlies this ethical vision of the world is the idea of a liberty entirely responsible and always at its own disposal. This notion is not worked out as such, but it is implicit in various themes, of a practical rather than a speculative character, which are found in all the rabbinical literature. The first of these is the theme of the two "inclinations" (or *yetzer*):[17] man is subject to

[17] For the theory of the two "inclinations" or "imaginations," besides the authors already cited (Moore, pp. 479–93, Herford, Bonsirven, Lagrange, etc.), see Norman Powell Williams, *Ideas of the Fall and of Original Sin* (New York and Toronto, 1927); Chap. II, entitled "The Adam Story and the Evil Imagination," traces the history of this symbol from Genesis 6:5 and 8:21, through Ecclesiasticus 15:11–17 and 27:5–6, down to the

GUILT   131

the duality of two tendencies, two impulses—a good inclination and
an evil inclination. The latter—*yetzer ha-ra*—is implanted by the
Creator in man; it is one of the things that God has made and
of which he has said that they were "very good." The evil inclination, then, is not a radical evil, engendered by man, from which
he is radically powerless to free himself; it is rather a permanent
temptation that gives opportunity for the exercise of freedom of
choice, an obstacle to be transformed into a springboard. "Evil
inclination" does not make sin something irreparable.

This interpretation is confirmed by the Jewish literature concerning "repentance." It has been remarked that the Old Testament has no abstract word for repentance, but the symbol of
"return." It was Judaism that raised it to the rank of a genuine
concept, making it the keystone of Jewish piety.[18] Now, "repentance" belongs to the same thematic universe as transgression and
merit, and it is no accident that it was precisely Judaism that laid
emphasis on this concept. For "repentance" signifies that "return"
to God, freely chosen, is always open to man; and the example of
great and impious men who have "returned" to the Eternal attests
that it is always *possible* for a man to "change his way." This
emphasis on repentance is in conformity with the interpretation
of "evil inclination" as occasion of sin and not as radical evil. The
ethical universe of Pharisaism is already that of Pelagius: no great
contrasts, as in Paul, Augustine, and Luther, between radical evil

---

rabbinical literature. From the beginning this notion oscillates between the
voluntary and the involuntary, the responsible and the irresponsible, fault
and weakness, man's share and God's share; it is imprinted in the heart of
every man, although it cannot be called hereditary; it is evil because it
inclines to evil, but it can be used for good. N. P. Williams sees in it an
alternative to the theme of the fall of Adam; he judges that Jesus' words
about the evil heart of man are compatible with the theory of the *yetzer
ha-ra* and that it was St. Paul who gave precedence to the Adamic theory.

[18] G. F. Moore, *Judaism,* Vol. I, pp. 507 ff.: repentance is both "turning
back" and "being sorry"; it is also making amends and having the firm
resolve to renew one's obedience, and sometimes it is also suffering for the
sake of atonement. It should be remarked, in this connection, that the
ritual atonement described by Leviticus never excused from repentance;
that is why Judaism could survive the disappearance of the Temple and
the discontinuance of the sacrificial cult. Cf. G. F. Moore, *ibid.,* Vol. I,
pp. 497–506.

and radical deliverance, but a slow and progressive process of salvation, in which "pardon" is not lacking to "repentance," grace to the good will.

Such is the greatness of scrupulousness, of its sense of guilt, and of its sense of responsibility. As to the limitation of the scrupulous conscience, it is to be sought for nowhere else than in that which is the principle of its greatness, namely, the thoroughgoing and freely accepted heteronomy that defines it. And this limitation, which was ignorant of itself, was to give rise to a new *peripeteia* of the guilty conscience—that which St. Paul brought to light in his two letters to the Romans and to the Galatians. In itself and for itself, that limitation is not yet guilt, but constitutes a part of the training in holiness and consequently of the quest for innocence that characterizes the "type" of the scrupulous conscience.

To locate the point of deflection, if one may so call it, of the scrupulous conscience, we must start from that which appeared essential to the doctors of Pharisaism, namely, the elaboration of an oral tradition that could keep the written Torah alive and that could be taken in its turn for an aspect of the eternal Torah which had been taught to Moses. Actually, by attaching itself to the written Torah, the oral Torah not only profits by the sacred character of the latter, but projects upon it the procedure by which the tradition was constituted. Now, in what does the work of interpretation that the sages pursued during the centuries when they were "fixing" the *halachah* consist? Essentially in a judicatory activity, in jurisprudential labors. It remains true that it was this *judicatory* activity, this long discipline of the faculty of judgment, this cultivation of moral *correctness* or *exactitude,* which maintained the Torah as a living instruction and fashioned the Jewish character practically and effectively. But, conversely, it appears that the Torah, although it is teaching rather than law, became dependent on the essentially definitive and legislative operation of the sages; and it was this operation which in fact became divinized under the title of unwritten Torah. Thus the unwritten Torah guaranteed and placed too high a value on a precise and limited type of relation between man and the divine, namely, correctness of judgment, discernment, which is the soul of casuistry. That this discernment was exercised by the sages of the Pharisean school with the zeal of obedience, and for the sole purpose of recognizing the will of God in all circumstances, is now indubitable. Nevertheless, it remains true that the sages divinized casuistic discernment and thus placed it in the same rank as the undivided and unlimited call of the Prophets to perfection and holiness.

It will be objected that the *halachah* does not cover the whole interpretation of the Torah, but only its imperative part, and that the *haggadah* covers all that which is not of the order of precepts; it was there that the sages gave free rein to their meditations and to their imagination, employing the freer forms of story, parable, and fantasy. Only a Jew experienced in the double play of *halachah* and *haggadah* can say how they are fitted together in the mentality of Judaism. It remains true, nevertheless, that the most fervent rehabilitations of the Pharisees do not deny that the *halachah* is binding and the *haggadah* free, that the first is more coherent and the second more improvised, that the first is submitted to collegiate judgment and the second is left to opinion and imagination; that the Pharisees were lay preachers and not theologians; that, moreover, they made scarcely any innovation in speculative theology; and, finally, that the Pharisees are men of a practical religion; so that, in the end, Pharisaism stakes its fate on the *halachah*.[19]

That is the point: if the Pharisees have been the educators of the human race through the Jewish people, their pedagogy shows clearly the greatness and the limitation of the *scrupulous conscience* or, more exactly, of *religious scruple*. Its fundamental limitation is that it confines the God-man relation to a relation of instruction—that is to say, in the last resort, a relation of a will that commands to a will that obeys. This is the very essence of a "practical" religion. Now, does the will to complete and exact obedience, even when prompted by the joyous acceptance of a

---

[19] "And though the Haggadah was its indispensable accompaniment, yet it was the Halachah which, so to speak, gave the word of command. . . . It was the peculiar genius of Pharisaism that developed them both, and that put Halachah first" (Travers Herford, *op. cit.*, p. 185).

grateful heart, exhaust the dialogal situation expressed of old by the conjugal symbolism of the Prophets? Is the bond between God and man solely or even essentially "practical"?

Judaism itself has lived only by that which overflows and exceeds religious *praxis*. Many authors celebrate the sweetness, yes, the tenderness, reserved and circumspect, of the best sages and the best rabbis; they say how spontaneous in all of them was the exercise of justice and friendliness. For its part, the lyricism of the Psalms, which nourished the liturgy of the synagogue long before it fed the liturgy of the Christian churches, expresses all the more than "practical" aspects of the dialogal situation which is the background for the teaching of the Torah.

But if we put in question the "tradition of the Ancients" (Mark 7:1–13), which impresses its juridical style on all the relations of the human to the divine, how far back must we trace the origin of this aberration? Only to the oral tradition? But did not the written law issue from a like process? Is it not evident that very early in the history of Israel the *Mosaic* aspect of the dialogal situation was overvalued? The limitation of all scrupulous conscientiousness seems to me to be exemplified by what I should like to call the construction of a Mosaic fantasy: Moses is placed above all the Prophets; it is granted that he knew all the law for all times and for all men, and that the Prophets only repeated it; all the successive legislations—the Decalogue, Deuteronomy, Leviticus—are attributed to him; lastly, the oral law itself is absorbed into the Mosaic revelation. Thus all the modalities and all the stages of the religious experience are contracted into the figure of *the* legislator and into the *single* event of the giving of the Law. This absorption of all the outbursts of prophecy into the Mosaic figure seems to me to be the key to the formation of any scrupulous conscience; in every case you can find this movement of contraction of an actual tradition into something like an absolute "event," by which this conscience was supposedly given to itself in the past; this gift of its ethos plays for it the role of a Torah, a divine instruction; the scrupulous conscience swears to be faithful, with understanding, zeal, humility, and joy, to this divine instruction in which, to its eyes, its absolute Origin is summed up. Its wholehearted fidelity is its greatness; the Mosaic fantasy (or whatever takes its place) is its limitation. But this limitation is not experienced as a fault; it is an integral part of that technique of innocence, that cultivation of justice, the purpose of which is precisely to reduce guilt.

With this schema of juridicization, which I see represented in Judaism by what I have called the Mosaic fantasy, we can connect certain other traits that will enrich our description of scrupulousness. The first is the coincidence of ritual and morality in scrupulousness.[20]

Scrupulousness could as well have been defined as a ritualization of the moral life or a moralization of ritual; but this trait cannot be grasped directly. Why, in the scrupulous conscience, does one see a certain esotericism that is characteristic of ritual take over, step by step, every obligation that must be performed thus and not otherwise, while rites receive an accent of obligation that confers upon them the sense of a duty? The historicist and progressivist interpretation, according to which the Judaism of the second Temple fell back to a bygone stage of the moral consciousness, to the archaism of the pure and the impure, is not sufficient; it accounts at best for the origin of the ritual content, but not for the decisive fact that those archaic modes of behavior were *resumed* after the ethical stage represented by propheticism. It seems to me that this resumption, this resurgence of a post-ethical ritualism, so to speak, cannot be understood unless we take as our point of departure the project of a consistent and voluntary heteronomy. The esotericism of the rite bears witness to conscience that conscience is not the source of the Law, since the Law is not transparent to conscience. In performing the rite, the conscience gives proof of its will to obey the Law not because it commands this rather than that, but because it makes manifest the will of God. Thus the ritualization of ethics is a corollary of its heteronomy: the scrupu-

---

[20] Moore (*op. cit.*, Vol. II, pp. 3 ff., 79 ff.) gives a clear and complete exposition of this mutual overlapping, in Judaism, of moral precepts and religious "observances" (circumcision, Sabbath, festivals, public fasts, payment of tithes, dietary laws, various purifications).

lous conscience desires to be exact in its accepted dependence, and the rite is the instrument of that exactness, which is the ethical equivalent of scientific exactness.

It seems to me, then, that the concern for levitical *purity* can be understood as an aspect of the will to practical *holiness* that is at the heart of Judaism. Thereby the illuminating example of Judaism reveals the whole method of scrupulousness: every scrupulous conscience tests its rigor by the touchstone of its *observances*. Perhaps an ethical life worthy of that name is not even possible without some ceremonial, public, domestic, or private—in short, without some observance. At the same time, the spirit of exactness reveals the dangers peculiar to the scrupulous conscience: to the danger of juridicization is added the danger of ritualization, when it begins to forget the intention of the commandment in the letter of the commandment. The scrupulous conscience is then threatened with the abolition of its own intention to obey in attention to the form of its obedience. This danger is the price it pays for its greatness; the scrupulous conscience does not see it as a fault.

A third trait must be added to this double process of juridicization and ritualization of the scrupulous conscience: under the regime of a thoroughgoing and willing heteronomy, obligation has an enumerative and cumulative character opposed to the simplicity and sobriety of the command to love God and men. What strikes the reader who penetrates into the rabbinical literature is the incessant multiplication of the collections of interpretative decrees; the collection of *halachoth* gives the Mishnah, which, confronted with the Torah and explicated in its turn, gives the Gemara, which, joined to the Mishnah, constitutes the Babylonian and Palestinian Talmud. Now this process represents the movement of every conscience for which commandments do not cease to multiply; the scrupulous conscience is an increasingly articulated and subtle conscience that forgets nothing and adds incessantly to its obligations; it is a manifold and sedimented conscience that finds salvation only in movement; it accumulates behind itself an enormous past that makes tradition; it is alive only at its point, at the forward end of tradition, where it "interprets," in new circumstances, equivocations or contradictions. This is not a conscience that begins or begins anew, but a conscience that continues and adds to. If its work of minute and often minuscule innovation stops, the conscience is caught in the trap of its own tradition, which becomes its yoke.

A final trait of the scrupulous conscience will complete the portrait: the scrupulous man is a "separated" man. We recall that "Pharisee" means separated; his separation is the reflection, on the level of relations to others, of the separation of the pure and the impure, inherent in the ritualization of the moral life. Of course rites bind together a community to which they furnish symbols as rallying points and as signs of mutual recognition; but this internal bond among observants does not prevent the class of observants from being separated from the class of non-observants as the pure is separated from the impure. Thus the Jew among the nations; thus the Pharisee himself among the "provincials," the common people, the heathen, the *am ha-aretz*. That is why the scrupulous man can safeguard his "urbanity" only by a consuming zeal for proselytism,[21] in order to reduce the separation between observance and non-observance and to make, of his own people at least, "a kingdom of saints and a holy nation." But the frontier of strict observance can only be pushed back; it reappears further on. The scrupulous man is then placed before the alternative of fanaticism or encystment. Sometimes he takes the first road (Louis Finkelstein cites some astonishing imprecations of the Pharisees with regard to the *am ha-aretz*, I, 24–37),[22] but more often he takes the second. Then he gives up the attempt to universalize the maxim of his own particularity and becomes for others a stumbling block and

[21] Louis Finkelstein joins these two traits together: "it was probably the first organization to admit plebeians and patricians on an equal footing; and it was the first definitely propagandist" (*op. cit.,* p. 75).

[22] Faithful to his sociological method, the author explains that the laws of Levitical purity could be observed only in Jerusalem and its vicinity: "Consequently, the whole nation, except those living in or near Jerusalem, was Levitically impure" (p. 26). Moreover, they were suspected of violating the law of tithes, did not know the use of writing, etc.: "as late as the Mishnah, compiled three and a half centuries after the organization of the society, the term Pharisee was still used as the antonym of *am ha-arez*" (p. 76). Is this a key to the conflict between Jesus and the Pharisees? Finkelstein suggests that it was (p. 32), and so does Travers Herford: "so far as he was outside the Pharisaic circle, he himself [Jesus] was an Am-ha-aretz" (p. 206).

for himself a solitary. This also the scrupulous man cannot regard as his fault; it is the bitter fruit of his obedience; it is his destiny.

Ritualization, sedimentation, separation of the scrupulous conscience—these traits do not make the scrupulous man a monster: the limitations of scrupulousness are the counterpart of its depth. Scrupulousness is the advanced point of the experience of fault, the recapitulation, in the subtle and delicate conscience, of defilement, sin, and guilt; but it is at this advance-post that the whole of that experience is on the point of capsizing.

The counterproof of our analysis would be furnished by the description of the specific failing of the scrupulous conscience. That failing is "hypocrisy"; hypocrisy is, so to speak, the grimace of scrupulousness. Everyone is familiar with the accusation ascribed to Jesus in the Synoptic Gospels, particularly Matthew's, the most anti-Pharisean of the three (Chap. 23): "Woe unto you, scribes and Pharisees, hypocrites!"[23] We cannot understand the Pharisees if we start from this attack; but we can arrive at it by starting from what we have described as the greatness of Pharisaism; we can arrive at it by a sort of schematic genesis of "hypocrisy," starting from "scrupulousness"; scrupulousness turns toward hypocrisy as soon as the scrupulous conscience ceases to be in movement.

In fact, its heteronomy is justified only if it is accepted right to the end; its juridicization is justified only as long as casuistry continues to conquer new domains; its ritualization, only if its exactitude is complete; its sedimentation, only while interpretation remains living; and its separation is rendered supportable only by missionary zeal. The scrupulous conscience, precisely because it looks to the past, because revelation is for it something already completed, is condemned to perpetual movement. Let it cease to practice, to make additions, to conquer new fields, and all the stigmas of hypocrisy begin to appear, one by one: its heteronomy is only a sham, the pretense of speech without the substance of the deed: "For they say, and do not"; the law that is no longer interpreted ceases to provide the happiness of study and becomes a yoke: "They bind heavy burdens and lay them on men's shoulders; but they

[23] Similar accusations are found between the schools of Hillel and Shammai (Finkelstein, *op. cit.*, Vol. I, p. 98).

themselves will not move them with one of their fingers"; the
authority of the teacher eclipses the living relation to God and men;
the minutiae of observance overshadow the great concerns of life,
"justice, mercy, and faith"; the purpose of the rules, namely, one's
neighbor, his freedom and his happiness, is sacrificed to exactness
of observance; merit, by which conscience gains worth, becomes
an advantage, a possession, on which conscience presumes; and,
finally, the outside loses contact with the inside and zeal in *praxis*
hides the death of the heart, "full of dead men's bones, and of all
uncleanness." Then the consistent and willingly accepted heteronomy becomes alienation.

The dilemma, then, is evident: Shall we say that this schematic
genesis of "hypocrisy" reveals nothing essential about the structure
of "scrupulousness," that the picture of the false Pharisee leaves
intact that of the true, the authentic Pharisee? Or shall we say that
the spiritual regime of the law does not know its own abysses until
they are revealed by means of the specific failing of scrupulousness,
and that the distinction between the false and the true Pharisee is
of little importance in the view of a radical critique of the law and
of "the justice that is obtained by the law"? In the first case, our
viewpoint is that of Hillel; in the second, that of St. Paul.

4. THE IMPASSE OF GUILT

It was necessary to raise the glory of the Pharisee to such heights,
in order to make manifest the inversion of "for" and "against"
that was effected in the consciousness of fault by the sort of experience exemplified in St. Paul and repeated by Augustine and Luther.

Let us present, without transition, this accusation of the accusation. Afterward we shall have to reread the whole of the preceding
analysis in the light of this ultimate *peripeteia,* which can be
summed up under the Pauline title of the "curse of the law" (Gal.
3:13).

The Pauline itinerary, as it is reported in Galatians 3 and 4, and
especially in Romans 7:1–13, can be stylized in the following
manner.[24] The starting-point is the experience of the powerlessness

[24] R. Bultmann, *Theologie des N. T.,* Vol. I (Tübingen, 1948), Part II:

of man to satisfy all the demands of the law. The observance of
the law is nothing if it is not whole and complete; but we are
never done: perfection is infinite and the commandments are unlimited in number. Man, then, will never be justified by the law;
he would be if the observance could be total: "As many as are of
the works of the law are under a curse. For it is written: Cursed is
everyone that continueth not in all things which are written in the
book of the law to do them" (Gal. 3:10).

It is here that the hell of guilt begins. Not only is the road that
leads to justice an endless one, but the law itself increases the distance. The great discovery of Paul is that the law itself is a source
of sin: it "was added because of transgressions"; far from "giving
life," it can only "give knowledge of sin." Indeed, it even begets sin.
How? St. Paul, long before Nietzsche—who nevertheless thought
he was blasting the first "theologian,"—dismounted the spring of
that infernal machine. He compares Law and Sin, as two imagined
entities, and reveals their deadly circularity; entering the vicious
circle by way of the law, he writes: "The law entered in, that sin
might abound. . . ." (Rom. 5:20); the commandment, when it
came, "gave life to sin" and so "slew me" (7:9). But this first
reading is the reverse of the other, the true one; it is sin that,
"taking occasion," makes use of the law to bestir itself and work
concupiscence in me; it is sin that, "utilizing the law, seduced me
and by its means slew me" (7:8, 11). Thus the law is that which
exhibits sin, that which makes sin manifest: "It was sin which, in
order that it might appear sin, made use of a good thing to procure
death for me, in order that sin might exert all its sinful power
through the commandment" (7:13).

By means of this circle that sin forms with itself and with the
law, Paul poses, in all its breadth and radicalness, the problem of
the commandment (ἐντολή), of the law (νόμος) as such. This dialectic, in fact, carries the law beyond the opposition between
ethical behavior and ritual-cultual behavior, beyond the opposition
between Jewish law and the law of the Gentiles, which is written

---

"The Theology of St. Paul." Karl Barth, *Der Römerbrief* (Berne, 1919).
Lagrange, *Saint Paul, Épître aux Romains,* 3d ed. (Paris, 1922). Prat, *La
Théologie de saint Paul* (Paris, 1943).

in their hearts, and finally beyond the opposition between the good will of the Jew and the "wisdom" or "knowledge" of the Greek. The problem of the commandment arises beyond all these dichotomies, and it is this: how is it possible that the law, although good in itself and recognized as good by "the inward man" in his "understanding," which "rejoices in it," how is it possible that this law, meant to gain life, is converted into a "minister of condemnation," a "minister of death"? It is while he is working out the answer to this root question that St. Paul brings to light a dimension of sin, a new quality of evil, which is not the "transgression" of a definite commandment, nor even transgression at all, but the will to save oneself by satisfying the law—what Paul calls "justice of the law" or "justice that comes by the law." Thus sin itself is carried beyond the opposition between concupiscence and zeal for the law. Paul calls this will to self-justification "boasting in the law." By that he does not mean ordinary boasting, but the pretension of living in reliance on that which of right is meant to give life, but which in fact is condemned to lead to death. By this pretension, morality and immorality are henceforth included in the same existential category, which is called "flesh" (we shall return to this word further on), "desires of the flesh," "care," "fear," "sorrows of this world"; all of these words denote the opposite of liberty, slavery, bondage to the "weak and beggarly elements."

Finally, by this double generalization of the law and the flesh a new and radical sense of death itself is revealed. St. Paul is the heir of the Hebrew thesis according to which sin is punished by death; but through this penal and consequently extrinsic interpretation of death, he discerns a ministry of death exactly proportionate to that of the law. Death is the result of the law for a being who, aiming at life, misses it; it is the "fruit," the "harvest" of the regime of existence that we have called sin, boasting, justification by the law, flesh: "to live according to the flesh" is death, just as "to mortify the deeds of the body" is "life" (Rom. 8:13). Thus the whole of existence, when it is placed under the law, becomes altogether "the body of this death" (7:24): "For when we were dead in the flesh, the sinful passions that make use of the law did work in our members so that we might bring forth fruit unto death" (7:5). Death, then, is no longer added to sin in a juridical sense; it is secreted by it in accordance with an organic law of existence.

What do we know of this death? In part, it is a death that does not know itself;[25] it is the living death of those who believe themselves living. But in part, also, it is a death that is suffered: "When the commandment came, sin revived and I died" (Rom. 7:9–10). What shall we say? Without doubt it is legitimate to compare this death that is suffered with the experience of division and conflict described in the pericope of the Epistle to the Romans (7:14–19), which follows the dialectic of sin and the law reported above. Death, then, is the actualized dualism of the Spirit and the flesh.

This dualism is far from being a primordial ontological structure;[26] it is rather a regime of existence issuing from the will to live under the law and to be justified by the law. This will is sufficiently enlightened to recognize the truth and the goodness of the law, but too weak to fulfill it: "To will the good is present with me, but not to accomplish it; for the good which I will, I do not; but the evil which I will not, that I do" (Rom. 7:18–19). At the same time, by contrast, that which I do not wish to do and yet do, stands before me as an alienated part of myself. St. Paul expresses well, by the very hesitation of his language, this cleavage in the personal pronoun. There is the I that acknowledges itself: "but I am a being of flesh, sold into the power of sin" (7:14); but, acknowledging itself, it disowns itself: "it is no longer I who perform the action" (7:20); disowning itself, it establishes itself within: "I delight in the law of God after the inward man" (7:22); but honesty requires me to take both the I of reason and the I of flesh for myself: "It is, then, I myself who by reason serve a law of God and by the flesh a law of sin" (7:25). This cleavage in myself is the key to the Pauline concept of flesh. Far from being a primordially accursed part of myself—the bodily part, sexuality for example,—the flesh is myself alienated from itself,

[25] Perhaps it should be said that physical death itself is the "fruit" of sin—not, of course, merely as a biological event, but in the human character of dying, as an event in communal existence, and as the anguish of solitude. We shall come back to this in connection with the Adamic myth.

[26] Cf. Part II, Chap. V, on the confrontation of the Adamic myth and the myth of exile.

opposed to itself and projected outward: "Now if I do that which I will not, it is no more I that do it, but sin that dwelleth in me" (7:20). This powerlessness of myself, thus reflected in "the power of sin that is in my members," is the flesh, whose desires are contrary to those of the spirit. That is why we could not begin with the flesh, as the root of evil, but had to arrive at it, as the flower of evil.

Such, in brief, is the Pauline itinerary. With this experience we have arrived at the farthest limit of the whole cycle of guilt. Of this limiting experience one can only say two things: on the one hand, it makes intelligible all that precedes it insofar as it itself goes beyond the whole history of guilt; on the other hand, it cannot be understood itself except insofar as one gets beyond it.

Let us consider, one after the other, these two aspects of the question.

The "curse of the law" reveals the meaning of the whole prior development of the consciousness of fault. To understand this point, let us go back not only to the Pharisees, but to the core of the notion of guilt. Guilt, we have said, is the completed internalization of sin. With guilt, "conscience" is born; a responsible agent appears, to face the prophetic call and its demand for holiness. But with the factor of "conscience" man the measure likewise comes into being; the realism of sin, measured by the eye of God, is absorbed into the phenomenalism of the guilty conscience, which is the measure of itself. If this analysis is brought to the light of the Pauline experience of justification by the works of the law, it appears that the promotion of guilt—with its acute sense of individual responsibility, its taste for degrees and nuances in imputation, its moral tact—is at the same time the advent of self-righteousness and the curse attached thereto. Simultaneously, the experience of scrupulousness itself undergoes a radical re-interpretation: that in it which had not been felt as fault, becomes fault; the attempt to reduce sin by observance becomes sin. That is the real meaning of the curse of the law.

The curse is twofold: it affects the structure of the accusation and that of the accused conscience.

The change in the accusation, when we pass from sin to guilt, is itself manifold. In the first place, it consists in the atomization of the law in a multitude of commandments. This phenomenon is very ambiguous; for it was already present in the dialectics of the prophetic accusation which, by turns, summons man to a total and indivisible perfection and itemizes his wickedness according to the many dimensions of his existence for himself and for others, and according to the many spheres in which he acts—worship, politics, marriage, trade, hospitality, etc. But under the regime of sin, the tension between *radical* demand and *differentiated* prescription is preserved, and the principal emphasis falls on the *radical* demand. With the consciousness of guilt, the equilibrium is destroyed, to the advantage of the differentiated prescription; an indefinite enumeration is substituted for the radicalness of the infinite demand, and from this multiplication of commandments there comes an indictment that is itself indefinite. We might call this indefinite enumeration and indictment, which make the law "accursed," an "evil infinite."

At the same time as the law becomes indefinitely atomized, it becomes completely "juridicized." We said above what was essential and not merely accidental in the juridical symbolism of guilt; it is not by chance that the notions of law, judgment, tribunal, verdict, sanction, embrace both the public domain of penal justice and the private domain of moral conscience. But the same process that we considered above as an advance belongs also to the progress of the "curse of the law." In becoming "juridicized," the dialogal relation of the Covenant, which culminates in the conjugal metaphor dear to Hosea, undergoes a profound change. It is enough that the sense of sin as being before God be abolished for guilt to work its havoc; at the limit, it is an accusation without an accuser, a tribunal without a judge, and a verdict without an author. To be accursed without being cursed by anybody is the highest degree of accursedness, as Kafka shows. By the semblance of intention that remains in a radically anonymous condemnation, the verdict is hardened into fate. There is no longer any place for that astonishing reversal that the Jews called "God's repentance," or for the conversion of the Erinyes into Eumenides, celebrated in Greek tragedy; God's repentance is the counterpart of our own advance from discovering God as wrath to encountering him as mercy. To become oneself the tribunal of oneself is to be alienated. We shall have to say later how this alienation, upon which we have been attempting to throw light through the notion of justification by works, can also be understood after the fashion of Hegel, Marx, Nietzsche, Freud, Sartre; but the Pauline stratum underlies all these stratifications of our ethical history. It may be that the introduction of all these other interpretations of ethical alienation is itself the counterpart of forgetting its most radical meaning, just as guilt, with its rational indictment, is at once an advance and a forgetting in relation to sin understood as a crisis in the Covenant.

But the curse of the accused conscience is the replica of the curse of the accusation, and so we can regard the passage from sin to guilt from this second point of view also. For the confession of sin as affecting the person as a whole there is substituted a detailed and indefinite examination of the purity of intentions; scrupulousness, reinterpreted by the Pauline experience of the curse of the law, appears in a new light: it too becomes the expression of an "evil infinite" that answers, from the side of conscience, to the "evil infinite" of the indefinite enumeration of commandments. At the limit, distrust, suspicion, and finally contempt for oneself and abjectness are substituted for the humble confession of the sinner.

The two curses give impetus to each other unceasingly. The zealous penitent gives himself the infinite task of satisfying all the prescriptions of the law; the failure of this undertaking gives impetus to the feeling of guilt; the integral observance by which the conscience seeks to exculpate itself increases the indictment; and as the atomization of the law tends to shift moral vigilance and direct it towards isolated and sometimes minute prescriptions, conscience consumes its energy in single combats with each of them.

It is not surprising, then, that these tactics for avoiding fault enlist in their service the ritualized modes of behavior inherited from the cultual stratum governed by the notion of defilement. Ritualism, the significance of which as obedience we saw above, reveals its own guilt, for the precise interdictions of the ritual-cultual type propose a satisfaction that is finite and verifiable, and so conscience throws itself into a technique of elusion in order to counter the failure to win exculpation. But this enlistment of the interdictions of "purity" under the banner of ethics, such as we saw, for example, in Israel at the time of the second Temple, results in an extra load of prescriptions; the ritualization of conduct, undertaken for the purpose of providing a less costly substitute for the indefinite ethical demand, only adds a new code to the other. Thus a complicated and disparate miscellany of ethical *and* ritual prescriptions is put together, in which the scruples of the cult are moralized through contact with a subtle ethics, but ethics is diluted in the letter of the minute prescriptions of the ritual. Thus cultual scrupulousness multiplies the law and guilt at the same time.

While it is indefinite, the guilty conscience is also a conscience that is shut in. Many myths have expressed this paradoxical co-incidence of reiteration with absence of any result; the futile activity of Sisyphus and the Danaïdes is well known, and Plato already interpreted it as a symbol of condemnation that is both eternal and without any result. St. Paul also speaks of an existence "shut up under the guard of the law." The guilty conscience is shut in first of all because it is an isolated conscience that breaks the communion of sinners. It "separates" itself in the very act by which it takes upon itself, and upon itself alone, the whole weight of evil. The guilty conscience is shut in even more secretly by an obscure acquiescence in its evil, by which it makes itself its own tormentor. It is in this sense that the guilty conscience is a slave and not only consciousness of enslavement; it is the conscience without "promise." It is here that what Kierkegaard called the sin of despair presents itself; not despair concerning the things of this world, which is only regret for lost things turned toward the future, but despair of being saved. Such is the sin of sins: no longer transgression, but a despairing and desperate will to shut oneself up in the circle of interdiction and desire. It is in this sense that it is a desire for death.[27] That this desire for death coincides with

[27] This hell of guilt, engendered by the law and its curse, finds its supreme symbol in the Satanic figure itself. We know that the Devil was understood not only as the Tempter but as the Accuser of man at the last judgment (while Christ becomes the Advocate, the Paraclete). Thus the demon stands not only behind transgression, but behind the law itself, inasmuch as it is a law of death.

the good will is something that conscience could not discover by following the forward movement from defilement to sin and from sin to guilt, but only by looking back from "justification by faith" to the curse of the law. We shall see later how the psychology of self-accusation, narcissism, and masochism explains these subtle procedures, not without having itself lost the key to them.

We are now to discover that the curse of the law, the condition of the divided man, and his march toward death could not be described except in terms of a completed situation. In the language of St. Paul, the final experience of sin is recounted in the past: "Once you were dead in your sins, but now. . . ." This is most astonishing. Death, which in the ordinary experience of human beings is pre-eminently the always future event, the imminence of the end, is here death in the past. This extreme symbol of a death that one has got beyond could be won only in the context of a new set of problems that itself gravitates around another symbol, as enigmatic as it is fundamental—the symbol of "justification."

The philosopher must recognize from the outset how shocking this symbol is for a mind educated by the Greeks. Far from its denoting the ethical quality of a person, the supremely disposable thing among those things at his disposal, in short, far from its being the case that justice is the architectonic virtue of a man, as in Book IV of Plato's *Republic,* "justice" according to St. Paul is something that comes to a man—from the future to the present, from the outward to the inward, from the transcendent to the immanent. A true exegesis compels us to start from what is most foreign to the knowledge, will, and power of a man, and to overtake the human only by starting from the more than human. To be "just" is to be justified by an Other; more precisely, it is to be "declared" just, to be "counted as" just. This forensic sense, as has been said, is bound up with all the symbolism concerning the eschatological judgment; justice, in fact, is the verdict of acquittal, having the effect of a decision of a public court (hence the forensic expression). It is only when the transcendent, forensic, eschatological dimension of "justification" has been recognized that the immanent, subjective, and present import of justification can be understood. For St. Paul, in fact, the eschatological event is present, already there, in such a way that justice, although it is extrinsic to a man as far as its origin is concerned, has become something that dwells within him, as far as its operation is concerned; the "future" justice is already imputed to the man who believes; and so the man who is "declared" just is "made" just, really and vitally. Thus there is no ground for opposing the forensic and eschatological sense of justice to its immanent and present sense: for Paul the first is the cause of the second, but the second is the full manifestation of the first; the paradox is that the acme of outwardness is the acme of inwardness, of that inwardness that Paul calls new creature, or liberty. Liberty, considered from the point of view of last things, is not the power of hesitating and choosing between contraries, nor is it effort, good will, responsibility. For St. Paul, as for Hegel, it is being at home with oneself, in the whole, in the recapitulation of Christ.

Such is the symbol in the light of which the final experience of fault is perceived as something in the past that one has got beyond. It is because "justification" is the present which dominates the backward look on sin, that the supreme sin consists, in the last resort, in the vain attempt to justify *oneself*. There is the key to the break with Judaism: man is justified "without the works of the law": "But now without the law the justice of God is made manifest. . . . For we account a man to be justified by faith, without the practice of the law" (Rom. 3:21–28). Justification by faith, then, is what makes manifest the failure of justification by the law, and the failure of the justice of works is what reveals the unity of the entire domain of sin. Only a retrospective view discloses the profound identity of ethics and cultual-ritual behavior, of morality and immorality, of obedience or good will and knowledge or wisdom.

It is, then, impossible to reflect philosophically on fault while omitting the fact, embarrassing for reflection, that the ultimate meaning of fault could be manifested only by means of the great contrasts set up by the first passionate thinker of Christianity: justification by the practice of the law and justification by faith; boasting and believing; works and grace. Whatever weakens those contrasts dissipates their meaning.

Sin, thus described in the past tense and related to the experience that goes beyond it, now gets its final meaning of *ambiguous threshold*. In itself and for itself, it is the impasse and the hell of guilt; it is a curse. But seen from the point of view of "justification," the curse of the law constitutes the supreme pedagogy. But this meaning can be recognized only after the event.

St. Paul's language is familiar: "Before faith came, we were kept under the law, shut up unto the faith which should afterwards be revealed. Wherefore the law was our schoolmaster to bring us unto Christ, that we might be justified by faith. But after that faith is come, we are no longer under a schoolmaster" (Gal. 3:23–24). It would be a serious misunderstanding of the Pauline paradox if we interpreted this schooling as a tranquil growth from childhood to adulthood; the childhood that is here in question is enslavement under the law: "Now I say that the heir, as long as he is a child, differeth nothing from a servant, though he be lord of all" (4:1), and the schoolmaster is the law of death. Consequently, the passage from one regime to the other must not be thought of in terms of development; rather, there is a sort of *inversion through excess:* "The law entered, that the offense might abound; but where sin abounded, grace did much more abound" (Rom. 5:20). In a text that is even more striking, because it emphasizes the divine origin of this schooling for liberty, St. Paul declares: "God hath shut up all men in disobedience, that he might have mercy upon all" (Rom. 11:32). This pedagogy of excess and increase, which draws the superabundance of grace from the abundance of sin,[28] is not at the disposal of anyone; no one can make a technique out of it and pretend that he sins abundantly *in order that* grace may superabound. After the event, the delivered conscience recognizes in the ethical stage, experienced as slavery, the tortuous road to its liberation; but it is not permissible to turn the paradox, which can be read only from the top downward, into some sort of technique that would make the cultivation of sin a means of obtaining grace.

[28] We shall return to this point when we speak of the Adamic symbol. The advance from the first to the second Adam will express this "superabundance" on the plane of the rich symbolism of the *Anthropos*. Cf. Part II, Chap. III, § 4.

Such Satanism would only be the most sophistical form of the ethical enterprise; for man would still be giving glory to himself, as when he boasted in the ritual and the law.

The last word, then, of a reflection on guilt, must be this: the promotion of guilt marks the entry of man into the circle of condemnation; the meaning of that condemnation appears only after the event to the "justified" conscience; it is granted to that conscience to understand its past condemnation as a sort of pedagogy; but, to the conscience still kept under the guard of the law, its real meaning is unknown.

Conclusion: Recapitulation of the Symbolism of Evil in the Concept of the Servile Will

AT THE END of this survey, it is possible to say both what horizon the whole chain of symbols that we have run through is oriented toward and how the most archaic are retained and reaffirmed by the most advanced of these symbols.

The concept toward which the whole series of the primary symbols of evil tends may be called the *servile will*. But that concept is not directly accessible; if one tries to give it an object, the object destroys itself, for it short-circuits the idea of will, which can only signify free choice, and so free will, always intact and young, always available—and the idea of servitude, that is to say, the unavailability of freedom to itself. *The concept of the servile will, then, cannot be represented as the concept of fallibility,* which we considered at the beginning of this work; for we should have to be able to think of free will and servitude as coinciding in the same existent. That is why the concept of the servile will must remain an indirect concept, which gets all its meaning from the symbolism that we have run through and which tries to raise that symbolism to the level of *speculation*. Hence, this concept, which will occupy our attention in the third volume of the present work, can be viewed only as the Idea, the intentional *telos* of the whole symbolism of evil. Moreover, we shall not be able to get closer to it except through the mediation of the second-order symbols supplied by the myths of evil.

For the present, we can at least say that the concept of the servile will, to which the most differentiated, the most subtle, the most internalized experience of guilt draws near, was already aimed at by the most archaic experience of all, that of defilement. The final symbol indicates its limiting concept only by taking up into itself all the wealth of the prior symbols. Thus there is a *circular* relation among all the symbols: the last bring out the meaning of the preceding ones, but the first lend to the last all their power of symbolization.

It is possible to show this by going through the whole series of symbols in the opposite direction. It is remarkable, indeed, that guilt turns to its own account the symbolic language in which the experiences of defilement and sin took shape.

Guilt cannot, in fact, *express* itself except in the indirect language of "captivity" and "infection," inherited from the two prior stages. Thus both symbols are transposed "inward" to express a freedom that enslaves itself, affects itself, and infects itself by its own choice. Conversely, the symbolic and non-literal character of the captivity of sin and the infection of defilement becomes quite clear when these symbols are used to denote a dimension of freedom itself; then and only then do we know that they are symbols, when they reveal a situation that is centered in the relation of oneself to oneself. Why this recourse to the prior symbolism? Because the paradox of a captive free will—the paradox of a *servile will*—is insupportable for thought. That freedom must be delivered and that this deliverance is deliverance from self-enslavement cannot be said directly; yet it is the central theme of "salvation."

The symbol of captivity, borrowed, as we know, from the theology of history, first designated a communal situation, that of a people made prisoner by its sins. This communal situation is still attached to the historical event that is re-enacted in the liturgy, as the unhappy fate from which the Exodus delivered them. In becoming a symbol of the guilty individual, the notion of captivity is detached from the memory of the historical event and gets the quality of a pure symbol; it designates an event in freedom.

This symbolism is central in the Jewish experience; but if it can be understood, that is because it belongs, at least as a lateral growth, to all cultures. The experience or the belief that furnishes the literal meaning may be manifold and varied, but the aim of the symbol remains the same. Thus the representation of demons as the origin of the state of *being bound,* among the Babylonians, furnishes the initial schema of possession; but this wholly corporeal possession can, in its turn, furnish the basic image through which the enslavement of free will is denoted. The same image of possession can be followed through various degrees of symbolization. At the lowest degree, possession is represented as a physical hold on the body and its members: "May the evil that is in my body, in my muscles and my tendons, depart today," implores the Babylonian suppliant; "deliver me from the spell that is upon me . . . for an evil spell and an impure disease and transgression and iniquity and sin are in my body, and a wicked spectre is attached to me." You may say as much as you will that this supplication still bears the mark of the confusion of sickness and sin, and of both with physical possession by a real demonic power. But the process of symbolization has undoubtedly already begun; the Babylonian suppliant "confesses" and "repents"; he knows obscurely that his bonds are in some way his own work; if not, why should he cry: "Undo the many sins that I have committed since my youth. I will fear the god; I will not commit offenses"? Why should the suppliant beg to be *released* from what he has *committed* if he did not know obscurely, if he did not know without knowing, if he did not know enigmatically and symbolically, that he has put upon himself the bonds from which he begs to be released?

What assures us that the symbolism of the servile will, although still submerged in the letter of demonic representations, is already at work in the confession of the Babylonian suppliant is that the same symbolism of a man with his limbs bound appears again in writers who employed this symbol with a clear awareness that it was a symbol. Thus St. Paul knows that man is "inexcusable," although sin is said to "reign" in his members, "in his mortal body" (Rom. 6:12), and the body itself is called "body of sin" (Rom. 6:6) and the whole man a "servant of sin." If St. Paul were not speaking symbolically of the body of sin as a figure for the servile will, how could he cry: "As you have yielded your members servants to uncleanness and to iniquity, unto iniquity; even so now yield your members servants to justice, unto sanctification" (Rom. 6:19)? The symbol of the enslaved body is the symbol of a sinful being who is at the same time *act* and *state;* that is to say, a sinful being in whom the very act of self-enslavement suppresses itself as "act" and relapses into a "state." The body is the symbol of this obliterated freedom, of a building from which the builder has withdrawn. In the language of St. Paul, the *act* is the "yielding" of the body to servitude (as you have yielded your members as servants), the state is the reign (let not sin therefore reign in your mortal bodies). A "yielding" *of* myself that is at the same time a "reign" *over* myself—there is the enigma of the servile will, of the will that makes itself a slave.

Finally, Plato himself, in spite of the Orphic myth of the soul exiled in a body that is its tomb, in spite of the temptation to harden the symbol of bodily captivity into a gnosis of the body as evil, in spite even of the guarantees that he gives to that gnosis for the future, knows perfectly well that the bodily captivity must not be taken literally, but as a sign of the servile will; the "prison" of the body is in the end only "the work of desire," and "he who co-operates most in putting on the chains is perhaps the chained man himself" (*Phaedo, 82d–e*). Thus, the captivity of the body and even the captivity of the soul in the body are the symbol of the evil that the soul inflicts on itself, the symbol of the affection of freedom by itself; the "loosing" of the soul assures us retrospectively that its "bonds" were the bonds of desire, active-passive fascination, autocaptivity; "to be lost" means the same thing.

The expression that we have just used—the affection of freedom by itself—helps us to understand how the most internalized guilt can recapitulate all the symbolism prior to it, including the symbolism of defilement; it turns it to its own account through the symbolism of captivity. I would even venture to say that defilement becomes a pure symbol when it no longer suggests a real stain at all, but only signifies the servile will. The symbolic sense of defilement is complete only at the end of all its repeated appearances.

I see in the pure symbol of defilement three intentions which constitute the triple "schematism" of the servile will:

1. The first schema of the servile will, according to the symbol of defilement, is the schema of "positiveness": evil is not nothing; it is not a simple lack, a simple absence of order; it is the power of darkness; it is posited; in this sense it is something to be "taken away": "I am the Lamb of God who takes away the sins of the world," says the interior Master. Hence, every reduction of evil to a simple lack of being remains outside the symbolism of defilement, which is complete only when defilement has become guilt.

2. The second schema of the servile will is that of "externality"; however internal guilt may be, it is only reflected in the symbol of its own externality. Evil comes to a man as the "outside" of freedom, as the other than itself in which freedom is taken captive. "Every man is tempted by his own lust, which draws and entices him" (Jas. 1:14). This is the schema of seduction; it signifies that evil, although it is something that is brought about, is already there, enticing. This externality is so essential to human evil that man, Kant says, cannot be absolutely wicked, cannot be the Evil One; his wickedness is always secondary; he is wicked through seduction. Evil is both something brought about now and something that is always already there; to begin is to continue. It is this being seduced that is symbolized in the externality of unclean contact. It is essential that evil be in some way undergone; this is the deposit of truth, among other errors, in any identification of human evil as a *pathos,* a "passion." Consequently, to extirpate the symbol of defilement, it would be necessary to eliminate from the human experience of evil this schema of externality. The magical conceptions of contagion and contamination may be demythized as much as necessary; but they will be survived by the ever more subtle modalities of the seductive "outside," which still belong to the servile will at its furthermost point of internality.

3. The third schema of the servile will is the schema of "in-

fection" itself. At first glance, this idea is the most difficult to save; it seems forever bound up with the magic of contact. And yet it is the ultimate symbol of the servile will, of the bad choice that binds itself. This schema of infection is in the first place a consequence of the preceding one; it signifies that seduction *from the outside* is ultimately an affection of the self by the self, an auto-infection, by which the act of binding oneself is transformed into the state of being bound. It is evident that the symbol of enslavement is a necessary step for this taking up of the symbol of defilement into the experience of the servile will; it is by thinking of the yielding of myself to slavery and the reign over myself of the power of evil as identical that I discover the profound significance of a tarnishing of freedom. But perhaps the schema of infection already signifies more than this binding of the self by the self. To infect is not to destroy, to tarnish is not to ruin. The symbol here points toward the relation of radical evil to the very being of man, to the primordial destination of man; it suggests that evil, however positive, however seductive, however affective and infective it may be, cannot make a man something other than a man; infection cannot be a defection, in the sense that the dispositions and functions that make the humanity of man might be unmade, undone, to the point where a reality other than the human reality would be produced. We are still not in a position to understand this ultimate intention of the symbol of defilement; it cannot be brought to light and elaborated except by means of the second-order symbols, especially the myth of the fall. Then we shall understand that evil is not symmetrical with the good, wickedness is not something that replaces the goodness of a man; it is the staining, the darkening, the disfiguring of an innocence, a light, and a beauty that remain. However *radical* evil may be, it cannot be as *primordial* as goodness. The symbol of defilement already says this about the servile will, and it says it through the symbol of captivity; for when a country falls intact into the hands of the enemy, it continues to work, to produce, to create, to exist, but for the enemy; it is responsible, but its work is alienated. This superimposition of servitude on self-determination, which an occupied country may experience, suggests the similar idea of an existential superimposition of radical evil on primordial good; and it is this superimposition that is already indicated in the schema of infection, in which we propose to recognize the ultimate intention of the symbol of defilement. But this intention becomes apparent only when the magical world that supported the symbol of defilement has been done away with, and when the experience of sin has itself been internalized in the experience of the servile will. Then defilement, having become the language of the servile will, discloses its ultimate intention. But it still does not disclose all the implications of the schema of infection. It does this only through all the symbolic levels that we have still to examine: mythical symbols and speculative symbols.

Part Two

The "Myths" of the Beginning
and of the End

Introduction: The Symbolic
Function of Myths

1. From the Primary Symbols to Myths

UP TO THE PRESENT we have been trying to "re-enact" in imagination and sympathetically the *experience* of fault. Have we really reached, under the name of experience, an immediate datum? Not at all. What is experienced as defilement, as sin, as guilt, requires the mediation of a specific language, the language of symbols. Without the help of that language, the experience would remain mute, obscure, and shut up in its implicit contradictions (thus defilement is expressed as something that infects from without, and sin as a ruptured relation and as a power, etc.). These elementary symbols, in their turn, have been reached only at the price of an abstraction that has uprooted them from the rich world of myths. In order to attempt a purely semantic exegesis of the expressions that best reveal the experience of fault (stain and defilement, deviation, revolt, transgression, straying, etc.), we have had to bracket the second-degree symbols which are the medium for the primary symbols, which are themselves the medium for the living experience of defilement, of sin, and of guilt.

This new level of expression embarrasses the modern man. In one sense, he alone can recognize the myth as myth, because he alone has reached the point where history and myth become separate. This "crisis," this decision, after which myth and history are dissociated, may signify the loss of the mythical dimension:

because mythical time can no longer be co-ordinated with the time of events that are "historical" in the sense required by historical method and historical criticism, because mythical space can no longer be co-ordinated with the places of our geography, we are tempted to give ourselves up to a radical demythization of all our thinking. But another possibility offers itself to us: precisely because we are living and thinking after the separation of myth and history, the demythization of our history can become the other side of an understanding of myth as myth, and the conquest, for the first time in the history of culture, of the mythical dimension. That is why we never speak here of demythization, but strictly of demythologization, it being well understood that what is lost is the pseudo-knowledge, the false logos of the myth, such as we find expressed, for example, in the etiological function of myths. But when we lose the myth as immediate logos, we rediscover it as myth. Only at the price and by the roundabout way of philosophical exegesis and understanding, can the myth create a new *peripeteia* of the logos.

This conquest of myth as myth is only one aspect of the recognition of symbols and their power to reveal. To understand the myth as myth is to understand what the myth, with its time, its space, its events, its personages, its drama, adds to the revelatory function of the primary symbols worked out above.

Without pretending to give here a general theory of symbols and myths, and limiting ourselves voluntarily and systematically to that group of mythical symbols which concern human evil, we can set forth in the following terms our working hypothesis, which is to be employed in the whole course of our analysis and verified in the performance:

1. The first function of the myths of evil is to embrace mankind as a whole in one ideal history. By means of a time that represents all times, "man" is manifested as a concrete universal; Adam signifies man. "In" Adam, says Saint Paul, we have all sinned. Thus experience escapes its singularity; it is transmuted in its own "archetype." Through the figure of the hero, the ancestor, the Titan, the first man, the demigod, experience is put on the track of existential structures: one can now *say* man, existence, human

being, because in the myth the human type is recapitulated, summed up.

2. The universality of man, manifested through the myths, gets its concrete character from the *movement* which is introduced into human experience by narration; in recounting the *Beginning* and the *End* of fault, the myth confers upon this experience an orientation, a character, a tension. Experience is no longer reduced to a present experience; this present was only an instantaneous cross-section in an evolution stretching from an origin to a fulfillment, from a "Genesis" to an "Apocalypse." Thanks to the myth, experience is traversed by the essential history of the perdition and the salvation of man.

3. Still more fundamentally, the myth tries to get at the enigma of human existence, namely, the discordance between the fundamental reality—state of innocence, status of a creature, essential being—and the actual modality of man, as defiled, sinful, guilty. The myth accounts for this transition by means of a narration. But it is a narration precisely because there is no deduction, no logical transition, between the fundamental reality of man and his present existence, between his ontological status as a being created good and destined for happiness and his existential or historical status, experienced under the sign of alienation. Thus the myth has an ontological bearing: it points to the relation—that is to say, both the leap and the passage, the cut and the suture— between the essential being of man and his historical existence.

In all these ways, the myth makes the experience of fault the center of a whole, the center of a world: the world of fault.

It can already be guessed how far we are from a purely allegorical interpretation of the myth. An allegory can always be *translated* into a text that can be understood by itself; once this better text has been made out, the allegory falls away like a useless garment; what the allegory showed, while concealing it, can be said in a direct discourse that replaces the allegory. By its triple function of concrete universality, temporal orientation, and finally ontological exploration, the myth has a way of *revealing* things that is not reducible to any translation from a language in cipher to a clear language. As Schelling has shown in his *Philosophy of*

Mythology, the myth is autonomous and immediate; it means what it says.[1]

It is essential, therefore, for a critical understanding of the myth to respect its irreducibility to the allegory.

2. MYTH AND GNOSIS: THE SYMBOLIC FUNCTION OF THE NARRATION

For a critical understanding of the myth it is first necessary that the myth be entirely divorced from the "etiological" function with which it appears to be identified. This distinction is fundamental for a philosophical handling of the myth; for the principal objection that philosophy addresses to myth is that the mythical explanation is incompatible with the rationality discovered or invented by the Pre-Socratics; from that time on, it represents the simulacrum of rationality.

The distinction between rationality and its imitation is, in fact, as decisive as that between history and myth. Indeed, it is the foundation of the latter; for history is history only because its search for "causes" leans upon the *Epistêmê* of the geometers and the physicists, even when it is distinguished from it. If, then, the myth is to survive this double distinction of history and myth as well as of explanation and myth, the myth must not be either history, happening in a definite time and place, or explanation.

My working hypothesis is that criticism of the pseudo-rational is fatal not to myth, but to gnosis. It is in gnosis that the simulacrum of reason attains realization. Gnosis is what seizes upon and develops the etiological element in myths. The gnosis of evil in particular takes its stand on the ground of reason; as the word itself makes clear, gnosis tries to be "knowledge." Between gnosis

---

[1] As the third book of this work will show, the refusal to reduce the myth to an allegory that can be translated into an intelligible language does not exclude all "interpretation" of myths. We shall propose a type of "interpretation" that is not a "translation"; let us say, to be brief, that the very process of discovery of the field of experience *opened up* by the myth can constitute an *existential verification* comparable to the transcendental deduction of the categories of the understanding. Cf. the final chaper of the second book: "The Symbol Gives Rise to Thought."

and reason a choice must be made. But perhaps there is a way of recovering the myth as myth, before it slipped into gnosis, in the nakedness and poverty of a symbol that is not an explanation but an opening up and a disclosure. Our whole effort will be directed toward dissociating myth and gnosis.

We are encouraged in this attempt by the great example of Plato. Plato inserts myths into his philosophy; he adopts them as myths, in their natural state, so to speak, without trying to disguise them as explanations; they are there in his discourse, full of enigmas; they are there as myths, without any possibility of confusing them with Knowledge.

It is true that the myth is in itself an invitation to gnosis. Furthermore, the problem of evil seems to be the principal occasion of this passage from myth to gnosis. We already know what a powerful incitement to questioning springs from suffering and sin: "How long, O Lord?" "Have I sinned against some divinity?" "Was my act pure?" One might say that the problem of evil offers at the same time the most considerable challenge to think and the most deceptive invitation to talk nonsense, as if evil were an always premature problem where the ends of reason always exceed its means. Long before nature made reason rave and threw it into the transcendental illusion, the contradiction felt between the destination of man, projected in the image of primordial innocence and final perfection, and the actual situation of man, acknowledged and confessed, gave rise to a gigantic "Why?" at the center of the experience of existing. Hence, the greatest explanatory ravings, which compose the considerable literature of gnosis, came into being in connection with that "question."

What, then, was the myth prior to its "etiological" pretensions? What is myth if it is not gnosis? Once more we are brought back to the function of the symbol. The symbol, we have said, opens up and discloses a dimension of experience that, without it, would remain closed and hidden. We must show, then, in what sense the myth is a second-degree function of the primary symbols that we have been exploring up to the present.

For that purpose we must rediscover this function of opening up and disclosing—which we here set in opposition to the explanatory function of gnosis—right down to the most specific traits that distinguish the myth from the primary symbols. Now, it is the *narration* that adds a new stage of meaning to that of the primary symbols.

How can the narration *mean* in a symbolic and non-etiological mode?

We shall have recourse here to the interpretation of the mythical consciousness proposed by the phenomenology of religion (Van der Leeuw, Leenhardt, Eliade). At first glance, that interpretation seems to dissolve the myth-narration in an undivided consciousness that consists less in telling stories, making myths, than in relating itself affectively and practically to the whole of things. What is essential for us here is to understand why that consciousness, structured lower than any narration, any fable or legend, nevertheless breaks out into language under the form of narration. If the phenomenologists of religion have been more concerned to go back from the narration to the pre-narrative root of the myth, we shall follow the opposite course from the pre-narrative consciousness to the mythical narration. It is in this transition that the whole enigma of the symbolic function of myths is centered.

There are two characteristics of the myth for which we must account: that it is an expression in language and that in it the symbol takes the form of narration.

Let us transport ourselves behind the myth. According to the phenomenology of religion, the myth-narration is only the verbal envelope of a form of life, felt and lived before being formulated; this form of life expresses itself first in an inclusive mode of behavior relative to the whole of things; it is in the rite rather than in the narration that this behavior is expressed most completely, and the language of the myth is only the verbal segment of this total action.[2] Still more fundamentally, ritual action and mythical

[2] "It is necessary to accustom oneself," says Eliade, "to dissociating the notion of myth from the notions of speech and fable, in order to relate it to the notions of sacred action and significant gesture. The mythical includes not only everything that is told about certain events that happened and certain personages who lived *in illo tempore,* but also everything that is

language, taken together, point beyond themselves to a model, an archetype, which they imitate or repeat; imitation in gestures and verbal repetition are only the broken expressions of a living participation in an original Act which is the common exemplar of the rite and of the myth.

There is no doubt that the phenomenology of religion has profoundly affected the problem of myths by thus going back to a mythical structure which would be the matrix of all the images and all the particular narrations peculiar to this or that mythology, and relating to this diffuse mythical structure the fundamental categories of the myth: participation, relation to the Sacred, etc.

It is this mythical structure itself that leads to the diversity of myths. What, in fact, is the ultimate significance of this mythical structure? It indicates, we are told, the intimate accord of the man of cult and myth with the whole of being; it signifies an indivisible plenitude, in which the supernatural, the natural, and the psychological are not yet torn apart. But *how* does the myth signify this plenitude? The essential fact is that this intuition of a cosmic whole, from which man is not separated, and this undivided plenitude, anterior to the division into supernatural, natural, and human, are not *given,* but simply *aimed at.* It is only in intention that the myth restores some wholeness; it is because he himself has lost that wholeness that man re-enacts and imitates it in myth and rite. The primitive man is already a man of division. Hence the myth can only be an intentional restoration or reinstatement and in this sense already symbolical.

This distance between experience and intention has been recognized by all the authors who have attributed to the myth a biological role of protection against anxiety. If myth-making is an antidote to distress, that is because the man of myths is already an unhappy consciousness;[3] for him, unity, conciliation, and recon-

---

related directly or indirectly to such events and to the primordial personages" (*Traité d'Histoire des Religions,* p. 355).

[3] One cannot hold at the same time, as G. Gusdorf does in *Mythe et Métaphysique* (Paris, 1953), that the myth has a biological, protective role (pp. 12, 21) and that it is "the spontaneous form of being in the world." All the excessive overestimations of the mythical consciousness come from

ciliation are things to be *spoken of* and *acted out,* precisely because they are not *given.* Myth-making is primordial, contemporaneous with the mythical structure, since participation is signified rather than experienced.

Now, in manifesting the purely symbolic character of the relation of man to the lost totality, the myth is condemned from the beginning to division into multiple cycles. There does not exist, in fact, any act of signifying that is equal to its aim. As the study of the primary symbols of fault has already suggested, it is always with something that plays the role of analogon as starting point that the symbol symbolizes; the multiplicity of the symbols is the immediate consequence of their subservience to a stock of analoga, which altogether are necessarily limited in extension and individually are equally limited in comprehension.

Lévi-Strauss has insisted strongly on the initial discrepancy between the limitation of experience and the totality signified by the myth: "The Universe," he writes,[4] "signified long before man began to know what it signified . . . ; it signified from the beginning the totality of what humanity might expect to know about it"; "man has at his disposal from the beginning an integrality in the *significans,* about which he is greatly perplexed as to how to allocate it to a *significatum,* given as such without, however, being known." This totality, thus signified but so little experienced, becomes available only when it is condensed in sacred beings and objects which become the privileged signs of the significant whole. Hence the primordial diversification of symbols. In fact, there does not exist anywhere in the world a civilization in which this surplus of signification is aimed at apart from any mythical form or definite ritual. The Sacred takes contingent forms precisely because it is "floating"; and so it cannot be divined except through the

---

this forgetfulness of the distance between experienced conciliation and aimed-at reconciliation. If it is true that "the primitive man is still the man of conciliation and reconciliation, the man of plenitude," and that he preserves the mark of "that concordance of reality and value that primitive mankind found without difficulty in the myth," one can no longer understand why the mythical consciousness gives itself up to the tale, to the image, and, in general, to significant speech.

[4] Quoted by G. Gusdorf, *op. cit.,* p. 45.

indefinite diversity of mythologies and rituals. The chaotic and arbitrary aspect of the world of myths is thus the exact counterpart of the discrepancy between the purely symbolic plenitude and the finiteness of the experience that furnishes man with "analogues" of that which is signified. Narrations and rites, then, are needed to consecrate the contour of the signs of the sacred: holy places and sacred objects, epochs and feasts, are other aspects of the contingency that we find in the narration. If the plenitude were experienced, it would be everywhere in space and time; but because it is only aimed at symbolically, it requires special signs and a discourse on the signs; their heterogeneity bears witness to the significant whole by its contingent outcroppings. Hence, the myth has the function of guarding the finite contours of the signs which, in their turn, refer to the plenitude that man aims at rather than experiences. That is why, although the primitive civilizations have in common almost the same mythical structure, this undifferentiated structure exists nowhere without a diversity of myths; the polarity of the one mythical structure and the many myths is a consequence of the *symbolic* character of the totality and the plenitude that myths and rites reproduce. Because it is symbolized and not lived, the sacred is broken up into a multiplicity of myths.

But why does the myth, when it is broken up, take the form of narration? What we have to understand now is why the original model, in which the myth and the rite lead us to participate, itself affects the character of a drama. It is, in fact, because that which is ultimately signified by every myth is itself in the form of a drama that the narrations in which the mythical consciousness is fragmented are themselves woven of happenings and personages; because its paradigm is dramatic, the myth itself is a tissue of events and is found nowhere except in the plastic form of narration. But why does the narration-myth refer symbolically to a drama?

It is because the mythical consciousness not only does not experience the plenitude, but does not even indicate it except at the beginning or the end of a fundamental *History*. The plenitude that the myth points to symbolically is established, lost, and re-established dangerously, painfully. Thus it is not given, not only because it is signified and not experienced, but because it is signified through a combat. The myth, as well as the rite, receives from this primordial drama the mode of discourse peculiar to narration. The plastic character of the myth, with its images and events, results, then, both from the necessity of providing contingent signs for a purely symbolic Sacred and from the dramatic character of the primordial time. Thus the time of the myth is diversified from the beginning by the primordial drama.

The myths concerning the origin and the end of evil that we are now going to study constitute only a limited sector of myths and furnish only a partial verification of the working hypothesis set forth in this introduction. At least they give us direct access to the primordially dramatic structure of the world of myths. We recall the three fundamental characteristics ascribed above to the myths of evil: the concrete universality conferred upon human experience by means of archetypal personages, the tension of an ideal history oriented from a Beginning toward an End, and finally the transition from an essential nature to an alienated history; these three functions of the myths of evil are three aspects of one and the same dramatic structure. Hence, the narrative form is neither secondary nor accidental, but primitive and essential. The myth performs its symbolic function by the specific means of narration because what it wants to express is already a drama. It is this primordial drama that opens up and discloses the hidden meaning of human experience; and so the myth that recounts it assumes the irreplaceable function of narration.

The two characteristics of myths that we have just emphasized are fundamental for our investigation of the world of fault.

In the first place, the surplus of signification, the "floating *significans*," constituted by the Sacred, attests that the experience of fault, as we have described it in Part I, is from its origin in relation or in tension with a totality of meaning, with an all-inclusive meaning of the universe. The relation, or the tension, is an integral part of the experience; or, rather, the experience subsists only in connection with *symbols* that place fault in a totality which is not perceived, not experienced, but signified, aimed at, conjured up. The language of the confession of sins, then, is only a fragment of a vaster language that indicates mythically the origin and the end of fault, and the totality in which it arose. If we detach the living experience from the symbol, we take away from the experience that which completes its meaning. Now, it is the myth as narration that puts the present experience of fault into relation with the totality of meaning.

On the other hand, this total meaning, which is the background of fault, is linked to the primordial drama by the mythical consciousness. The fundamental symbols that impregnate the experience of fault are the symbols of the distress, the struggle, and the victory which, once upon a time, marked the foundation of the world. Totality of meaning and cosmic drama are the two keys that will help us unlock the myths of the Beginning and the End.

3. Toward a "Typology" of the Myths of the Beginning and the End of Evil

But if the mythical consciousness in primitive civilizations remains very much *like itself,* and if, on the other hand, mythologies are *unlimited in number,* how shall we make our way between the One and the Many? How shall we escape getting lost, either in a vague phenomenology of the mythical consciousness which finds "mana" and repetition and participation everywhere, or in an indefinitely diversified comparative mythology? We shall try to follow the counsel of Plato in the *Philebus,* when he tells us not to imitate the "eristics," who make "one too quickly and many too quickly," but always to seek an intermediate number that "multiplicity realizes in the interval between the Infinite and the One"; regard for these intermediate numbers, said Plato, "is what distinguishes the dialectic method in our discussions from the eristic method."

This "numbered multiplicity," intermediate between an undifferentiated mythical consciousness and the too much differentiated mythologies, must be sought by means of a "typology." The "types" which we propose are at the same time *a priori,* permitting us to go to the encounter with experience with a key for deciphering it in our hands and to orient ourselves in the labyrinth of the mythologies of evil, and *a posteriori,* always subject to correction and amendment through contact with experience. I should like to think, as Cl. Lévi-Strauss does in *Tristes Tropiques,* that the images which the myth-making imagination and the institutional activity of man can produce are not infinite in number, and that it is possible to work out, at least as a working hypothesis, a sort of morphology of the principal images.

We shall consider here four mythical "types" of representation concerning the origin and the end of evil.

1. According to the first, which we call the drama of creation, the origin of evil is coextensive with the origin of things; it is the *"chaos" with which the creative act of the god struggles.* The counterpart of this view of things is that *salvation is identical with creation itself;* the act that founds the world is at the same time the liberating act. We shall verify this in the structure of the cult that corresponds to this "type" of the origin and end of evil; the cult can only be a *ritual re-enactment* of the combats at the origin of the world. The identity of evil and "chaos," and the identity of salvation with "creation," have seemed to us to constitute the two fundamental traits of this first type. The other traits will be corollaries of these dominant traits.

2. It has seemed to us that there is a change of type with the idea of a "fall" of man that arises as an irrational event in a *creation already completed;* and consequently we shall try to show that the dramas of creation *exclude* the idea of a "fall" of man. Any indication of a doctrine of the "fall"—if there be any—within the dramas of creation is held in check by the whole of the interpretation and heralds the transition to another "type"; and, inversely, the idea of a "fall" of man becomes fully developed only in a cosmology from which any creation-drama has been eliminated. The counterpart of a schema based on the notion of a "fall" is that salvation is a new peripeteia in relation to the primordial creation; salvation unrolls a new and open history on the basis of a creation already completed and, in that sense, closed.

Thus the cleavage effected, with the second type, between the irrational event of the fall and the ancient drama of creation provokes a parallel cleavage between the theme of salvation, which becomes eminently historical, and the theme of creation, which recedes to the position of "cosmological" background for the *temporal* drama played in the foreground of the world. Salvation, understood as the sum of the initiatives of the divinity and of the believer tending toward the elimination of evil, aims henceforth at a specific end distinct from the end of creation. That specific end, around which gravitate the "eschatological" representations, can no longer be identified with the end of creation, and we arrive at a strange tension between two representations: that of a creation brought to a close with the "rest on the seventh day," and that of a work of salvation still pending, until the "Last Day." The separation of the problematics of evil from the problematics of creation is carried out along the whole line, beginning with the idea of a fall that supervened upon a perfect creation. It is, then, the event of the fall that carries the whole weight of this mythology, like the point of an inverted pyramid.

3. Between the myth of chaos, belonging to the creation-drama, and the myth of the fall, we shall insert an intermediate type that may be called "tragic," because it attains its full manifestation all at once in Greek tragedy. Behind the tragic vision of man we shall look for an implicit, and perhaps unavowable, theology: the tragic theology of the god who tempts, blinds, leads astray. Here the fault appears to be indistinguishable from the very existence of the tragic hero; he does not commit the fault, he is guilty. What, then, can salvation be? Not the "remission of sins," for there is no pardon for an inevitable fault. Nevertheless, there is a tragic salvation, which consists in a sort of aesthetic deliverance issuing from the tragic spectacle itself, internalized in the depths of existence and converted into pity with respect to oneself. Salvation of this sort makes freedom coincide with understood necessity.

Between the chaos of the drama of creation, the inevitable fault of the tragic hero, and the fall of the primeval man there are complex relations of exclusion and inclusion, which we shall try to understand and to recapture in ourselves; but even the relation of exclusion occurs within a common space, thanks to which these three myths have a common fate.

4. Altogether marginal to this triad of myths, there is a solitary myth that has played a considerable part in our Western culture, because it presided, if not over the birth, at least over the growth of Greek philosophy. This myth, which we shall call "the *myth of the exiled soul*," differs from all the others in that it divides man into *soul* and *body* and concentrates on the destiny of the soul, which it depicts as coming from elsewhere and straying here below, while the cosmogonic, or theogonic, background of the other myths receives little emphasis. One test of our typology— and that not the least—will be to understand why the myth of the exiled soul and the myth of the fault of a primeval man could sometimes merge and blend their influences in an indistinct myth of the fall, although these two myths are profoundly heterogeneous, and the secret affinities of the Biblical myth of the fall carry it toward the myth of chaos and the tragic myth rather than toward the myth of the exiled soul.

Thus our "typology" ought not to be confined to an attempt at classification; we must go beyond the statics of classification to a dynamics that has as its task the discovery of the latent life of the myths and the play of their secret affinities. It is this dynamics that must prepare the way for a philosophic recapture of the myth.

I. The Drama of Creation
and the "Ritual" Vision
of the World

1. PRIMORDIAL CHAOS

THE FIRST "TYPE" OF MYTH concerning the origin and the end of evil is illustrated in a striking manner by the Sumero-Akkadian theogonic myths, which have come down to us in a version dating, perhaps, from the beginning of the second millennium before our era. These myths recount the final victory of order over chaos. The Homeric and particularly the Hesiodic theogonies belong to the same type, but less strikingly so; and besides they did not determine the whole vision of the world as completely as the Babylonian epic did.

To illustrate this "type" and to discover the motivation that determined it, we will present without preliminaries the great drama of creation called *Enuma elish* (after the first two words of the poem, "When on high. . . .").[1] The first noteworthy trait exhibited by this creation-myth is that, before recounting the

[1] P. Dhorme, *Choix de textes religieux assyro-babyloniens* (Paris, 1907), pp. 3–81. R. Labat, *Le Poème babylonien de la création* (Paris, 1935). Heidel, *The Babylonian Genesis and Old Testament Parallels* (Chicago, 1942; 2d ed., 1951). The reference edition here will be the one in James B. Pritchard, ed., *Ancient Near Eastern Texts Relating to the Old Testament* (Princeton, 1950; 2d ed., 1955), pp. 60–72 (reproduced partially in his *Anthology of Texts and Pictures*, 1958, pp. 31–39, and completely in Isaac Mendelsohn, ed., *The Religions of the Ancient Near East: Sumero-Akkadian Religious Texts and Ugaritic Epics*, New York, 1955, pp. 17–47).

genesis of the world, it recounts the genesis of the divine; the
birth of the present world order and the appearance of man, such
as he exists now, are the last act of a drama that concerns the
generation of the gods. This coming-to-be of the divine has a considerable significance on the level of "types";[2] this myth, which

---

Theodore H. Gaster has translated this story and told it anew in *The
Oldest Stories in the World* (Boston, 1952), pp. 52–70.

[2] Various authors (S. N. Kramer, *Sumerian Mythology*, Philadelphia,
1944; Thorkild Jacobsen, in *The Intellectual Adventure of Ancient Man,*
by H. and H. A. Frankfort, J. A. Wilson, and Thorkild Jacobsen, Chicago,
1947) have reconstructed the background of the Akkadian myth that we
are studying here. It appears from this investigation that the question of
the origin of order was a relatively late question, and that it was order
itself that was first celebrated. That order has been represented as a cosmic
State, or a Cosmos-State, in which the fundamental forces of the universe
have a determinate rank: at the top, authority, majesty, reign (Anu, the
Sky); then force, ambiguous might (Enlil, Lord of the Storm), who brings
devastation and aid by turns (it is he, as we shall see, who vanquishes the
monstrous power of Tiamat in the Akkadian poem of creation); then the
passive fertility of Mother Earth; then active and ingenious creativity
(Enki, lord of the earth, the sweet waters of wells, springs, and rivers). No
doubt this vision of order must be kept in mind when one reads the later
myths of which Marduk is the hero, where order is challenged; but the later
theogonic and cosmogonic myth is contained in germ in the oldest myths.
In the first place, the vision of the cosmic hierarchy contains a drama from
the beginning, even if only by the conjunction of these multiple forces,
which change their respective places. Second, there was always a place for
myths of origin, even if only with respect to secondary divinities; matings,
conflicts, divine decrees put the hierarchy of the cosmos in flux. But above
all, majesty, deposited in the power of the supreme god, passes from one
god to another by delegation of the assembly of the gods, and thus movement is introduced into the system. That explains why the successive
apogees of the Mesopotamian cities were related to the enthronement of a
series of divinities within the flexible framework of the divine hierarchy.
The enthronement of Marduk, who is at the center of the myth that we take
here as an example of the first type, belongs in this evolution of kingship
within the Mesopotamian pantheon. Thus there is continuity, and not
contradiction, between a vision in which order is primordial, and another,
which we are going to examine, in which order is won by strife on high.
Éd. Dhorme, in *Les Religions de Babylonie et d'Assyrie* (Paris, 1945),
also proposes a description of the "gods of the world" (pp. 20–52) which
is modeled on the four divisions of visible and invisible space—sky, earth,
waters, underworld—and puts the study of the cosmogonic and heroic myths
at the end of his work (pp. 299–330). On the contrary, in *La littérature
babylonienne et assyrienne* (Paris, 1937), the study of the "cosmogonic
literature" (and of *Enuma elish,* pp. 27–34) comes at the beginning, before

appears most naïve in its execution, most indebted to the models provided by fictile production and sexual production, and so most dependent on the narrative form, anticipates typologically the most subtle ontogeneses of modern philosophy, especially those of German idealism. That is why we must not allow ourselves to be turned away from the typological interpretation by the most legitimate sociological explanations, even if it is true that Babylonia emphasized its political supremacy by making Marduk, hitherto a minor divinity, the hero of the cosmic struggle. That explanation does not exhaust the meaning of the poem; there remains the task of understanding the epic schema itself, through which the political supremacy was expressed, and the vision of the world that was worked out by means of that schema. In short, it is the "epic" mode of ontogenesis that requires interpretation—a mode of thought according to which order comes at the end and not at the beginning. That cosmology completes theogony, that what there is to *say* about the world is the result of the *genesis* of the divine —this is the intention that must be recaptured and understood "in" and "beyond" the images of the myth.

This first trait leads to a second: if the divine came into being, then chaos is anterior to order and the principle of evil is primordial, coextensive with the generation of the divine. Order came to pass in the divine itself, and it came to pass by the victory of the latest over the earliest forces of divinity. The anterior disorder is represented in our poem by various figures and episodes, and first of all by Tiamat, the primordial mother—"mother of them all" (I, 4)—who with Apsu, the primordial father, represents the initial commingling of the vastness of the marine waters with the fresh waters. But this liquid chaos has a surcharge of meaning, in which the myth of the origin of evil takes shape. For Tiamat is more than the visible immensity of the waters; she has the power to produce. Moreover, she is capable of plotting against the other gods. According to the story, the younger gods disturbed the primeval peace of the old couple:

---

the "mythological," "epic," "lyric" literature, etc. In G. Contenau, *La Civilisation d'Assur et de Babylone* (Paris, 1937), the point of view is more archeological and sociological (on *Enuma elish,* see pp. 77 ff.).

> Yea, they troubled the mood of Tiamat
> By their hilarity in the Abode of Heaven.
>
> I, 23–24*

Thereupon Apsu wished to destroy them, and Mummu, his son and vizier, proposed a plan.

> When Apsu heard this, his face grew radiant
> Because of the evil he planned against the gods, his sons.
>
> I, 51–52

But the old god was killed before this plan could be carried out. And when Marduk had been created ("A god was engendered, most able and wisest of gods," I, 80), Tiamat, inflamed with rage, gave birth to monsters—viper, dragon, sphinx, great lion, mad dog, scorpion-man (I, 140–141). Then,

> When Tiamat had thus lent import to her handiwork,
> She prepared for battle against the gods, her offspring.
> To avenge Apsu, Tiamat wrought evil.
>
> II, 1–3

This savage recital evokes a terrible possibility: that the Origin of things is so far on the other side of good and evil that it engenders at the same time the late principle of order—Marduk—and the belated representatives of the monstrous, and that it must be destroyed, surmounted, as a blind origin. This promotion of the divine at the expense of the primordial brutality is found again in Greek mythology; tragedy and philosophy will have to struggle with this possibility in diverse ways.

What is signified by this possibility, this terrible possibility? Negatively, that man is not the origin of evil; man finds evil and continues it. The question will be to know whether the confession of man as sinner will have the power to take up the origin of evil completely into the evil will of which he accuses himself and of which he recognizes himself as author. Positively, that evil is as old as the oldest of beings; that evil is the past of being; that it is that which was overcome by the establishment of the world; that God is the future of being. The question will be to know whether the

---

* This and the following quotations are from the English translation of *Enuma elish* by E. A. Speiser, in Pritchard, *op. cit.*, pp. 60 ff.—Tr.

confession of God as Holy will have the power to exclude the origin of evil completely from the sphere of the divine.

The two questions complement each other; only the confession of the Holiness of God and the confession of man as sinner could pretend to exorcise this possibility radically. We shall see how far they succeed; for, besides the possibility that man is not capable of going all the way to the end in this twofold confession, there is the possibility that the confession cannot retain its peculiar significance, apart from any legalistic and moralistic reduction, except by preserving something of the terrible epic of being.[3]

But we have not yet come to the end of this investigation of primordial evil, for it is still by disorder that disorder is overcome; it is by violence that the youngest of the gods establishes order. Thus the principle of evil is twice designated: as the chaos anterior to order, and as the struggle by which chaos is overcome. That is what makes the theogony "epic": it is by War and Murder that the original Enemy is finally vanquished.

In the Babylonian poem, the first murder, that of Apsu massacred in his sleep, serves as prologue to the decisive combat in which Tiamat is vanquished by Marduk. That combat, for which the way is solemnly prepared by the enthronement of Marduk in the assembly of the gods, is really the center of the poem;[4] it makes the creation of the world follow upon the salvation of the gods, menaced by the original disorder from which they came forth:

> . . . Tiamat, she who bore us, detests us.
> She has set up the [Assembly] and is furious with rage.
>
> III, 15–16

The gods need to be confirmed in existence—saved—by the victory of the Lord.

---

[3] A. Heidel (*op. cit.*, p. 127) insists strongly on the subordinate character of the story of creation in relation to the story of Marduk and his enthronement. Marduk, in contrast with the crude violence of Tiamat, is the origin of a habitable world, of a cosmos measured by the stars and the calendar, as in the *Timaeus*, and finally the author of the establishment of mankind. In the same vein is Éd. Dhorme, *Les Religions de Babylonie et d'Assyrie* (Paris, 1945), p. 308.

[4] Heidel, *op. cit.*, pp. 102–114.

Each time that the poem was recited, with great solemnity, on the fourth day of the New Year's Festival, it was this perilous advent of order that was re-enacted, this coming into existence of the very being of the gods that was celebrated. With all the gods who proclaim Marduk their Lord, the faithful cry out:

> "Go and cut off the life of Tiamat.
> May the winds bear her blood to places undisclosed."
>
> IV, 31–32

> Then the lord raised up the flood-storm, his mighty weapon.
> He mounted the storm-chariot irresistible [and] terrifying.
>
> IV, 49–50[5]

It is by the violence of the evil winds that he drives into her body that Marduk vanquishes Tiamat.

Then the Cosmos is born: Tiamat is cut in two, and from her divided corpse the distinct parts of the Cosmos are formed (IV, end, and V). Thus the creative act, which distinguishes, separates, measures, and puts in order, is inseparable from the criminal act that puts an end to the life of the oldest gods, inseparable from a deicide inherent in the divine. And man himself[6] is born from a new crime: the chief of the rebel gods is declared guilty, brought to trial, and slain; from his blood Ea, on the counsel of Marduk, creates man; man has now the task of serving and nourishing the great gods in place of the vanquished gods. Thus man is made from the blood of an assassinated god, that is to say from the life of a god, but from his life ravished by a murder:

---

[5] Cf. below, Chap. V, § 3. Also, read Marduk's invectives against Tiamat: "Against Anshar, king of the gods, thou seekest evil; [Against] the gods, my fathers, thou hast confirmed thy wickedness" (IV, 83–84); and see the rhythmical and rhymed translation of this passage by T. H. Gaster (*op. cit.,* pp. 62–63).

[6] "Blood I will mass and cause bones to be.
I will establish a savage, 'man' shall be his name.
Verily, savage-man I will create.
He shall be charged with the service of the gods
   That they might be at ease!"

VI, 5–9

> Out of his blood they fashioned mankind.
> He [Ea] imposed the service and let free the gods.
>   VI, 33–34[7]

This role of violence at the origin of the divine itself, and subsequently at the origin of the world and of man, appears still more striking if one remarks the filiation between Enlil, Sumerian god of the storm as well as of help, and Marduk. The creative act that separates the mass of the upper waters from the mass of the lower waters, in the manner of a powerful wind inflating an orderly space, a solid sky and a habitable earth, between the liquid reserves,—this act is also the devastating act of the Storm, which finds expression in another way in great historical catastrophes. The barbarians who destroyed Ur are the Storm, and the Storm is Enlil.

> Enlil called the storm.
>   The people mourn . . .
>
> He summoned evil winds.
>   The people mourn . . .
>
> The storm ordered by Enlil in hate, the storm
>   Which wears away the country,
> Covered Ur like a cloth, enveloped it like a linen sheet.[8]

It is also by the violence of the winds that he drives into her body, ready to devour it, that Marduk overcomes the might of Tiamat—perhaps as the wind drives back the threatening might of the waters.

The Sumerians had noticed the ambiguity of this great divinity. By turns Enlil spreads terror ("What has he planned against me in his holy mind? A net he spread: that is the net of an enemy") and trust ("Wise instructor of the people. . . . Counselor of gods on earth, judicious prince"). In another Sumerian myth, the myth

---

[7] Gaster (*op. cit.,* p. 69) compares this story with the Orphic one, in which man is born from the ashes of the Titans, struck down by lightning. We shall speak of it later.

[8] Tr. by Mrs. H. A. Frankfort, quoted by Thorkild Jacobsen, *loc. cit.,* pp. 141–42.

of Enlil and Ninhil, we see Enlil committing rape. Even if rape
has not, in Babylonian morality, the significance of a wrong done
to a woman, it gives evidence of the contradictory nature of
Enlil.

Shall we say that the power of chaos represented by Tiamat, by
the strife among the gods, by the succession of deicides, even by
the victory of Marduk, was not identified with evil in the Babylonian consciousness, and that we do not have the right to employ
these myths of origin in the framework of a genesis of evil?

Of course, the Babylonians did not form the idea of *guilty* gods,
and even less did the Sumerians. Nevertheless, they named "evil"
in naming the gods, their tricks, their plots, their acts of violence:

> When Apsu heard this [his vizier's advice to kill his
>   sons], his face grew radiant
> Because of the evil he planned against the gods, his sons.
> *Enuma elish*, I, 51–52

> To avenge Apsu, Tiamat wrought this evil.
> II, 3

"But pour out the life of the god who seized evil" (IV, 18), say
the gods when they grant kingship to Marduk, their avenger.

The intentions and actions which the mythographers ascribe to
the gods are the same as those which man recognizes as evil for
himself and which the penitent repents. In the course of the
struggle that opposes Marduk to Tiamat, Marduk appears as brute
force, as little ethical as the wrath of Tiamat. Marduk personifies
the identity of creation and destruction; when he is enthroned by
the gods, before the decisive combat with Tiamat, all cry out:

> "Lord, truly thy decree is first among the gods.
> Say but to wreck or create; it shall be."
> IV, 21–22

It will be seen what human violence is thus justified by the primordial violence. Creation is a victory over an Enemy older than the
creator; that Enemy, immanent in the divine, will be represented
in history by all the enemies whom the king in his turn, as servant
of the god, will have as his mission to destroy. Thus Violence is

inscribed in the origin of things, in the principle that establishes while it destroys.

If our interpretation of the "type" that presides over the Babylonian myth of creation is exact, the counterproof should be furnished by an examination of the so-called myths of the fall in Sumerian and Akkadian mythology. The "type" of primordial violence excludes, in fact, the "type" of the fall—that is to say, in the precise meaning of the term, a degradation in order which is distinct from the institution of order and which, in mythical terms, is "posterior" to creation.

Now, it was believed at first that one could recognize in Babylonian literature the first expression of that which was to become the Biblical narrative of Paradise and the fall.[9] The old Sumerian myth, retranslated, reinterpreted, broken up into several fragments, and now attached to the "cycle of Enki and Ninhursag," does, in fact, depict a land of bliss, "pure," "clean," and "bright," in which there are apparently no death, no sickness, no life-and-death struggles among the animals. The water-god begets a series of divinities born of his spouse, "the mother of the land," then of his daughter, then of his granddaughter, until his spouse, taking his seed at the moment when he is embracing his great-granddaughter, causes eight plants to sprout from it. But before the goddess has named them, Enki plucks and eats them. The goddess curses him in these words: "Until he is dead I shall not look upon him with the 'eye of life' " (vs. 219). This curse makes the god weak and ill. Finally the fox reconciles the two, and the goddess cures the eight ills of Enki by creating an appropriate deity for each sick organ. If it is true that the images of the Biblical Paradise are already formed in this poem, which has wrongly received the title of "A Paradise

[9] S. Langdon, *Sumerian Epic of Paradise, the Flood, and the Fall of Man* (University Museum, University of Pennsylvania, *Publications of the Babylonian Section*, X, Pt. I, 1915; French translation by Ch. Virolleaud, Paris, 1919). See the review by P. Dhorme, *Révue Biblique* (1921), pp. 309–12; Kramer, *Sumerian Mythology*, pp. 54–59; Contenau, *Le Déluge babylonien*, new ed. (1951), pp. 50–54. There is a new translation by S. N. Kramer, giving a quite different interpretation of this difficult Sumerian text, in Pritchard, *op. cit.*, pp. 37–41, and Mendelsohn, *op. cit.*, pp. 3–11.

Myth" on the strength of its first thirty verses, it is impossible to
recognize the schema of the fall in the episode of Enki eating the
eight plants. It is to know their "heart" and to name them in
accordance with their true natures that he assimilates them: "Of
the plants, [Enki] decreed their fate, *knew* their 'heart' " (vs.
217). And the consequence is not the entrance of evil into the
world, but the banishment into darkness of the might of the waters.
We are still dealing, therefore, with a fragment of theogony, gravitating around cosmic forces, earth and water, and not with an
event relative to the appearance of human evil.[10]

As to the Flood, Babylonian as well as Sumerian, it cannot be
said that the narrations which have come down to us[11] put the
accent on a fault committed by men, for which the cosmic catastrophe is the punishment. Indeed, it is here that we see most
clearly how like images can belong to different types. Where the
Biblical myth appears to be closest to a Babylonian source—
whether that source be one of the accounts with which we are
acquainted or a still more primitive tradition,[12]—the images that
it seems to derive from its Babylonian source receive a distinctive
mark from the general intention of the type of the fall; the flood is
the close of a long series of stories (Abel and Cain, the tower of
Babel, etc.) designed to illustrate the growing wickedness of men.
There is nothing of the sort in our Babylonian sources: the same
stock of images lends support to a radically different vision of

[10] According to Kramer, what is involved is an explanation concerning
the origins of vegetation. G. Contenau sees, in the central theme, a "sacred
marriage," an old fertility rite, which insures life on this earth.

[11] P. Dhorme, *Choix de textes religieux assyro-babyloniens* (Paris, 1907),
pp. 100–20. R. Campbell Thompson, *The Epic of Gilgamesh* (Oxford,
1938). G. Contenau, *Le Déluge babylonien, Ishtar aux enfers, La Tour de
Babel* (Paris, 1941; new ed., 1952), texts on pp. 90–121; the author's
archeological interest is evident in his care to distinguish the different strata
of the story. Cf. the critical edition in Pritchard, *op. cit.*, pp. 42–52, for the
Sumerian myth, tr. by A. S. Kramer, and pp. 72–99, for the Akkadian myth
inserted in the Gilgamesh epic, tr. by E. A. Speiser (reproduced in the
Anthology cited above, pp. 65–75, and in Mendelsohn, *op. cit.*, pp. 100–
109). A. Heidel, *The Gilgamesh Epic and Old Testament Parallels* (Chicago, 1945), has Tablet XI (pp. 80–93) and the Atrahasis epic (pp. 106–
16).

[12] G. Contenau, *op. cit.*, pp. 110–12.

things; the flood plunges once more into theogony and its primordial violence.

The Babylonian account of the flood[13] is inserted into the Gilgamesh epic (we will come back later to the meaning of the Babylonian Odyssey, and we shall then understand better how this epic context fits the story of the flood that was belatedly included in it). The motive of the flood remains obscure: "their heart led the great gods to produce the flood" (XI, 14; Speiser's translation, in Pritchard). Divine caprice? So it seems. Now, at the height of the catastrophe, the gods are panic-stricken:

> The gods were frightened by the deluge,
> And, shrinking back, they ascended to the heaven of Anu.
> The gods cowered like dogs
>   Crouched against the outer wall.
> Ishtar cried out like a woman in travail,
> The sweet-voiced mistress of the [gods] moans aloud:
> "The olden days are alas turned to clay,
> Because I bespoke evil in the Assembly of the gods.
> How could I bespeak evil in the Assembly of the gods,
> Ordering battle for the destruction of my people,
> When it is I myself who give birth to my people!
> Like the spawn of the fishes they fill the sea!"
>
> XI, 113–123

The flood is attributed expressly to Enlil, in whom we have already recognized primordial Violence; the flood is the Storm which, instead of separating the waters as in the creative act, reduces all things to primitive chaos, as if in a fury of uncreation. The Babylonian Noah, Un-napishti, or Utnapishtim (that is to say, "day of life"), the Akkadian hero who succeeds the Sumerian

---

[13] The Sumerian version, the oldest we possess, is too mutilated to allow a sure interpretation. In particular, it presents a lacuna at the moment when the gods make the decision to destroy mankind. Nintu, goddess of birth, is heard weeping, and Enki, god of wisdom and friend of man, contrives to save his protégé Zinsudra, the Sumerian Noah. It is true that Zinsudra is presented as a pious and god-fearing king; but there is nothing to indicate that he is saved for any other reason than the same divine arbitrariness which produces the flood. After the flood he receives "life like a god's" and "eternal breath"; he is transported to Dilmun, "the place where the sun rises." The end is destroyed.

Zinsuddu or Zinsudra (that is to say, "prolonged day of life"[14]), when he has been saved from the waters, offers a sacrifice that is pleasing to the gods: "The gods smelled the savor, the gods smelled the sweet savor, the gods crowded like flies about the sacrificer" (XI, 159–61). But Ishtar wants to exclude Enlil: "For he [Enlil], unreasoning, brought on the deluge and my people consigned to destruction" (168–69). And Enlil is furious because a mortal has escaped: "Has some living soul escaped? No man was to survive the destruction!" (173–74). Ea reprimands him severely: "How couldst thou, unreasoning, bring on the deluge? On the sinner impose his sin, on the transgressor impose his transgression! (Yet) be lenient, lest he be cut off, be patient, lest he be dis[lodged]!" (179–83). Of course, an allusion to the sins of human beings can be seen here; but the flood is precisely not connected with human faults, since it proceeds from an excess of wrath on the part of a god who, instead of sending the flood, could have warned men by calamities commensurate with their faults. And Enlil repents, blesses Un-napishti (Utnapishtim), and confers immortality on him. The flood is not a demonstration that death is the wages of sin, and Un-napishti (Utnapishtim) is not "saved by grace."

It is true that the poem *Atrahasis* is more explicit concerning the motive of the flood:

> The land became wide, the peop[le became nu]merous,
> The land *bellowed* like wild oxen.
> The god [Enlil] was disturbed by their uproar.
> [Enlil] heard their clamor
> (And) said to the great gods:
> "Oppressive has become the clamor of mankind.
> By their uproar they prevent sleep."
>   A, 2–8 Speiser's translation, in Pritchard, *op. cit.*

It is evident that an ethical motive has not yet succeeded in breaking through, even though men are held responsible. It is not the holiness of God that is offended!

Finally, the episode of the flood is still caught in the divine chaos; instead of the one, holy God of Genesis, confronted with

[14] G. Contenau, p. 71.

human disorder, there is a confrontation of gods who blame one another, tremble like dogs, and crowd about the sacrifice of the old Sage like flies. The theme of human fault, which the epic of Atrahasis approaches and which the Akkadian epic is on the point of evoking toward the end, in the reproaches of Ea, is, so to speak, masked, impeded, by the dominant structure of the myth. It must be admitted that the same folkloric foundation supports two different theologies.[15]

That the intention of the myth is not to illustrate the wickedness of men is confirmed further by its insertion in the famous *Epic of Gilgamesh*.[16] The quest of Gilgamesh has nothing to do with sin, but only with death, completely stripped of any ethical significance, and with the desire for immortality.

Gilgamesh is the epic of the "human, all too human"; it is the quest for immortality that reveals mortality as fate.[17] Evil is death.

---

[15] Heidel, *op. cit.*, places the difference of motive between the Babylonian flood and the Biblical flood among the multiple differences that betray an opposition in the intentions; he contrasts the caprice of the Babylonian gods with the holiness of the Biblical God and the "regret" of the first with the "repentance" of the second. G. Contenau, less sensible of the typological difference, writes: "All the civilizations that have preserved the memory of the flood see in it a punishment from the gods for a fault committed by men. This was certainly the case for the Babylonian flood; but we still lack the exposition of the fault; we see the gods displeased with mankind, but we do not know the reason. Twenty years ago, however, it was thought that the explanation had been found" (*op. cit.*, p. 50).

[16] P. Dhorme, *Choix de textes religieux assyro-babyloniens,* pp. 182–325. G. Contenau, *L'Épopée de Gilgamesh, poème babylonien* (Paris, 1939). A. Heidel, *The Gilgamesh Epic and Old Testament Parallels* (Chicago, 1945). Our text is the translation in Pritchard, *op. cit.*: Sumerian fragments, pp. 42–52; Akkadian version, pp. 72–99, reproduced in the same editor's *Anthology* (except Tablet XII), pp. 40–75, and in I. Mendelsohn, *op. cit.,* pp. 47–115. T. H. Gaster tells the adventures anew in *The Oldest Stories in the World,* pp. 21–51. Éd. Dhorme comments on them in *La littérature babylonienne et assyrienne* (Paris, 1937), pp. 51–73.

[17] The Orphic myth of the twofold descent of man—divine and Titanic—does not seem to be paralleled by the description of Gilgamesh given by the scorpion-man who guards the gates to the abode of the Babylonian Noah: "He who has come to us—his body is the flesh of the gods"; to which the wife of the monster replies: "Two-thirds of him is god, one-third of him is human" (IX, ii, 14 and 16). Apart from the ironic tone, this trait explains the heroic character of the undertaking, but does not guarantee its success. J. Bottéro, *La religion babylonienne* (Paris, 1952), p. 85, has

Its terrors are represented, before the grievous experience of the death of his friend, death in the second person, by the monster Huwawa, placed by the god in the midst of the cedar forest "as a terror to mortals"; the two friends must destroy him to exorcize their weakness: "Let us, me and thee, slay him, that all evil from the land we may banish!" (III, iii, 6–7). "Huwawa—his roaring is the flood-storm, his mouth is fire, his breath is death!" (III, iii, 18–20). And already Gilgamesh has a foreboding of the secret which he will have to take as the reason for his mortal life:

> "Who, my friend, is superior to death?
> Only the gods live forever under the sun.
> As for mankind, numbered are their days;
> Whatever they achieve is but the wind!"
>
> III, iv, 5–8

Here the epic becomes indistinguishable from an elegy on mortal time.

It is true that Gilgamesh and his companion kill the giant of the forest and also the "Bull of Heaven" sent against them for having insulted the gods. But these murders do not imply any guilt; they, too, must be interpreted within the perspective of the desire for eternity; they signify that the desire of man is to share in the immortality of the gods; and it is the jealousy of the gods that makes this desire for immortality the transgression of a limit, represented by the destruction of the giant and of the Bull of Heaven.

The gods say to one another:

> "Because the Bull of Heaven they have slain, and Huwawa
> They have slain, therefore"—said Anu—"the one of them
> Who stripped the mountains of the cedar
> [Must die!]"
>
> VII, 6–8

It is then that Gilgamesh has the first and only experience of death that is given to a man to have, that of the death of a friend:

> "Hear me, O elders [and give ear] unto me!

---

clearly seen the difference between the Orphic myth and the Babylonian myth of men created with the blood of a god.

> It is for Enkidu, my [friend], that I weep,
> Moaning bitterly like a wailing woman [etc.]. . . ."
>
> VIII, ii, 1 ff.

And again:

> "When I die, shall I not be like Enkidu?
> Woe has entered my belly.
> Fearing death, I roam over the steppe."
>
> IX, i, 3–5[18]

It is within the framework of this passionate and vain quest, radically foreign to the problematics of fault, that the voyage to the land of Utnapishtim, the Akkadian Noah, is situated:

> "About death and life [I wish to ask him]."
>
> IX, iii, 5

But even before the meeting he is warned by various terrible signs:

> "Never was there, Gilgamesh, [a mortal who could
>   achieve that]."
>
> IX, iii, 8

says the scorpion-man. And Shamash:

> "Gilgamesh, whither rovest thou?
> The life thou pursuest thou shalt not find."
>
> X, i, 7–8

And Siduri, the alewife, "who dwells by the deep sea," repeats the litany:

> "The life thou pursuest thou shalt not find.
> When the gods created mankind,
> Death for mankind they set aside,
> Life in their own hands retaining."
>
> X, iii, 2–5

[18] Nowhere is the epic closer to tragedy. Enlil has decreed the death of the friend, and the god Shamash cries out: "Was it not at my command/ That they slew the Bull of Heaven and Huwawa?/Should now innocent/ Enkidu die?" (VII, 12–15). Nevertheless, the tragic theme is not complete; there lacks the blinding of man by the god; here the interplay of innocence and fault is still incidental to the theogonic conflict.

The advice she gives him is that of Ecclesiastes: make merry, feast and dance:

> "Let thy spouse delight in thy bosom!
> For this is the task of [mankind]!"
>
>   X, iii, 13–14

Utnapishtim gives evidence only of an exceptional and incommunicable immortality, which makes the quest of Gilgamesh all the more distressing and absurd.[19] The sorrowful hero is separated from the blessed hero by the abyss of sleep (XI, 200 ff.); and this sleep is also the harbinger of death (233–34). For Gilgamesh there is only one way: Return, return to finitude, to the city of Uruk, to toil and care.

Failing immortality, he will at least carry back from the blessed land the plant named "Man Becomes Young in Old Age" (XI, 282). Even that is denied him by a supreme irony of fate; while he is bathing, a serpent steals the plant of youth from him before he could taste it himself. This plant evidently has nothing in common with the forbidden fruit;[20] it is a symbol belonging to the same cycle as the murders of Huwawa and the Bull of Heaven, as well as the encounter with the immortal saint; it is the final symbol of Deception, not of Fault. In Genesis, too, man is frustrated of the fruit of the tree of life, but that is because of the other tree, the tree of the knowledge of good and evil, which belongs to another "type" than the Babylonian cycle. In the epic of Gilgamesh, the checkmate is a fate without ethical significance and foreign to any idea of a fall; death, in which the checkmate of man culminates, represents the original difference between men and gods.

It seems to me, then, that the absence of a genuine myth of the fall in the Sumero-Babylonian culture is the counterpart of the vision of the world set forth in their myths of creation. Where evil is primordial and primordially involved in the very coming-to-be of the gods, the problem that might be resolved by a myth of the

---

[19] Heidel, *op. cit.*, pp. 10–13: because the immortality of the Babylonian Noah is unattainable, only the epicureanism recommended by the alewife, or the strenuous mode of life to which the hero returns, are left.

[20] In spite of E. Dhorme, *op. cit.*, p. 69: "As in Eden, it is the serpent that robs man of the gift of immortal life. . . . Only the serpent has profited by the tribulations of the hero."

fall is already resolved. That is why there is no place for a myth of the fall alongside a creation-myth of this sort; the problem of evil is resolved from the beginning and even, as we have seen, before the beginning: before the creation of man, before the creation of the world, even before the birth of the god who establishes order.

2. THE RITUAL RE-ENACTMENT OF THE CREATION AND THE FIGURE OF THE KING

If evil is coextensive with the origin of things, as primeval chaos and theogonic strife, then the elimination of evil and of the wicked must belong to the creative act as such. In this "type" there is no problem of salvation distinct from the problem of creation; there is no history of salvation distinct from the drama of creation.

Consequently, every historical drama, every historical conflict, must be attached by a bond of *re-enactment* of the cultual-ritual type to the drama of creation. Let us try to understand this re-enactment of the foundation of the world and its implications step by step in all the spheres of human existence, from worship to politics. It is there, in fact, that we shall find the type of *man* corresponding to this vision of theogonic strife and that we shall discover the equivalent of what soteriology is for other types of myth.

It has been said too quickly that the cultual-ritual re-enactment excludes time and history. It only excludes a historicity of a contingent type, bound up, as we shall see, with the interpretation of evil as "entering into the world" by means of a contingent act. The "cultual-ritual" vision of human existence develops a specific sort of history attached to the cult—and hence to the re-enactment of the drama of creation—by means of the King. Because royalty stands between gods and men, it provides the figure that ties history to the cult, as the cult is itself tied to the theogonic drama. Relying on contemporary works devoted to the "religious character of Assyro-Babylonian kingship,"[21] we shall try to show the conformity

[21] René Labat, *Le caractère religieux de la royauté assyro-babylonienne* (Paris, 1939); Henri Frankfort, *Kingship and the Gods* (Chicago, 1948); Engnell, *Studies in Divine Kingship in the Ancient Near East* (Uppsala,

that exists between this type of history and the type of evil that we shall study here.

The first entrance of the drama of creation into the History of men is the cult and the ensemble of ritual practices that surround all human activities.[22] Now the cult is already a kind of action— not only a fictive re-enactment, but a renewal of the drama by active participation. Mankind, says the creation-myth,[23] was created for the service of the gods, for which the gods founded Babylon, its temple, and its cult; and this service, when it is addressed to the god who established order, evoking this attribute explicitly, calls for the real re-enactment of the drama of creation. The magnitude of the New Year's festival at Babylon is well known.[24] A whole people, in the presence of the gods assembled in effigy, re-enacts the original battle in which the world order was won and relives the fundamental emotions of the poem—the cosmic anguish, the exaltation of battle, the jubilation in triumph. By the celebration of the festival, the people place their whole existence under the sign of the drama of creation. The connection with the poem is recalled by the recitation of it on the fourth day. The mimed dramatization of the poem in the rite of the festival is further amplified by the identification of Marduk with Tammuz, the dying and reviving god. Like the popular god, the national god is lost, held prisoner in the "mountain"; the people, thrown into confusion, weep for him as for a suffering and dying god; it is at once the death of a god and the return of the creation to chaos. The people "descend" to the imprisoned god; then the god revives with the aid of the ritual; Marduk is liberated and released; his enthronement is re-enacted and the people participate in his deliverance by the great procession that marks the approach of the culminating point of the festival. The procession symbolizes Marduk's

---

1943); Thorkild Jacobsen, "Mesopotamia," in *The Intellectual Adventure of Ancient Man* (Chicago, 1946).

[22] On the cult, cf. Éd. Dhorme, *Les religions de Babylonie et d'Assyrie,* pp. 220–57.

[23] *Enuma elish,* VI, 49–70.

[24] Frankfort, *op. cit.;* Labat, *op. cit.,* pp. 167–76; Engnell, *op. cit.,* p. 33.

going forth to the encounter with the hostile forces; the banquet of the gods celebrates the victory over chaos; and, finally, the sacred marriage revives all the life-giving forces in nature and man. By this fusion with the vegetation liturgy the epic myth becomes charged with all the symbolism suggested to man by the periodic decay and renewal of natural life,[25] while the agrarian rite is inserted into a cosmic epic that can be extended not only in the direction of nature, but in the direction of the history and political destiny of mankind.

Its influence on human life is exhibited not only by the role of expiations, prayers of appeasement, and sacrifices throughout the festival, but by the two ceremonies of "determination of destiny," the first after the liberation of Marduk, to express the fact that men are the slaves of the gods, the second at the end of the ritual, so that the renewal of society may coincide with the rejuvenation of nature. Thus the cosmic order is also the judgment of mankind.

But it is especially by the role of the king in the festival that the transition from cosmic drama to history is effected. The king is both the grand penitent, in whom the service of the gods is epitomized, and the personification of the bound and delivered god. On the fifth day of the festival, the king is stripped of his emblems and struck by the priest; he makes a declaration of innocence; the priest speaks words of appeasement to him, reclothes him in his insignia, strikes him again to draw from him tears that probably signify the good will of the god; the king, thus reinstalled, can play the role of officiant in the great ceremony of renewal. This scene of humiliation is a kind of deposition which associates the precariousness of his kingship with the captivity of the dying god and bases the renewal of his sovereignty on the victory of the delivered god.

[25] Engnell shows that the fusion of the supreme god with the god of fertility can easily take place in either direction, without the necessity of supposing a transposition from the agrarian theme to the theme of sovereignty through the king as intermediary; on the contrary, it is the figure of the king that is the beneficiary of this mutual encroachment upon each other of the two "divine" epithets (*op. cit.,* pp. 18–23). Similarly Frankfort: "The recital of the gods' victory over chaos at the beginning of time cast a spell of accomplishment over the hazardous and all-important renewal of natural life in the present" (*op. cit.,* p. 314).

This participation of the king in the festival is the epitome of all the ties that bind the human to the divine, the political to the cosmic, history to the cult. We can truly say that the king is Man. An Assyrian proverb says: "Man is the shadow of the god and [other] men are the shadow of Man; Man is the king, who is like the mirror of the god."[26]

Thus, Babylonian thought effects the passage from the cosmic drama to the history of men through a theology of sovereignty and through the figure of the King. Now we shall observe the effect this had on the conception of violence and its role in history.

This theology of sovereignty has deep roots in theogony. The god, in fact, is King; he is the master and owner of the land; the whole Cosmos is conceived as a State.[27] Thus the turn from the cosmic to the political is effected within the divine sphere itself; a pact with the earth, with men and history, is written in this attribute of Sovereignty.

But the sovereignty of the god over the city, the country, and the "four regions of the world," that is to say, the entire universe,[28]

[26] Labat, *op. cit.*, p. 222. The king "occupied a privileged place between gods and men; he was, in a way, the bond that unites the world of mortals with the sublime sphere of the gods" (*ibid.*). "He is chosen by the gods, not to be a god himself but to be the Man *par excellence*" (p. 362). We are referred to the celebrated analyses in Frazer's *Golden Bough,* VI. This theme is taken up vigorously by Engnell, who goes so far as to identify the king with the god; he sees this identity of the king and the god of vegetation ratified by the symbol of the tree, or the plant of life, which connects heaven and earth; like the tree, the king is a giver of life (*op. cit.,* pp. 23–30).

[27] Thorkild Jacobsen, "Mesopotamia," in *The Intellectual Adventure of Ancient Man.* The author (who, like Frankfort, insists on the contrast with Egypt and links this contrast with a difference of attitude towards nature) shows that the cosmic order is represented as an integration of gigantic and frightening powers, and so as a Cosmos-State. Anu represents the essence of authority in his terrible greatness, "the very centre and source of all majesty"; the devastating violence of Enlil is co-ordinated with it as catastrophe with sovereignty, or, says the author, quoting Max Weber, as violence with the essence of the State. The manifestations of fertility and creation, in the figures of Mother Earth and Water, are also included in this complex of wills and elevated to the dignity of powers in the Cosmos-State.

[28] On the evolution of the conception of kingship from the Sumerians to the Babylonians and the Assyrians, cf. Labat, *op. cit.,* introduction.

is fully manifested only in the person of the king who, without being personally a god, holds his sovereignty by divine favor. The king is the place where the primordial kingship descends from heaven to earth; kingship is communicated to him by the choice of the gods who look with kindness upon him, by calling upon a favorable name, by the determination of a propitious destiny—in short, by investiture and adoption rather than by actual filiation. The ritual of enthronement is only the manifestation of this predestination.

Can an echo of the creation-drama be found in this theology of power? Yes, in the essentially precarious conception of Babylonian kingship, on which Frankfort and Th. Jacobsen insist so much, in contrast with the Egyptian conception.[29] Now, the Mesopotamian and Egyptian theologies of power both conform to their respective views of creation; in contrast with the "serene splendor of the Egyptian creator rising from the primeval ocean on the first morning to shape the world he was to rule,"[30] there is the long conflict, of which the Babylonian creation is only the final episode; Marduk becomes king only at the height of the crisis in order to save the assembly of the gods; thus the divine monarchy itself is the product of confusion and anxiety. The kingship of the terrestrial monarch reflects this painful parturition; after his enthronement, "the task which he now faced was hazardous in the extreme."[31] He has to interpret the will of the gods unceasingly, through signs and omens; he represents the people before the gods, offering to them an epitome of human piety encased in a very complicated daily ritual; he is legislator and judge in the name of the gods. He is responsible for the whole life of the country: he is man *par excellence,* and the unique being in whom all the life-giving forces of the land are concentrated;[32] being responsible for the relations between heaven and earth, he will also be the victim of any discord and will have to humble himself unceasingly for it, "as if the cause of the evil from which the universe suffers were in him and had to be extir-

[29] Frankfort, *op. cit., passim;* Thorkild Jacobsen, *op. cit.,* pp. 185–200.
[30] Frankfort, *op. cit.,* p. 232.
[31] *Ibid.,* p. 247.
[32] Labat, *op. cit.,* p. 277.

pated from his body by confession and various rites of elimination";[33] that is why the royal priest, the royal worshiper, becomes the royal penitent.[34] Thus placed in the perspective of the creation-myth, against the background of the pain of being, the kingship, in which the humanity of man is epitomized, appears as wretched as it is great—dominated, finally, by the anguish arising from the instability of order. The revocable investiture of the king introduces a factor of unforeseeability into history; the gods have changed and can change their earthly servant. They have only to transfer the kingship to another city or another state, to raise up the scourge of a tyrant or a foreign avenger, just as among themselves they grant supremacy now to one, now to another.

Can the verification of the myth by the mode of life be pushed further? The structure of the myth permits us to anticipate what may be called a theology of the Holy War. If the King represents the god who overcomes chaos, the Enemy should represent the forces of evil in our history and his insolence should represent a resurgence of the ancient chaos.

At first sight, the facts do not seem to confirm this expectation: "In general, the Babylonian king is not a warrior. He more willingly occupies himself with pious works and the labors of peace. He builds temples and palaces. . . ."[35] It is the Assyrian civilization that develops this vindictive aspect of the theology of power: "It was above all as a leader in war, avenger of the divine right, that the sovereign of Assur realized his power to the full."[36] Even if the Babylonian sovereign is not chiefly a leader in war, nevertheless the fate on which the gods have deliberated requires him "to make justice prevail, to protect the weak, and to hold the wicked in check."[37] Hammurabi, in the exordium of his famous Code, declares that he has been named by Anu and Marduk "to cause justice to prevail in the land, to destroy the wicked and the evil,

---

[33] *Ibid.*, p. 279.

[34] Should one go so far as to say, with Engnell, that the psalm literature (hymns and psalms of repentance and lamentation) gravitates around the king, that the psalms are primarily royal psalms (*op. cit.*, pp. 45–51)?

[35] Labat, *op. cit.*, p. 14.

[36] *Ibid.*, p. 22.

[37] *Ibid.*, p. 51.

that the strong might not oppress the weak. . . ."* Thus the king cannot be judge, laborer, penitent, without wielding the sword against the wicked in his kingdom and outside it; violence is included in the fate that has made him the Man *par excellence*. Among the insignia conferred upon him at the time of his enthronement, the king receives the sacred arms of the divine conqueror and the divine avenger; "the invincible bow" of the king of Assyria, "the terrible bow of Ishtar, Lady of Combats," is, then, not without precedents.[38] From this to regarding the enemy himself as representing the primordial chaos, there is only a step. That step was taken with greater alacrity by the Assyrians[39] than by the Babylonians.[40] The enemy must be punished because he does not obey the word of Assur, because he is impious and sacrilegious (and so he will first have his tongue cut out); his death will be evidence of the power of the god, while his pardon, if he is pardoned, will be a sign of the fear inspired by the god.

So I see the ultimate outcome of this type of myth in a theology of war founded on the identification of the Enemy with the powers that the god has vanquished and continues to vanquish in the drama of creation. Through the mediation of the king, the drama of creation becomes significant for the whole history of mankind, and particularly for all of that aspect of human life which is characterized by combat. In other words, the mythological type of the drama of creation is marked by the *King-Enemy* relation,

* Tr. by T. J. Meek, in Pritchard, *Ancient Near Eastern Texts*, p. 164.—TR.

[38] The reliefs in the British Museum, in which the position of the royal archer duplicates exactly the position of the divine bowman, whose figure dominates his, are well known. Thus the historical violence of the king imitates the primordial violence of the god.

[39] In the chapter entitled "Guerre Sainte," Labat (*op. cit.*, pp. 253–74) takes his examples principally from the Assyrian period.

[40] E. Dhorme (*op. cit.*, p. 145) recalls the enumeration of the arms of Marduk in *Enuma elish*, IV. Thorkild Jacobsen (*op. cit.*), who insists on the anteriority of Enlil, god of the storm and of counsel, to Marduk, sees in the function of Enlil the source of historical violence; he cites numerous contemporary texts concerning the city-state in which Enlil is invoked as the executor of punitive justice; it is the passing of sovereignty from one city to another which manifests the arbitrament of violence in this epoch; then the god of the city weeps over it, as Ningal grieves for the "day of storm" that sees the destruction of her city, Ur.

which becomes the political relation *par excellence*. This phenomenological filiation is fundamental, for it introduces us through the myth to the problem of political evil, which will hold an important place in our later research. Even if, as it seems, this theology of war was not developed explicitly and systematically by the Assyro-Babylonians, it can be said inversely that any coherent theology of the holy war is founded on the first mythological "type" of Evil. According to that theology, the Enemy is a Wicked One, war is his punishment, and there are wicked ones because first there is evil and then order. In the final analysis, evil is not an accident that upsets a previous order; it belongs constitutionally to the foundation of order. Indeed, it is doubly original: first, in the role of the Enemy, whom the forces of chaos have never ceased to incarnate, although they were crushed at the beginning of the world; second, in the figure of the King, sent to "destroy the wicked and the evil" by the same ambiguous power of devastation and of prudence that once upon a time established order.

3. A "Recessive" Form of the Drama of Creation: The Hebrew King

We have supported our analysis of the first type of myth by the example of the Babylonian creation-drama. In that myth not only is the "type" *dominant,* but it succeeded in animating the whole of a culture, since it furnished it with an understanding of its political existence.

Now we shall verify our typological method with the help of two mythical schemata, one Hebrew and one Hellenic, in which the exemplification of the "type" is less pure and more complex. In the first case the creation-drama is pushed back by another "type" and subsists only in a *recessive* form. In the second, the conception of the world and of evil *hesitates* between several types and begins to veer toward the mythical forms that we shall study further on. We have here two modalities of what might be called the phenomenological "transition" between types: the superimposition of a dominant form on a recessive form, and indetermination among several forms.

Are we right in speaking of a recessive form in connection with certain themes of the Hebrew Bible that are still enlisted, it seems, under the phenomenological type of the creation-drama? Certain exegetes, chiefly Scandinavian,[41] have gone much further and have shown the strict dependence of the Messianic theme and even of the theme of the primordial man on the "ideology of the king," the meaning of which in the drama of creation we have seen. Let us begin by following them. Perhaps the typological method will bring to light a discontinuity in meaning where the historical and exegetic method is more sensitive to the weight of influences and to the continuity of images and literary expression. Historical continuity and phenomenological or typological discontinuity are not mutually exclusive, if they are brought into play from different points of view and at different levels.

The "ritual-cultual" schema of the drama of creation, repeated in the combats of the king against his enemies, is certainly the key to a certain number of the Psalms, which insinuate at the same time that the evil in history, represented by the enemies of Yahweh and the King, also has its roots in a primordial enmity overcome by Yahweh when he founded the world and established the firmament, above which his throne is securely set.

Thus the cultual frame of the celebration of the enthronement of Yahweh is still related to the drama of creation: the Psalms of God's reign (Ps. 47, 93, 95, 100) develop the acclamation "God is King!"; and as his kingdom embraces the peoples of history as well as the physical universe, the schema of reign, subjugation, contests against enemies, characteristic of a theology of history, willingly avails itself of the imagery of the creation-drama. In Psalm 8, the firmament appears as the strong place that Yahweh opposes to the aggressor in order to destroy enemies and rebels. The formless might of the waters, as well as certain monstrous figures—Rahab, the Dragon—associated with the figure of the primeval sea, continue to represent the primordial adversary opposed to the unshakable firmament: "Yahweh on high is mightier than the noise of many waters, yea, than the mighty waves of the sea" (Ps. 93:4); "Thou rulest the raging of the sea: when the waves thereof arise,

[41] Mowinckel, Engnell, Widengren, Pedersen.

thou stillest them. Thou hast broken Rahab in pieces, as one that is slain; thou has scattered thine enemies with thy strong arm" (Ps. 89:9–10). The overflowing of great waters can become a symbol of anguish—"in the floods of great waters they shall not come nigh unto thee [the pardoned sinner]" (Ps. 32:6)—and of death—"the waves of death enveloped me" (Ps. 18:5). This "spiritual" theme preserves the mark of the mysterious primordial Peril.

Still more important for our purpose than the epic theme of the Reign of Yahweh is the theme of the oriental king who wages war in the name of God against the common enemies of God, of his anointed, and of his chosen people. It is here, as we have seen, that the evil of history is linked with cosmic evil, the Enemy representing the outcropping, in history, of the primordial Peril. The cosmic drama becomes a Messianic drama: "Why do the heathen rage, and the people imagine a vain thing? The kings of the earth rise up, and the rulers take counsel together, against the Lord, and against his anointed. . . ." But Yahweh, in his wrath, speaks to them: "I myself have set my king upon Zion, my holy mountain. . . ." And to his king he says: "Thou shalt break them with a sceptre of iron; thou shalt dash them in pieces like a potter's vessel" (Ps. 2). To David, "his servant," Yahweh says again in Psalm 89: "The enemy shall not deceive him, nor the son of wickedness afflict him. And I will beat down his foes before his face, and plague them that hate him. . . ." Have we not here a recollection of the "cultual-ritual" combat of the god-king? Is not the historical enemy the primordial enemy of God and the king? Is not the king himself chosen "from the beginning," at the time when chaos was overcome?

Thus placed in the sequence of the drama of creation, the theme of the *enemy* stands out strongly: "I will make thine enemies thy footstool . . . rule thou in the midst of thine enemies . . . [the Messiah] will break kings in the day of his wrath," says Psalm 110. At the same time it is easy to see how the ritual combat, which re-enacts the drama of creation, can be extended in three different directions. In the first place, the paradigm of the King may move toward that of the primeval man, who likewise "reigns" over the earth, because he also is the "image" of God. Again, it is Psalm 8 that says of the son of Adam: "Thou hast made him little less than a god, crowning him with glory and splendor; thou madest him to have dominion over the works of thy hands, putting all things under his feet. . . ." The line from the original King to the primordial man seems well established.

In the second place, the paradigm of the King can be "historicized"—and, in the same measure, "demythologized"—in virtue of the same combats that put to the test his kingship, established from the beginning. We have seen above that the King does not only "re-enact" the drama of creation, he evolves a genuine "history"; from the ritual combat one passes insensibly to the historical combat. Royal laments—for example, Psalm 89:39–52, which celebrates in the minor mode the sufferings of the king—favored this historicization more than anything else, while the hymn of enthronement leads more naturally to the primordial establishment of the kingship. While it revives the primordial anguish of the time when chaos had not yet been overcome, the royal lament plunges into the thick of genuine historical perils. It is David, fleeing before his son Absalom, who cries: "Yahweh, how are they increased that trouble me! Many are they that rise up against me. Many there be which say of my soul, There is no salvation for him in his God" (Ps. 3:1–2). "How long, Yahweh, wilt thou forget me? Unto the end?" (Ps. 13:1). At the limit, the theme may be "demythologized" and "moralized" to such a degree that it loses all connection with any precise history; the faithful of Judaism and Christianity could legitimately interpret "the adversary," "the oppressor," in the sense of adversity—that is to say, misfortune—or of diabolical temptation—that is to say, temptation by the Evil One. But the "demythologization" of the Enemy and his "historicization" in the guise of Egypt, or the Philistines, or the Assyrians, were a necessary stage on the road to this "moral" and once again "mythical" transposition of the Adversary. Moreover, the Christians gave a "Christological" interpretation to the lament of the innocent one persecuted, closer to the "suffering servant," according to Second Isaiah, than to the king threatened by an historical enemy: "My God, my God, why hast thou forsaken me?" (Ps. 22:1). In this cry, the epitome of all distress, in this lamentation of the universal Good Friday, may we not recognize the echo of the cultal drama at its most intense moment, when the primordial Peril seems on the point of gaining the victory?

But the historical derivation of the themes can be followed in a third direction: that of the "eschatological" Kingdom. In the cultal schema salvation *has been* won, the King *has* conquered, creation *has been* completed; history, with its perils, is not truly new; it "re-enacts" the moment of tension of the cultal drama. Now let history become real, and the final victory is no longer an already attained moment of the drama, but a moment waited for at "the end of time." We see how the drama, in being demythologized, becomes historicized, and, in becoming historicized, effects a sort of "eschatological" carrying forward of its dénouement. Thus the creation-drama was to break out nòt only in the direction of primordial Man or historical contingency, but in the direction of the much more recent figure of the "Son of Man," whose coming from heaven is awaited by Daniel and Enoch; from the Messianic King within history to the transcendent, heavenly "Son of Man" the line of descent is continuous. Moreover, we can find an important stage in this "eschatological" transposition: the Child, the Prince of Peace, foretold by Isaiah (9:6), is already a figure of the End; he will restore the peace of Paradise; the wolf will dwell with the lamb, the baby will play on the hole of the cobra. The Man of the end-time and primeval Man ultimately coincide; is this not because both are derived from the figure of the King, established *from* everlasting *to* everlasting?

It is evident that the paradigm of the King and the Enemy can be drawn out in various directions. But it must be noticed that this result is bound up with a certain method, more attentive to survivals than to new directions; once you have decided to explain the new by the old, the event by its historical "sources," you will find everywhere, even in its most remote derivatives, the initial nucleus that you have decided to take as the basis of "explanation."

A method more attentive to typological differences[42] will start from a different observation: these resemblances with the theme

[42] Aage Bentzen, *Messias, Moses redivivus, Menschensohn* (Zürich, 1948).

of the King in the drama of creation can no longer be anything but
survivals, because the cornerstone of the "ritual of the King" has
been broken; *fundamentally* there is no longer a drama of creation
because there is no longer a theogony, no longer any vanquished
gods; the images of the old system can no longer survive except as
cut flowers. It is the series of "images" that is continuous; the
series of "significations" is no longer so. A different system of
"significations" is at work with the same representations.

In the new system[43] creation is good from the first; it proceeds
from a Word and not from a Drama; it is complete. Evil, then,
can no longer be identical with a prior and resurgent chaos; a
different myth will be needed to account for its appearance, its
"entrance into the world." History too, then, is an original dimension and not a "re-enactment" of the drama of creation. It is
History, not Creation, that is a Drama. Thus Evil and History are
contemporaneous; neither Evil nor History can any longer be
referred to some primordial disorder; Evil becomes scandalous at
the same time as it becomes historical. But, if neither Evil nor
History "re-enacts" a primordial disorder, neither can Salvation
any longer be identified with the foundation of the world; it can
no longer be an aspect of the drama of creation re-enacted in the
cult; it becomes itself an original historical dimension like evil.

Such, in our opinion, is the discontinuity at the level of "types"
of myth; this new "type" organizes itself around new "significations" concerning creation, evil, history, salvation. But as a "type"
does not become explicit all at once, it is perfectly understandable
that it should at first avail itself of the "images" deposited by the

[43] See the chapter on the Adamic myth. A. Heidel has seen this discontinuity very clearly (*op. cit.*, p. 126): the essential point in the
Babylonian theme is the victory of Marduk over the savage earlier gods,
and the cosmogony is a part of the theogony; in the Bible, the essential
point is the creation of the world, and cosmogony is divorced from theogony. The first verse of Genesis expresses this typological difference;
Heidel gives an exegesis of it (*op. cit.*, pp. 128–40). The creation of man
also ceases to belong to theogony; autonomy and responsibility are aimed
at, rather than service to the gods (*ibid.*, pp. 118–22). Finally, the author
has seen clearly that the fall of man is substituted for the guilt of the gods
(*ibid.*, pp. 122–26).

vanquished myth in the culture of the people; aided by this sort
of inertia of images, the new myth works a slow transmutation in
them until it carries them to the level of the new "myth."

We can, therefore, relate to this subterranean work of the new
myth certain of the developments described above as the damped
waves of the old myth. We shall review them in the reverse order.

1. We will not dwell here on the transition from the Messiah
immanent in history to the transcendent and heavenly Son of Man.
The series of figures stretching from the King to the Son of Man,
and then to the Lord of the Gospels, does not simply perpetuate
the initial figure, but constantly adds new dimensions: that of the
sacrificed Prophet—Moses "redivivus"—above all, that of the "Servant of Yahweh." Now, the novelty of those figures is inseparable
from the novelty of history, the novelty of evil, and the novelty
of salvation, with respect to any drama of creation.

2. The emancipation of history from the "cultual-ritual" drama
is the second aspect of that obscure mutation which affects all the
images inherited from the ideology of the King. A purely historical
combat takes the place of the theogonic combat. The Exodus—that
is to say, the departure from Egypt—the key event of the whole
Biblical theology of history, has acquired a consistency of its own,
a new signification with regard to the primordial creation; it is
an event without any reference in principle to any drama of creation. The Exodus, as we have seen, itself became a source of
"symbolization" for the whole Hebrew experience of deliverance
from sins, which were themselves compared to the servitude in
Egypt; it is History, and no longer the drama of creation, that
becomes the active center of symbolism. At the same time, the
Enemy ceases to represent primeval chaos; he undergoes a sort of
reduction to the purely historical, as a function of the action of
Yahweh. Egypt in relation to the Exodus, the Philistines in relation
to the settlement in Canaan are now simply components of the
history of Israel. Thus, one sees the image of the sea-monster itself
turn from the cosmic to the historical when it enters into the field
of attraction of the new *Völkerkampfmythus*.[44]

---

[44] It can be added that the downfall of the ideology of kingship was
accelerated by the discrediting of monarchy, which, too, was considered as

3. But if the Enemy loses his cosmic position to become historical, nothing but historical, the primordial Man must himself become human, nothing but human, and human, purely human evil must find a new myth capable of taking over the wickedness of the Enemy and, even more than that of the Enemy, the wickedness of man in every man.

The ideology of the king may, indeed, continue to nourish the theme of the kingship of man, or that of man as the son of God, image of God, little lower than a God; but the wickedness of man, however kingly, discovered in the course of several centuries of prophetic accusation, remains without roots in the creation, now that the creation is without drama. A new myth, purely anthropological, will be needed to take the place of the old cosmic myth. The figure of the *Urmensch* will then have to be detached from the figure of the King; his fault will have to constitute a radical novelty in the good creation. It is this need which will be fulfilled by the Adamic myth.

Now one may legitimately ask whether this mythical substitution can be carried through right to the end, and whether man can bear the burden of evil in the world all by himself. The Serpent, whose "guile" precedes the fall, is perhaps the last evidence of the drama of creation. But even so it remains true that it is not in *man,* in the figure of Adam, king of creation, that the drama of creation is prolonged, but in the Other than Man, in that Other who will later be called Satan, the Adversary. We will speak of him when the time comes. For the moment, let us leave in suspense this "remythologization" of human evil; it cannot very well be understood until after the "demythologization" of cosmic evil—

---

a ruined and condemned historical magnitude. At the same time, the oriental king appears as the figure of false greatness, as the caricature and no longer the image of God. Read, for example, the prophecy of Ezekiel against the king of Tyre (28:1 ff.): "Because you are swollen with pride, you have said: 'I am a god, I am seated on the throne of God, in the midst of the sea.' Although you are a man and not a god, you set your heart as the heart of God." The figure of the king, then, had to diminish in order that those of the Prophet, of a new Moses connected with a second Exodus, of the servant of Yahweh, and finally of the Son of Man might increase.

that is to say, the movement of thought that liberated three components which the cosmic drama cannot take upon itself: the
"eschatological" component of salvation, the "historical" component of the human drama, and the "anthropological" component
of human evil.

4. A "MUTANT" FORM OF THE DRAMA OF CREATION: THE HELLENIC TITAN

Greek theogony, Homeric and Hesiodic, belongs essentially to
the creation-drama "type," so magnificently illustrated by the
Babylonian poem. That is why we shall not spend much time on
it here, and why we shall seek in it not so much new testimony concerning this "type" of myth of origin, but rather the signs of a
phenomenological transition towards other mythical "types." The
theme of the Titan, which can turn in the direction of the tragic
myth, or of the Orphic myth, or even of the Biblical myth of the
fall, will interest us just because of its indeterminateness.

We will not stop to consider the theogonic theme in the *Iliad*.
Homer has little taste for such stories, and so the episodes that
concern the radical origin of evil have a toned-down and, so to
speak, muted air. Okeanos and Tethys are, no doubt, the equivalents of Apsu and Tiamat; their procreative faculty is inexhaustible; even after the inauguration of the reign of Zeus, these representatives of the formless subsist, in the words of Kerenyi,[45] as a
"current, a barrier, and a frontier between us and the beyond."
But the episode corresponding to the murder of Tiamat in the
Babylonian poem is reduced to the "quarrel" between Tethys and
Okeanos, "father of all beings" (*Iliad*, XIV, 246: ὅς περ γένεσις
πάντεσσι τέτυκται), a quarrel that stops procreation.[46] Here there
comes to light a profound view according to which order is a limit
imposed on the power of procreation and a sort of repose, or rest;
all the philosophical dialectics of the "unlimited" and the "limited"

[45] Kerenyi, *La mythologie des Grecs*, p. 19.
[46] "For a long time now they have stayed apart from each other, from
bed and love, since wrath (χόλος) has invaded their souls (θυμῷ)" (*Iliad*,
XIV, 206–207).

is anticipated here. At the same time, this limitation of formless power hardly appears to be connected with the eruption of a young violence that was to overcome disorder.

It was Hesiod who brought into the foreground the bloody theme which concerns us here. In that peasant fresco concerning origins, the union of Ouranos and Gaia—Sky and Earth—takes the place of the marine couple. Let us leave aside Hesiod's effort to carry the origin back beyond what he nevertheless calls the beginning (ἀρχή), namely, "those to whom Earth and the vast Sky had given birth" (*Theogony*, 45). The anteriority of the Abyss (χαός) and its offspring—Erebos, Night, Aither, Light of Day, etc.—anticipate a stage that goes beyond the theogonic myth in the direction of powers and principles that break away from the story-form and consequently from the myth itself. But the same myth that points in the direction of physics and dialectics immerses itself in the horror of primordial Crimes. The "terrible" sons, born of Earth and Sky —Sky "hated them from the beginning"; he denies them access to the light and conceals them in the caves of the earth; "and while Sky took pleasure in that evil (κακῷ) deed, the enormous Earth choked and groaned in her depths" (158–59). Into the hands of her sons she puts the sickle of vengeance: "Children, my offspring and a raving father's, if you will follow my advice, we shall punish the criminal offense (κακήν... λώβην) of a father, though he be your father, since he first conceived foul deeds" (163–65). The abject episode of the mutilation of Ouranos by the hand of Kronos "of the crafty thoughts" is well known. Similar monstrous episodes occur again in the reign of Kronos, who devours his children. The victory of Zeus himself, like that of Marduk, is the fruit of trickery and violence. Thus order borrows from primordial violence the impulsion by which it gains the victory. And the earlier disorder survives its defeat in a thousand figures of distress and terror: "odious Death," the Parcae, the Keres, "implacable avengers who pursue all faults against the gods or men, goddesses whose dreadful anger never ceases before they have inflicted on the guilty, whoever he may be, a cruel blow,"—and Nemesis, "scourge of mortal men," —and "violent-hearted Strife." "And odious Strife bore grievous Pain—Forgetfulness, Hunger, tearful Woes—Conflicts, Combats,

Murders, Slaughters—Quarrels, lying Words, Disputes—Anarchy and Disaster, which go together—and finally Oaths, the worst of scourges for any mortal here below who has deliberately committed perjury" (226–32).

What shall we say of all these "irresistible" monsters, "which resemble neither mortal men nor the immortal gods," Dog with fifty heads, Nemean Lion, Lernean Hydra, Chimera that spits out an "invincible fire"? Everywhere there rise up the formless, the terrible, the irresistible.[47]

It is here that the figures of the Titans present themselves to us. They are very interesting for a typological investigation. On the one hand, they are rooted in the cosmogonic myth; they are representatives of the old, vanquished gods: "But their father, the vast Sky, calling them to account, gave to the sons he had engendered the name of Titans; by stretching (τιταίνοντας) their hands too high, they had, he said, committed in their folly a horrible offense and the future would take vengeance (τίσιν) for it" (207, 210). In this sense the theogonic stories just cited were also stories of Titans, of archaic and savage forces which obeyed no law. But the image of the Titans moves in the direction of other mythical "types" as soon as it is associated with the origin of man: the Titans are no longer witnesses only of the ancient era, of primordial disorder, but of a subversion posterior to the establishment of order. It is to be noted that in Hesiod the episode of "crafty-minded" Kronos begins with the disputes between the gods and men about the distribution of sacrificed victims (535 ff.). And it is because Zeus has withdrawn from human beings the fire of the lightning that Prometheus steals, in the hollow of a fennel stalk, "the bright gleam of the untiring fire." Thus Hesiod's stories concerning the struggle of the Titans against the Olympians have this ambiguous character of continuing the creation-drama and of presaging what one might call the post-divine drama—in a word, anthropogony, whether it be of the tragic type, the Orphic type, or the Adamic type.

[47] This work had already been printed before I became acquainted with the remarkable essay of Clémence Ramnoux on *La Nuit et les Enfants de la Nuit de la tradition grecque* (Paris, 1959; especially pp. 62–109).

Hesiod's Prometheus is almost an *Urmensch,* a "primordial man."

This movement toward more anthropogonic myths takes various routes. In the first place, it is favored by the anthropomorphism in the creation-drama itself; with the purely physical violence of the old gods there is already associated what may be called the "psychological" violence of guile, or trickery. In the second place, as the ouranian aspect of divinity becomes more clearly defined, all the chthonic violence which has been expelled from the sphere of the divine is left in suspense, like an unused waste-product of the divine; and it is this less than divine that is gathered up in the image of the Titans. Finally, the figure of the Giant—a very large, very strong, and very savage man—furnishes a plastic representation of this inferior kind of divinity and contributes to its attraction toward a sort of primordial man.

Nevertheless, the Promethean myth, at least in Hesiod, is not completely emancipated from its theogonic matrix; it continues to share in the defeat of the Titanic and chthonian elements belonging to the origin of things and to the genesis of the divine itself. Prometheus does not invent evil; he continues it; his guile is a sequel to the guile displayed in the theogonic combats.

It was Aeschylus who transformed Prometheus into a "tragic" figure. While he keeps the theogonic setting, he really makes Prometheus the vis-à-vis of Zeus, who himself becomes the hidden god, or the κακὸς δαίμων; and so Prometheus becomes the "Hero" pursued by the wrath of the god. On the other hand, in accentuating his philanthropic character, Aeschylus makes him, if not a man, at least the demigod who gives man his humanity. Thus Prometheus becomes a sort of model of man, as the German *Sturm und Drang* rightly saw. In Aeschylus himself this transformation is not yet complete, for at the end of the trilogy, now lost, Prometheus is again exalted as a god and given back, so to speak, to theogony. But the direction in which the theme of the Titan evolved is not doubtful.

Perhaps it is among the Orphics that the myth of the Titan gets its closest association with an anthropogony. The Orphic myth, we shall see, is in general a myth of man, a myth of "soul" and "body"; "the crime of the Titans," who dismembered and devoured the young god Dionysos, becomes the origin of man; from their ashes Zeus raised up the present race of men, who thus have a twofold inheritance from god and Titan; the myth of the Titan is henceforth an etiological myth, designed to account for the present condition of man; it is detached completely from the theogonic background to become the first link in an anthropogony. Plato's words in the *Laws* about the "Titanic nature" of man are perhaps the best testimony for this shift in the theme of the Titan from theogony towards anthropogony.

Finally, it would appear that a theme akin to that of the Titans served the Hebrews for a while as a myth of the fall, at least in an obscure tradition, a trace of which is found in the Bible in the sixth chapter of Genesis (vss. 1–4). The Giants—Nephilim,—to whom the Yahwist account alludes, appear to be derived from oriental Titans born of the union between mortals and heavenly beings; but the origin of the legend is less interesting than the use which the Yahwist makes of it. It is to be noted that the Yahwist incorporated this popular legend into his description of the growing corruption in human history, which was to provide a motive for the Flood. Here, then, the theme of the Titans is brought into the story of the fall.

Thus the myth of the insolent race of the Titans is incorporated by turns in the tragic type, the Orphic type, and the Biblical type. It is a sort of evasive myth that hesitates between several types of anthropogony, while remaining a captive of its primitive theogonic matrix. It represents an uncertain attempt to situate the origin of evil in a region of being intermediate between the divine and the human. That is why it remains unusual, close both to chaos and to the *Urmensch*. It signifies, perhaps, an attempt to tie the antiquity of human evil, which is always already there, to those aspects of brute reality which testify of themselves to a resistance to order and beauty—masses of shapeless rocks, the Caucasus battered by storms, to which Aeschylus' Prometheus is nailed.

II. The Wicked God and the "Tragic" Vision of Existence

THE SECOND TYPE OF MYTHS of beginning and end gets its name from its most famous "example": Greek tragedy.

How is this "example" related to the "essence of the tragic"?

One would like to think that the task of the philosopher is to approach Greek tragedy with a category of the tragic already in mind, or at least with a working definition broad enough to include all tragic works: Greek, Christian, Elizabethan, modern. It would seem that this method, proceeding from essence to example, is the only one capable of avoiding the questionable procedure of advancing, by way of induction, from the particular case to the general structure.

Nevertheless, one must start with Greek tragedy. For several reasons. In the first place, because the Greek example is not one example among others; Greek tragedy is not at all an example in the inductive sense, but the sudden and complete manifestation of the essence of the tragic; to understand the tragic is to relive in oneself the Greek experience of the tragic, not as a particular case of tragedy, but as the origin of tragedy—that is to say, both its beginning and its authentic emergence. It is far from being the case that this approach to the tragic through Greek tragedy condemns us to a doubtful process of induction and amplification; rather, it is by grasping the essence in its Greek phenomenon that we can understand all other tragedy as analogous to Greek tragedy.

For, as Max Scheler himself says,[1] although he proposes to go from the essence to the example, the problem here is not to prove but to "make see," to show; Greek tragedy is the most advantageous place for getting "the perception of the phenomenon itself."[2]

Besides, the Greek example, in showing us the tragic itself, has the advantage of revealing to us, without any attenuation, its connection with theology.[3] If there is a tragic vision of man in Aeschylus, that is because it is the other face of a tragic vision of the divine; it is in Greek tragedy that the theme of the man "blinded" and led to his destruction by the gods is carried all at once to the uttermost limit of its virulence, so that thereafter the analogues of Greek tragedy are perhaps only muted expressions of the same *insupportable* revelation.

Finally, the Greek example is especially fitted to persuade us that the tragic vision of the world is tied to a spectacle and not to a speculation. This third trait is not without relation to the preceding one; for, if the secret of tragic anthropology is theological, that theology of making blind is perhaps unavowable, unacceptable for *thought*. The plastic and dramatic expression of the tragic would not, then, be a reclothing, much less an incidental disguise, of a conception of man that could have been expressed otherwise in plain language.

It is of the essence of the tragic that it must be exhibited in a tragic hero, a tragic action, a tragic dénouement. Perhaps the tragic cannot tolerate transcription into a theory which—let us say it immediately—could only be the scandalous theology of predestination to evil. Perhaps the tragic theology must be rejected as soon as it is thought. Perhaps also it is capable of surviving, as spectacle, all the destructions that follow upon its transcription into the plain language of speculation. This connection with a spectacle, then, would be the specific means by which the *symbolic* power that resides in every tragic myth could be protected. At the same time, the connection with a spectacle, with the theatre, would have the

[1] Max Scheler, *Le Phénomène du tragique,* tr. into French by M. Dupuy (Paris, 1952).

[2] *Ibid.,* p. 110.

[3] This chapter owes much to the reading of Gerhard Nebel, *Weltangst und Götterzorn; eine Deutung der griechischen Tragödie* (Stuttgart, 1951).

value of a warning and of an invitation. The philosopher would be put on guard by the invincible tragic spectacle against the illusion that he has done with the tragic vision of the world when he has unmasked—with the Plato of the second book of the *Republic,* for example—the scandalous theology implicit in tragedy. At the same time, he would be invited to try to discover a hermeneutics of the tragic symbol that would take into account the invincibility of the spectacle in the face of any reductive criticism based on the transposition from "theatre" to "theory."

1. THE PRE-TRAGIC THEMES

The tragic theology is inseparable from the tragic spectacle. Its themes, taken one by one, come from further back than tragedy; but tragedy introduces the final trait, the decisive trait, from which the plastic form of the drama and the spectacle itself are born.

We shall call pre-tragic those themes which are anterior to the drama and the spectacle.[4] The first and principal pre-tragic theme is not specifically Greek; it appears in all cultures, every time that the initiative in fault is traced back into the divine and that this divine initiative works through the weakness of man and appears as divine possession. Under this quite undifferentiated form, it is indistinguishable from the preceding theme, since in both of them the principle of evil is as primordial as the principle of good; and so in the figure of the Babylonian god Enlil, whose ambiguous might was the source both of devastation and of good counsel, we could see the beginning of the first and of the second type. But a typological differentiation occurs in the direction of a myth of chaos, enveloped in a drama of creation, when the principle of evil is polarly opposed to the divine as its original Enemy; while the ambiguous figure tends toward the tragic when such a polarization does not occur and when the same divine power appears both as

[4] Kurt Latte, "Schuld und Sünde in der griechischen Religion," *Arch. f. Rel.* 20 (1920–21), pp. 254–298. William C. Greene, *Moira: Fate, Good and Evil in Greek Thought* (Harvard Univ. Press, 1944). E. R. Dodds, *The Greeks and the Irrational* (Univ. of California Press, 1951). H. Fränkel, *Dichtung und Philosophie des frühen Griechentums* (Am. Phil. Ass., XIII, 1951).

a source of good counsel and as a power to lead man astray. Thus the non-distinction between the divine and the diabolical is the implicit theme of the tragic theology and anthropology. Perhaps, as we shall see, it was this non-distinction that could not be *thought through* right to the end and that caused the downfall of tragedy and its vehement condemnation by philosophy in the second book of the *Republic*. But if the feeling that good and evil are identical in God resists thought, it is projected in dramatic works that give rise to indirect, but nevertheless troubling, reflection.

It is astonishing to find this theology of blindness avowed by Homer, who is so far from exemplifying what has aptly been called the "guilt-pattern," which imposed itself after him and which dominated the literature of continental Greece. Few Greek writers were as little concerned as he about purification and expiation; and yet it is in him, in the *Iliad*, that one finds expressed with surprising force and constancy this theme of infatuating blindness, of some god laying violent hold on a human act.[5] This darkening, this leading astray, this seizure, is not a punishment for some fault; it is the fault itself, the origin of the fault.

The fault itself is part of a complex of misfortunes, to which death and birth contribute a note of contingency and ineluctability that contaminates human action, so to speak, with their fatality. Man is essentially mortal, and his mortality is his lot; the pale and unsubstantial reality of the world of the dead heightens more than it weakens the character of mortality as an insurmountable obstacle; the gods, as powers brought to a focus in distinct and precise shapes, can do nothing about it. This note of impotence is reflected back from death upon birth, which is the first day of reckoning, the first fateful event; birth is represented on the model of death, and all of one's destiny appears fated, beginning from its end. Thus the fatality of death and of birth haunts all our acts, which are thereby rendered impotent and irresponsible. The psychological "lability" of the Homeric hero has often been emphasized

[5] E. R. Dodds, *op. cit.*, Chap. I, "Agamemnon's Apology"; *Iliad*, XIX, 86 ff. An important study of the psychology and theology of being led astray is Nilsson's "Götter und Psychologie bei Homer," *Arch. f. Rel.* 22 (1924), pp. 363 ff.; summarized in his *History of Greek Religion*, pp. 122 ff.

—the feebleness of the psychological synthesis of his acts, which makes them seem like happenings without a personal subject and consequently the prey of superior powers.[6] It is by a passive verb— ἀᾶσθαι—that the blinding is expressed; the blinding itself—Ἄτη —is its other side, positive and active, its projection into a world of transcendent powers.

It remains an open question whether it is a very impulsive psychological temperament that favors the belief in the "psychological intervention" of the divine, or whether it is the cultural conception determined by myth that begets this representation of the self and brings man into conformity with its own image.

What concerns us here is precisely this self-representation of man by means of myths.

In the Homeric world, the origin of such blindness is related indeterminately to Zeus, to Μοῖρα,[7] to Erinys. All these mythical expressions resemble each other in designating a reserve of non-personalized power. When the divine, with Homer, finally gets divided into plastic figures like human beings, blindness is related to the surplus of power not distributed among the most distinctly anthropomorphized gods.

Μοῖρα denotes the most impersonal aspect of that power; it is the "portion," the "share," the "lot" imparted to a man beyond his choice; it is the non-choice of choice, the necessity that surcharges and over-determines his acts. The expression δαίμων says the same thing. Although it developed in the opposite direction from μοῖρα, toward personalization and not toward the anonymity of fate and abstract legality, it nevertheless represents the divine as

[6] Bruno Snell, *Die Entdeckung des Geistes* (English translation, *The Discovery of the Mind,* Harvard Univ. Press, 1953), Chap. I, studies the representation of man through the Homeric vocabulary, and shows the absence of a term to designate the unity of the body, as the word σῶμα did later. He shows also that the case is the same for the psychological vocabulary: the ψυχή leaves a man at death, but its role in the living body is not perceived; θυμός generates emotional movements and νόος produces thoughts; the unity of the soul is as unknown to Homer as the unity of the body and the opposition of body and soul. These remarks are important for our typology. Cf. below, Chap. IV.

[7] Homer represents the Moirai with the attributes of spinners; thus they are the dispensers of the inevitable, mighty goddesses, hard to bear, destructive (Greene, *op. cit.,* pp. 10–28).

close to undifferentiated power; and so it provides an apt designation for the sudden, irrational, invincible apparition of the divine in the emotional and volitional life of man.

Thus the theology of fault tends to sustain a reserve of divinity that resists the tendency, triumphant everywhere else, to individualize and visualize divine powers.

The attribution to Zeus of the origin of evil does not contradict these remarks. If Zeus has relatively determinate functions, more or less co-ordinated with those of the other divinities, nevertheless, as supreme god, he represents a greater extension of the divine and less division of power; he is not a partisan god like the others, although the particular wills of the gods are not well subordinated to his government. It is this Zeus who takes upon himself the burden of fault; Até is his daughter: θεὸς διὰ πάντα τελευτᾷ· πρέσβα Διὸς θυγάτηρ Ἄτη, ἣ πάντας ἀᾶται, οὐλομένη (Iliad, XIX, 90–92). At the end of this fusion of divine Blinding with the figure of the supreme divinity, the tragic figure of Zeus in the *Prometheus Unbound* of Aeschylus will take shape; the tragic poets, too, will say θεοί, ὁ θεός, θεός τις. While the myth of chaos tends to dissociate a more recent kind of divinity, ethical in character, from an older and more brutal kind, the tragic myth tends to concentrate good and evil at the summit of the divine.[8] The transition to the tragic

---

[8] Hesiod tends toward the "non-tragic" type, when he makes the maleficent forces issue from the oldest race of the gods; Moros and Thanatos are children of Night (*Theog.*, 211), but so are Momos (blame), Oizys (distress), the Hesperides who guard the golden apples beyond Okeanos, and Nemesis—but so are Apate and Philotes, Geras and Eris (Kerenyi, *La mythologie des Grecs*, French translation, Paris, 1952, pp. 35–36). This mythological ensemble that Kerenyi gathers together under the title of pre-Olympian divinities is a fantastic assemblage of terrifying figures who gear down the world from its original violence, from which the just reign of Zeus will rescue it. It is interesting to see these figures waver between two types, the creation-drama "type" toward which they are drawn by theogony, and the wicked-god "type" toward which they are drawn by the epic. Clémence Ramnoux, in *La Nuit et les Enfants de la Nuit,* shows that these figures of fright also waver between two "levels," that of archaic images (or infantile images, such as the ogre father and the castrated father) and that of the incipient physical concepts. The story of the mutilation of Kronos still belongs to naïve mytho-poetic creation; the cosmogonic

in the strict sense is linked with the progressive personalization of that ambiguous sort of divinity which, while remaining μοῖρα, involuntary and hyper-divine, irrational and ineluctable fatality, takes the quasi-psychological form of malevolence. It may be said that divine malevolence has two poles, an impersonal one in μοῖρα and a personal one in the will of Zeus.

The decisive moment in this personalization of divine hostility is represented by the concept of divine φθόνος: the "jealous" gods cannot endure any greatness beside theirs; man, then, feels himself thrust back into his humanity. Here is the birth of the "tragic," contemporaneous with the famous Greek notion of measure, or moderation; that seemingly tranquil and happy modesty preached by wise men, that acceptance of finiteness, is haunted by the fear of an immoderation that divine "jealousy" cannot tolerate. It is divine jealousy that denounces immoderation, and it is fear of immoderation that instigates the ethical riposte of "modesty."

Of course, the wise men tried to moralize divine φθόνος by reducing it to a punishment for *hybris* and proposing a non-tragic genesis for *hybris:* success begets a desire for more and more—πλεονεξία,—greed begets complacence, and complacence begets arrogance. Thus evil does not come from φθόνος; it is *hybris* that is first. But in demythologizing *hybris,* the moralist makes it ready for a new tragic interpretation; for is there no mystery in the giddiness that lays hold on complacence, makes it clearly excessive, and sets it on the perilous road of the endless desire for more? The πρῶτον κακόν of human *hybris,*[9] as Theognis says, who appears to come close to the Biblical conception of the fall, will become tragic again, as soon as human *hybris* is not only the initiative that provokes the jealousy of the gods, but the initiative that is caused by that jealousy through the intermediary of blindness.

---

fragment (115–38, 211–32) is already close to speculation on being (*op. cit.,* pp. 62–108).

[9] E. R. Dodds, *op. cit.,* puts Simonides, Theognis, and Solon at the sources of this tragic sense of φθόνος. The moralization of φθόνος proceeds at the same time as that of ὕβρις; the surplus of good produces the complacency that engenders pride, which unleashes the jealousy of the gods. We shall see what the tragedians made of this pair—pride and jealousy.

2. The Crux of the Tragic

Thus we have all the elements of the tragic: "blindness" sent by the gods, "daimon," "lot" on the one hand, "jealousy" and "immoderation" on the other.

It was the tragedies of Aeschylus that tied these themes together in a sheaf and added the *quid proprium* that makes tragedy tragic.

What is this germ that causes the tragic to crystallize?

The tragic properly so called does not appear until the theme of predestination to evil—to call it by its name—comes up against the theme of *heroic* greatness; fate must first feel the resistance of freedom, rebound (so to speak) from the hardness of the hero, and finally crush him, before the pre-eminently tragic emotion—φόβος—can be born. (We shall speak later of the other emotion, tragic compassion, in the setting of tragic purification.) Tragedy was the result of magnifying to the breaking point a twofold set of problems: those concerning the "wicked god" and those concerning the "hero"; the Zeus of *Prometheus Bound* and Prometheus himself are the two poles of the tragic theology and anthropology. With the figure of Zeus the movement tending to incorporate the diffused satanism of the δαίμονες into the supreme figure of the "divine" is brought to completion; and with him, consequently, the problematics of the "wicked god," the undivided unity of the divine and the satanic, reaches its highest pitch. All the lines of the tragic theology converge upon this figure of the wicked Zeus, which is already adumbrated in *The Persians.*

It is well known that that tragedy celebrates not the victory of the Greeks at Salamis, but the defeat of the Persians. Now, how could an Athenian rise above his victory and, through tragic compassion, share in the catastrophe of his enemy? Because his enemy, in the person of Xerxes, appeared to him not only as a wicked man justly punished—that would only have made a patriotic drama—but as an example of a man crushed by the gods; Xerxes manifests the mystery of iniquity: "What began all our misfortune, mistress, was an avenging genius (ἀλάστωρ), an evil god (κακὸς δαίμων), appearing from I know not where (ποθέν)." "Ah! hostile fate

($\sigma\tau\nu\gamma\nu\grave{\epsilon}$ $\delta\alpha\hat{\iota}\mu o\nu$)," the old queen Atossa could cry out, "how hast thou deceived ($\grave{\epsilon}\psi\epsilon\acute{\nu}\sigma\alpha\varsigma$) the Persians in their hope!" And the leader of the chorus: "Ah! cruel divinity ($\delta\alpha\hat{\iota}\mu o\nu$), with what weight hast thou fallen upon all the Persian race!" (Note the various renderings of $\delta\alpha\acute{\iota}\mu\omega\nu$, based on the French translation of M. Mazon: god, fate, divinity. The Greek language itself swings from one to another among $\delta\alpha\acute{\iota}\mu\omega\nu$, $\theta\epsilon\acute{o}\varsigma$, $\theta\epsilon o\acute{\iota}$, $\tau\nu\chi\acute{\eta}$, and $^{*}A\tau\eta$. No doubt such an evasive theology cannot be worked out with precision, since, in order to express primordial incoherence, speech must become out of joint and obscured, as Plotinus says of the thought of non-being, of the "lying essence.") "With what weight hast thou fallen . . .": here, then, is man as the victim of a transcendent aggression. The fall is not the fall of man; rather, it is being that, so to speak, falls on him. The figurative uses of net, snare, bird of prey that swoops down upon the smaller bird, belong to the same cycle of fault-misfortune. "Here are we, stricken —with what eternal ills!" Evil as *ictus*. . . . That is why Xerxes is not only the accused but the victim. That, too, is why ethical denunciation and reform is not the business of tragedy, as it was to be the business of comedy; the exegesis of moral evil is so much a part of its theological exegesis that the hero is shielded from moral condemnation and offered as an object of pity to the chorus and the spectator.

Thus *anguish*—the $\phi\acute{o}\beta o\varsigma$ of tragedy—is linked from the beginning with the *wrath of the gods,* according to the excellent title of Gerhard Nebel's book.[10]

The $\kappa\alpha\kappa\grave{o}\varsigma$ $\delta\alpha\acute{\iota}\mu\omega\nu$ of *The Persians* is the key to the Zeus of the *Prometheus.* But the limited and discrete intuition of *The Persians* here takes on gigantic proportions, bringing together two elements which belong to the first "type" of etiology of evil, the drama of creation, and which the tragic poet found in the Greek theogonies. The first is the theme of the genealogies of the gods (Ouranos, Kronos, Zeus). This theme was taken over from epic poetry, but tragedy converted it into a tragic view of the divine; the gods, born of conflict and destined to suffering, have a sort of finitude which is consonant with their immortality; there is a

[10] G. Nebel, *op. cit.,* pp. 11–48.

history of the divine; the divine comes to be through anger and suffering. The second element is constituted by the polarity of the Olympic and the Titanic. The Olympian wins his way against a chaotic and indeed chthonic background, a symbolic vision of which Aeschylus found in the fires and the rumblings of Etna—"hundred-headed Typhon." The sphere of the sacred, then, admits the polarity of night and day, the passion of the night and the lawfulness of the day, to speak with K. Jaspers. The κακὸς δαίμων of *The Persians* gets enriched by these two harmonics: suffering in history and the Titanic abyss. Without doubt it is the same theology, non-thematized, that secretly animates the drama of the *Oresteia* and the ethical terror which inhabits it; that chain of cruelty, which from crime begets crime and which finds its image in the Erinyes, emerges from a sort of fundamental badness in the nature of things. The Erinys pursues the guilty because, if I may venture to say so, she *is* the guiltiness of being.

It is to this guiltiness of being that Aeschylus has given a plastic form in the Zeus of the *Prometheus*.

Facing Zeus stands Prometheus.

We have, in fact, thrown light only on one side of the drama of Prometheus: the problematics of the wicked god and, if we are willing to use the expression, the guiltiness of being. But the guiltiness of being, in its turn, is only one side of a paradox of guiltiness, whose other side is the "immoderation" or "excess" of the "hero," treated as authentic greatness and not as unwarranted exaltation. The Greek tragedians came close to a paradox which resembles the Pauline paradox of grace and freedom, but at the same time is in opposition to it. There is an Aeschylean paradox of the wicked god and human guilt. Let us approach the other side of the paradox.

Without the dialectics of fate and freedom there would be no tragedy. Tragedy requires, on the one hand, transcendence and, more precisely, hostile transcendence—"pitiless god, thy hand alone has guided all," says Racine's Athalia,—and, on the other hand, the upsurge of a freedom that *delays* the fulfillment of fate, causes it to hesitate and to appear contingent at the height of the crisis, in order finally to make it break out in a "dénouement," where its

fatal character is ultimately revealed. Without the delaying action
of the freedom of the hero, fate would be comparable to a dis-
charge of lightning, according to Solon's figure of speech;[11] the
freedom of the hero introduces into the heart of the inevitable
a germ of uncertainty, a temporary delay, thanks to which there is
a "drama"—that is to say, an action the outcome of which, while
it is taking place, is uncertain. Thus delayed by the hero, fate,
implacable in itself, deploys itself in a venture that seems contingent to us; thus is born the tragic action with its peculiar
cruelty that Antonin Artaud knew so well; the unstable mixture
of certainty and surprise is turned to terror by the drop of transcendent perfidy that tragic theology lets fall on it. The tragic emotion of terror reflects, in the soul of the spectator, the cruel play of
the wicked god and the hero; the spectator re-enacts through his
feelings the paradox of the "tragic": all is past, he knows the
story, it is over and done with, it has taken place; and yet he waits
for the certainty of the past absolute to supervene upon chance
events and the uncertainty of the future as if it were something
new: now the hero is broken.

In temporal language, the past absolute of fate—as one sees in
the tragedy of *Oedipus,* which is wholly a tragedy of retrospection,
of the recognition of self in an alien past—the past absolute of
fate reveals itself with the uncertainty of the future: the servant
arrives, the baleful news is heard, and all that which has been true
in itself becomes true for Oedipus, in the pain of identification.
Suppress either side of the tragic, fate or human action, and the
emotion of terror vanishes. Neither would pity be tragic if it did
not spring from that fear in the face of destiny which joins freedom with transcendence. Pity proceeds from that fear as a suffering in the face of destiny; it encounters in man that enormous
opacity of suffering which man opposes to the divine act; it bears
witness that man must have been originally constituted as a counterpole of the misfortune that descends on him. The suffering, or
rather the act of suffering, is revealed as that liminal action which
is already setting itself up in opposition to fate. It is as a response,

[11] Werner Jaeger, *Paideia,* Vol. I, pp. 307–43 (on the drama of Aeschylus), emphasizes strongly the connection between Aeschylus and Solon.

a counterthrust, a defiance, that suffering begins to be tragic and not only lyric.

The tragedy of *The Persians* already showed the conjunction of the theology of the malign genius with the anthropology of immoderation, or excess; Xerxes is at once the victim of an error of divine origin and the transgressor of a prohibition (which is also called δαίμων, *Persians,* 825) inscribed in geography, which destines various peoples for various places.

Thus, taken alone, *hybris* is not tragic; and so one finds it before Aeschylus, without the tragic accent, in Solon. In the thought of the moralist, *hybris* is denounced so that it may be avoided and because it is avoidable; that is why it is not tragic. In sketching the genesis of misfortune from good fortune. Solon was performing an essentially profane and didactic task: good fortune begets a desire for more (πλεονεξία), this begets immoderation (ὕβρις), and this begets misfortune. This malignancy of good fortune, which is turned into misfortune by greed and pride, does not become tragic until it is brought into conjunction with the mystery of iniquity of the wicked god. In return, the immoderation introduces a human movement, a contrast, a tension into the heart of the mystery. "Man's share" must at least begin to be discerned if the ethical moment in evil is to appear; there must be at least an indication of a dawn of responsibility, of avoidable fault, and guilt must begin to be distinguished from finiteness. But this distinction tends to be muted, annulled by predestination; the indistinctness of divine and human guilt is an incipient and annulled distinction.

Henceforth, then, the wrath of the gods is faced by the wrath of man.

The figure of Prometheus completes and crowns the series of heroic figures on whom transcendent misfortune is poured. Within the *Prometheus Bound* he stands at the summit of a hierarchy of free men. At the bottom—lower than freedom, lower than the tragic—are the figures of Bia and Kratos, simple executors of fate; then Ocean and the importunate friends, speaking the language of the friends of Job and of explanatory theodicy: "Know yourself, adapt yourself to the facts, and learn new ways"; then Io, the

young woman transformed into a cow, the victim of divine lewdness, who presents the passive and suffering side of the tragic. Io is
the image of man suffering under the wicked god; but Io is not
yet completely tragic, because she only suffers; she is tragic only
in conjunction with Prometheus; only Prometheus confers the
tragic dimension upon the passion of Io, mute and crushed obla-
tion; action is joined to pure suffering—the supreme action of
a will that says No.

We must imagine the power of the scene and its violent contrasts.[12] He, the Titan, riveted to a rock above the empty *orchestra;*
she in a frenzy, leaping into the great, level space, stung by the
gadfly; he nailed, she wandering; he virile and lucid, she a woman
broken and alienated; he active in his passion, she pure passion,
a simple witness to the divine *hybris.*

And Prometheus himself is a figure with a twofold significance.
On the one hand, he heightens by his innocence—that innocence
which is complete in Io—the guiltiness of being. Prometheus is
the benefactor of mankind; he is the humanity of man; he suffers
because he has loved the human race too much. Even if his autonomy is also his fault, it expresses first his generosity; for the fire
that he has given to men is the fire of the hearth, the fire of the
household cult that would be relighted each year from the fire of
the community cult, the fire of the arts and crafts, and finally the
fire of reason, of culture, and of the heart. In that fire is summed
up what it is to be a man, breaking with the immobility of nature
and the dreary repetition of animal life and extending his empire
over things, beasts, and human relations. It is to be noted, in this
connection, that the myth attained its maturity at the moment
when Aeschylus, taking it over from Hesiod, elevated the figure of
Prometheus above the roguery of "coarse rustic mischievousness"[13]

[12] Wilamowitz-Moellendorf, *Aischylos Interpretationen,* pp. 114–62, on
Prometheus. Maurice Croiset, *Eschyle; Études sur l'invention dramatique
dans son théâtre* (Paris, 1928) is also very useful for understanding the
bond between the tragic and spectacle.

[13] Louis Séchan, *Le mythe de Prométhée* (Paris, 1951). This book is
very valuable for placing the myth in the tradition of the cult of fire and
the renewal of fire, for putting the theme of Prometheus' fault into the
context of the theomachies, and, finally, for discerning the double equivoca-

to the tragic grandeur of a suffering savior. It is Prometheus the
lover of mankind who is tragic, for his love is the cause of his
misfortune and theirs.

But, on the other hand, there is not only the innocent passion
of man, prey to a malign genius; there is also the wrath of man,
rising up against the wrath of god. True, Prometheus is powerless;
crucified on his rock, he does nothing; but he has the power of the
word and the hardness of a will that withholds consent. There is
no doubt that in the eyes of the pious Aeschylus the freedom of
Prometheus is an impure freedom and, as it were, the lowest degree
of freedom. Neither Prometheus nor Zeus, according to him, is
absolutely free. The freedom of Prometheus is a freedom of *defiance*
and not of *participation*. Aeschylus has expressed this maleficence
of Prometheus' freedom in the theme of the "secret." Prometheus
has a formidable weapon against Zeus: he knows what union of
the king of the gods with a mortal would result in the birth of
the son who would dethrone him; he possesses the secret of the fall
of Zeus, the secret of the Twilight of the Gods; he has the means
for *annihilating* being. A destructive freedom like this is not, for
Aeschylus, the last word of freedom; it is only its first word. And
so the final defiance of Prometheus, as we know, provokes a thun-
derous reply; Prometheus tumbles with his rock into the gaping
abyss. For Aeschylus, this disaster is part of a hard schooling, which
the choruses of the *Agamemnon* summarized in the πάθει μάθος.
The end of the trilogy, unfortunately lost, described, we know, the
final reconciliation: when Zeus acceded to true justice, Prometheus,
unbound, gave his consent to the luminous, Olympian side of the
divinity.

There is, then, guilt on the part of Prometheus, guilt which is
overshadowed by that of Zeus in consequence of the torment to
which he is subjected by him and which in turn overshadows that
of Zeus in consequence of the secret with which he threatens him.
It seems to me that it was this guilt that Aeschylus wished to ex-

---

tion in Prometheus, guilty benefactor, and Zeus, god of wrath on the way
toward a religion of justice and wisdom.

press by the Titanic nature of Prometheus.[14] Freedom has its roots in the chaotic depths of being; it is a moment in the Titanomachy. Prometheus calls unceasingly upon Gaia, symbol and epitome of the chthonic powers; from the beginning he summons ether, winds, springs, earth, and sun to bear witness; his defiance is in keeping with the gigantic character of mountains and waves. In his freedom, elementary wrath looms up. And that elementary wrath, which is expressed in his defiance, does not differ fundamentally from the dark power which animates Clytemnestra, in whom the dreadful powers of a maternal bosom, of the earth, and of the dead are united. Neither does it differ essentially from the ethical terror represented by the Erinyes, which shuts man up in the cycle of vengeance. All that is chaos, and so is freedom in its first appearance.

Thus Prometheus bound bears witness not so much to the paradox as to the deep-seated complicity of the wrath of God and the wrath of man, of the wicked god and Titanic freedom. Both taste the bitterness of the "grapes of wrath."

It seems to me, then, that this *hybris* of innocence, if I may call it so, this violence that makes Prometheus a guilty victim, throws light retrospectively on the original theme of the myth, the theme of the theft of fire. The drama, it is true, begins afterward; it falls within the period of punishment (just as the incest and the murder are anterior to the tragedy of Oedipus, which is a tragedy of discovery and recognition, a tragedy of truth). The tragedy of Prometheus begins with the unjust suffering. Nevertheless, by a retrograde motion, it makes contact with the original germ of the drama: the theft was a benefaction, but the benefaction was a theft. Prometheus was initially a guilty innocent.

Is the tragic theology thinkable? The tragic drama does not work it out reflectively; it exhibits it by means of the characters in a spectacle, in the vestments of poetry, and through the specific emotions of terror and pity. Nevertheless, the wisdom-literature, half-way between dramatic performance and reflective wisdom, did

[14] G. Nebel, *op. cit.*, pp. 49–88.

succeed in stating the tragic theology sententiously: "When the wrath of the daemons attacks a man," says Lycurgus, "it begins by taking away his understanding and inclining him to the worse judgment, so that he is not aware of his own errors."[15] The tragic choruses chant similar maxims.[16] Perhaps this is the only theology that cannot be avowed or, at any rate, defended. Plato's indignation at the tragic theme, when it is worked out and stated clearly, might make us think so. Let us hear him.

"God, since he is good, is not the cause of everything, as is commonly said; he is the cause of only a part of the things that happen to men and has no responsibility for the greater part of them, for the bad far outweighs the good in our lives." And so "we will not allow the young to hear the words of Aeschylus: 'God implants crime in men when he wishes to ruin their house completely'" (*Rep.* 379c–380a).[17]

If, then, the religious consciousness hesitates to *formulate* the tragic theology, that is because elsewhere it professes "the innocence of God," to speak in Platonic language, or his "holiness," in Biblical language. Explicit formulation of the tragic theology would mean self-destruction for the religious consciousness.

[15] *In Leocratem,* 92, cited by E. R. Dodds, *op. cit.,* p. 39. Here already is the *quem deus vult perdere, prius dementat.*

[16] Lyrical expressions of this tragic theology are numerous: *Persians,* 354, 472, 808, 821; *Agamemnon,* 160 ff., 1486, 1563 ff.; etc. Nowhere was it expressed more openly than in the chorus of the *Antigone* with which Dodds ends his study of "guilt-culture": "Happy are they whose life has not tasted the fruits of evil. When the gods shake a house, misfortune pursues the multitude of its descendants without respite. . . . Forever, as in the past, this law will prevail: in the life of mortals, excessive prosperity never comes without misfortune (ἐκτὸς ἄτας). Inconstant hope is a good for many men; but for many, also, it is only a deception practiced by their credulous desires; destruction creeps upon a man who knows nothing of it until he burns his feet in the flame. With wisdom was the well-known saying first uttered by someone: the evil seems to be a good to him whose mind the divinity is leading to destruction (ὅτῳ φρένας θεὸς ἄγει πρὸς ἄταν); only for a little time is he sheltered from destruction (ἐκτὸς ἄτας)" (*Antigone,* 582–625).

[17] E. R. Dodds remarks (*op. cit.,* p. 57) that Plato omits to quote the end of this fragment (162) of the *Niobe* concerning ὕβρις, which supposes some contribution by a man to his own fate (μὴ θρασυστομεῖν: that "arrogance" is ours).

3. Deliverance from the Tragic or Deliverance within the Tragic?

In the creation-drama, evil was, so to speak, the reverse, the other, of the act of creation. Salvation, then, was creation itself, as the establishment of the present world-order; it was re-enacted in the battles of the king and in every conflict where the eye of faith could make out, behind the face of the enemy, the ancient Adversary vanquished at the beginning by the deeds of the gods.

What can the end of evil be like in the tragic vision?

It seems to me that the tragic vision, when it remains true to its "type," excludes any other deliverance than "sympathy," than tragic "pity"—that is to say, an impotent emotion of participation in the misfortunes of the hero, a sort of weeping with him and purifying the tears by the beauty of song.

It is true that Aeschylean tragedy seems to propose a different outcome, as we see in the trilogy of Orestes: the *Eumenides* gives a new answer to the question raised in the last verse of the *Choephori:* "Where, then, will the wrath of Até stop, where will it finally stop and be stilled?"; and the last part of the trilogy answers: Terror has an end, the chain of vengeance can be broken, God is just, God is merciful; his Justice is expressed in the purification by Apollo, which brings divine Vengeance to an end, and his benevolence is manifested in the severe but measured law of the city, which takes upon itself retribution for criminal faults. Likewise, a *Prometheus Delivered* terminated the trilogy of the Titan. This piece is lost, but we know enough about its action to say that time—the long space of thirty thousand years which separated this drama from the preceding one—had "worn out the wrath" of the celestial tyrant and the suffering Titan. "Worn out the wrath"—it is the same expression that Sophocles uses in *Oedipus at Colonus* in speaking of the effect of the meditation that leads from bitter grief to calm acquiescence; the passage of time in the Greek tragedies suggests the thought of a redemption by time, which wears out the claws and teeth of the wrath of gods and men. It is within this common cosmic space of time that Zeus the tyrant *becomes* Zeus the father of Justice.

Thus the coming-to-be of the divine appears as the analogue of the "repentance" of God in the Hebrew Bible. Is it not a sort of repentance of being that the *Eumenides* and the *Prometheus Delivered* portend?

There is no doubt that, for Aeschylus at least, tragedy is both a representation of the tragic and an impulse toward the end of the tragic.

That is true, but only up to a certain point. It is striking that, even in Aeschylus, who went furthest in this direction (and the trilogic structure of his tragedy well expresses the movement of tragedy toward the end of the tragic), that end of the tragic is not a real deliverance for the hero; at the end of the *Eumenides* Orestes is volatilized, so to speak, in the great debate that takes place over his head among Athena, Apollo, and the Erinyes. That end of the tragic was glimpsed by the poet only at the price of the destruction of the tragic theology itself: it was not true, in the end, that Zeus was wicked. Now, how is this destruction of tragic theology possible? By a transition to the other etiological "type," by a transition to the drama of creation; holiness wins out over the primordial badness, as Marduk vanquished Tiamat. It is this theogonic schema that subtends the conversion of Zeus in the trilogy of *Prometheus* and the conversion of Erinyes to Eumenides in the *Oresteia*. Thus it is the "epic" that saves "tragedy" by delivering it from the "tragic"; the "wicked god" is reabsorbed in the suffering of the divine, which must attain its Olympian pole at the expense of its Titanic pole.

But in Sophocles there is no longer an end of the tragic, and in this sense Sophocles is more purely tragic than Aeschylus.[18] The hostile god makes himself felt less by pressure than by his absence, abandoning man to his own resources. This doubly tragic view bars the way to the solutions sketched by Aeschylus. Thus the tragedy of Antigone, which is a tragedy of insoluble contradiction,

---

[18] Nebel, *op. cit.*, pp. 169–231: "Antigone and the savage world of the dead," "King Oedipus and the god of wrath"; Werner Jaeger, *Paideia*, I, 343–63.

begins precisely at the point where Aeschylus, in the *Eumenides*, saw a way out of the tragic; the city is no longer the place of reconciliation; it is the closed city which drives Antigone into defiance and the invocation of laws incompatible with the historic existence of the city.

There is one exception, it is true, but one that confirms our interpretation indirectly. Sophocles too, in *Oedipus at Colonus*, hailed the end of the tragic;[19] the old Oedipus, after a long meditation on his misfortunes, is led by Sophocles to the threshold of a non-tragic death; he is removed from the sight of the profane, after having been accompanied by Theseus, the royal sacrificer, to the boundaries of the sacred territory of the city. Weinstock justly compared this sacred drama to a "legend of the saints"; but the death of the aged Oedipus, the glorious death of a hero grown wiser, is a suspension of the human condition rather than its cure.

In truth, salvation, in the tragic vision, is not outside the tragic but within it. This is the meaning of the tragic φρονεῖν, of that "suffering for the sake of understanding" which is celebrated by the chorus in Aeschylus' *Agamemnon*: "Zeus, whatever be his true name, if that name please him, upon him I call. I have pondered all; I recognize only Zeus as he who can relieve me of the burden of my sterile anguish. . . . He has opened up to men the ways of prudence, giving them the law of *suffering for the sake of understanding*. When in sleep, in the sight of the heart, painful remorse descends, wisdom enters into them in spite of themselves. And that, I think, is the benevolent violence of the gods, seated at the bar of heaven" (*Ag.*, 160 ff.). "Suffering for the sake of understanding" —that is tragic wisdom, that is "tragic knowledge," to speak like Karl Jaspers.[20]

I do not believe that Greek religion in its highest expressions, beyond the cults, ever offered a genuine end for the tragic; it always proceeds by substituting some other religious schema and not by resolving the internal tensions that issue from the tragic schema itself. Whether it becomes a religion of "divine possession" —that is to say, penetration of the divine into the human,—or a

---

[19] Nebel, *op. cit.*, pp. 233–53: "Blessed death in the *Oedipus at Colonus*."
[20] Karl Jaspers, *Von der Wahrheit*, pp. 915–60. Cf. below, Chap. V.

religion of "divine ecstasy"—that is to say, escape from the human into the divine,—religion in its Apollonian or Dionysiac form is not a resolution of the tragic. The authority of the Delphic oracle does indeed reassure, guide, and in this sense pacify; Apollo was the great pacifier insofar as he was, through the intermediary of the oracle, the great counselor, the guarantor of the legislative activity of the great founders of laws; but Apollo is also the great master of ritual purifications, which means that his counsel, although it gives some security to the human word, does not heal the "tragic" soul, since recourse to the old purifications is necessary after all. Apollo, the counselor, could not forgive sins but only wash away the stains of defilement, because the tragic vision of the world excludes forgiveness of sins.[21]

Dionysos seeks even less to make the wounded soul whole again; he provides an outlet for the anguish due to faults by drawing the soul out of itself and out of its solitude. Thus his ecstasy relieves man of the weight of his responsibility by changing him into someone else. Dionysos does not confirm man in the truth of his finiteness; he offers him an exaltation, a sort of sacred immoderation, by which he escapes from himself rather than becoming reconciled with himself.[22]

---

[21] On this role of Apollo in expiation, see Nilsson, *A History of Greek Religion* (Oxford, 1925), Chap. VI: Apollo remains the master of sacred expiation in the case of blood-guilt, even when the state has already taken upon itself the office of meting out punishment. Nilsson, while emphasizing the role of the Apollonian cult in favor of moral purity and rectitude of intention, confirms the inability of Apollonism to go beyond external ritualism and reach the level of the requirements of justice: "He was the authority who restored and maintained peace with the gods. His task was not to arouse consciences, as the prophets did, but to calm them" (pp. 199–200); hence its cautious reformism, its moderate actions with respect to Dionysianism; but it created no new values.

[22] Nilsson, *ibid.,* pp. 205–206. We shall return to this point in Chap. IV. Everything that one says about Greek religion must always be tempered by the following consideration: there was never one Greek theology, but an overlapping not only of cults properly so called, but also of diverse religious syntheses attempted by reformers, poets, and religious propagandists, none of which ever succeeded in bringing the others into a single system. There is the authority of Delphi and there is the "telestic madness" of Dionysos; the latter invades the domain of the former; but Apollo restrains Dionysos and embraces him by legislating for his cult and moderating his ecstasy.

There remains the tragic *spectacle* itself, to purify whoever yields himself to the sublimity of the poetic word. It is neither counsel in the Apollonian sense, nor an alteration of personality in the Dionysiac sense, except, perhaps, in a very remote sense—for example, in the sense that the spectacle fosters "illusion." Through the spectacle the ordinary man enters into the "chorus" which weeps and sings with the hero; the place of tragic reconciliation is the "chorus" and its lyricism. By entering into the tragic "chorus" ourselves, we pass from the Dionysiac illusion to the specific ecstasy of tragic wisdom. Then the myth is among us; it is we who are frightened and lament, because we have put ourselves into the scene. One must become a member of the chorus in order to yield himself to the feelings which are specifically those of the tragic reconciliation. The ordinary man knows only fear and the sort of bashful sympathy that the spectacle of misfortune calls forth; in becoming a member of the chorus, he enters a sphere of feelings that may be called symbolic and mythic, in consideration of the type of utterance to which they are proportionate. These feelings, as we have known since Aristotle, are, first, tragic φόβος, the specific sort of fear which comes over us when we are suddenly faced with the conjunction of freedom and empirical ruin; and then tragic ἔλεος, that merciful gaze which no longer accuses or condemns but shows pity. Terror and Pity are both modalities of suffering, but of a suffering that may be called suffering in the face of destiny, since it needs the retardation and the acceleration of a hostile fate and the agency of a heroic freedom. That is why those feelings come to birth only in the aura of a tragic myth. But they are also a modality of understanding: the hero becomes a seer; when he loses his sight, Oedipus attains to the vision of Tiresias. But he does not know that which he understands in any objective and systematic way. Hesiod said long ago: παθὼν δέ τε νήπιος ἔγνω—suffering makes wise the simple (*Works*, 218).

Such is the deliverance which is not outside the tragic, but within it: an aesthetic transposition of fear and pity by virtue of a tragic myth turned into poetry and by the grace of an ecstasy born of a spectacle.

III. The "Adamic" Myth and the "Eschatological" Vision of History

THE "ADAMIC" MYTH is the anthropological myth *par excellence;* Adam means Man. But not every myth of "the primordial man" is an "Adamic" myth. Each of the other types of myth includes some reference to man: thus the figure of the King, in the theogonic myth, gives substance to a certain sort of history and to a certain sort of political reality; but the origin of evil is not attributed to man in any peculiar sense in that myth. Likewise, the figure of the Titan, which fluctuates among the various types of myth, is very close to changing into the figure of the primordial man; but the Orphic "anthropogony," which annexed the myth of the Titans to itself—at a late date, no doubt,—does not constitute an anthropogonic myth of evil: the being of man is itself the result of a drama anterior to man; the evil is that there are human beings; the genesis of evil coincides with anthropogony. Many other representations of the primordial man will be found at the gnostic level of speculation; but those speculations differ fundamentally from the Adamic theme because in them the genesis of the present condition of man is regularly considered as identical with the evil process displayed in the "eons" anterior to the present condition of man.

Only the "Adamic" myth is strictly anthropological. This means that it has three characteristics. In the first place, the etiological myth relates the origin of evil to an *ancestor* of the human race as it is now whose condition is homogeneous with ours. All the speculations on the supernatural perfection of Adam before the fall are adventitious contrivances which profoundly alter the original naïve, brute meaning; they tend to make Adam superior and hence a stranger to our condition, and at the same time they reduce the Adamic myth to a genesis of man from a primordial superhumanity. There is no doubt that the very word "fall," which is foreign to the Biblical vocabulary, is contemporaneous with the elevation of the "Adamic" condition above the present human condition; only what has first been elevated falls. The symbol of the fall, then, is not the authentic symbol of the "Adamic" myth; moreover, it is found in Plato, in gnosis, in Plotinus. That is why we have not called this chapter "The Myth of the Fall," but "The Adamic Myth." When we have traced the roots of the symbolism of the Adamic myth back to the more fundamental symbolism of sin, we shall see that the Adamic myth is a myth of "deviation," or "going astray," rather than a myth of the "fall."

Second characteristic: the etiological myth of Adam is the most extreme attempt to separate the origin of evil from the origin of the good; its intention is to set up a *radical* origin of evil distinct from the more *primordial* origin of the goodness of things. Whatever the strictly philosophical difficulties of this attempt may be, the distinction between radical and primordial is essential to the anthropological character of the Adamic myth; it is that which makes man a *beginning* of evil in the bosom of a creation which has already had its absolute *beginning* in the creative act of God. At the time when the Adamic myth was composed, the concept of freedom had not yet been elaborated as a support for this, so to speak, second beginning, although the Deuteronomic idea of a radical choice imposed by the prophetic summons portends the evolution of the Adamic myth toward a speculation of a higher degree, in which freedom will be not only a sort of beginning, but the power of the creature to defect—that is to say, in the strict sense, the power of the human creature to undo (*défaire*), and to unmake

himself (*se défaire*), after he has been made (*fait*) and made perfect (*par-fait*). On the level of the myth, to which we confine ourselves here, this power of defection which belongs to freedom is
still only implicit in the structure of the *story;* it is represented by
a happening that looms up, one does not know where from, and
that distinguishes a before from an after. In the terminology of the
fall, about which we have expressed reservations above, there is a
supralapsarian state of innocence and an infralapsarian state of
peccability. (Let us note, in passing, that fallibility and peccability
are not identical. "Fallibility," in the sense given to it in Book I,
denotes the human structure capable of departing from the right
way out of malignancy, while "peccability" describes the condition
of mankind when they are already inclined to evil. That is why we
speak of peccability here in the sense of a *habitus* of the species;
we shall discuss it at length in Book III.) The passage from innocence to sin as the status of a man destined for good and inclined
to evil is *narrated* by the Adamic myth as something that happened.
But because the origin of evil is narrated as a story about something
that happened, and because that story is connected with a legendary character, Adam, we are not yet in the presence of speculation,
but only of an etiological myth. No doubt the myth is ready to be
taken over by speculation, but it is still immersed in mythical space
and time; and so it must be understood as a myth, half-way between the primordial symbols and the speculative symbols created
by gnosis, or against gnosis.

Finally—third characteristic—the Adamic myth subordinates to
the central figure of the primordial man some other figures which
tend to decentralize the story, but without suppressing the primacy
of the Adamic figure. It is noteworthy, in fact, that the Adamic
myth does not succeed in concentrating and absorbing the origin
of evil in the figure of a primordial man alone; it speaks also of
the adversary, the Serpent, who will become the devil, and of another personage, Eve, who represents the vis-à-vis of that Other,
Serpent or Devil. Thus the Adamic myth raises up one or more
counterpoles to the central figure of the primordial Man, and from
those counterpoles it gets an enigmatic depth by which it communicates subterraneously with the other myths of evil and makes

possible what we shall call further on a system of the myths of evil. But, however far it may be possible to go in the direction of this multiplication of the centers of proliferation of evil, the central intention of the myth is to order all the *other* figures in relation to the figure of Adam, and to understand them in conjunction with him and as peripheral figures in the story which has Adam as its principal protagonist.

1. THE PENITENTIAL MOTIVATION OF THE "ADAMIC" MYTH

What does it mean to "understand" the Adamic myth?

In the first place, it means accepting the fact that it is a myth. We shall say further on how Jewish thought could work out this chronicle of a first human pair; but it must be well understood *from the outset* that, for the modern man who has learned the distinction between myth and history, this chronicle of the first man and the first pair can no longer be co-ordinated with the time of history and the space of geography as these have been irreversibly constituted by critical awareness. It must be well understood that the question, Where and when did Adam eat the forbidden fruit?, no longer has meaning for us; every effort to save the letter of the story as a true history is vain and hopeless. What we know, as men of science, about the beginnings of mankind leaves no place for such a primordial event.[1] I am convinced that the full accept-

---

[1] A clear attitude is preferable to the attitude of authors like A. M. Dubarle (*op. cit.*, pp. 45–60) who try to evade the choice between history and myth and to find in this story "a history of a special type, which employs traditional imagery as a means of expression while profoundly transforming its import" (p. 49). It is true that Israel, whose religion is founded on an historical event, the exodus from Egypt, could not appeal to some non-temporal "archetype" for an explanation of evil, but only to events supposed to be the source of the present; but to say that Israel rediscovered past events by faith is inevitably to come back to the idea that Adam was a real person and that the fall was an event that really took place. We must keep the idea of *event* as a symbol of the break between two ontological regimes and abandon the idea of *past fact.* In particular, we must recognize the mythical character of the figure of the ancestor of the human race, supposed to be for all mankind what the eponymous ancestor is for Moab, Edom, etc. It is in this schematization that there arises the idea of a sin supposed to be *first* and *inherited,* as well as the false rationalizations to which it gave rise.

ance of the non-historical character of the myth—non-historical if
we take history in the sense it has for the critical method—is the
other side of a great discovery: the discovery of the *symbolic*
function of the myth. But then we should not say, "The story of
the 'fall' is *only* a myth"—that is to say, something less than history—but, "The story of the fall has the greatness of myth"—that
is to say, has more meaning than a true history. But what meaning?

We have suggested repeatedly that the meaning resides in the
power of the myth to evoke *speculation* on the power of defection
that freedom has. Hence, that meaning is to be sought in the relation of the pre-philosophical to the philosophical, according to the

---

An echo of the discussions that shook Catholic exegesis at the beginning
of the century can be found in Y. Laurent, "Le caractère historique de
Genèse, 2–3, dans l'exégèse française au tournant du XIXe siècle," in
Analecta Lovaniensia Biblica et Orientalia, 1947, pp. 37–69; justice is
rendered to the works of F. Lenormant (1880–84); and the eclectic attempt
of Father M. J. Lagrange, in his famous article in the *Revue biblique*
(1897), "L'innocence et le péché," is well characterized. When we reread
that notable article today, we are struck at the same time by its boldness
in detail and its timidity as a whole. Father Lagrange rejects both literalism
and the interpretation which he calls allegorical, and regards the story of
the fall as "a true history told in a popular or symbolic way" (p. 358): "It
has always been understood in the Church that this very true history was
not a history like others, but a history clothed in figures—metaphors,
symbols—or popular language" (p. 361); hence the attempt to separate the
"substantial elements" and the "symbolic forms" (p. 361). Like Origen and
Cajetan, he extends the role of symbolism very far. But it is hard to see
how the story as a whole could have a bearing on real history when all the
circumstances, taken one by one, are interpreted symbolically (pp. 343–
58). Perhaps Father Lagrange has too narrow an idea of the symbol, which
he seems not to distinguish from allegory; thus, faced with the alternative,
allegory or history, he chooses history, while distinguishing the form and
the content of the story. Nevertheless, it is true that Father Lagrange did
see, long before we were acquainted with the whole Babylonian background
of the creation-stories, that what is significant is not what is corroborated
by historical parallels, but what is without parallel. Thus he broke decisively
with the sort of apologetic exegesis which relied on such parallels to prove
a so-called oral tradition descending from Adam to our first written sources.
Moreover, Father Lagrange perceived that the genius of the sacred writer
consisted very often in transforming into symbols something that had been
literal belief in the popular imagination. That insight goes very far, but it
is not carried out to its ultimate consequences. Still, Father Lagrange does
write: "Symbolic language does not have the same laws as familiar language
and should not be interpreted by the same method" (p. 354).

maxim which has been and will be our guiding star throughout this book: "The symbol gives rise to thought." But this heuristic, exploratory power of the myth turned in the direction of the speculation that follows it cannot be disengaged from the etiological function of the myth unless we first treat the myth as a rehandling of the fundamental symbols elaborated in the living experience of defilement, sin, and guilt. The myth anticipates speculation only because it is already an interpretation, a hermeneutics of the primordial symbols in which the prior consciousness of sin gave itself form. That it gives rise, in its turn, to thought is a consequence of the fact that it itself interprets other symbols. It is thus that we shall seek to understand it in this chapter, reserving for a later investigation the second-degree rehandling of it in the more intellectualized symbols of "original sin." So we shall distinguish three levels: first that of the primorial symbols of sin, then that of the Adamic myth, and finally the speculative cipher of original sin; and we shall understand the second as first-degree hermeneutics, the third as second-degree hermeneutics.

This way of understanding is supported by the historical experience of the Jewish people. So far is the Adamic myth from being the point of departure for their experience of sin and guilt that it presupposes that experience and marks its maturity. That is why it was possible to understand the experience and to interpret its fundamental symbols—deviation, revolt, going astray, perdition, captivity—without recourse to that myth. Our problem will be to understand what the "Adamic" myth adds to those first symbols. In every way the addition is belated and, in certain respects, nonessential, as the history of Hebrew literature superabundantly proves. Adam is not an important figure in the Old Testament: the Prophets ignore him; various texts do, indeed, name Adam (subject of a verb in the plural) and the sons of Adam, but without allusion to the story of the fall; Abraham, the father of believers, and Noah, the father of mankind as recreated after the flood, are more important figures; and even for the editor of the account in Genesis it is not certain that Adam bears the entire responsibility for the evil in the world;[2] he is perhaps only the first example of evil. In

[2] Ben Sirach, author of Ecclesiasticus, and Wisdom allude to the account

any case the story of Adam should not be separated from the ensemble of the first eleven chapters which, through the legends of Abel and Cain, of Babel, of Noah, the supreme threat—the Flood, —and the supreme promise—the regeneration beyond the waters, —lead to the election of Abraham, father of believers.

In the New Testament Jesus himself never refers to the Adamic story; he takes the existence of evil for a fact, as the situation which is presupposed by the call to repentance: "If you do not repent, you shall all alike perish." In the Synoptic Gospels, equal emphasis is laid on the evil "heart" (Mark 7:21–22; Matt. 7:11; 12:33–34) and on "the Adversary": to the disciples asking who sowed the tares among the good seed, Jesus answers: "An Enemy has done this." The Lord's Prayer emphasizes temptation and the oppressive power of the Evil One: "Lead us not into temptation, but deliver us from the Evil One." In sickness, as in temptation, man is attacked by "the unclean spirit." The Passion itself is under the influence of the Evil One: "Simon, Simon, behold, Satan has desired to have you, that he may sift you as wheat" (Luke 22:31). Was not Christ himself delivered up to the assaults of the Demon? There is nothing, then, in all this, which points toward an "Adamic" interpretation of the beginning of evil. It was St. Paul who roused the Adamic theme from its lethargy; by means of the *contrast* between the "old man" and the "new man," he set up the figure of Adam as the inverse of that of Christ, called the second Adam (I Cor. 15:21–22, 45–49; Rom. 5:12–21). At the same time, the figure of Adam was not only raised higher in comparison with all the other figures of the first eleven chapters of Genesis, but was personalized on the model of the figure of Christ, to which it serves as contrast. From this, two conclusions must be drawn: that it was Christology that consolidated Adamology, and that the demythologization of the Adamic figure, as an individualized personage from whom all mankind would be descended physically, does not imply any conclusion concerning the figure of Christ, which was not constructed with reference to the figure of

in Genesis (Sir. 25:24; Wisd. 2:23–24; 10:1–2), but do not relate the fall of man or all the evils of the human condition to a first sin.

Adam but which, on the contrary, gave individuality to the latter by retroaction.

Hence, it is false that the "Adamic" myth is the keystone of the Judeo-Christian edifice; it is only a flying buttress, articulated upon the ogival crossing of the Jewish penitential spirit. With even more reason, original sin, being a rationalization of the second degree, is only a false column. The harm that has been done to souls, during the centuries of Christianity, first by the literal interpretation of the story of Adam, and then by the confusion of this myth, treated as history, with later speculations, principally Augustinian, about original sin, will never be adequately told. In asking the faithful to confess belief in this mythico-speculative mass and to accept it as a self-sufficient explanation, the theologians have unduly required a *sacrificium intellectus* where what was needed was to awaken believers to a symbolic superintelligence of their actual condition.

Not that the myth is a vain repetition of the penitential experience of the Jews; we have insisted too much on the triple function of the myth—as universalization of experience, as establishment of a tension between a beginning and an end, and as investigation of the relations between the primordial and the historical—to scorn the contribution of the myth. But this contribution cannot be understood except by starting from the impulsion that the myth receives from the experience which precedes it and from the symbols in which that experience took shape.

The living experience of the Jewish confession doubly prepares the way for the emergence of the myth: negatively and positively.

On the one hand, it entails the dissolution of the theological presuppositions of two other myths, the theogonic and the tragic; nowhere else has criticism of the fundamental representations on which the myths of chaos and of the wicked god are built been pushed as far as in Israel. Hebrew monotheism and, more particularly, the ethical character of that monotheism undermined theogony and the tragic god, who is still theogonic, and made them impossible. Conflicts and crimes, trickery and adultery are expelled from the sphere of the divine: animal-headed gods, demigods, titans, giants, and heroes are ruthlessly excluded from the field of religious consciousness. Creation is no longer conflict but "word": God says, and it is so. The "jealousy" of Yahweh is no longer that of the tragic god offended by heroic greatness; it is the "jealousy" of holiness with regard to "idols"; it is the monotheistic "jealousy" which reveals the vanity, the nothingness of false gods.[3] Isaiah's vision in the Temple (Is. 6) bears witness both to the new discovery of the Holy God and to the waning of the theogonic and tragic god. The purely anthropological conception of the origin of evil is the counterpart of this general "demythologization" of theogony: *because* "Yahweh reigns by his Word," *because* "God is Holy," evil must enter into the world by a sort of catastrophe in the created, a catastrophe that the new myth will endeavor to gather up into one event and one story in which original badness is dissociated from primordial goodness. This motivation is not without analogy to that of Plàto in Book II of the *Republic:* because God is the Good, he is innocent. But whereas Plato concludes: God, then, is not the cause of everything, nor even of the greater part of existing things, the Jewish thinker continues: God is the cause of everything that is good and man is the cause of everything that is vain.

Now, at the same time as the ethical monotheism of the Jews was destroying the basis of all the other myths, it was working out the positive motifs of a strictly "anthropological" myth of the origin of evil.

The "Adamic" myth is the fruit of the prophetic accusation directed against man; the same theology that makes God innocent accuses man. Now that accusation, more and more integrated and assimilated into the consciousness of the Jew, developed into a spirit of repentance, the depth of which we have seen in our study of sin and guilt. The Jew repents not only for his actions, but for

[3] Nevertheless, one might discover in the Bible certain traces of a "tragic" conception of life and certain recessive forms of the "jealousy" of the tragic god; the destruction of Babel, the condemnation of Cain, and even the expulsion of Adam and Eve from the garden of Eden contain, perhaps, an element of clerical resentment against the heroic greatness of the man of action. But we shall attach more importance to the more secret affinities of the Adamic myth with the two other myths; we shall not seek them in resentment against greatness, but in the role of the Serpent and in the structure of the drama of the fall.

the root of his actions. I do not venture to say "for his *being*"—first, because he never formed that ontological concept, and, second, because the purpose of the myth of the fall is to dissociate the historical starting point of evil from the starting point, which we moderns can call ontological, of creation. At least his repentance penetrates to the "heart" of man, to his purpose—that is to say, to the monadic source of his many actions. Furthermore, at the same time as his piety discovers the personal dimension of sin, it also discovers its communal dimension; the evil "heart" of *each* is also the evil "heart" of *all;* a specific *we,* namely, "we sinners," unifies all mankind in an undivided guilt. Thus the spirit of repentance discovered something beyond our acts, an evil root that is both individual and collective, such as a choice that each would make for all and all for each.

It was because the confession of sins involved this virtual universalization that the Adamic myth was possible: the myth, in naming Adam, man, makes explicit the concrete universality of human evil; the spirit of repentance gives to itself, in the Adamic myth, the symbol of that universality.

Thus we find again what we have called the universalizing function of myth. But at the same time we find the other two functions, likewise evoked by the experience of repentance. We know that the theology of history, around which the fundamental representations of guilt and salvation in the Old Testament revolve, alternates between extreme threats and extreme promises: "Woe unto them that desire the Day of Yahweh! What do you look for from the Day of Yahweh? It will be darkness and not light" (Amos 5:18). And then: "Behold, the days come, saith Yahweh, when I will make a new covenant with the house of Israel, and with the house of Judah. . . . I will put my law in their inward parts, and write it in their hearts; and I will be their God, and they shall be my people" (Jer. 31:31–34). This dialectic of judgment and mercy is read into contemporary history, into the actual history of the Exile and the Return, by the Jewish Prophet; and in interpreting history he makes it significant at the same time that he really bends it to his purposes. The same dialectic of judgment and mercy, beginning from an interpretation of the actual history of the prophetic

epoch, is projected into a mythical representation of the "beginning" and the "end." Already the exodus from Egypt, reinterpreted
in the light of the prophetic experience, had furnished, as we have
seen, the fundamental symbolism of captivity and deliverance; in
its turn the calling of Abraham, torn from the country of his birth
and set upon the paths of his vocation, is understood on the model
of the Prophet's obedience to an irresistible inner call; and finally,
the prologue to history in the garden of Eden contains in epitome
all that the dramatic destiny of Israel had revealed about the meaning of human existence: call, disobedience, exile; Adam and Eve
are driven from Paradise as Israel is banished from Canaan. But,
just as "a remnant will return," so the myth of the flood, intentionally welded to the myth of Paradise lost, symbolically shows
the new creation emerging from the disaster of the waters and
made pure by the judgment which both condemns and pardons.
Noah is still Adam, is still Man, by turns exiled and saved from
the waters—that is to say, recreated.

The proto-historical myth thus served not only to generalize the
experience of Israel, applying it to all mankind, at all times and
in all places, but also to extend to all mankind the great tension
between condemnation and mercy that the teaching of the Prophets
had revealed in the particular destiny of Israel.[4]

Finally, there is the last function of the myth as it was motivated
in the faith of Israel: the myth prepares the way for speculation
by exploring the point of rupture between the ontological and the
historical. The confession of sins drew nearer to this point of
rupture as it gained in depth, and it discovered it by means of a
paradox. It is the holiness of God that reveals the abyss of sin in
man; but, on the other hand, if the root of sin is in the "nature,"
in the "being" of man, then the sin revealed by the holiness of

---

[4] I subscribe whole-heartedly to the view of C. H. Dodd, *The Bible Today*
(Cambridge Univ. Press, 1946): "Thus the stories with which the Bible
begins may be regarded as adaptations of primitive myths by writers who
used them as symbols of truths learned in history. Nominally they refer to
pre-history. In fact, they apply the principles of divine action revealed in
the history of a particular people to mankind at all times and in all places.
They universalize the idea of the Word of God, which is both judgement
and renewal" (p. 115).

God returns upon Him and accuses the Creator of having made man evil. If I repent of my being, I accuse God in the same moment in which he accuses me, and the spirit of repentance explodes under the pressure of that paradox. Thus, the myth appears at a point of high tension in the penitential experience; its function is to posit a "beginning" of evil distinct from the "beginning" of creation, to posit an event by which sin entered into the world and, by sin, death. The myth of the fall is thus the myth of the first appearance of evil in a creation already completed and good. By thus dividing the Origin into an origin of the goodness of the created and an origin of the wickedness in history, the myth tends to satisfy the twofold confession of the Jewish believer, who acknowledges, on the one hand, the absolute perfection of God and, on the other hand, the radical wickedness of man. This twofold confession is the very essence of his repentance.

2. The Structure of the Myth: The "Instant" of the Fall

Let us try now to understand the structure of the myth by beginning with its *intention,* suggested by the primary experience of sin. The Adamic myth, as narrated by the "Yahwist" editor of Genesis III, obeys a twofold rhythm. On the one hand, it tends to concentrate all the evil of history in a single man, in a single act—in short, in a unique event. That is how St. Paul understood it: "As by one man sin entered into the world. . . ." By this extreme contraction of the origin of evil into one point the Biblical account emphasizes the irrationality of that cleavage, that deflection, that leap, which tradition, not without ambiguity, has called the fall.

On the other hand, the myth spreads out the event in a "drama," which takes time, introduces a succession of incidents, and brings several characters into the action. In being extended in time and scattered among several roles, the drama gets a turbid ambiguity which contrasts with the frank rupture of the evil event. Let us try to comprehend this dialectical play between the "event" of the fall and the "space of time" of the temptation.

"One" man, "one" act—that is the first schema of the myth,

which we have called the schema of the "event."

"One" man; the chronicler called the "Yahwist" in Biblical criticism found the idea for him in a myth which was no doubt very primitive and which may even have had a very different meaning —the myth of a first man or, rather, of a first pair driven out of a wonderful garden because they had disobeyed a taboo. The myth is very old, but its significance is new; and that significance comes to it from a retrograde motion in the understanding of history that starts from contemporary history as a nucleus. It would seem that the myth was seized upon in the course of meditation on the origins of the chosen people and annexed to that meditation through the intermediary of a folklore in which the different ethnic groups are represented by a single family, by a single ancestor. The time of the patriarchs, before Abraham, points in its turn to a still older time, in which all the eponymous ancestors of all the peoples spring from a single pair who would be to the whole of mankind what each patriarch is to the whole of his people—namely, the founding ancestor of a great family now broken up into many peoples with many languages. That chronicle of the first man furnishes the symbol of the concrete universal, the model of man exiled from the kingdom, the paradigm of the beginning of evil. In Adam we are one and all; the mythical figure of the first man provides a focal point at the beginning of history for man's unity-in-multiplicity.

The first man, in his turn, is summed up in one act: he took the fruit and ate of it. About that event there is nothing to say; one can only tell it; it happens and henceforth evil has arrived. About the instant, as a caesura, one can only say what it *ends* and what it *begins*. On the one hand, it brings to an end a time of innocence; on the other, it begins a time of malediction.

This reference of the instant of the fall to an innocent past, to a paradise which is spoken of only as lost, is secured by the insertion of the story of the fall into a story of creation.[5] In virtue of

[5] I take for granted the results of the textual criticism which, since Gunkel (*Genesis übersetzt und erklärt*, Göttingen, 1900; 5th ed., 1922) and Budde (*Die biblische Urgeschichte*, Giessen, 1883; *Die biblische Paradiesgeschichte*, in *Beih. Zeitsch. Altt. Wiss.*, 1932), distinguishes two sources underlying the present story of the fall and thus accounts for the

that preliminary myth the first sin appears as the loss of a prior mode of being, as the loss of innocence. The creation-story with which our story of the fall is integrated is not the admirable story with which our Bible opens, and which is articulated around the following verses: "God said, Let there be light: and there was light"; "Let us make man in our image, after our likeness"; "God saw everything that he had made, and, behold, it was very good." This story is the fruit of a long maturation. Yahweh had to become the master of universal history before he could be recognized as the master of the earth and the heavens without any risk of his being confounded with a natural force; but before he could be acclaimed as the master of history, Jewish thought had to integrate the terrible ordeal of the national destruction and exile. The older story that we read in the second chapter of Genesis antedates that catastrophe and the greater depth in religion that resulted from it; and so it is of a more rudimentary make (we need only compare the creative act of 2:7 with that of 1:26 ff.).

Nevertheless, this myth is not negligible; for, if we may believe M. Humbert, whose interpretation I adopt here, it entailed a view of man that was suppressed by the Yahwist editor, but not so completely that we cannot discover some traces of it in certain manifest "doublets" of Chapter 3. It seems that the story of creation

---

doublets and inconsistencies of our story concerning the status of Adam before the fall, the place of the fall, the role of the two trees, the nature of the curses, the role of the various protagonists. There are discussions of the problem in Paul Humbert, *Études sur le récit du Paradis et de la chute dans la Genèse* (Neuchâtel, 1940); Zimmerli, *I Mose I–XI, die Urgeschichte* (Zürich, 1943); and J. Coppens, "La connaissance du bien et du mal et le péché du paradis," in *Analecta Lovaniensia Biblica et Orientalia,* 1948, App. I, pp. 47–72. The distinction of two traditions, two sources, or two different documents should serve to improve our understanding of the story as it has come down to us in its final compilation; the question of sources should prepare the way for the question of meaning. That is why I try to incorporate in the meaning of the story itself the tension that comes from the concurrence of the two sources according to P. Humbert; Zimmerli is a very good methodological guide on this point (*op. cit.,* p. 145). For the theological significance of the story of the fall, I have used Eichrodt, *Theologie des alten Testaments,* III, § 23, "Sünde und Vergebung"; Edmond Jacob, *Les Thèmes essentiels d'une théologie de l'ancien Testament* (Neuchâtel & Paris, 1955), pp. 226–39; G. von Rad, *Theologie des alten Testaments,* I (Munich, 1957), pp. 157 ff., 261 ff.

placed man, at his first appearance, not in the center of a "garden" in the midst of a steppe (Eden), but on the soil (the Adama) from which man (Adam) was drawn. He cultivated that soil industriously and intelligently. Furthermore, the man of the first story must have been an adult, sexually awakened; for he cries out in exultation, in the presence of his new companion: "This is now bone of my bones, and flesh of my flesh: she shall be called Woman (*ischa*), because she was taken out of man (*isch*)." The Yahwist would seem to have suppressed all the traits of discernment or intelligence connected with the state of innocence, and to have assigned all of man's cultural aptitudes to his fallen state. The creation-man becomes, for him, a sort of child-man, innocent in every sense of the word, who had only to stretch out his hands to gather the fruits of the wonderful garden, and who was awakened sexually only after the fall and in shame. Intelligence, work, and sexuality, then, would be the flowers of evil.

This discrepancy at the heart of our story is of great interest. Far from leading us to consider the suppressed myth as a residue and a survival, it invites us to interrogate the tension between the cultural and sexual implications of creation and the implications of the fall. The fact that there are two interpretations of civilization and of sexuality is by itself full of meaning; every dimension of man—language, work, institutions, sexuality—is stamped with the twofold mark of being destined for the good and inclined toward evil. This duality is spread out by the myth in mythical time, just as Plato, in the myth of the *Politicus,* supposes a succession of two periods of the Cosmos, the movement forward and the movement backward, which we experience in the inextricable mélange of the temporal *intentio* and *distentio*.

The ambiguity in man, created good and become evil, pervades all the registers of human life. The power of naming all beings, which is the royal prerogative of a being created scarcely inferior to God, is so profoundly altered that we now know it only under the regime of division of idioms and separation of cultures. Likewise, if we compare the sober description of innocence with the more explicit enumeration of maledictions, we see the opposition of the two ontological regimes invading the other aspects of the human condition. The nakedness of the innocent pair and the shame that follows fault express the human mutation of all communication, marked henceforth by dissimulation.[6] Work ceases to be joyous and becomes toilsome, placing man in an attitude of hostility toward nature. The pain of child-bearing darkens the joy of procreation. The conflict between the woman's seed and the serpent's symbolizes the militant and suffering condition of freedom, henceforth a prey to the guile of desires (compare with Genesis 4:7). Even death is altered: the curse is not that man shall die ("for dust thou art, and unto dust shalt thou return"), but that he shall face death with the anguished awareness of its imminence; the curse is the human modality of dying.

Thus the whole condition of man appears to be subjected to the rule of hardship; it is the *hardship* of being a man which, in the striking brevity of the myth, makes manifest his fallen state. Thus an anthropology of ambiguity issues from the myth; henceforth the greatness *and* the guilt of man are inextricably mingled, so that it is impossible to say: here is the primordial man, there is the evil result of his contingent history.

This ambiguity, this twofold reference of human "nature" to its original destination and to radical evil, stands out in high relief in the case of the divine interdiction. The Yahwist's account presents the interdiction—"But of the fruit of the tree of the knowledge of good and evil thou shalt not eat"—as if it were a structure of innocence. That seems surprising at first. Is not a life subject to prohibitions, to the Law that represses the passions and thus excites them, precisely the life of the sinful man? St. Paul gave striking expression to the experience of being cursed by the Law in the sort of spiritual autobiography which we find in Romans 7:7-14, and which we have commented on above.[7]

What shall we say then? Is the law sin? God forbid. Nay, I had not known sin, but by the law: for I had not known lust, except the law

---

[6] A. M. Dubarle, *Le péché originel dans l'Écriture* (Paris, 1958): "Thus clothing sums up all the dissimulations that make social life possible, and not only the precautions taken to avoid sexual excitations" (p. 64); "The language of the story, so discreet, indicates an ambiguity and a constraint invading all the relationships of human life" (p. 65).

[7] Cf. above, Part I, Chap. III, § 4, on "the curse of the law."

had said, Thou shalt not covet. But sin, taking occasion by the commandment, wrought in me all manner of concupiscence. For without the law
sin was dead.

For I was alive without the law once: but when the commandment
came, sin revived, and I died. And the commandment, which was or-
dained to life, I found to be unto death. For sin, taking occasion by the
commandment, deceived me, and by it slew me.

Wherefore the law is holy, and the commandment holy, and just, and
good. Was then that which is good made death unto me? God forbid.
But sin, that it might appear sin, working death in me by that which
is good; that sin by the commandment might become exceeding sinful.

For we know that the law is spiritual: but I am carnal, sold under sin.

Such is the dialectic of sin and the law, which Luther and
Nietzsche also knew well. How, then, can an interdiction belong
to the order of innocence? No doubt we must understand that, in
making man free, God gives him a finite freedom. The finiteness
of that freedom consists in the fact that it is a freedom primordially
oriented not, of course, by what we call "values," which are
already much elaborated cultural products, but by a hierarchical
principle of preference among values. This ethical structure of
freedom constitutes the authority of values in general. Perhaps that
is why the Yahwist, who elsewhere relates the *crime* of Cain and
who therefore knows the gravity of murder, retained the naïve
motif of the forbidden fruit, which may have had a different meaning in the older legend. In the new and peculiarly Hebraic myth,
the forbidden fruit stands for prohibition in general; compared to
murder, eating forbidden fruit is a peccadillo.[8] Hence the mon-

---

[8] J. Coppens has tried to restate the problem of the "knowledge of good
and evil"; he rejects the idea of omniscience or divine knowledge as well as
the idea of a purely human judgment. The important thing, according to
him, is the sudden irruption of evil into knowledge; more precisely, its
addition to the good in a "combined, intermixed, additive, cumulative
knowledge" (*op. cit.,* p. 16). It is not a discriminating or exhaustive knowledge, but a "cumulative knowledge of good and evil" (*ibid.,* p. 17). To
this first thesis he adds a second: that guilty knowledge is related to sexuality. Far from being a peccadillo, a childish fault as far as its *object* is
concerned and a mortal sin only because of the relation to *Him who* forbids,
the fault of Adam has a particular content. Is not Eve punished in her life
as woman and mother? Is not man punished in his life of desire? But above
all the triangle formed by Eve, the serpent, and the tree suggests a fault

strousness of the act as such is less important than the alteration of the relation of trust between man and God. In this sense it may be said that, in taking up the myth of the tree and its fruit in this new theological context, the Yahwist demystifies the old theme of the magic potion, the magic fruit; he demystifies it by calling the fruit "the fruit of the tree of the knowledge of good and evil." These

---

of this kind: the serpent is the symbol of the gods of vegetation; without being the representative of sex as such, he represents the temptation of the divinities that sacralize sex. Coppens is even more precise: the fault must have to do with the only commandment reported in Genesis before the fall, the command to procreate. Thus the serpent would represent the temptation to place sexual life under the influence of the licentious pagan cults and so to surrender it to dissoluteness (*op. cit.*, pp. 13–28, 73–91, and, in the same collection, *Analecta Lovaniensia Biblica et Orientalia*, II, 8, pp. 396–408). It must be said that M. Coppens rests his interpretation on a vast and solid inquiry concerning the significance of the serpent as associated with the divinities of vegetation (*ibid.*, pp. 91–117 and 409–42). But, in my opinion, he passes too quickly over the question whether it is really the existence of sexual transgression that the sacred author *teaches*. When he encounters this question, which ought to dominate the discussion, he answers in the negative: "Does the sacred author teach the existence of the sexual transgression of which we have spoken? I think not. The development of that theme is muted. It was much clearer, I think, in the source known to the author. The hagiographer dropped the theme; but there remain some traces of it which must be made out as in a palimpsest. Or one may suppose that he did not abandon it entirely for his own part, but that he abstained from inculcating it. He may have contented himself with insinuating it, either because he preferred not to rend the veil or because he deliberately made it thicker" (*ibid.*, p. 26). These remarks make me think that the sexual interpretation is a *recessive* interpretation of the sin of Adam. If it belongs to the most archaic level, the editor has suppressed it not in order to conceal the meaning, but in order to say something much more important. It seems to me that the intention of the text is to reduce the *content* of the fault to the extent of making it a peccadillo, in order to emphasize the fact that man has broken the filial dependence that united him to his Father. That is why, finally, the question of the tree is not important, as Zimmerli has clearly seen (pp. 165–66, 235–38). The decisive argument, in my opinion, is the place of this story, at the head of the series formed by Genesis 1–11. The sin of Adam is the first, in the sense that it is at the root of all the others: Adam breaks with God, as Cain separates himself from his brother and the men of Babel are confounded. We shall take up this problem again in Book III, when we examine the psychoanalytic interpretation of guilt; it will then be possible to discover the positive value of the sexual interpretation and to assign Coppens' interpretation to its right place, which is not that of intentional instruction.

250 THE SYMBOLISM OF EVIL

two words, "good" and "evil,"[9] place the hidden meaning far
beyond any magic, at the very foundation of the discrimination
between being good and being evil; what is forbidden is not this
or that, but a state of autonomy which would make man the
creator of the distinction between good and evil.

There is more to be said. For an innocent freedom, this limitation would not be felt as an interdiction; but we no longer know
what that primordial authority, contemporaneous with the birth of
finite freedom, is; in particular, we no longer know what a *limit* that
does not repress, but orients and guards freedom, could be like;
we no longer have access to that creative limit. We are acquainted
only with the limit that constrains; authority becomes interdiction
under the regime of fallen freedom. That is why the naïve author
of the Biblical story projects into the state of innocence the sort
of interdiction that we experience "after" the fall; the God who
says Yes—"Let there be light: and there was light"—now says
No—"As for the tree of the knowledge of good and evil, thou shalt
not eat of it." The fall is at the same time a fall of man and a fall
of the "law"; as St. Paul says, again, "The commandment that
was to give me life has led me to sin." Thus the fall is a caesura
cutting across everything that makes man human; everything—
sexuality and death, work and civilization, culture and ethics—
depends on both a primordial nature, lost but yet still lying there
underneath, and an evil which, although radical, is nonetheless
contingent.

If now we ask the meaning of that innocence which the myth
projects as a "before," we can answer: to say that it is lost is still
to say something about it; it is to posit it in order at least to cancel
it. Innocence here plays the role of the Kantian thing-in-itself: it
is thought of to the extent of being posited, but it is not known;
that is enough to give it the negative role of a limit in relation
to the pretensions of the phenomenon to be coextensive with being.
To posit the world as that *into which* sin entered, or innocence as

[9] M. Humbert translates: "l'arbre du connaître bien et mal." He thinks
that it is a question of judgment in its full extent: "Knowledge both
theoretical and practical, experimental; knowledge in general, making one
experienced, capable, and prudent in all fields. An exclusively moral sense
is excluded" (*op. cit.*, p. 90).

that *from which* sin strayed, or again, in figurative language, Paradise as the place *from which* man was driven, is to attest that sin is not our original reality, does not constitute our first ontological status; sin does not define what it is to be a man; beyond his becoming a sinner there is his being created. That is the radical intuition which the future editor of the second creation-story (Gen. 1) will sanction by the word of the Lord God: "Let us make man in our image, after our likeness." The *imago Dei*—there we have both our being-created and our innocence; for the "goodness" of the creation is no other than its status as "creature." All creation is good, and the goodness that belongs to man is his being the image of God. Seen retrospectively, from the point of view of sin, as a "prior" state in mythical language, the likeness appears as an absence of guilt, as innocence; but his goodness is altogether positive; it is sin that is the nothingness of vanity.

Thereby the possibility arises of interpreting the two states of innocence and sin no longer as successive, but as superimposed; sin does not *succeed* innocence, but, in the *Instant,* loses it. In the Instant I am created, in the Instant I fall. In the Instant I am created: my pristine goodness is my status as a created being; but I do not cease to be a created being unless I cease to be; therefore I do not cease to be good. Then the "event" of sin terminates innocence in the Instant; it is, in the Instant, the discontinuity, the breach between my having been created and my becoming evil. The myth puts in succession that which is contemporaneous and cannot not be contemporaneous; it makes an "earlier" state of innocence terminate in an instant that begins the "later" state of accursedness. But that is how it attains its depth; in telling of the fall as an event, springing up from an unknown source, it furnishes anthropology with a key concept: the *contingency* of that radical evil which the penitent is always on the point of calling his evil nature. Thereby the myth proclaims the purely "historical" character of that radical evil; it prevents it from being regarded as primordial evil. Sin may be "older" than sins, but innocence is still "older." The "anteriority" of innocence to the "oldest" sin is, as it were, the temporal cipher of a profound anthropological fact. By the myth anthropology is invited, in the first place, to gather all the sins of the world into a sort of transhistorical unity, symbolized by the first man; then to put the stamp of contingency on that radical evil; and finally to preserve, superimposed on one another, the goodness of created man and the wickedness of historical man, while "separating" the one from the other by the "event" which the myth tells of as the first sin of the first man.

That is what Rousseau genially understood: man is "naturally good," but we know him under the regime of civilization—that is to say, of history—only as "depraved." Above all, that is what Kant understood with admirable rigor in the *Essay on Radical Evil:* man is "destined" for the good and "inclined" to evil; in this paradox of "destination" and "inclination" the whole meaning of the symbol of the fall is concentrated.

3. The "Lapse of Time" of the Drama of Temptation

But the same myth that focuses the "event" of the fall in one man, one act, one instant, also spreads it out among several characters—Adam, Eve, the serpent—and several episodes—the seduction of the woman and the fall of the man. Hence, a second reading offers itself, in which the "passage" from innocence to fault gets the sense of an insensible transition and no longer that of a sudden occurrence. The myth is both the myth of the caesura and the myth of transition, the myth of the act and that of motivation, the myth of an evil choice and that of temptation, the myth of the Instant and that of a lapse of time. Under this second aspect the myth tries to fill up the interval between innocence and the fall by a sort of dizziness from which the evil act emerges as if by fascination. But in articulating the event of the fall upon the duration of the dizziness, the Yahwist gives his story a second pole— the serpent; the serpent is a figure of the transition. Furthermore, the mediation of the serpent is itself linked with another figure— that of the woman, Eve, Life. Thus the myth multiplies intermediaries, countering the irrationality of the Instant.

Let us not ask first *who* the serpent is. Let us see what he does.

The drama begins between the serpent and the woman. The serpent raises a question and that question insinuates a doubt:

"Has God truly said . . . ?" Now the question is an interrogation concerning the *Interdict;* it is a question that seizes upon the interdiction and transforms it into an occasion for falling; or rather, if our analysis of the creative limit is exact, the question makes the limit suddenly appear as an interdiction. Dizziness begins with alienation from the commandment, which suddenly becomes my "Other," whereas it had been my "Orient." Floating at a distance from me, the commandment becomes insupportable; the creative limit becomes hostile negativity and, as such, problematic: Has God truly said . . . ? At the same time as the meaning of the ethical limit becomes hazy, the meaning of finiteness is obscured. A "desire" has sprung up, the desire for infinity; but that infinity is not the infinity of reason and happiness, as we have interpreted it at the beginning of this work; it is the infinity of desire itself; it is the desire of desire, taking possession of knowing, of willing, of doing, and of being: "Your eyes shall be opened, and ye shall be as gods, knowing good and evil." It is in relation to this "desire" that finiteness is insupportable, the finiteness which consists simply in being created being. The soul of the serpent's question is the "evil infinite," which simultaneously perverts the meaning of the limit by which freedom was oriented and the meaning of the finiteness of the freedom thus oriented by the limit.

This likeness to gods by means of transgression is something very profound:[10] when the limit ceases to be creative and God seems to

[10] What is the meaning of Genesis 3:22: "Behold, the man has become as one of us, to know good and evil! And now let him not put forth his hand, and take also of the tree of life, and eat, and live forever"? Does God hold himself for vanquished? Does he speak ironically? Several authors have retreated before the consequences of those two hypotheses and preferred either to ascribe the verse to a distinct document (Zimmerli) or to propose another translation (J. Coppens): "Behold, the man, and whoever is born of him, will have to endure good and evil." Why not take seriously this affirmation that, in acquiring discernment, man effectively realized his likeness to God, which remained dormant, as it were, in his innocence? Now man has become conscious of it, but in an alienated mode, in the mode of contest and strife. Everything we shall say later, with St. Paul, about the "how much more" of grace—which "superabounds" where sin has "abounded"—inclines us to say that sin represents a certain advance in self-consciousness. Thus there begins an irreversible adventure, a crisis in the becoming of man, which will not reach its dénouement until the final process of justification.

bar the way against man by his prohibitions, man seeks his freedom in the unlimitedness of the Principle of existence and forms the wish to posit himself in being as a creator of himself by himself. Moreover, the serpent has not spoken altogether falsely; the era opened up to freedom by fault is a certain experience of infinity that hides from us the finite situation of the creature, the ethical finiteness of man. Henceforth the evil infinite of human desire— always something else, always something more—which animates the movement of civilizations, the appetite for pleasure, for possessions, for power, for knowledge—*seems* to constitute the reality of man. The restlessness that makes us discontented with the present *seems* to be our true nature, or rather the absence of nature that makes us free. In a way, the promise of the serpent marks the birth of a human history drawn by its idols towards the infinite; all phenomenology develops in this enchanted precinct of vanity, under the category of the *Pseudo*. That is why no phenomenology, no science of appearances, can take the place of a critique of the illusion of appearance. The myth is the symbolic form of that critique.

And now, why is the woman chosen for the confrontation of interdict and desire? In the Biblical account she represents the point of weakness and giving way in the presence of the seducer; the serpent tempts the man through the woman.

No doubt it must be granted that the story gives evidence of a very masculine resentment, which serves to justify the state of dependence in which all, or almost all, societies have kept women. Moreover, that resentment is quite in the style of the "divine jealousy" in which we have recognized a sort of residual tragic myth; there is undoubtedly some trace of the god's jealousy of human greatness in the clerical hatred of curiosity, of boldness, of the spirit of invention and freedom, which animates those pessimistic pages, if it is true that they tend, contrary to the myth of creation, to eliminate the ambiguity of civilization and to place it unequivocally under the sign of guilt.

But beyond the legitimate criticism that a Nietzschean spirit might level against the resentment of the Yahwist, the story points to an "eternal feminine" which is more than sex and which might be called the *mediation of the weakness*, the frailty of man. The flesh is "weak," says the Gospel. The essence of that frailty is to be found in the type of finiteness belonging to man. His finiteness is an unstable finiteness belonging to man. His finiteness is an unstable finiteness, ready to veer towards the "evil infinite"; insofar as it is an ethical finiteness, it is easily seduced by perversion of the limit that constitutes it. The cause of man's fall is not the human libido, but the structure of a finite freedom. It is in this sense that evil was *possible* through freedom. Here the woman represents the point of least resistance of finite freedom to the appeal of the *Pseudo,* of the evil infinite.

Eve, then, does not stand for woman in the sense of "second sex." Every woman and every man are Adam; every man and every woman are Eve; every woman sins "in" Adam, every man is seduced "in" Eve.

"Frailty, thy name is woman!" says the tragedy of *Hamlet.*

What we have just said about ethical finiteness as the occasion for man's fall and about the breaking out of this finiteness into an infinite desire and a hostile law leads us to the decisive question: What does the serpent signify?

The serpent does not seem to have posed any problem for the author of the story: he is there and he is already cunning—"the most cunning of the beasts of the fields"—before Adam's fault; the Yahwist does not speculate further on his nature or the origin of his cunning; we are still far from the Satan of the Persian and Greek period. In particular, the idea of a test imposed upon man, such as we read of in the book of Job, has not yet been formed. Besides, such a test would appeal to a power of discernment which the innocent man does not have, and it would also suppose that God himself takes the initiative in questioning man's childlike dependence on him. Nevertheless, the Yahwist appears to have *kept* the serpent intentionally; the only monster who survived from the theogonic myths, the chthonic animal, has *not* been demythologized.[11] The Yahwist only says—and it is a capital point—that he also is a creature.

---

[11] On the serpent as symbol of chthonian divinities and divinities of vegetation, J. Coppens, *op. cit.,* pp. 92–117; W. F. Albright, "The Goddess of Life and Wisdom," *Am. Journ. Sem. Lang. Lit.,* 1920–21, pp. 258–94;

It is this limit introduced into the demythologization of demons by Jewish thought that creates a problem. Why was the origin of evil *not* restricted to Adam? Why was an extraneous figure retained and introduced?

We can give a first answer—which remains only a partial answer —to that question: in the figure of the serpent, the Yahwist may have been dramatizing an important aspect of the experience of temptation—the experience of quasi-externality. Temptation would be a sort of seduction from without; it would develop into compliance with the apparition that lays siege to the "heart"; and, finally, to sin would be to *yield*. The serpent, then, would be a part of ourselves which we do not recognize; he would be the seduction of ourselves by ourselves, projected into the seductive object. This interpretation is so much the less irrelevant as it has already been invoked by the apostle James: "Let no man say when he is tempted, I am tempted of God: for God cannot be tempted with evil, neither tempteth he any man. But every man is tempted, when he is drawn away of his own lust, and enticed" (1:13–14). Likewise, St. Paul identified the quasi-externality of desire with the "flesh," with the law of sin that is in my members. The serpent, then, represents this passive aspect of temptation, hovering on the border between the outer and the inner; the Decalogue calls it "covetousness" (Tenth Commandment). We might even say, following St. James's line of thought, that this pseudo-outer becomes an alien reality only through bad faith; arguing from the fact that our freedom is beset by desire, we seek to exculpate ourselves and make ourselves appear innocent by accusing an Other. Thus we allege the irresistibility of our passions in order to justify ourselves. That is what the woman does when she is asked by God, after the fatal deed: "Why have you done this?" She answers: "The serpent beguiled me." Bad faith, then, seizes upon the quasi-externality of desire in order to make it an alibi for freedom. The artfulness of the excuse is that it puts temptation, which had been hovering on the border between the inside and the outside, completely outside. Carrying out this interpretation to the end, we might say that the serpent represents the psychological projection of desire.[12] He is the image of the "fruit"—plus the bad faith of the excuse. Our own desire projects itself into the desirable object, reveals itself through the object; and so, when he *binds himself*— and that is the evil thing—a man accuses the object in order to exculpate himself. It is this subtle procedure that the serpent dramatizes, as the ghost in *Hamlet* dramatizes the obscure call of vengeance and the reproachfulness of the father-image assailing Hamlet's indecisiveness. The *Phaedo* says the same thing: "And the extraordinary thing about the prison [the prison made by the bodily passions], as philosophy has seen, is that it is the work of desire and that he who co-operates the most in loading the prisoner with chains is perhaps the prisoner himself" (82*e*).

This reduction of the serpent to a part of ourselves does not, perhaps, exhaust the symbol of the serpent. The serpent is not only the projection of man's seduction by himself, not only our animal nature goaded by interdictions, maddened by the vertigo of infinity, corrupted by the preference each man gives to himself and to that in which he differs from others, and beguiling his properly human nature. The serpent is also "outside" in a more radical fashion and in various ways.

In the first place, the serpent represents the following situation: in the historical experience of man, every individual finds evil *already there;* nobody begins it absolutely. If Adam is not the first man, in the naïvely temporal sense of the word, but the typical man, he can symbolize both the experience of the "beginning" of humanity with each individual and the experience of the "succes-

---

[12] I shall say later what is to be thought of the psychoanalytic interpretations of the myth of Genesis; but it is already clear that the dialectic of lust overflows the adventure of the *libido* on every side. The struggle of the Prophets against injustice and insolence, St. Paul's struggle against the pretensions of the "just," warn us that the symbolism of the serpent opens up and uncovers an immense field for "lust," of which sexuality is only one sector. But we are not yet prepared to situate sexuality exactly in relation to injustice and justification.

On psychoanalytic interpretations of the serpent, cf. Ludwig Levy, "Sexuale Symbolik in der Paradiesgeschichte," in *Imago,* 1917–19, pp. 16–30; R. F. Fortune, "The Symbolic of the Serpent," in *Intern. Journ. of Psychoanalysis,* 1926, pp. 237–43; Abraham Cronbach, *The Psychoanalytic Study of Judaism.*

sion" of men. Evil is part of the interhuman relationship, like language, tools, institutions; it is transmitted; it is tradition, and not only something that happens. There is thus an anteriority of evil to itself, as if evil were that which always precedes itself, that which each man finds and continues while beginning it, but beginning it in his turn. That is why, in the Garden of Eden, the serpent is already there; he is the other side of that which begins.

Let us go further: behind the *projection* of our lust, beyond the *tradition* of evil already there, there is perhaps an even more radical externality of evil, a cosmic structure of evil—not, doubtless, the lawfulness of the world as such, but its relation of indifference to the ethical demands of which man is both author and servant. From the spectacle of things, from the course of history, from the cruelty of nature and men, there comes a feeling of universal absurdity which invites man to doubt his destination; Gabriel Marcel speaks of the "invitation to betray" which seems inherent in the structure of our universe when we confront it with the fundamental intention of man's being and with his desire for truth and happiness. There is thus a side of our world that confronts us as chaos and that is symbolized by the chthonic animal. For a human existent, this aspect of chaos is a structure of the universe; Aeschylus recognized it in the volcano Etna, in the thousand-headed Typhon, in the horror that adheres to gods and men, feeding the essential tragedy of the human condition. Prometheus and Oedipus on the one hand, Job on the other, recognized the cosmic dimensions of brute chaos. We shall return in the following chapter to this proximity of the theme of the serpent to tragedy.

Thus the serpent symbolizes something of man *and* something of the world, a side of the microcosm and a side of the macrocosm, the chaos *in* me, *among* us, and *outside*. But it is always chaos for me, a human existent destined for goodness and happiness.

This triple "sketch of a serpent" explains why the chthonic animal resisted the demythologization of theogony; he represents the aspect of evil that could not be absorbed into the responsible freedom of man, which is perhaps also the aspect that Greek tragedy tried to purify by spectacle, song, and choral invocation. The Jews themselves, although they were well armed against demonology by their intransigent monotheism, were constrained by truth, as Aristotle would say, to concede something, to concede as much as they could without destroying the monotheistic basis of their faith, to the great dualisms which they were to discover after the Exile. The theme of the serpent represents the first landmark along the road of the Satanic theme which, in the Persian epoch, permitted the inclusion of a near-dualism in the faith of Israel. Of course, Satan will never be another god; the Jews will always remember that the serpent is a part of the creation; but at least the symbol of Satan allowed them to balance the movement toward the concentration of evil in man by a second movement which attributed its origin to a prehuman, demonic reality.

If we follow the intention of the serpent theme all the way to the end, it must be said that man is not the absolute evil one, but the evil one of second rank, the evil one through seduction; he is not *the* Evil One, the Wicked One, substantivally, so to speak, but evil, wicked, adjectivally; he makes himself wicked by a sort of counter-participation, counter-imitation, by consenting to a source of evil that the naïve author of the Biblical tale depicts as animal cunning. To sin is to yield.

From here on, speculation becomes very risky—at least religious speculation; for it must venture upon ground inaccessible to the sort of verification proper to it, namely, verification through the spirit of repentance. Beyond what the believer can repent of, speculation has nothing to lean on. Placed in the perspective of the confession of sins and the symbolism that illuminates it, the theme of the Evil One is never anything more than a limiting figure, which denotes the evil that I continue when I, too, begin it and introduce it into the world; the always-already-there of evil is the *other* aspect of the evil for which, nevertheless, *I* am responsible. The situation of a *victim*, which the iconography of temptations developed to satiety in the baroque art of Hieronymus Bosch, is the reverse of the position of a sinner, of which man accuses himself under the guidance of the prophet. The sobriety of the penitent conscience excludes the possibility of ever cutting off speculation about Satan from the anthropology of evil. Man knows evil only as that which he inaugurates; that is why a first step in "Satanology," on the confines of the experience of being tempted, is always necessary. But it is impossible to take the second step beyond the borders between Satanology and anthropology; outside the quasi-external structure of temptation, which is still a structure of man's sin, I do not know what Satan is, who Satan is, or even whether he is Someone. For if he were someone, it would be necessary to intercede for him, which makes no sense.

That is why the Biblical myth, in spite of Eve and the serpent, remains "Adamic"—that is to say, anthropological.

4. Justification and Eschatological Symbols

We have penetrated into the forest of meanings created by the Adamic symbol. The moment has come to restore to that symbol its motion: it is a symbol of the beginning and it was adopted by the Biblical writer whom we call the Yahwist with a lively awareness that it is a *retrospective* symbol closely bound up with a whole historical experience turned toward the *future*. We are not concerned here to reconstruct the whole theology of history underlying that experience, but to find a solution to a precise problem, which is this: Are there, in that experience and that theology of history, symbols of the End which are homogeneous with the symbolism of the Beginning developed by the Adamic myth? Hence the problem we are proposing here is a problem of agreement of symbol with symbol; what is at stake is the coherence of the "type" for which the Adamic symbol is the ultimate retrospective symbol. In other words, we are trying to discover that which corresponds, in the Biblical type, to the "cultual-ritual" re-enactment (and to the figure of the King which is subordinate to it) in the cosmic-drama "type," or that which corresponds to the spectacle, the emotion, and the wisdom of tragedy, or, again, that which corresponds to the odyssey of the soul in the Orphic myth. We shall attempt to answer this question within the limits of an investigation of symbols.

At the same time as we complete the meaning of the Adamic symbolism by replacing it in the temporal whole from which we have abstracted it, we are going to find again, at the second degree, the symbolism of "pardon" which we began to sketch in Part I. It will be remembered that the notion of "pardon" evolved a history parallel to the history that leads from defilement to sin and to guilt. We have marked the route of that ideal history of pardon by the themes of purification, mercy (*hesed*), and justification. Now, that history rested on a primary symbolism: to wash or to take away, to unbind, to liberate, to buy back, etc.; but although we were able to perceive the wealth of the symbol of the "exodus" from Egypt with no other resources than a theological reinterpretation of the historical past of Israel, the symbol of justification could not be worked out completely for want of an elucidation of the system of images concerning the end of time. Hence it is to the symbolism of justification that we are going to relate the eschatological symbolism. Through this second symbolism the living experience of pardon will continue to unfold; in passing through the metaphysical imagination, the experience will be enriched by a meaning that could not be expressed in the direct language of religious experience. It is on this long road of the hermeneutics of symbols that the experience comes to the light of speech.

The dominant symbols of eschatology are the symbols of the "Son of Man" and the "second Adam" (we will not yet raise the question of their unity); extraordinarily striking symbols, since they answer, term for term, to the Adamic symbol and permit us to discover at a single stroke the mutual agreement between the symbols of the fall that happened at the Beginning and the symbols of the salvation that will come at the End of time.

But it is difficult to put oneself all at once in the presence of this symbolism, to which it can be justly objected that it is not at the level of the Adamic symbol, since it acquired literary existence only in late and esoteric Judaism (book of Daniel, IV Ezra, Ethiopian book of Enoch), in the Gospels, and in the Pauline epistles. We must place ourselves, then, at the level of the Adamic myth, begin with the response to that myth in the same cultural milieu, and then try to follow the progressive enrichment of the figures or images that answer from the beginning to that of Adam, in order to overtake the symbols of the Son of Man and the Second Adam.

Of course, it is not the literary history of those figures or images that interests us but, through that history, their phenomenological filiation.

The tension towards the future is discerned by the Yahwist editor (who knows nothing of a "second Adam") in an event which also belongs to the *Urgeschichte* and in a sense brings it to a close, at the same time that it opens the *Heilsgeschichte*.[13] That event is the calling of Abraham:

> Yahweh said unto Abram, Get thee out of thy country, and from thy kindred, and from thy father's house, unto a land that I will shew thee. And I will make of thee a great nation, and I will bless thee, and make thy name great; and thou shalt be a blessing.
>
> I will bless them that bless thee,
> I will curse them that curse thee.
> Through thee shall be blessed
> all the nations of the earth.
>
> Gen. 12:1–3

The figure of Abraham may be said to be the first answer to the figure of Adam,[14] and indeed it is much elaborated upon in its theological significance: "Abraham believed in Yahweh, who counted it to him as justice" (Gen. 15:6).

Thus, in his past, when he thinks back on it, the Israelite finds a sign of hope; even before any eschatology he represents the history of his "fathers" to himself as a history directed by a "promise" and moving toward a "fulfillment." No doubt that hope is dependent on Land and Blood: You shall possess a land, the Promised Land,

---

[13] Gerhard von Rad, *Theologie des alten Testaments,* I, p. 164.

[14] The figure of Noah already has a similar significance as an anticipation of the perfect man: the "Noachic" covenant anticipates what is most universal in the promise to Abraham; it is, indeed, a covenant with everything living, which announces the great reconciliation hailed by the Prophets, even before the later eschatologies. As to the flood itself, it signifies not only the wrath of God but the advent of a new creation; it is the symbolism the baptism develops in connection with the symbolism of burial and resurrection. It is noteworthy that the "sacerdotal" editor attaches all the races of the earth to Noah as their begetter, thus placing the dispersion of peoples and languages (Gen. 10:32) under the sign of the promise made to Noah (Gen. 9:1 ff.), and not only, as the "Yahwist" editor does, under the sign of the fall. The calling of Abraham is in direct contrast with this final ambiguity of the *Urgeschichte* (G. von Rad, *op. cit.,* pp. 165–68).

and your posterity will be as innumerable as the dust of the earth; but at least the movement from promise to fulfillment furnishes the clew that makes it possible to put in order the disparate stories concerning Abraham, Jacob, and Joseph.

What interests us here is that that historical schema was sufficiently charged with meaning to support a whole series of transpositions which, step by step, could lead to the eschatological figures and images.

The transposition is effected first in the ancestral history itself, and, consequently, still in retrospection: the fulfillment of the Promise, which at first appears to be at hand ("All the land which thou seest, to thee will I give it, and to thy seed forever. . . . Arise, walk through the land in the length of it and in the breadth of it; for I will give it unto thee" [Gen. 13:15–17]), is constantly postponed. In the meantime, the revelation of Sinai, the knowledge of the Law, the setting up of a cult, and the experience in the wilderness take place. The wealth of the interval is such that the end itself changes its meaning.[15]

It was the experience of historical stalemate that was to "eschatologize" the Promise in a decisive manner. The meaning of the Promise made to Abraham—"In thee all the nations of the earth shall be blessed" (Gen. 12:3)—had not been exhausted in the conquest of Canaan under Joshua; new dimensions of meaning, concealed under the carnal desire for land and posterity, continually come into view as political success becomes more problematic and Israel ceases to exist as an independent state. Then the look that anticipates is no longer only a look that interprets the past; the eye of hope is an eye that turns away from the *Urgeschichte* and sees the meaning of salvation coming from the future toward the present.

Henceforth the "Promise" will express its tension through the mythical images of the end; those images and the figures in which they will be crystallized will supply the true answer to the images and figures of the beginning. J. Héring[16] proposed not long ago to define "eschatology" as "the ensemble of the thoughts that

15 G. von Rad, *op. cit.*, pp. 169–77.
16 J. Héring, *Le royaume de Dieu et sa venue* (Strasbourg, 1937).

express religious hopes concerning the coming of a world regarded as ideal, that world being habitually presented as one which must be preceded by a 'Judgment' (which implies the destruction of the present world or of the powers that dominate it)."[17] It is the affinity of the eschatological representations of the Judeo-Christian world with the representations concerning the *Urgeschichte* which will be the theme of our reflections from now on.

As the ritual-cultual vision of life was coherent with the creation-drama, as the spectacle of Terror and Pity went with the wicked god of tragedy, and as the odyssey of the soul is the answer to the wretchedness of bodily existence, so it can be shown that the eschatological representations of the Man to come are homogeneous with the fall of the first Man.

There is no better illustration of the cleavage between the "ritual-cultual" type and the "eschatological" type than the evolution undergone by the figure of the King: the kingship founded "in those times" becomes little by little "the Kingdom to come," as the eschatological type possesses itself more completely of the images deposited by the ritual-cultual type. We have already spoken of this inversion within the framework of the "ritual-cultual" type, and we have considered the evolution of the figure of the King from the point of view of the decomposition of the anterior ideology. We can now comprehend better the new dynamism that carries those old images along toward a new horizon. The King, the Anointed One, still charged with earthly and political hopes in the oracles concerning the permanence of David's line (for example, II Samuel 7:12–16), begins to be "eschatologized" in Jeremiah 23:1–8, Ezekiel 34:23 ff. and 37:20 ff., and above all in Isaiah 9:1–6 (which does not prevent it from becoming more and more strongly "political" under the Greek domination, while remaining within the horizon of history, as one sees in the psalms of Solomon). The beautiful words of Isaiah deserve to be quoted:

> The people that walked in darkness
> have seen a great light:

[17] J. Héring, *op. cit.*, p. 51. On the relation with the figure of the King, cf. A. Bentzen, *op. cit.*, pp. 32–42. Cullmann, *Christologie du Nouveau Testament* (Paris, 1958), p. 97.

> they that dwell in the land of the shadow of death,
> upon them hath the light shined.
>
> . . . .
>
> For unto us a child is born,
> unto us a son is given:
> and the government shall be upon his shoulder:
> and his name shall be called
> Wonderful Counsellor, The mighty God,
> The everlasting Father, The Prince of Peace.
> Of the increase of his government and peace
> there shall be no end,
> upon the throne of David,
> and upon his kingdom,
> to order it, and to establish it
> with judgment and with justice
> from henceforth even for ever.
> The zeal of the Lord of hosts will perform this.
>
> Is. 9:2, 6–7

In this text, as in the preceding ones, the King, the Shepherd, the Son of David is in no wise a mysterious personage "coming from heaven," like the Son of Man in the later eschatologies; eschatological does not mean transcendent, heavenly, but final. The important thing for us is that the representation of a reconciled cosmos which accompanies this image of the coming Reign expresses not at all the regret for a lost golden age, but the expectation of a perfection the like of which will not have been seen before.

While the Messianic figure is becoming "eschatologized," other historically important figures appear. Two among them deserve to be introduced here: that of the "Servant of Yahweh" and that of the "Son of Man," in which the eschatological accent is particularly evident. The Second Isaiah celebrates the sorrowful servant in four upsetting "songs" (42:1–9; 49:1–6; 50:1–11; 52:13—53:12).[18] In many of its traits, this theme is original in relation to

---

[18] On the suffering servant of God (*Ebed Yahweh*): H. H. Rowley, *The Servant of the Lord and Other Essays on the Old Testament*, 2d ed. (1954); J. Jeremias, art. παῖς, in *Theol. Wörterbuch z. N. T.*, V, 636 ff.; J.

the ideology of the King; it needs a new ear to understand the song of the suffering servant who gives himself for the remission of sins: "Surely he hath borne our griefs, and carried our sorrows. . . . He was wounded for our transgressions, he was bruised for our iniquities"; we can no longer use the ideology of the King to understand the role of disciple, or that of the inspired sage, or the wretched appearance, the absolute patience, the non-resistance to the wicked of the *Ebed Yahweh.* It is true that the eschatological emphasis is weak in this figure; and yet it is said that this "slave of tyrants" is the one who will "restore the survivors of Israel" and be "the light of the nations, so that my salvation may reach to the ends of the Earth." It is noteworthy that this canticle "speaks" without our being able to say *who* this Servant of Yahweh is, or even whether he is a people taken in a body, a "remnant," or an exceptional individual.

And yet, in spite of this enigma—or in virtue of this enigma—we need the figure of the *Ebed Yahweh* to lead us to the idea of "pardon," the examination of which we postponed because we rejected the short cut of religious psychology and chose the long road of symbolic figures. It is through an enigmatic personage who substitutes his suffering for our sins that pardon is announced. Pardon does not appear here as a wholly inward change, psychological and moral, but as an interpersonal relation to that immolated personality (individual or collective); this interpersonal relation rests on the reciprocity of a gift ("in place of," "for our sins") and an acceptance ("we did esteem him stricken, smitten of God, and afflicted"); this alliance supposes that the substitutive suffering is not the simple transfer of defilement to a passive object, such as the scapegoat, nor yet the ineluctable destiny of a misunderstood and rejected prophet,[19] but the voluntary "gift" of a suffering taken upon himself and offered to others: "Yet it was our sufferings that he bore, our griefs with which he was laden." "Having given his life as a sacrifice for sin, he will see a posterity and prolong his days,

---

Héring, *op. cit.,* pp. 83–85; A. Bentzen, *op. cit.,* pp. 42 ff.; Théo Preiss, *Le Fils de l'Homme,* fragments d'un cours sur la christologie du N. T. (Montpellier, 1951), pp. 51 ff.; O. Cullmann, *op. cit.,* pp. 48–73.

[19] O. Cullmann, *op. cit.,* pp. 52 and 64.

and the work of the Eternal will prosper in his hands. Because of the travail of his soul, he will see and be satisfied; through his knowledge my just servant will justify many men and he will take their iniquities upon himself." Expiation through the voluntary suffering of another, however mysterious the *Ebed Yahweh* may be, is an essential key to the idea of pardon; it will be relayed through all the successive mediations developed by the other figures.[20]

Other, profoundly other, is the apocalyptic figure indicated in Daniel 7:13 and in the extra-canonical apocalypses (book of Ezra, Ethiopian book of Enoch). "I watched during my visions in the night, and behold, on the clouds of heaven there came one like a son of man; he advanced toward the Ancient of Days, and they brought him near to him. And there was given him dominion, glory, and kingship; and all peoples, nations, and men of every language served him. His eternal dominion will never pass away, and his kingship will never be destroyed" (Dan. 7:13–14). According to the ensuing explanation given by the visionary (vss. 15 ff.), the "Son of Man" represents the "saints of the Most High." This figure, of heavenly origin, comes to assemble the holy people of the end of time and to share his reign with them. This figure, the most distant from the figure of the earthly King,[21] will lead us back, at

[20] The eschatological aspect of two other figures might also be emphasized: (1) the figure of the prophet of the last times: Moses Redivivus, Elia Redivivus in Judaism, the "Master of Justice" in the Qumran sect. Preaching proclaims the end of the world and offers the last chance for repentance. Héring, *op. cit.*, p. 68; A. Bentzen, pp. 42 ff. (the latter seeks the unity of the two figures of the prophet and the Messiah in the figure of the Son of Man, rather than in that of the Messiah-King, counter to the ideology of the King); O. Cullmann, *op. cit.*, pp. 18–47, insists on the importance of this Christological title of Jesus in Judeo-Christianity. (2) The figure of the "high priest" of Genesis 14:18–20 and Psalm 110:4 ("Thou art a priest forever, after the order of Melchizedek"), a figure which, as the ideal high priest expected at the end of time, is akin to the Prophet, the Priest-King, and the Man. Héring, *op. cit.*, p. 72; A. Bentzen, pp. 67 ff., O. Cullmann, *op. cit.*, pp. 76–94.

[21] I leave aside the problem whether this figure belongs to a Zoroastrian, Mandaean, or gnostic tradition, as Reitzenstein, Bousset, and Bultmann have tried to establish. In any case, it did not affect Christianity except through esoteric circles in Judaism. Moreover, knowledge of the origins of the Son of Man "could add nothing of importance to the meaning he acquired in Judaism" (J. Héring, *op. cit.*, p. 81). See further A. Bentzen,

the end of this chapter, to the initial figure: to Man, to Anthropos. The Son of Man is Man; but he is no longer the First Man, but a Man who is coming; he is the Man of the end, whether he be an an individual or the personification of a collective entity, of the remnant of Israel, or of the whole of humanity. As such, he is the replica of the first Man, created in the image of God (O. Cullmann supposes that the theme of the *imago Dei* may have made the adoption of this figure that comes from elsewhere easier for Judaism); he is the replica of the first Man, but he is new in relation to him and cannot be the return, pure and simple, of a first Man, supposed perfect and not a sinner, as in certain gnostic speculations on Adam.[22]

What draws this figure toward the most ultimate future is his twofold function of Judge of the world and King to come. The Kingdom is to come, and the Apocalypses present it in the great setting of the last judgment, when the Man is proclaimed king and receives the power, the glory, and the kingship over all nations. It is to this eschatological role that the revelation of the assembly of the just is joined; the "collective component" in the figure of the Son of Man is manifested thereby. Thus the true meaning of present humanity is revealed, so to say, in the light of what lies ahead, starting from that true Man who "is coming"; as Théo Preiss insists: "The meaning is not mythical (in the sense of a repetition of a primordial Event) and anthropological, but eschatological: a savior who establishes a new world. The interest is turned towards the future, towards the second creation which will

---

op. cit., pp. 37–42; E. Sjöberg, *Der Menschensohn im ethiopischen Henochbuch* (1946); O. Cullmann, *op. cit.,* pp. 118–66; and especially Théo Preiss, *Le Fils de l'Homme.*

[22] O. Cullmann (*op. cit.,* pp. 124–28) insists on the incompatibility, even from the point of view of *the conception of time,* between the gnostic thesis of the return of Adam and the conception of the Son of Man. That is why the Son of Man is not called Adam in Judaism and in the New Testament; and that is why St. Paul will speak of the "second Adam" and not of the perfect return of the Man of the first age, even divided, in the manner of Philo, into a heavenly Adam, created in the image of God (according to Genesis 1:27), and an earthly Adam, drawn from the dust (according to Genesis 2:7) and sinful. As we shall see, the "second Adam," according to St. Paul, is the figure of the *new* Man.

surpass the first creation in the very act of completing it."[23]

It is the problem of the theologian, not of the philosopher, to understand what can be meant by the following two affirmations from the New Testament: at first, Jesus refers to himself in the third person by the title of Son of Man (Mark 13:26–27 is a direct echo of Daniel 7:13), and consequently the theme of the Son of Man gives the clew to the first Christology, that of Jesus himself; afterwards Jesus for the first time unites the idea of suffering and death, which had previously pertained to the theme of the servant of Yahweh, with the figure of the Son of Man; thus he makes the theology of glory follow the road of the theology of the Cross, and profoundly transforms the function of the Judge (connected with the figure of the Son of Man) by bringing it into contact with the suffering of the "servant," thereby making him both judge and advocate. That Jesus could be the point of convergence of all the figures without himself being a "figure" is an Event that exceeds the resources of our phenomenology of images. All the images we have examined are subject to our hermeneutic method insofar as they are scattered images, but their temporal and personal unity is not; the event announced in the Gospel, the "fulfillment," is properly the content of the Christian Kerygma.[24] Hence, our exegesis of the figures stays on the hither side of the Christian Kerygma; this is possible because "no Christological title, no Christian concept was invented by Jesus or by the Christians."[25] On the other hand, we can very well give an account of the enrichment that those fundamental images received from their being remolded by Jesus in the Synoptic Gospels and from their convergence in his own person.

[23] Théo Preiss, *Le Fils de l'Homme*, p. 70.

[24] *Ibid.*, p. 21. On the relation between the "Christological titles" and the problem of the person and nature of Jesus, cf. O. Cullmann, *op. cit.*, pp. 9–16, and conclusion, pp. 276–87.

[25] Théo Preiss, *op. cit.*, p. 7. The author continues: "On the surface, everything was borrowed; but, in reality, there was a conversion and modification of concepts and images through their convergent application to Jesus of Nazareth" (*ibid.*). At the end of his study: "The notion of the Son of Man, simple enough in its beginnings, was enriched first in Jewish thought and then in the thought of Jesus by so many new elements that it becomes difficult to see simultaneously all its implications" (p. 70).

It is to be remarked, in the first place, that pardon and healing are the two signs of the irruption of the new regime into the old. "The Son of Man has power on earth to forgive sins" (Mark 2:10). Thus "pardon" is not the movement of the "soul" separating itself from the "body"; it is the beginning of the new creation in the midst of men on earth, the penetration of the new era into ours. But what is most striking is that this power of "pardon" issues from the eschatological focus constituted by the cosmic judgment.[26]

We can see what the idea of "pardon" receives from its contact with the figure of the Son of Man. The figure of the Suffering Servant had contributed the idea of a substitutive suffering that is voluntary in character; the figure of the Son of Man at first accentuates the heavenly or transcendent character of that initiative to such a degree that, in the tradition of Judaism, this figure does not seem susceptible of incarnation; but at the same time it confirms the belief that what is highest above man is what is most inward to him. That heavenly figure is precisely Man; even more, it is the identity of one man with men taken in a body. Henceforth, the substitution of the suffering servant itself rests on the profound identity of the Man and men. Théo Preiss has made much of this: the identity of the Son of Man and men is the great "mystery" revealed in the prophecy of the last judgment upon the sheep and the goats; the verdict is based on the attitude of men toward the lowly, who *are* the Son of Man: "Inasmuch as you have done it unto one of the least of these my brethren, you have done it unto me" (Matt. 25:40). The Judge of men is identical with men insofar as they come face to face in action and insofar as they are crushed by the "greater" ones. This "mystery" is augmented by another one, to which we have already alluded: in the great act of Justification, the Son of Man figures at the same time as judge and as witness, Parakletos and Kategoros, while Satan is the Antidikos, the Adversary—an astonishing end for the figure

[26] "The notion of the Son of Man requires a juridical setting; it designates the central figure of a trial in which some are justified, others condemned. The juridical setting of the great judgment . . . is foreign to the myth of the Anthropos as we find it in oriental and gnostic syncretism. This juridical character is one of the distinctive traits of the Jewish and Christian notion of the Son of Man" (Théo Preiss, *ibid.*, p. 40).

of the Serpent who, from Tempter, becomes, within the juridical framework of the cosmic judgment, the prosecuting attorney, while the Judge becomes the intercessor; and he becomes the intercessor because he is also the substituted victim. This series of equivalences is the result of the identification of the Son of Man, judge and king at the End, with the suffering servant: "The Son of Man came not to be ministered unto, but to minister, and to give his life a ransom for many" (Mark 10:45). Whether this verse be a saying of Jesus, an interpretation by the Palestinian church, or a gloss of the Hellenistic church, it expresses completely the fusion of the two figures—the servant of the Eternal and the Son of Man. At the same time, this fusion introduces a new note of tragedy:[27] "How is it written of the Son of Man that he must suffer many things and be set at nought?" (Mark 9:12). The new note of tragedy is that the King is the Victim, "must" (δεῖ) be the Victim. That is "the mystery of Jesus."

Perhaps it is necessary to have assimilated this succession of figures in order to understand the one which insures the ultimate symmetry between the Adamic figure of the myth of origin and the series of eschatological figures—namely, the figure of the "second Adam," dear to St. Paul. If Son of Man means Man and if Adam also means Man, the question is fundamentally of the same thing (although St. Paul never uses the expression Son of Man, but speaks only of the "second Adam," the "last Adam," the "Adam who is to come"). This new figure at the same time consecrates the preceding ones and adds a decisive trait to them. On the one hand, it supposes the fusion of the two figures of the Son of Man and the suffering servant,[28] as well as the relation between a single figure of Man and the whole of mankind, between "one" and "many." On the other hand, the new meaning that St. Paul gives to the comparison of the two Adams is decisive for a retrospective understanding of the whole series of the earlier eschatological figures. What particularly interests us here is that, in

[27] On the taking up of the tragic into the Adamic and eschatological type, see below, Chap. V.

[28] K. Barth, *Christus und Adam nach Röm. 5; ein Beitrag zur Frage nach dem Menschen und der Menschheit,* in *Theol. Stud.* 35 (1952); French translation, Paris, 1958.

Romans 5:12–21, the comparison between the first and the second Adam not only establishes a similitude ("As the fault of one brought condemnation upon all men, so also the justice of one procures for all a justification that gives life," Rom. 5:18), but the apostle, by means of the similitude, brings to light a progression: "But not as the fault, so also the gift. For if by the fault of one many died, *how much more* the grace of God and the gift conferred by the grace of one man, Jesus Christ, have abounded unto many" (5:15).[29] This "how much more," which overturns the "as . . . so also," gives to the movement from the first to the second Adam its tension and its temporal impulsion; it excludes the possibility that the "gift" should be a simple restoration of the order that prevailed before the "fault"; the gift is the establishment of a new creation. We have already spoken of the role of the law in this experience of a break. We shall not go back to that point, but we shall insist on the irreversibility of that movement which, beyond the breaking off of the regime of the law, leads to the abundance of sin, and from the abundance of sin to the superabundance of grace: "The law entered in, that offense might abound. But where sin abounded, grace did much more abound, in order that as sin has reigned in death, even so grace might reign through justice unto eternal life through Jesus Christ our Lord" (Rom. 5:20–21). The sense of "as . . . so also," then, is "how much more," and the sense of "how much more" is "in order that": "God has shut up all in unbelief in order that he may have mercy on all" (Rom. 11:32).

In transcribing the movement from the "old man" to the "new man" in Adamological terms,[30] St. Paul opened the way to all the

[29] O. Cullmann (*op. cit.*, pp. 147 ff.) insists on two points. In the first place, the second Adam is heavenly as the Son of Man, and he suffers in place of men as the servant of Yahweh; "We understand how Paul could and must have seen, in the coupling of the ideas of 'Son of Man' and *Ebed Yahweh*, the solution to the problem 'Son of Man-Adam,' which the Jews had not been able to solve" (*ibid.*, p. 149). On the other hand, Romans 5:12, 17, and 18, erects the parallelism of the two "men" on the fact that in both cases "one man" ("one offense," "one act of justice") affects the destiny of "all." Now, the Servant and the Son of Man were both figures representative of all mankind, inclusive of a community.

[30] I leave aside, for the present, the problem whether St. Paul did not introduce into Adamology a Hellenistic theme closer to the gnostic dualism

"progressivist" theologies of history which, even if they go considerably beyond the intentions of the first Christian theologian, are manifestly prolongations of his "how much more" and his "in order that." The Church itself in its liturgy sings: *O certe necessarium Adae peccatum quod Christi morte deletum est! O felix culpa, quae talem ac tantum meruit habere Redemptorem!* That hymn celebrates only the greatness of the Redeemer; but the "greatness" of the Redeemer is also the "greatness" of the new creation. That is why there is less of error in the interpretation of the Adamic myth given by German idealism[31] than in all the dreams of a return to an earlier paradise. Kant, in the *Muthmasslicher Anfang der Menschengeschichte,* sees the good of the species issuing from the evil of the individual; and, in the *Religion within the Limits of Pure Reason* (I, IV), he understands the fall, free and fated, of man as the painful road of all ethical life that is of an adult character and on an adult level. What is properly Paulinian, and what the Greek and Latin Fathers commented on fervently,[32] is that, by a miraculous initiative on the part of God, the

---

of the "spiritual" and the "earthly" (or "the psychic") than to the Hebrew tradition. It is above all the other Adamological passage in St. Paul (I Cor. 15:35–55) that poses the problem: "The first man Adam was made a living soul: the last Adam is a spirit who gives life. . . . The first man, sprung from the earth, is earthy; the second man is from heaven." On this hypothesis, we shall attempt further on to account for the attraction of the Adamic type in the direction of the type of the exiled soul (cf. below, Chap. V, § 4); what we have said about the dualism of "spirit" and "flesh" in St. Paul (Part I, Chap. III, § 4) has prepared the way. For the moment, let us say only that St. Paul does not break with the Hebrew tradition of the Son of Man, who there, too, is "heavenly" (Dan. 7:13). Furthermore, as Héring has suggested (*op. cit.,* p. 153), followed by Cullmann (*op. cit.,* pp. 144–45), the key to the text might be to regard it as a polemic against the interpretation of Philo, who distinguished two "first men," the first heavenly and perfect (according to Genesis 1:26), the second earthly and fallen (according to Genesis 2:7). For St. Paul, it is the first who is earthly, and there is no other first; it is the second who is heavenly, and he is the last. The movement, the progression, from the earthly Adam to the heavenly Adam is only more striking; there is no longer, behind us, a "heavenly" Adam; the perfect man is wholly signified by the Man to Come.

[31] A. M. Dubarle, *Le péché originel dans l'Écriture* (Paris, 1958), p. 4, notes 1 and 2.

[32] Texts from John Chrysostom and Irenaeus in Stanislas Lyonnet, *De Peccato et Redemptione,* I (Rome, 1957), pp. 36–37.

fall is turned into growth and progress; the curse of paradise lost becomes a test and a medicine. It is, therefore, St. Paul's "how much more" and "in order that" which confer its truth upon that vision of history according to which man's access to his humanity, his passage from infancy to maturity, both on the individual level and on the level of the species, proceed through awareness of his limitations, his conflicts, and his sufferings. Salvation evolves a history; in symbolic terms: the second Adam is *greater than* the first Adam; the first Adam is *with a view to* the second Adam. We must go this far in order to understand that the Bible never speaks of sin except in the perspective of the salvation that delivers from sin. This "pedagogy" of the human race makes the pessimism of the fall abound in order that the optimism of salvation may superabound.

This detour through the "images of the End" permits us to give the notion of "pardon" all its richness. It has been said too readily that pardon is God's answer to man's avowal of fault. But pardon cannot be understood directly as a psychological event; in order to arrive at the experience, one must have come from the symbolic universe constituted by the accumulation of figures stretching from the Adam of the Yahwist editor to the two Adams of the Pauline epistles and including the figures of the Messiah-King, the Shepherd-King, the Prince of Peace, the Servant of Yahweh, and the Son of Man, to say nothing of the Lord and the Logos of the apostolic Church. Pardon, as something experienced, gets its meaning from the participation of the individual in the "type" of the fundamental Man. Without that reference to the symbol of the Man, the experience is shut up in that which is most inward and most individual. Something essential is then lost, something that cannot be conveyed except by the over-determined figure of a Man who is himself and all men, as the figures of the Servant and of the Son of Man already were. In Pauline language, the passage from the "old man" to the "new man" is the psychological event which expresses the incorporation of the individual in the reality signified by the "types" of the first and the second Adam; the inner mutation—"putting on the new man"—is the shadow cast on the plane of experience by a transformation which cannot be wholly experienced subjectively, nor observed from outside, but can only be signified symbolically as a participation in the "types" of the first and the second Adam. It is in this sense that St. Paul says that the individual is "transformed [μεταμορφοῦσθαι—metamorphosed] into the same image [εἰκών]" (2 Cor. 3:18), "conformed [σύμμορφος] to the image [εἰκών]" of the Son (Rom. 8:29), and that he "bears the image of the heavenly" after having "borne the image of the earthy" (I Cor. 15:49).[33] Of course, what gives ontological weight to these "types" in St. Paul is the faith that Jesus himself, a historical man, "exists in the form of God," that he fulfills the type, the form, the image. The plenary sense of those images is therefore inseparable from that faith, and the phenomenology of the images as such remains an abstraction in relation to that faith. At least, a simple comprehension of the symbols, such as we are pursuing in this book, is sufficient to make it understood that the psychology of religious experience does not render an account of the phenomenon of pardon. It is not that the individual undergoes a certain experience and then projects it into a world of images; on the contrary, it is because he is incorporated into that which those "images" signify that the individual attains the experience of pardon. The experience of pardon is, so to speak, the psychological trace of that which happens in reality, and which can only be spoken of in an enigma and signified as the passage from incorporation in the first Adam to incorporation in the second Adam.

Now this transfiguration, this metamorphosis, or rather this symmorphosis, is itself so rich in meaning that even on the level of "types" it gives rise to a series of symbolic equivalents which enrich the experience in their turn. We should like to dwell on the interplay between two significant symbolisms which develop in two divergent directions, but without exhausting it, the same theme of the assimilation of the individual to the εἰκών, the μορφή, of the Man: the more "juridical" symbolism of acquittal and the

[33] O. Cullmann, *op. cit.*, pp. 130–33, with reference to the third Pauline passage on the Man (Phil. 2:5–11), which, according to Héring, may likewise be regarded as associating the figure of the Son of Man ("in the form of God") with the figure of the Servant ("he humbled himself").

more "mystical" symbolism of the living graft. It must not be thought that the first is the poorer, because "juridical"; "juridical" does not mean "legalistic." On the contrary, this symbolism reaches its culmination in St. Paul, who pushed furthest the criticism of the Law and of justification by works, and in St. John, who does not concern himself with the problem of the Law. The "juridical" symbolism conveys some fundamental significations without which the "mystical" symbolism itself would lose its force. It can be traced very far back, to the archaic theme of retribution as well as to the contractual aspects of the "Covenant." This, perhaps, is what explains the appearance, in later Judaism and in the Septuagint, of the idea of "debt" (ὀφείλημα) and the idea of "remission" (ἀφιέναι, remittere, to remit a debt), which in the Septuagint covers the Messianic "propitiation," and even sometimes the Messianic "liberation."[34] The notion of "debt" has, it is true, a short career in the New Testament (it appears only in the enunciation of the Our Father in Matthew [6:12]—"forgive us our debts as we have forgiven our debtors"); on the other hand, ἄφεσις, the remission of sins in the sense of forgiving a debt, plays a considerable role in the writings of the primitive Church. Now this theme of "remission"—associated with the themes of "unbinding," "taking away," "destruction," "purification"—receives a considerable amplification when it is inserted into the eschatological context of the cosmic judgment; the "remission" of the debt is the acquittal at the great trial in which the fundamental Man is Judge and Advocate.

The symbolism of the eschatological judgment swells the meaning of the notion of pardon, because it relays to the level of symbols of mythical degree the primary symbolism of "justification" which we have interpreted in our study of guilt.[35] On the one hand, the primary symbolism provides a first foundation of meaning: gracious initiative, movement from transcendence toward immanence; but it is the second-degree symbolism of the eschatological judgment that supplies the cosmic and communal dimension, along with the temporal tension of hope. Without that relay of the images of the

---

[34] On this point, cf. Stanislas Lyonnet, *op. cit.,* pp. 52–54.
[35] Cf. above, Part I, Chap. III, § 4.

End, justification would relapse into biography, subjective and individual, as in the pietism of all times. By the *mise en scène* "of the great proceedings between God and his elect on the one hand, and the adversary and his on the other,"[36] something unique is signified, something that does not appear in the individualistic and subjective reductions of "pardon."

In the first place, man is an "acquitted" being. Rembrandt understood thus the parable of the prodigal son, in which he saw above all the mercy of the Father.[37] Thus the "return" preached by the Prophets and the "conversion" preached by the Baptist, insofar as they are psychological events and the work of human initiative, are enveloped in the eschatological event of "acquittal," in which the divine initiative is manifested.

The symbolism of the Judgment says also that men are pardoned in a body, not each one for himself; the individualism of religious experience is encompassed in the collective adventure of the history of salvation; the relation of "one only" to "all," characteristic of the symbol of the Man, unites mankind by a "how much more" essential bond than their sharing in the disobedience of the first Adam. This bond among men was already implicit in the symbolism of the departure from Egypt, the Exodus, which answers, in the Yahwist's account, to the banishment from Eden; it is a whole people that is delivered; and now it is all mankind, enumeratively and structurally, which is implicated in the "type" of the cosmic judgment.

The symbolism of the Judgment says, finally, that the fulfillment of humanity is mysteriously linked to a redemption of bodies and

[36] Théo Preiss, "La justification dans la pensée johannique," *Hommage et reconnaissance à K. Barth* (Neuchâtel & Paris, 1946); reproduced in *La Vie en Christ*, p. 50. The author, in discovering this "juridical" aspect of Johannine thought, lessens the distance between that thought and the thought of St. Paul, and places it in the continuation of Jewish eschatology. The "juridical" aspect is all the more interesting because it is nowise centered on the problem of the law and turns principally about the ideas of "testimony," "witness," "truth," and "falsehood," of συνήγορος or παράκλητος, that is to say, witness for the defense; here, too, the final judge is at the same time advocate and victim.

[37] Lyonnet, *op. cit.*, p. 61.

of the whole Cosmos; the soul cannot be saved without the body, the inner cannot be saved without the outer, the subjective cannot be saved without the totality.

As we see, the "juridical" symbolism of acquittal is not dry and sterile; the "mystical" symbolism of the graft of life completes it only on the condition that it receive from it its transcendent, communal, and cosmic dimensions. It is the inclusive character of the figure of the Son of Man, representative of a collectivity, which makes possible the living communion between the Spirit and spirits. Now, the Son of Man is the central figure in the justification at the great cosmic Judgment; what the symbol of "grafting" adds is the intimate connection of the infusion of life with the gratuitousness of the grace of acquittal. Thus we find, at the end of our long detour, that which the mystical interpretation of St. Paul, dear to Schweitzer, has brought to light and which religious experience has been able to verify, namely, the mystical immanence of life by the Spirit. But even so it is still the power of the symbol, giving what it says, that secretly animates the experience of the "life in Christ," the feeling of the continuity of life between "the vine and the branches." One lives only that which one imagines, and metaphysical imagination resides in symbols; even Life is a symbol, an image, before being experienced and lived. And the symbol of life is saved as a symbol only through communication with the ensemble of the eschatological symbols of "justification."

It is still an open question whether and how a philosophy and a psychology of "pardon" are possible on the basis of this rich symbolism of "justification" and "acquittal" at the cosmic judgment.

IV. The Myth of the
Exiled Soul and Salvation
Through Knowledge

THE NEW "TYPE" OF MYTH that we have now to consider is the
one which all *anthropological dualism* endeavors to transpose and
rationalize. What distinguishes it from all the other types is that it
divides man into "soul" and "body"; it is on the basis of this myth
that man understands himself as the *same* as his "soul" and *"other"*
than his "body."

Let us disregard for the moment the difficult question where
and when this myth attained its final literary form. It has been
said that the type which we are here setting forth was perfectly
exemplified by archaic Orphism; there has even been an inclination
to identify the myth of the exiled soul purely and simply with the
Orphic myth. But, as we know, the problems raised by Orphism
for the history of religions and the history of Greek thought are
considerable, and we shall not attempt to conceal them. We know
that all of Platonic and Neo-Platonic philosophy presupposes
Orphism and draws nourishment from its substance, but we do
not know exactly what sort of Orphism Plato was acquainted with
and what the παλαιὸς λόγος of Orphism was like before the
late revisions of the myth. That is why we must approach history
armed with a theory of types such as we find in Max Weber's
Idealtypen, but prepared to correct the ideal outline of the "myth

of the exiled soul" by a sort of give-and-take between the typological stylization and the patient investigation of history. Hence we shall give the first word to the conception of "type" before turning to the documents, with the understanding that only a certain familiarity with the historical and critical problems posed by archaic Orphism authorizes this heuristic and didactic boldness.

The mythical schema of the exiled soul can be understood through a comparison with the three other schemata which we have examined. It then becomes apparent that this myth is the only one which is, in the proper sense of the word, a myth of the "soul" and at the same time a myth of the "body." It tells how the "soul," divine in its origin, became human—how the "body," a stranger to the soul and bad in many ways, falls to the lot of the soul—how the mixture of the soul and the body is the event that inaugurates the humanity of man and makes man the place of forgetting, the place where the primordial difference between soul and body is abolished. Divine as to his soul, earthly as to his body, man is the forgetting of the difference; and the myth tells how that happened.

None of the other myths is a myth of the "soul"; even when they speak of a rupture in the condition of the human being, they never divide man into two realities. The drama of creation does not concern man as soul; it presents him as an undivided reality; it makes him as a whole the seat of the drama and an author of the drama, even if only by means of the ritual re-enactment. The tragic vision of the world is just as little a myth of the psyche; it takes man as an undivided whole just as much as the creation-drama does; it is the hero as a whole and, so to speak, without remainder, who is stricken and condemned. It is true that the esthetic contemplation of misfortune, which is the specific "consolation" in tragedy, can be considered as a detachment of the soul, akin to one of those "madnesses," ecstatic or phrenetic, that Plato enumerates in the *Phaedrus* (244*a*) and that reveal the supernatural, divine origin of the soul; but tragic enthusiasm, as such, is not a departure toward another region, but ecstasy in the spectacle itself and in meditation upon finitude and misfortune. That is why the enthusiasm of the tragic spectacle never gave birth to a myth of origin which would make evil the contrary of that enthusiasm, the reverse of that madness, and which would declare that our sojourn here below is itself intrinsically evil.

Finally, no myth is fundamentally less "psychic" than the Biblical myth of the fall. It is, of course, an anthropological myth, and even the anthropological myth *par excellence,* the only one, perhaps, that expressly makes man the origin (or the co-origin) of evil; but it is not in any degree a myth of the adventures of the "soul" considered as a separate entity. On the contrary, it is a myth of the "flesh," of the undivided existence of man. Whatever may be the later confusions of Christianity and Neo-Platonism, which in a certain fashion retains the essential traits of the Orphic myth, the dualistic myth and the myth of the fall are radically heterogeneous, and the task of typology is to complete that difference by stylizing the myths.

If now we turn to the literary documents,[1] we find the following situation: the Platonic philosophy presupposes a παλαιὸς λόγος —an "ancient discourse"—distinct from the Homeric and Hesiodic theogonies and traditionally called Orphic, which it transposes, integrates with its reflection on the soul, and rationalizes. Thus it makes the myth its origin, one of the non-philosophical origins of philosophy. Moreover, as we shall insist at the end of this chapter, there is a pact between this myth and philosophy which has no equivalent in any other myth. Philosophy breaks with the theogonic myth, it breaks with the tragic myth and its unavowable theology; but, after the sophistic crisis, it recharges itself in the Orphic myth and draws therefrom a new substance and a new depth. Plato himself shattered the tragic myth and transposed the παλαιὸς λόγος from Orphism; it is in this sense that "philosophy" presupposes Orphism. Unfortunately that παλαιὸς λόγος is not to be

[1] O. Kern, *Orphicorum Fragmenta et Testimonia;* W. K. C. Guthrie, *Orpheus and Greek Religion* (London, 1935); Nilsson, *Geschichte der griechischen Religion,* I (1941), Pt. IV, Chap. IV; Jeanmaire, *Dionysos, histoire du culte de Bacchus* (Paris, 1951); A. Boulanger, *Orphée, rapports de l'orphisme et du christianisme* (Paris, 1925); Delatte, *Études sur la littérature pythagoricienne* (Paris, 1915); Festugière, "Les mystères de Dionysos," in *Rev. biblique,* XLIV (1935); Moulinier, *Orphée et l'orphisme à l'époque classique* (Paris, 1955); Guthrie, *The Greeks and Their Gods* (1950), pp. 145–83 ("Dionysos"), pp. 307–32 ("The Orphics").

found, and one is tempted to ask whether it was not philosophy
that caused it to crystallize in order to give itself a borrowed
authority, the authority of archaic revelations.

We do, indeed, possess an etiological myth that is called "Orphic"; but that myth is attested, in its *complete* form, only by the
Neo-Platonists, by Damascius and Proclus. This is an astonishing
situation: the perfect Orphic myth is post-philosophical. The myth
is well known: the infant Dionysos was assassinated by the cunning
and cruel Titans, who thereupon boiled and devoured the members
of the god; Zeus, to punish them, blasted them with lightning and
from their ashes created the present race of men. That is *why* men
today participate both in the evil nature of the Titans and in the
divine nature of Dionysos, whom the Titans had assimilated in the
course of their horrible feast. It is a very fine myth, a true myth
of original sin. The mixture that constitutes the present condition
of human beings stems from an anterior, pre-human, superhuman
crime, and so evil is inherited; it points back to an event that
inaugurates the confusion of two natures which had before been
separate. That event is a murder which signifies both the death of
a god and participation in the divine. Yes, it is a very fine myth.
Unfortunately we have no means of proving that it belonged, in
this final form, to the "ancient discourse" of Orphism; indeed, we
have reasons for suspecting that it is a Neo-Platonic invention,
created for the pleasure and the profit of a philosophizing exegesis
of myths.

Caught between a myth that is pre-philosophical, but not to be
found, and a myth that is perfect, but post-philosophical, the
phenomenologist is indeed embarrassed. The situation would be
desperate if it were not possible to distinguish from the fully worked
out *etiological* myth, which is perhaps contemporaneous with the
philosophical exegesis of it, a *myth of situation*—a myth of the
present situation of man—which reveals "soul" and "body" as distinct magnitudes and powers, although it remains silent concerning
the origin of their confusion. This myth of a primordial distinction
is not undiscoverable; it can be reconstructed on the sole basis of
the documents of the archaic and classical epoch; it is, by itself,
the "ancient discourse" presupposed by philosophy. With respect to

the etiological myth and in comparison with the other etiological myths of evil, it is an embryonic myth; but perhaps it will be possible to show that the famous later myth is an orthodox explication of the archaic schema and that it is in perfect agreement with it. Thus we have no need to suppose that the *etiological* myth is ancient in order to give substance to the παλαιὸς λόγος invoked by Plato.

1. THE ARCHAIC MYTH: "SOUL" AND "BODY"

The ancient discourse of Orphism is precisely the invention of "soul" and "body."

It is noteworthy that Plato, in the fanciful etymology he proposes for "body" in the *Cratylus,* does not ascribe to the Orphics the exegesis of σῶμα by σῆμα, but declares that the Orphics "imposed that name"; and this is the important thing. It has already been remarked that the Homeric hero does not have a "body," but "members";[2] the body becomes a simple entity only in contrast with the "soul" and in virtue of the mythical symbolism which confers upon it a destiny other than that of the soul. Through the myth the body became an eschatological force:

It was the Orphics in particular, I think, who imposed that name, in the belief that the soul atones for the faults for which it is punished, and that, for its safekeeping [ἵνα σῴζηται], it has, round about it, the body in the likeness of a prison; hence, that it is, as its name implies, the *sôma* [the jail] of the soul, until the soul has paid its debt, and there is no need to change a single letter.

Cratylus, 400c.

We have here the nucleus of the situational myth, prior to the anthropogony of the myth of origin. It does not yet make the body the origin of evil; the soul seems rather to bring with it an anterior evil, which it expiates in the body. But this enclosure "in the likeness of a prison" receives from its penal character its own peculiar significance of alienation; in becoming an instrument of expiation, the body becomes a place of exile. It is no longer an expressive sign, according to another fanciful etymology which also identifies

[2] Cf. above, Chap. II, p. 215, n. 6.

σῶμα and σῆμα. More than the ship for the pilot, the jail is for the prisoner a strange, alien, hostile place; it stands, in closest proximity to the prisoner, for the inimical transcendence of the judge and of his sentence.

Starting with this first nucleus of meaning, we can reconstruct other traits of the ancient discourse. The place of punishment is also a place of temptation and contamination. It is not said, in fact, that for the soul to "pay its debt" (δίκην διδόναι, ἐκτείνειν) is to receive purification; the Jewish idea of reconciliation or propitiation must not be confused with the Orphic idea of expiation; the punishment appears rather to be a degrading sanction. As such, it is both an effect of evil and a new evil; the soul in prison becomes a secondary delinquent, continually subject to the hardening effect of the regime of the penitentiary. To understand this second trait, we must understand how the schema of *reiteration* interferes with the jail-schema. The *Phaedo* (70c ff.) evokes this transmutation in the meaning of life, when it ceases to be unique, and of death, when it ceases to be the limit of that unique life. Life and death alternate as two states: life comes from death and death comes from life, like waking and sleeping; the one may be the dream of the other, and each borrows its meaning from the other. Hence, the punishment is not only incarnation, but reincarnation; and so existence, under the sign of repetition, appears to be a perpetual backsliding.

Here we must introduce a third theme, which does not flow necessarily from the second and which, in fact, is not absolutely consistent with it: the theme of infernal punishment. Nilsson attaches a good deal of importance to it; indeed, he thinks that preaching about the punishments in the infernal world—the abode of the impure in the mire—was the center of the missionary activity of the Orphics and the point of departure of their preaching, which hinged upon punishment (*op. cit.,* p. 632). While the Eleusinians promised beatitude for the pure and the blessed and seem to have been silent on the subject of punishment, the Orphics took seriously the Homeric theme of the punishment of great criminals and made of it an imminent threat that weighs upon everyone. Plato attests that the traffickers in initiation who, at least in his time, usurped the name and the writings of Musaeus and Orpheus, speculated on this fear of punishment after death. "They call initiation those ceremonies which deliver us from the evils of the other world and which one cannot neglect without expecting dreadful torments" (*Rep.*, 364*d*). This speculation on the fear of the living surely does not exhaust the meaning of the preaching, which must have included, before it reached the decadence of Plato's day, both an appeal to a purity that was moral rather than ritual, as Plato himself understood it in the *Phaedo,* and also concern for a punishment which would fall upon the guilty and not upon the innocent, as commonly happens in this life.

At first sight there appears to be no connection between the theme of expiation in and through the body and the theme of expiation in the lower world. It is necessary to get beyond those two half-themes in order to understand their profound unity. It must be understood that life is a repetition of hell, as hell is a doublet of life, which gives a punitive meaning to those non-ethical torments the terrifying spectacle of which is displayed in life and history. The circularity of life and death is without doubt the more profound myth that subtends the two myths of punishment in the body (σῶμα) and punishment in Hades. To be born is to ascend from death to life, and to die is to descend from life to death. Thus the "body" can be the place of expiation for that other life which we call death, and Hades the place of expiation for the evil committed in this life which, for the profane, is the only life. Orphism, then, revived an old Indo-European theme of migration and reincarnation and at the same time plunged again into the depths of the old agrarian myths, which have always hinted at a hidden relation between the vernal rebirth of vital forces and the re-ascent of energies accumulated in the other realm, as if death increased the "wealth" (*Ploûtos*) of the prince of darkness (Pluto) and as if life could grow only by the forces granted to it by the other realm.[3] But only a religion or a religious movement such as Orphism, which ascribes to the soul an occult reality in this life, could understand that circularity not only as a succession of two states external to one another, but as an alternation which appears

[3] Jeanmaire, *Dionysos,* p. 54.

in our present life in the condensed form of a superimposition; if fragment 133 of Pindar represents Orphism correctly,[4] the soul of the sleeping wakes and the soul of the waking sleeps. Soul and body, then, have inverse possibilities, which conceal each other. The soul is the witness of the other world, hidden while we are awake in this life and revealed in dreams, ecstasies, love, and death. The circularity of death and life and the coincidence of their inverted values give the body-tomb a fullness of meaning. If one life conceals the other, we must say with fragment 62 of Heraclitus: "Immortals, mortals; mortals, immortals; our life is their death and our death is their life," and with the verses of Euripides cited in Plato's *Gorgias* (492*e*):

> Who knows whether living is not dying
> And whether dying is not living?

This permutation of meaning between life and death in this life itself—which Plato sums up thus: "Perhaps in reality we are dead" (492*b*)—completes the meaning of the body that was adumbrated in the theme of the body-prison. For the aspect of the other world that is repeated in the body is not its divinity, but precisely its penal function. Here, again, the *Gorgias* (493*a*) is very illuminating: the *reiterative* penalties that the Greeks were pleased to imagine— Sisyphus' rock, the vessel of the Danaïdes,—which are penalties in virtue of their character as impotent, vain, perpetual labors, are reflected in this world, after having been projected into the other world, and become a cipher for the body, insofar as the body itself is an experience of reiteration. We see in the *Gorgias* that the vessel which the uninitiated man fails to fill with the water of purification, and which is therefore the figure of an impossible purification,

---

[4] "For those who have paid to Persephone the ransom for their old faults [ποινὰν παλαιοῦ πένθεος], she sends their souls anew to the sunlight above at the ninth year; and from those souls there rise up illustrious kings, men mighty in their strength or great through their knowledge, who are honored among mortals forever as heroes without stain" (cited by Plato, *Meno,* 81*b–c*). Nilsson compares this fragment, 133, with fragment 62 of Heraclitus and with *Gorgias,* 492*c*. From these passages, he concludes: "it follows that the idea according to which the body is the tomb of the soul is so closely bound to the migration of souls that the Orphics must have shared those beliefs" (*op. cit.,* p. 694).

becomes the image of desire itself. Thus the punishment for desire is desire itself; the reiterative penalty that punishes in the other world the disordered life of this world is the cipher of that disorder itself.

This play of reflection between hell and the body is at the center of the understanding of the body; it explains that expiation in the body is quite the contrary of a purification; the soul in prison becomes a secondary delinquent corrupted by punishment; and so existence appears as an eternal relapse. The schema of exile, heightened by the schema of repetition, tends to make of the body the symbol of the misfortune of existence; for is there a more frightening idea than that which makes life a rebirth to punishment? In propagating itself from one life to the other, from a life to a death and from a death to a life, evil becomes the coincidence of self-inculpation and self-punishment. This mixture of condemnation and reiteration is the very figure of despair.

The interpretation of the "body" as an instrument of reiterated punishment provokes, as a reaction, a new interpretation of the soul, which may be called "puritanical" with E. R. Dodds: the soul is not from here; it comes from elsewhere; it is divine; in its present body it leads an occult existence, the existence of an exiled being that longs for its liberation.

Archaic Greek culture did not unify the soul any more than the body. Neither for the Ionians nor for the tragedians is the soul the unique existential root of thinking, meditating, feeling, suffering, and willing; it is scarcely more than the breath that the dying man gives back to the air, and that breath is not identified in a unique destiny with the scant and shadowy existence of death. "Soul" and "body" took substance together as the two dimensions, the two inverse vections of human existence.

Other cults taught enthusiasm, the possession of the soul by a god. What seems to be original in Orphism is that it interpreted this sudden alteration, this rapture, as an excursion from the body, as a voyage in the other world, rather than as a visitation or a possession. Ecstasy is now seen as manifesting the true nature of the soul, which daily existence hides. Other cults, too, taught the survival of the soul: Homer himself delights in painting the infernal punishments reserved for great sinners; the devotees of Eleusis meditate on the delights of Paradise. But the survival of the soul does not manifest a new "type," any more than possession by a god does, as long as survival is not understood as a return to its true condition, as an odyssey of the soul. The soul possessed becomes another, the sinner and the devout are in different places; the Orphic soul becomes again that which it is, divine and not human.[5]

Other seers, healers, purifiers exercised their followers in psychic excursions;[6] only the Orphics attained the revolutionary intuition that man is no longer to be defined as "mortal" but as "god." Wisdom is no longer "thinking as a mortal," but recognizing oneself as divine. The dividing line, the ontic difference, is no longer between the gods, who have kept immortality for themselves, and men, who have only vain hope for their share; it runs through man, separating his godlike immortality from the corruption of his body. Only this mutation in the very meaning of human existence made possible the legendary transcription of the life of Pythagoras and the death of Empedocles. It is the Orphic soul that cries out, in the *Purifications:* ἐγὼ δ'ὑμῖν θεὸς ἄμβροτος, οὐκέτι θνητός.

Perhaps we must go still further. If we compare what we have just said about the "divinity" of the soul with our previous remarks concerning the body as a jail and the mirror-play between the body and hell, it appears that the "divinity" of the soul does not consist simply in its capacity for survival; indeed, the idea of survival is on the way to being surpassed. The important thing now is to escape from the alternation of life and death, from reiteration; the "divine" soul is a soul that can be delivered from this reciprocal

[5] "It was here that the new religious pattern made its fateful contribution: by crediting man with an occult self of divine origin, and thus setting soul and body at odds, it introduced into European culture a new interpretation of human existence, the interpretation we call puritanical" (E .R. Dodds, *The Greeks and the Irrational,* p. 139). It is of little importance for us whether this type was foreign to Greece and whether it was shamanistic before being Orphic; what is important for us is that this type of "divine man" appeared in Greece, at the source of our occidental culture.

[6] For Abaris, Aristeas, Hermotimus of Clazomenae, and the ἰατρομάντεις in contact with the North, and, on the other hand, Epimenides of Crete, cf. E. R. Dodds, *op. cit.,* p. 141.

generation of contrary states, from the "wheel of birth and rebirth."

We are on the threshold of a new understanding of the self: the soul, having become the counterpole of the life-death pair, outlasts the time of repetition. It is true that before Plato, before the attempt in the *Phaedo* to link this perenniality of the soul with the non-temporality of the Forms, "immortality" is not yet "eternity"; it is only, so it seems, a force sufficient to keep the soul in existence through several bodies and several lives, as we see in Socrates' discussion with Simmias and Cebes. Before philosophy there does not yet exist a carefully thought-out model for an existence that remains *identical, the same as itself*. But at least the myth, in imagining a cycle of life and death, suggests a sort of carrying forward of the Self beyond contradiction, a sort of Repose beyond discord. Philosophy would not have tried to conceive the soul's identity with itself if the myth had not inspired it.

There is no doubt that this understanding of the self preceded Plato. Even if those to whom he refers in the *Meno* are not Orphics —or not only Orphics,—it is certainly the *type of the exiled soul* that he evokes in the following terms: "They are priests and priestesses who are anxious to be able to give reasons for the functions they perform, as well as Pindar and many other poets—all the truly divine ones. Here is what they say; consider whether you think they speak correctly. They say that the soul of man is immortal, and that it sometimes departs from life, which we call dying, and sometimes comes back to life, but that it is never destroyed; and that, for this reason, one's conduct in this life should be as holy as possible right to the end" (81*a–b*).

Of course, immortality is still tied to the imaginative schema of multiple rebirths ("thus the soul is immortal and reborn many times," ἀθάνατός τε οὖσα καὶ πολλάκις γεγονυῖα, *ibid.*, 81*c*); but the μῦθος is already λόγος; it gives reasons (λόγον . . . διδόναι). That is why those men and those women, "skilled in divine things," said "things which are true and beautiful" (81*a*).

2. THE FINAL MYTH

It was this myth of situation which evolved into a myth of origin in the anthropogony that the Neo-Platonists "quote" fragments of. Are we in the presence of an authentic restoration, or rather of a late construction which would permit the last philosophers of Greece to place their speculation under the authority of the poems from which their master, Plato, was supposed to have drawn his inspiration?

Are we in the presence of a pagan apologetics intended to turn the tables on Christianity by countering its stories concerning the origin and the fall of mankind with comparable stories?

Some points are certain: it is not disputed that the Orphic movement was distinguished from similar movements of the archaic era by the existence of *writings,* which broke with the oral and confidential teaching of other initiations or liturgies; and it is certain also that those books included theogonies. But the books must have been in perpetual flux; there was no fixed "canon" of them, and they were continually swelled by new speculations; the diversity of the Neo-Platonic versions is itself a sign of this. Besides, it cannot be proved that the archaic theogony was expanded into an anthropogony; this can only be conjectured on the basis of some allusions in classic authors, such as Plato's remark in the *Laws* about the "Titanic nature" of man. It is also a reasonable way of erecting a bridge between the theogony and the Orphic preaching, which was essentially turned toward man and his actual condition. It is those allusions and this argument of convenience which incline the majority of specialists on Orphism[7]—in spite of Wilamo-

---

[7] According to Guthrie (*Orpheus and Greek Religion,* 2d ed. rev., London, 1952), "The Orphic writers had taken what suited them from popular mythology. They had added something to its matter and much to its significance. It was a crystallization around a new centre, and the centre was the story of the dismemberment of Dionysos, the revenge of Zeus on the Titans, and the birth of mankind from the ashes" (p. 153). "The climax is original, is Orphic (and in this all our evidence concurs), because it enshrines the peculiarly Orphic thought of our own mixed earthy and heavenly nature" (*ibid.,* p. 120).

Nilsson, *Geschichte der griechischen Religion,* I, pp. 642–62, follows Guthrie in general. Not only does he maintain that the anthropogony was "fundamental for the Orphic religion" and that "in its broad outlines, it goes back to the archaic age" (pp. 647–48), but the episode of the sufferings of Dionysos at the hands of the Titans seems to him to be ancient, since otherwise we could not understand Plato's allusion to the Titanic nature: "this nucleus of the Orphic doctrine goes back to the ancient past" (p. 649).

witz and Festugière[8]—to think that the "quotations" by the Neo-

---

"Here," he says again, "we touch upon the most original part of the Orphic creation in religion: the addition to theogony of an anthropogony designed to explain the nature of man, composed of good and evil" (p. 650).

A. Boulanger, *Orphée, rapports de l'orphisme et du christianisme,* presents the same argument of convenience: the anthropogony reported by the Neo-Platonists "accounted for the twofold nature of the origin of evil on the earth, and thus gave the author an opportunity to expound the Orphic doctrine of salvation through expiation and purification" (p. 33). He does not go so far as to make of Onomacritus (the *chresmologos* of the era of the Pisistratidae, of whom Pausanias says that, "borrowing from Homer the name of the Titans, he made them the authors of the passion of Dionysos") the St. Paul of Orphism, and to ascribe to him a veritable doctrine of original sin and redemption, "which we know only from texts of a much later epoch" (p. 33). He grants, nevertheless, that the Orphic religion was formed by the end of the sixth century and that Onomacritus limited himself to bringing together two myths that had been independent before: the birth of men from the ashes of the giants struck down by the thunderbolts of Zeus, and the passion of Zagreus; that, however, is enough to justify the attribution to him of the discovery of "a new cause for the existence of evil on the earth" (p. 34). Such arguments authorize Boulanger to present as an Orphic doctrine all of the anthropogony which receives a complete exposition only in the last Neo-Platonists. There is an excellent summary on pp. 27–28. We shall see later that the fundamental argument of Boulanger has been contested. According to him, the myth of the murder of Dionysos by the Titans is etiological: "It was evidently created to explain a rite of which the celebrants no longer understood the meaning, namely, omophagy—that is to say, the sacrifice of an animal in which the spirit of a god of vegetation is incarnated and the consumption of its raw flesh by the participants, who believed that thereby they were assimilating a bit of the divine virtue" (p. 28). But is omophagy a "vegetation" rite? And, above all, is the myth of the dismemberment of Dionysos in harmony with this rite of tearing apart and eating raw flesh? Jeanmaire, in his *Dionysos* (pp. 384–90), contests both points. The second concerns us more here. Furthermore, Jeanmaire grants the antiquity of the myth of the passion and dismemberment of Dionysos: "To the extent that [the revelation contained in the Orphic writings] unquestionably proceeds from systematic thought, this myth appears inseparable from their conception of human nature, the origin of evil, and the conditions of individual salvation" (p. 404); but he regards the myth as adventitious in relation to the trance and the Dionysiac ritual; it represents rather a mutation of the legend of Dionysos in the direction of a "pre-philosophy still held captive by and, so to speak, still under the spell of the categories of immemorial myths" (p. 402).

[8] Wilamowitz-Moellendorf, *Der Glaube der Hellenen,* II (1932), pp. 199–202; Festugière, "Les mystères de Dionysos," in *Rev. biblique,* XLIV (1935). Here is Festugière's conclusion, after a careful examination of the archaic, classic, Hellenistic, and Neo-Platonic stages of the final myth:

Platonists preserve the essential character of the ancient poem.

Our typological method does not require us to settle the purely historical debate concerning the date when the anthropogonic myth was worked out. According to Glotz's formula, cited by Boulanger, the theory of sin preceded that of the fall among the Hellenes as

"Let us sum up the fruit of our inquiry. The historian finds himself in the presence of three kinds of documents.

"1) In the first place, a good number of inscriptions relative to the mysteries of Dionysos. Joined to the monuments decorated with figures in Italy, this material gives us a pretty good knowledge of the organization of the *thiasoi* and the rites of initiation. The best specialists, Cumont, Wilamowitz, Nilsson, have been able to pursue their studies without saying a word about Orphism. Issuing from the Thraco-Phrygian cults, the religion of the *thiasoi* is seen to depend more and more on public control: the rites are fixed, they are humanized. The same evolution is repeated everywhere. The initiate at first sought only to escape for some hours from the course of daily life. At the time of Christ, he is assured also of happiness as a reward after death. Orpheus is never named. Neither is Zagreus; there is only once an allusion to his legend, in the inscription of Perinthus, which is late and which, moreover, relates an oracle of the Sibyl.

"2) In the second place, a literary tradition about Orpheus. From the sixth to the third century before our era, Orpheus appears as an inspired singer, companion of the Argonauts, founder of the *teletai,* able to persuade rocks, wild beasts, and even Pluto. His disciples, in the fifth century, practice rules of abstinence and read poems attributed to him. In the fourth century, itinerant charlatans sell pseudo-orphic recipes. If Orpheus had his colleges, his mysteries, as some pretend, they have left no trace. The vogue of Orphism was born again only in the third and fourth centuries of our era. At that time there flourished a whole literature, the authenticity of which cannot be established.

"3) From the third century B.C. there circulated an 'Orphic' poem telling the myth of Dionysos Zagreus torn apart by the Titans. The identity of the Cretan and the Thraco-Phrygian seems then an accomplished fact, at least in a particular tradition, which does not exclude others. This legend of Zagreus copies the legend of Osiris; we do not know when and where it was formed. In an Egyptian ritual, it gives rise to special rites: the initiate deposits in the *kalathos* objects offered to the infant god by the Titan. Is a 'passion' of the god performed? Is omophagy practiced? We do not know. Plutarch connects the legend with the psychological dualism dear to the school of Pythagoras and to Plato. With Neoplatonism, the moral sense dominates and perhaps gives rise to rites that escape us. Unless new texts are discovered, nothing allows us to say that Orphism transformed the Bacchic mysteries constituted as we see them in the first two centuries of our era.

"To ask oneself whether the mysteries of Dionysos influenced Christianity is therefore a vain question. If one means the mysteries made known to us by epigraphy, no one dreams of a relation. For the rest. . . ."

well as among the Jews. Hence, it is to an intentional analysis of the myth of the fault of the Titans that we must now proceed, in order to show in what sense it explicates and completes the myth of situation. Such an intentional analysis presupposes that we take the myth in its final state (hence, in its late manifestation), and that we relate it retrospectively to the exegesis of the human condition that we have already reconstructed, without the aid of that myth, on the sole basis of the testimony of classic authors.

What do we find in that final myth? A theogony which, in itself, belongs to the type studied above under the heading of the drama of creation, but which veers in the direction of an anthropogony in agreement with the experience of the deep-seated discordance in man.

The drama of creation in which the new anthropogonic episode is set is not an indifferent frame; it imposes its presence and its general meaning on the new myth in a twofold manner. In the first place, it gives a cosmic dimension, an ontological depth to the misfortune which afflicts the soul. That misfortune is rooted in the pain of being, represented by the violent succession of the generations of great gods; the theogony gives Crime, Discord, and Guile a prehuman significance by associating them with the origin of things. In this regard, the figure of the Titans, which will be the pivot of the new myth, is a part of that pain of being; the Titan is the figure through which human evil is rooted in prehuman evil, at the same time as the pain of being is turned in the direction of anthropology through the same figure. But, in particular, the drama of creation preached to the Orphics already implies a possible interpretation of evil from which the strictly "Orphic" myth of the fault of the Titans stands out in contrast. The interpretation of evil through the theogony remained obscure in the poem of Hesiod, who hardly did more than to put the disparate primordial figures in a series. Some of those figures—Kronos, Ouranos, Zeus— are divinities from an earlier time who were now joined by means of dynastic succession, procreation, or murder; others—Night, Death, War—are aspects deemed primordial in our experience, joined together by a filiation comparable to the preceding; and others, finally, are regions or elements of nature such as Earth and

Sky. The myth attributed to the Orphics sketches, through similar images, a significant movement oriented from the one toward the many, from the confused toward the distinct—the same movement found in the Pre-Socratic cosmogonies. This kinship between the still mythical cosmogony of the Orphics and a more philosophical cosmogony can be explained in various ways: the philosophical cosmogonies may have been influenced by the Orphic myth, or more probably the theogonic myth, on contact with philosophy, may have turned in the direction of a genesis of being, while remaining a prisoner of the mythical imagination.

It is in the dominant figure of Phanes—"the most beautiful among the immortal gods"—that the "philosophical" tone of the Orphic myth is manifested. He is Protogonos, the first-born— Erikepaios, and so bisexual—Metis, counsel—Dionysos, Eros. Born of the primordial egg, representing the undifferentiated, he is both the difference among beings and the manifestation, the shining forth, of the totality of the world. He is truly "the unity of the whole and the separation of the parts."

But the same myth plunges back into naïve imagination. In order to identify with this rather esoteric Phanes the Zeus of common belief, the dying Zeus Zagreus and the dismembered and revived Dionysos of the sects of initiates, the myth resorts to a series of subterfuges. It tells of a second creation of the world by Zeus, who swallows Phanes and his creation and thus causes all his power to pass into himself; thus, says the myth, "all was created anew." Then the myth imagines that Zeus cedes his power to Dionysos: "O gods, lend your ears; this is he whom I have made your king." These concatenations are very much in accord with the taste of the most archaic theogony. Is Plato alluding to such a series of reigns when he exclaims ironically in the *Philebus:* "At the sixth generation, cease the order of your song" (66c)?

Toward what interpretation of evil is the myth oriented in its theogonic part? At first sight evil appears to be still included in the origin of things, as it was for Hesiod and particularly the Babylonians. But the figure of Phanes points to something different; in Phanes, the one and multiple manifestation, we have no longer a representation of the primordial contradiction between good and evil, but rather of progressive separation, of gradual differentiation, as one sees in the myth of the primordial Egg. This myth, in abandoning the contradiction and replacing it by a movement from the Confused to the Differentiated, ceases to account for the un-happiness of man, which consists, on the contrary, in the confusion of his twofold original nature. Consequently a myth of differentia-tion no longer suffices to explain the evil in man, which is a mixture; and it is not astonishing that the source of evil is dis-lodged from the sphere of the divine, which is in the process of concentrating itself in the figure of Phanes, and that theogony appeals to an anthropogony to explain an evil, the secret of which it no longer possesses. Thus the Orphic experience of an occult soul imprisoned in a body that is its enemy burst the bonds of the theogonic drama, which was itself in the process of orientation towards a rational cosmology. A new etiological myth was needed.

It is impossible to determine with any certainty what the Orphic anthropogony was in the archaic epoch. One must be content to cull the more and more precise quotations from later authors, which indicate pretty well the progressive construction of the theme, without our being able to tell whether they reflect an actual creation or a rediscovery of archaic themes. Nevertheless, some archaic traits can be made out among the manifestly later elabora-tions.

In the first place, it is significant that the origin of evil was re-lated to the "passion" of the youngest of the gods, Dionysos. The new myth, then, comes about from a strictly "theological" elabora-tion of the figure of Dionysos. Now, the infant god who is at the center of the original fault is not the Dionysos who inspires the μανία of the bacchantes, the rhythmic frenzy, their *joi de vivre;* he is a master of life, the young god who comes after Zeus. First, then, the madness of which Euripides' *Bacchantes* gives us a picture (itself no doubt mythical, but significant) had to be replaced by meditation, delirium had to become speculation. That the Orphics did thus turn Dionysianism against itself is very probable;[9] that they oriented it toward a sort of pre-philosophy,

[9] Nilsson, *Gesch. der gr. Rel.,* regards the legend that Orpheus died by being torn apart by the Maenads as an indication of the vindictiveness of

still captive to the mythical imagination, is all the more admissible
as the Dionysiac movement suffered other transpositions just as
extraordinary, if it is true that ritual action gave birth to the tragic
spectacle, by way of the dithyramb.[10] The possibility is not excluded
that Orphism from the beginning turned Dionysianism toward
speculation and placed Dionysos at the center both of creation, as
the *last* god, and of anthropogony, as the victim of the Titans. But
no doubt it was only later that Dionysos became explicitly the
conqueror of the Orient, and then master of the world, ready for
those great syncretisms, strongly tinctured with Orientalism, which
dominate the mystery religions centered on the death and resurrection of the god. The anthropogonic myth does not presuppose a
full explicitation of the consequences of the reform of Dionysianism
by the Orphics, but it does, surely, presuppose a decisive inversion
of the type of religious experience which was essential to it.

The second point to be considered is the role of the Titans in
the new myth. On the one hand they are associated with the passion of Dionysos as the "authors" of his murder; on the other hand

---

the devotees of Dionysos against the reformer. The prohibition of meat appears to him as another sign of the struggle of the Orphics against the
barbarous rite of tearing an animal apart (*diasparagmos*) and devouring it
raw (*omophagy*).

[10] Jeanmaire, *Dionysos,* pp. 220 ff. The author, a partisan of the antiquity
of the Orphic anthropogony, agrees that, "although there is no reason to
doubt that this introduction of Dionysos into the system that he exposed
goes back to the oldest Orphic writings, the consequences of it appeared
only in a future which at that date was still quite distant" (p. 401). The
author undermines one of Boulanger's arguments in favor of the antiquity
of the legend of the dismemberment of Dionysos. If one could show that
the dismemberment is the mythical explanation of the rite of tearing apart
(*diasparagmos*) the animal that the initiate devours raw (*omophagy*),
it would have a basis in the archaic ritual; but in the myth the infant-god
is not devoured raw; he is "boiled," and "the affirmation that the flesh was
consumed by the Titans (after being cooked) is found only in some witnesses and does not seem to be essential" (p. 384). The myth of the suffering of Dionysos is, then, not specifically Dionysiac; it is adventitious and
is only attached to, rather than integrated in, the legendary cycle of
Dionysos. Even if, independently of the cult of Dionysos, it has its own
archaic roots—as Jeanmaire believes, seeing in the sufferings of the young
god the memory of a ritual of initiation,—it would be necessary to show
that the myth of the "passion" of the young god was already incorporated
in the legendary cycle of Dionysos in archaic times.

they are incorporated in the genesis of mankind through their punishment and their "ashes." It is this progression in the myth that the literary expression permits us to follow from century to century. If the passion of Dionysos at the hands of the Titans is attested by several authors between the third century before our era and the first century of our era,[11] no text before Plutarch puts the crime of the Titans into relation with the birth of mankind. After having told how the Titans were struck by lightning as a punishment for the murder of Dionysos, Plutarch gives the following explanation: "This myth makes allusion to palingenesis. In fact, that part of us which is not amenable to reason or order, which is violent, not divine but demoniac, was called by the ancients Titans, and it is that part which is chastised and must pay the penalty" (*De Esu Carnium,* I, 996; Kern, *O. F.,* 231). Now it was Plutarch also who assimilated the Dionysos-Zagreus myth to the myth of Osiris; it is tempting to suppose, with Festugière, that he was the author of the Titanic origin of man as well. The Christian writers—Justin, Clement of Alexandria, Arnobius—who worry about the persistence of the ancient beliefs say nothing about

[11] The myth of Dionysos killed by the Titans seems to have been known in the third century before our era: "in the excess of their violence they [the Titans] put him to boil" (Euphorion). A recovered fragment of the Epicurean Philodemus, a contemporary of Cicero, after having spoken of the three births of Dionysos—"and the third when, after his dismemberment by the Titans, Rhea having reassembled the members, he came back to life"—confirms the third-century poet: "Euphorion, in the Mopsopia, confirms this legend, and Orpheus declares that the god has dwelt all this time in Hades" (Kern, *Orphicorum Fragmenta,* fr. 36). However, the authors of the romanced lives of the god, who flourished in the last centuries before our era, neglect this episode. Only Diodorus of Sicily (first century B.C.), in his vast review of myths, after having told the episode of the god torn apart by the sons of the earth, then boiled, and revived by Demeter, notes: "It is of this god [Dionysos] that Orpheus tells us in the *Teletai* that he was torn apart by the Titans" (Kern, *Orph. Frag.,* 301 and 303); but he interprets it in the allegorical manner of the Stoics, as a transcription of wine-making. Pausanias (first century A.D.), attributes the episode to the forger Onomacritus: "Borrowing the name of the Titans from Homer, Onomacritus compiled the mysteries (*orgia*), which he relates to Dionysos; it was the Titans, according to him, who were for the god the authors of his sufferings [παθήματα]" (Kern, *Testimonia,* 194). On all this, see Festugière, "Les mystères de Dionysos," *Rev. bibl.,* XLIV (1935), pp. 366–81, and Jeanmaire, *Dionysos,* pp. 372–416.

this Titanic origin of man (it is true that they do not say anything about Dionysos' return to life either); and sometimes they pass over, in silence, the sinister repast, although it is essential to the anthropogonic myth. Thus we arrive at Proclus' (fifth century; Kern, *O. F.,* 210) and Olympiodorus' (sixth century; *O. F.,* 209, 211–12, 220 f.) versions of the birth of mankind from the ashes of the Titans; it is here that the myth gets its final form: man is the inheritor both of the violent nature of the Titans, murderers of Dionysos, and of the nature of Dionysos, with which the Titans identified themselves by their horrible feast. Thus the myth is completed at the moment when the cycle of the Neo-Platonic philosophy reaches its end.

If we follow the progress of the myth through the successive quotations, we get the impression of a growth by addition of parts. The question now is whether this inflation of the Orphic myth at the beginning of our era also gave increasing explicitness to the myth of situation which we have elaborated without recourse to that anthropogony.

The myth of situation, as we have seen, tends to elevate the soul and to brand the body with a mark of infamy; it sets up the soul as the Same, and the body as the Other; the myth of situation is the imaginative expression of the dualism of soul and body, or rather the construction of that dualism in imagination. The question, then, that is raised by the myth is this: Why is that duality forgotten? Why is that twofold nature experienced as a confused existence? It was at this point that the myth in which the duality of the roots of existence was elaborated called for a myth which would recount the beginning of the confusion that makes necessary a constant effort to regain the vision of duality. It cannot be proved that this myth of origin was formulated explicitly in the archaic era, although Plato's allusion to "the Titanic nature" (*Laws,* 701*c*) is troublesome; but it can be shown, by an analysis of meanings, that the myth of origin completes the sense of the myth of situation.

If we confine ourselves to the citations in the classics, we find several times an allusion to an "ancient curse." Thus, in the fragment of Pindar cited by Plato in the *Meno* (81*b*), expiation in this body implies a prior fault—ποινὰν παλαιοῦ πένθεος. Now, the idea of a fault committed in another life, besides making it possible to safeguard the old law of retribution by spreading it out over a series of generations, as a text of the *Laws* (872*d–e*) on the vindictive justice of the gods says, implies a reference to a prior misfortune, to the transcendence of a choice which is both mine and older than I—in short, an evil that is both committed and undergone. Thus the prior life represents the unfathomable origin of an evil, the remembrance of which would be older than all memory. One might object, it is true, that the myth of the Titans points in another direction than that which is indicated in a Pythagorean verse quoted by Chrysippus, according to Aulus Gellius, VII, 2, 12: Γνώσει δ'ἀνθρώπους αὐθαίρετα πήματ' ἔχοντας.[12]

Contrary to this fragment of a Pythagorean ἱερὸς λόγος concerning a "freely chosen evil," does not the myth of the Titans entirely remove the blame for evil from man by referring the origin of evil to superhuman events and beings?

It may be remarked that the Biblical myth also distributes the origin of evil between a human figure—Adam—and a non-human figure—the serpent,—thus separating the willed from the suffered. The myth of the Titan, instead of dividing choice and fate between man and demon, concentrates them in a single, ambiguous figure on the border between the divine and the human. The Titan is not truly other than man: we are born from his ashes; he is the inherited and contracted part of evil choice, that which Plato calls our Titanic nature; he attests that the lowest degree of freedom is close to the brute, angry, inordinate force of the unleashed elements; Prometheus is in harmony only with the shapeless scenery of the Caucasus, not with the temperate landscape of Colonus, which bathes the aged, transfigured Oedipus in sweetness. This savage possibility in ourselves, beginning from which our freedom becomes humanized, is relegated by the myth to the origin and incarnated in a crime older than any human fault; and so the Titan represents the anteriority of evil in relation to actual human evil. There is no occasion for opposing it to those evils, evoked

[12] "You shall know that men have self-chosen woes." Quoted by Delatte, *Études sur la littérature pythagoricienne*, p. 25.

by the Pythagorean ἱερὸς λόγος, which are αὐθαίρετα—"willed by ourselves," "freely chosen"; the Orphic myth projects the temporal transcendence of evil into a mythical time; it gives a figurative expression to this experience: evil does not begin because it is always already there in some fashion; it is choice *and* heritage.

The Platonic myth in Book X of the *Republic* will give expression to the same fateful character attached to evil choice; it, too, will project this background implied in every actual choice into a choice that has already taken place, once upon a time, elsewhere. We shall return to this point later.

Even if the Orphic anthropogony is a late elaboration, even if it is only a philosophizing allegory invented after the beginning of our era, it reveals the profound intention of the myth of situation which undoubtedly existed, in Orphism and outside Orphism, much earlier than Plato. The anthropogonic myth exhibits, on the level of theogonic images, the complete unfolding of the myth of situation by means of which the Orphics *invented* the "soul" and the "body."

3. Salvation and Knowledge

If now, turning toward the future, toward deliverance, we ask what type of "salvation" goes with this type of "evil," one answer forces itself upon us: while the not-to-be-avowed theology of the wicked god excludes philosophy and finds fulfillment in the spectacle, the myth of the exiled soul is *par excellence* the principle and promise of "knowledge," of "gnosis." The Orphics, says Plato, "named" the body; in naming the body, they named the soul. Now the act in which man perceives himself as soul, or, better, makes himself the same as his soul and other than his body—other than the alternation of life and death,—this purifying act *par excellence* is knowledge. In this awareness, in this awakening to itself of the exiled soul, all "philosophy" of the Platonic and Neo-Platonic type is contained. If the body is desire and passion, the soul is the origin and principle of any withdrawal, of any attempt to put a distance between the λόγος on the one hand and the body and its πάθος on the other; and all knowledge of anything, every science, whatever its object, is rooted in the knowledge of the body as desire and of oneself as thought in contrast with desire.

Of course the Orphic movement itself seems not to have been capable of going explicitly beyond "myth" to "philosophy"; even on the level of the ἱερὸς λόγος the Orphic reform, as we have seen, does indeed bear on "meanings," as Guthrie says, but it remains a prisoner of cosmogonic imagery. But Orphism is not only a βίος λόγος ; it is also a βίος, a "way of life." This "way of life" is to the future what the myth is to the past; as the myth is the recollection of a human evil that is older than man, so the Orphic ἱερὸς is the prophecy of a deliverance that is more human than man. And just as the myth wavers between theogonic imagination and philosophical reflection, so the Orphic βίος hesitates between the old ritual purification and a new sort of purification in spirit and in truth. On the one hand, it looks to the *teletai* preached by so many other professional purifiers, so many other mendicant soothsayers and prophets of the sort judged so severely by Plato in Book II of the *Republic*:

For their part, mendicant priests and soothsayers go to the doors of the rich and persuade them that they have power, obtained from the gods by sacrifices and incantations, to repair by means of pleasurable rites and feasts any crime committed by a man or by his ancestors. . . . On the other hand, they produce a host of books by Musaeus and Orpheus, sons of the Moon and of the Muses, so they say. They follow these books in their sacrifices, and they make not only individual men but also states believe that there are ways of absolving and purifying men from their crimes through sacrifices and diversions, whether they be living or dead. They give the name of initiations to those ceremonies which deliver us from the evils of the other world, and they assert that dreadful things are in store for those who have not sacrificed.

Republic, 364b–365a

Nevertheless, one can discern, amid these equivocal activities, the attempt to discover a life more concerned with purity of heart.[13]

---

[13] Compare this severe fragment with the testimony of Pausanias, quoted by Guthrie, *op. cit.*, pp. 59–60: "Now in my opinion Orpheus was one who surpassed those who went before him in the composition of verses, and reached a position of great power owing to the belief that he had discovered how to initiate into communion with the gods, how to purify from

No doubt O. Kern's grandiose reconstruction, in *Die Religion der Griechen,* of an Orphic religion on the Christian model, with parishes, sacraments, hymns, and dogmas, must be rejected. It is possible that Orphism was less a homogeneous movement than the modification of several other movements dedicated to Apollo and Dionysos, themselves on the way to merging.[14] Orpheus himself seems to have been an Apollonian reformer of the wild cult of Dionysos before becoming the patron saint of the sects in Italy, which did not hesitate to place their own mystical compositions under his patronage. But it appears that some of them had begun to realize, before Plato, the "potential greatness," as Guthrie says (187), in Orphism. Otherwise, how can we explain the fact that Plato, so severe in *Republic* II, could write in the *Phaedo:*

Besides, it is possible that those to whom we owe the institution of initiations were not without merit, but that it is really the truth which has lain hidden from olden times under their enigmatic language: whoever arrives in Hades profane and uninitiated lies in the mud, while he who has been purified and initiated will dwell with the gods when he arrives there. For, as those who concern themselves with initiations say, *the thyrsus-bearers are many, the bacchantes are few.* Now the latter, in my opinion, are those whose occupation has been philosophy in the strict sense of the term.

Phaedo, 69c–d

Significant also is the famous passage of the *Meno* in which Plato speaks with reverential admiration of those "divine" men, those priests and those priestesses who have been concerned to "give reasons" (λόγον διδόναι) for their office. And even the bizarre rites traditionally ascribed to the Orphics must have wavered between the archaic form of taboos and a quite esoteric symbolism,

---

sin, to cure diseases and to avert divine vengeance." Kern, *Test.,* 142, 93, 116, 123, 120.

Guthrie himself writes: "The Orphic showed a genius for transforming the significance of his mythological or ritual material (he would not have been a Greek if he had not), and sometimes saw an opportunity of preaching his religion through the medium of symbols which were in their origin of the crudest and most primitive" (*ibid.,* p. 128).

[14] Guthrie, *op. cit.,* pp. 41–48.

such as Plato implies in his allusion to the "Orphic regime" and its abstinences (*Laws, 782c*).[15]

That Orphic "purification" was already on the road toward philosophy is suggested by the saying quoted by Plato: "Many bear the thyrsus, but few become bacchantes."

It is the Pythagorean literature that marks, decisively and explicitly, the passage from "purification" as rite and "purification" as "philosophy."[16] The "sacred discourse" of Pythagoreanism—as it can be reconstructed, or simply conjectured, on the basis of the testimony of the fourth and third centuries alone, without recourse to the Neo-Pythagorean apocrypha of about the beginning of our era, and still less to the even later "Golden Verses"—was preeminently a discourse of this sort, hesitating between myth and philosophy. That literature, situated at the crossroads of science and revelation—the division between "Mathematicians" and "Acousmatics" is very significant in that respect,—is connected on the one hand with the pessimistic myth of the fall and, on the other hand, points toward purification by knowledge. It is an echo of Orphism that we hear in the fragment of Chrysippus, which refers expressly to a Pythagorean maxim: γνώσει δ'ἀνθρώπους αὐθαίρετα πήματ' ἔχοντας.[17] It is Orphism that the Pythagoreans extend in the direction of Platonism when they proclaim that unity of the race of men and of gods which Pindar also sings: "One is the race of men, one the race of the gods" (frag. 131, *Nem.*, 6, 1). "To follow the god," to walk in the "traces of the di-

---

[15] Cf. also Euripides, *Hippolytus*, 952; Aristophanes, *Frogs*, 1032; Herodotus, II, 81. Nilsson (pp. 687–88) refers to all these texts.

See Nilsson's very reasonable conclusion on the significance of Orphism in general (*op. cit.*, p. 699): "They put man, with his nature composed of good and evil and his need for deliverance from the bonds of corporeity, at the center of their religious thinking. Thus Orphism is the creation of a religious genius whose work was in part obscured by gross myths and mercenary priests."

[16] Delatte, *Études sur la littérature pythagoricienne:* "He wavered between the Orphics and the philosophers, seeking his way; and, as his mind had affinities with both, he believed he could synthetize their work" (p. 26).

[17] Aulus Gellius, VII, 2, 12, S.V.F. 1000, quoted by Delatte, *op. cit.*, p. 25. Delatte finds a faithful comment on this fragment in Iamblichus' *Life of Pythagoras:* ἐπέδειξεν ὅτι οἱ θεοὶ τῶν κακῶν εἰσιν ἀναίτιοι καὶ ὅτι νόσοι καὶ ὅσα πάθη σώματος ἀκολασίας ἐστὶ σπέρματα.

vine"—this is already the scheme of deliverance of "philosophy."
Plato also will speak of the "traces of the Good" in the *Republic*.

The very word "philosophy" bears witness to what we have said:
rather than calling a man who meditates in pursuit of the god
σοφός or σοφιστής, the Pythagoreans preferred the rather esoteric term φιλόσοφος; it evokes the φιλία that is broken by "discord," by ἔρις, which sets man at variance with the divine and
with his own origin. Withdrawal of the soul, reunion of the soul
with the divine—there we have the philosophical intention before
Plato. The idea of happiness—εὐδαιμονεῖν—is at the point where
the magical vision and the philosophical vision meet; for "happiness" is the "good soul,"[18] and the "good soul" comes to a man
when he "knows," when knowledge is the "strongest" and desire
the weakest.[19]

Perhaps we can best sum up the whole μῦθος and the whole
βίος of the Orphico-Pythagoreans in the following exclamations,
taken from the *Purifications* of Empedocles: "What honors and
what heights of bliss have I left to wander here among mortals!"
And again: "I have wept and I have wailed upon seeing the un-
familiar place where Murder dwells, and Wrath, and tribes of
other woes—withering diseases, corruption, flood." And: "Of these
am I now one, exiled from the divine abode, a wanderer who has
placed his trust in raving Discord." And, finally, the famous words:
"I assure you that I am an immortal god, and no longer a mortal."

But these fragments not only testify to the carrying out of the
Orphico-Pythagorean tradition in the mingled light and shade of
the philosophizing myth (or mythicizing philosophy); they herald
something else. We cannot forget that the author of the *Purifications* is the author of a poem *On Nature*. For the first time, perhaps, the same principle—Discord, νεῖκος—is invoked both as a
cosmological principle, coupled with Friendship, and as the root of
human evils; the souls of mortals are long-lived gods who have
"erred, soiling their hands with murder," and who, "having vio-

---

[18] D. L., VIII, 32: εὐδαιμονεῖν τ'ἀνθρώπους ὅταν ἀγαθὴ ψυχὴ προσγένηται.
[19] "What is strongest?" the catechist asks the acousmatics. Answer:
"γνώμη." "What is most excellent? Happiness." "What is the truest
saying? That men are wicked." (From Iamblichus, *Life of Pythagoras*,
Chap. XVIII, quoted by Delatte, *op. cit.*, p. 282).

lated their oath," have "followed in the steps of Discord." Friendship and Discord emerge from the myth and are elevated to the
rank of Principles: "Good and Evil as principles," says Aristotle.[20]
With Empedocles' Discord, a principle of *things* which is manifested in *human* evil, we are on the threshold of a new peripeteia;
the "myth" rises to "speculation." We shall not now cross this
threshold of the symbolic knowledge of Evil.

---

[20] Aristotle, *Metaphysics*, A, 4, 985 a 8.

V. The Cycle of the Myths

1. FROM THE STATICS TO THE DYNAMICS OF THE MYTHS

AT THE END of these hermeneutic exercises, there is a question that must be troubling the reader as it has embarrassed the author. Can we live in all those mythical universes at the same time? Shall we, then, we children of criticism, we men with immense memories, be the Don Juans of the myth? Shall we court them all in turn?

And if we had some reason for preferring one of them, why did we have to lend so much attention and understanding to myths that we were going to declare abolished and dead?

We must try to get beyond this alternative. On the one hand, having familiarized ourselves successively with each of the myths, we are assured that they all speak to us in some fashion; this credit, this belief, are the presupposition of our enterprise; we would not have interrogated them if they had not challenged us and if they could not still address themselves to us. And yet, nobody asks questions from nowhere. One must be in a position to hear and to understand. It is a great illusion to think that one could make himself a pure spectator, without weight, without memory, without perspective, and regard everything with equal sympathy. Such indifference, in the strict sense of the word, destroys the possibility of appropriation.

The presupposition of my undertaking is that the place where one can best listen to, hear, and understand what all the myths together have to teach us is the place where the pre-eminence of one of those myths is proclaimed still today—namely, the Adamic myth. For that presupposition I must "give reasons," as Plato says in speaking of the initiates of the Orphico-Pythagorean tradition, and as St. Paul says in addressing the Christians of the Apostolic age.

How? By an exact awareness of the mode of belief attached to that proclamation. Three points need to be stated precisely in this order of ideas.

1. In the first place, the faith of the Christian believer is not concerned primarily with an interpretation of evil, its nature, its origin, and its end; the Christian does not say: I believe in sin, but: I believe in the remission of sins; sin gets its full meaning only retrospectively, from the present instant of "justification," in the language of St. Paul; on this point we have insisted sufficiently at the end of our study of the trilogy defilement-sin-guilt. It follows that the description of sin and the symbolization of its origin by means of the myth belong to the faith only secondarily and derivatively, as the best counterpart of a gospel of deliverance and hope. It is not without reason that we repeat this, in opposition to the tendency, issuing from Augustinianism, to confer upon the "dogma of original sin" the same sort of authority as upon justification by faith in the death and resurrection of Christ; like the church of the first centuries, we regard the interpretation of sin as a part of the "prolegomena of the faith," rather than as a part of the "deposit of the faith." All our effort to relate the dogma of original sin to the Adamic myth, and the latter to the penitential experience of Israel and of the Apostolic church, points in the same direction; in making apparent the intentional relation of the dogma to the myth and of the myth to the confession of sins, we have confirmed the subordination of the dogma of original sin to the preaching of salvation. The bond that unites the Adamic myth to the "Christological" nucleus of the faith is a bond of suitability; the symbolic description of man, in the doctrine of sin, suits the announcement of salvation, in the doctrine of justification and regeneration. To understand that bond of suitability is already to give a reason for the belief accorded to the Biblical *symbolization* of human evil.

2. That doctrine of sin, even when considered abstractly, detached from its soteriological context, is not an incomprehensible revelation; besides its relation of suitability to Christology, it is

revealed insofar as it is revealing. In fact, here again we find our interpretation of the myth as a symbol of the second degree. It is far from being the case that the Christian believer is obliged to limit himself to the alternative, either myth or revelation; rather, he should resolutely seek the meaning revealed in the story of the fall on the basis of its interpretation as myth, in the twofold sense of an etiological fable demythologized by history and a revealing symbol liberated by the very process of demythologization. Is not the revelation of this myth, then, precisely its power to challenge? St. Paul spoke of the "inner witness of the Holy Spirit." What can that witness signify, in the particular case of the understanding of evil, its nature, and its origin, if not the "discerning of spirits"? And is that, in its turn, anything other than the *election* of the best myth, the recognition of the most significant, the most reveal- ing myth, and, at the same time, the myth that can most appropri- ately be co-ordinated with the advent of salvation, serving as a prolegomenon to the faith? If it is in this sense that we must seek for some quality of revelation in the Biblical story of the fall, that quality is not irrational; it calls for verification of its revealed origin by its revealing power. The Holy Spirit is not an arbitrary and absurd commandment, it is discernment; as it addresses itself to my intelligence, it invites me, in my turn, to practice the *crisis,* the discernment of myths; and this is already a way of practicing the *crede ut intelligas* which we shall evoke in the following chap- ter. This discernment calls for a hermeneutics capable of bringing out the symbolic meaning of the myth. As we shall show in the methodological chapter that terminates this investigation of the myths of evil, the hermeneutics, in its turn, requires that the philosopher wager his belief, and that he lose or win the wager by putting the revealing power of the symbol to the test of self- understanding. In understanding himself better, the philosopher verifies, up to a certain point, the wager of his faith. All the rest of this work will be devoted to the verification of the wager through integral experience; thus the revealing power of the myth will be manifested. This is the second way in which the believer justifies his belief in the revealed character of the myth to which he ascribes pre-eminence.

3. The pre-eminence of the Adamic myth does not imply that the other myths are purely and simply abolished; rather, life, or new life, is given to them by the privileged myth. The appropriation of the Adamic myth involves the appropriation, one after the other, of the other myths, which begin to speak to us from the place from which the dominant myth addresses us. Not that the other myths are "true" in the same sense as the Adamic myth: we have seen that the Adamic myth is opposed to all the others in various ways, as they are opposed to one another; but the Adamic myth, by its complexity and its inner tensions, reaffirms *in varying degrees* the essential truths of the other myths. Thereby one catches sight of a specific manner of justifying the Adamic myth, which consists in displaying the relations of opposition and identification that attach the other myths to the Adamic myth. By thus putting all the other myths into perspective with relation to a dominant myth, we bring to light a circularity among the myths and we make possible the substitution of a dynamics for a statics of the myths; in place of a static view of myths regarded as having equal rights, the dynamic view makes manifest the struggle among the myths. The appropriation of the struggle among the myths is itself a struggle for appropriation.

This chapter is devoted to the dynamics of the myths. Of the three ways of accounting for the pre-eminence of the Adamic myth, this is the one that most naturally follows our mythical investigation of fault. The second way will be the object of the last volume of this work; it corresponds to the line of force of our whole undertaking and commands a philosophy of fault, distinct from a theology; the principle of it will be set forth in the concluding chapter of the present work. The dynamics of the myths which we are going to propose plays a propaedeutic role with relation to that philosophical interpretation of the symbols of evil; for it is not the Adamic myth alone, but the whole cycle of myths and its gravitation around the dominant myth, that provide the subject matter for reflection on the symbols of evil. As to the first way of justifying the Adamic myth, it belongs to theology and not to philosophy. The philosopher verifies what is revealed by that which reveals; the theologian testifies to the agreement of the Adamic myth with Christology. Like St. Paul, he places the "in Adam" with relation to the "in Christ," and determines the relevance of the symbol of the fall to the totality of the Kerygma; that relevance constitutes its authority in an ecclesiastical theology. The philosopher who does not pretend to annex Christology to his enterprise can have recourse only to the verification of the revealing character of the myth. The belief accorded to the pre-eminence of the Adamic myth is common to the way of the philosopher and the way of the theologian, but their modes of justifying the belief are different. We shall be concerned with the bifurcation between philosophy and theology only in the analyses of the final chapter. The dynamics of the myths, which we are about to sketch, still belongs to an undifferentiated mode of thinking that is common to the theologian and the philosopher.

The cycle of the myths can be compared to a gravitational space, in which masses attract and repel each other at various distances. Seen from the point of view of the Adamic myth, the oriented space of the myths presents a concentric structure, which puts the tragic myth nearest to the Adamic myth and the myth of the exiled soul farthest from it. Every time that we have anticipated the dynamics in the statics, we have affirmed the proximity of the tragic myth and, indeed, of the theogonic myth to the Adamic myth, and the isolation of the Orphic myth, which alone divides man, separates the soul, and invites us to flee from here to the beyond. We must now elaborate those scattered remarks systematically, following the order of increasing opposition. By means of and beyond that increasing opposition, the essential truths of the other myths will be reaffirmed with decreasing force.

2. The Reaffirmation of the Tragic

Let us, then, sketch the movement that leads from the Adamic myth to the tragic myth under its two aspects, anthropological and theological, and from the tragic myth to the most archaic and apparently most outmoded vision of the world, the vision of theogony.

The Adamic myth is anti-tragic; that is clear. The fated aberration of man, the indivisibility of the guilt of the hero and the guilt of the wicked god are no longer thinkable after the twofold confession, in the Augustinian sense of the word confession, of the holiness of God and the sin of man. And yet the Adamic myth does reaffirm something of the tragic man and even something of the tragic god.

There are several "tragic" aspects of the Adamic myth. We have already hinted at the "tragic" meaning of the figure of the serpent, which is *already* there and *already* evil. But before coming back to the serpent, we must note the tragic accent of the Adamic figure itself. That figure thematizes a mystery of iniquity which is not reducible to the clear consciousness of actual evil, of the evil beginning in the instant; it points towards an underlying *peccability* which, as Kierkegaard says in *The Concept of Dread,* endures and increases quantitatively. That underlying peccability is like the horizon of actual evil, and is perceived only as horizon, at the frontier of the avowal of present evil. Later speculation will endeavor to fix that underlying peccability in the false concept of inheritance. The rationalization of original sin as inherited sin was to encumber Western thought for centuries. It is necessary to undo this knot of speculation and to display the motivations deposited as a sediment in the pseudo-thought of an original sin which was supposed to be both a *first* sin and a *transmitted* heritage; it is necessary to come back to the limiting concept of an evil concerning which I confess that it is already there in the very instant in which I avow that I put it there. This other side, not posited, of an evil that is posited, is the "radical" in radical evil; but I know it only as implied.

The other myths speak of the anteriority (theogonic myth) of this reverse side of sin, the sin committed by all men in Adam, or of its passiveness and externality (Orphic myth), or, finally, of its fatedness, which is the contribution of the tragic myth. By means of an unavowable theology, aspects of the Ineluctable are made manifest which are not opposed to freedom, but are implied by it, and which cannot be made the objects of biological, psychological, or sociological knowledge, but are accessible only to symbolic and mythical expression. It is precisely the tragic myth which is the depository of the Ineluctable implied in the very exercise of freedom, and which awakens us to those fateful aspects which we are always stirring up and uncovering as we progress in maturity, autonomy, and the social engagement of our freedom. The myth regroups these fateful aspects, which come to the surface discontinuously through scattered signs. For example, it is not possible for me to aim at completeness without running the risk of losing myself in the indefinitely varied abundance of experience or in the niggardly narrowness of a perspective as restricted as it is consistent. Between chaos and the void, between ruinous wealth and destructive impoverishment, I must make my way by a road that is difficult and, in certain respects, impossible. It is Ineluctable that I lose the wealth in order to have unity, and vice versa. Kierkegaard clearly recognized the incompossibility of the requirements for becoming oneself; *The Concept of Dread* evokes the two ways in which a man may lose himself: in the infinite without finiteness or in the finite without infinity, in reality without possibility or in imagination without the efficacy of work, marriage, profession, political activity.

To this major sign of the fateful character of freedom many others can be added. Who can realize himself without excluding not only possibilities but realities and existences, and, consequently, without destroying? Who can join the intensity of friendship and love to the breadth of universal solidarity? It is a tragic aspect of existence that the history of self-awareness cannot begin with the sympathy of the Stoics, but must start with the struggle of master and slave, and that, once having consented to itself and to the universal, it must plunge anew into self-division.

Now, all these fateful aspects, because they are implied in freedom and not opposed to it, are necessarily experienced as fault. It is I who raise up the Ineluctable, within myself and outside myself, in developing my existence. Here, then, is a fault no longer in an ethical sense, in the sense of a transgression of the moral law, but in an existential sense: to become oneself is to fail to realize wholeness, which nevertheless remains the end, the dream, the horizon, and that which the Idea of happiness points to. Because fate belongs to freedom as the non-chosen portion of all our choices, it must be experienced as fault.

Thus the tragic myth is reaffirmed as an associated myth, revealing the fateful reverse side of the ethical confession of sins. Under the figure of the blinded and misled hero, it expresses the role of ineluctable guilt. This fateful aspect, joined to the aspects of antecedence and externality expressed by the other myths, points toward the quasi-nature of an evil already there, at the very heart of the evil that springs up now. It can only be represented dramatically, theatrically, as a "fate," as a fold or crease that freedom has contracted. That is why tragedy survived its destruction by Platonism and Christianity. What cannot be thought, can and must nevertheless be exhibited in the figure of the tragic hero; and that figure necessarily excites anew the great tragic emotions; for the non-posited aspect that any positing of evil involves can only awaken terror and compassion, beyond all judgment and all condemnation; a *merciful* vision of man comes to limit the accusation and save him from the wrath of the Judge.

It is here that the "tragic" light cast upon the Adamic myth enhances the enigma of the serpent. As we have said, it is not possible to absorb all the meanings revealed through that figure into the avowal of a purely human origin of evil. The serpent is more than the transcendence of sin over sins, more than the non-posited of the posited, more than the radical of radical evil; it is the Other, it is the Adversary, the pole of a counterparticipation, of a counterlikeness, about which one can say nothing except that the evil act, in positing itself, *lets itself be seduced* by the counterpositing of a source of iniquity represented by the Evil One, the Diabolical. When tragedy *shows* the hero blinded by a demonic power, it manifests the demonic side of the human experience of evil by means of the tragic action; it makes visible, without ever making it thinkable, the situation of the wicked who can never occupy any but the second place in wickedness, "after" the Adversary. Thus, the tragic *representation* continues to express not only the *reverse side* of all confession of sins, but the *other pole* of human evil; the evil for which I assume responsibility makes mani-

fest a source of evil for which I cannot assume responsibility, but
which I participate in every time that through me evil enters into
the world as if for the first time. It might be said that the avowal
of evil as human calls forth a second-degree avowal, that of evil
as non-human. Only tragedy can accept this avowal of the avowal
and exhibit it in a spectacle, for no coherent discourse can include
that Other.

But perhaps there is more to be said: it is not only something
of the tragic anthropology that is reaffirmed by the Adamic myth,
but something even of the tragic theology. The tragic element in
Biblical theology can be discovered in the following way. I will
start with the *ethical* sense to which the Covenant between Israel
and Yahweh was elevated. That ethical sense, which makes the
Law the bond between man and God, reacts upon the conception
of God himself; God is an ethical God. This "ethicization" of man
and God tends toward a moral vision of the world, according to
which History is a tribunal, pleasures and pains are retribution,
God himself is a judge. At the same time, the whole of human
experience assumes a penal character. Now, this moral vision of the
world was wrecked by Jewish thought itself, when it meditated on
the suffering of the innocent. The book of Job is the upsetting
document that records this shattering of the moral vision of the
world. The figure of Job bears witness to the irreducibility of the
evil of scandal to the evil of fault, at least on the scale of human
experience; the theory of retribution, which was the first, naïve expression of the moral vision of the world, does not account for all
the unhappiness in the world. Hence, it may be asked whether the
Hebrew and, more generally, the Near-Eastern theme of the "suffering Just One" does not lead back from the prophetic *accusation*
to tragic *pity*.

The movement of thought that we shall try to describe rests on
the ethical vision itself: where God is perceived as the origin of
justice and the source of legislation, the problem of just sanctions
is raised with a seriousness without precedent; suffering emerges
as an enigma when the demands of justice can no longer explain
it; this enigma is the product of the ethical theology itself. That is
why the virulence of the book of Job is without equivalent in any

culture; Job's complaint supposes the full maturity of an ethical vision of God; the clearer God becomes as legislator, the more obscure he becomes as creator; the irrationality of power balances the ethical rationalization of holiness; it becomes possible to turn the accusation back against God, against the ethical God of the accusation. Thereupon there begins the foolish business of trying to justify God: theodicy is born.

It is at this point of doubt, when the spontaneous ethical vision appeals to the arguments of theodicy and has recourse to a rhetoric of conviction, that the possibility of a tragic vision looms up again. That possibility is born of the impossibility of saving the ethical vision with the aid of any "proof." The friends of Job do, indeed, mobilize forgotten sins, unknown sins, ancestral sins, the sins of the people, in order to restore the equation of suffering and punishment; but Job refuses to close the gap. His innocence and his suffering are marginal to any ethical vision.[1]

Babylonian "wisdom" had already carried very far the dissolution that the ethical vision suffers when it comes into contact with meditation on suffering.[2] For the author of *A Pessimistic Dialogue between Master and Servant,* suffering is not so much unjust as senseless, and it has the result of making every undertaking sense-

---

[1] There is no need to ask whether such a just man existed, nor even whether such a just man is possible. Job is the *imaginary* personage who serves as touchstone for the ethical vision of the world and makes it fly to pieces. By hypothesis or by construction, Job is innocent; he must be just in order that the problem may be posed in all its intensity: how is it possible that a man so wholly just should be so totally suffering? Besides, such a product of the imagination was made possible precisely by the attainment of the idea of *degrees* of guilt (cf. Part I, Chap. III, § 1, p. 107); the imagining of the extremes of the just and the unjust is enveloped in the representation of gradual guilt; Job is the zero degree of guilt joined to the extreme of suffering; from this conjunction is born the scandal which also is extreme.

[2] S. Langdon, *Babylonian Wisdom* (London, 1923); J. J. Stamm, *Das Leiden des Unschuldigen in Babylon und Israel* (Zürich, 1948). For the texts we have used Robert H. Pfeiffer's English translation, in Pritchard, *Ancient Near Eastern Texts,* pp. 434–40: "I Will Praise the Lord of Wisdom" (the Babylonian Job); "A Pessimistic Dialogue between Master and Servant"; and "A Dialogue about Human Misery" (the Babylonian Ecclesiastes). They are reprinted in Mendelsohn, *op. cit.,* pp. 187–204. Only the "Pessimistic Dialogue" is reproduced in Pritchard's *Anthology* (pp. 250–52).

less; in the face of absurdity, everything is equal. Thus the ethical
vision is eaten away right down to the very core of action.³ In other
texts, such as the poem of the suffering just man ("I Will Praise
the Lord of Wisdom"), complaint is pushed to such a point of
despair that it rivals Job's complaint and protestation,⁴ but "wisdom" counsels mute resignation and a most extreme sacrifice of
the will to know; a theophany of Marduk, which fills the believer
with gratitude, but not with understanding, casts a ray of hope into
the darkness of distress.⁵

³ "A Pessimistic Dialogue between Master and Servant," Strophe I
(Pritchard, *op. cit.*, p. 438): "['Servant,] obey me.' Yes, my lord, yes.
['Bring me at once the] chariot, hitch it up. I will ride to the palace.' [Ride,
my lord, ride! All your wishes] will be realized for you. The king will be
gracious to you. ['No, servant,] I shall not ride [to] the palace.' [Do not
ride], my lord, do not ride. [To a place . . .] he will send you. [*In a land
which*] you know [not] he will let you be captured. [Day and] night he will
let you see trouble."
     The poem continues: To eat and drink? Yes and no. To speak, to be
silent? It's all the same. To love a woman? It's the ruin of a man. To help
his country? The mounds of ancient ruins and the skulls of former men
teach that benefactors and evildoers come to the same end.
     The poem ends thus: " 'Servant, obey me.' Yes my lord, yes. 'Now, what
is good? To break my neck, your neck, throw [both] into the river—[that]
is good.' Who is tall enough to ascend to heaven? Who is broad enough to
embrace the earth? 'No, servant, I shall kill you and send you ahead of me.'
[Then] would my lord [wish to] live even three days after me?" (Pritchard,
op. cit., p. 438).
     On this poem, cf. Langdon, *op. cit.*, pp. 67–81, and J. J. Stamm, *op. cit.*,
pp. 14–16.
⁴ "I Will Praise the Lord of Wisdom" (Pritchard, *op. cit.*, pp. 434–37):
"I look about me: evil upon evil!
My affliction increases, right I cannot find.
I implored the god, but he did not turn his countenance;
I prayed to my goddess, but she did not raise her head."
                                                        II, 2–5
"Whence come the evil things everywhere?"
                                                        II, 10
"Oh that I only knew that these things are well pleasing to a god!
What is good in one's sight is evil for a god.
What is bad in one's own mind is good for his god.
Who can understand the counsel of the gods in the midst of heaven?
The plan of a god is deep waters, who can comprehend it?"
                                                        II, 33–37
⁵ Langdon (*op. cit.*) shows well that the revolt is brought back, by means
of the consolation and restoration of the suffering just man, into the classic

Scepticism, surrender to the inscrutable, modest hedonism, expectation of a miracle—all these attitudes are already held in reserve and in suspense in the Babylonian "wisdom." The complainer, then, will sacrifice his complaint, will learn patience, will surrender himself humbly into the hands of an inscrutable god, and will forgo knowledge.

But the most extraordinary document of the ancient "wisdom" of the Near East, concerning the turn from ethical comprehension to tragic comprehension of God himself, is the book of Job. And since the "ethicization" of the divine had nowhere else been carried as far as in Israel, the *crisis* of that vision of the world was nowhere else as radical. Only the protestation of *Prometheus Bound* can perhaps be compared with that of Job; but the Zeus that Prometheus calls in question is not the holy God of the Prophets. To recover the hyperethical dimension of God, it was necessary that the alleged justice of the law of retribution should be turned against God and that God should appear unjustifiable from the point of view of the scheme of justification that had guided the whole process of "ethicization." Hence the tone of legal pleading in the book, which turns against the earlier theodicy invoked by the three "friends."

> I know as much as you; I yield to you in nothing.
> But I must speak to Shaddai;
> I wish to remonstrate with God. . . .
> He may slay me: I have no other hope
> than to justify my conduct before him.
>
> Job 13:2-3, 15

---

paths of the penitential Psalms, leaving the problem that had been raised unsolved. But although one finds here the Babylonian confession of divine inscrutability, common to all orthodox prayers ("Mankind is dumb and knows nothing. Mankind as many as bear names, what know they?") and to Greek wisdom, on the other hand the avowal of sin forgotten, unknown, communal or ancestral, already ceases in the sapiential literature of Babylon to support the old theory of retribution; that is why the problem remains open. Stamm (*op. cit.,* p. 19) emphasizes the value of this poem as an anticipation of Job: the theophany of Marduk attests that the incomprehensible god has the power to save when man does not expect it any longer; thus he will praise the Lord, even though the enigma persists.

> Oh! if I knew how to find him,
>   how to come to his dwelling place,
> I would present my case before him,
>   my mouth would be full of arguments.
> I would know the words of his defense,
>   I would be attentive to what he would say to me.
>
> Job 23:3–5

Job's admirable apology in Chapter 31—which is also an interesting document concerning the scrupulous conscience, in virtue of its enumeration of the faults that Job has not committed—ends with these proud words:

> Oh! who will make God listen to me?
> I have said my last word; let Shaddai answer me!
> If my adversary will write out an indictment,
> I will wear it upon my shoulder,
> I will put it on like a diadem.
>
> Job 31:35–36

The putting in question of the ethical God reaches its utmost virulence when it begins to disturb the dialogal situation which, in Israel, is at the very basis of the consciousness of sin. Man is before God as before his aggressor and his enemy. The eye of God, which represented for Israel the absolute measure of sin, as well as the watchfulness and the compassion of the Lord, becomes a source of terror:

> What is man, that you make so much of him,
>   that you fix your attention on him,
> that you inspect him every morning,
>   that you scrutinize him every instant?
> Will you ever stop looking at me
>   for the length of time it takes to swallow my spittle?
>
> Job 7:17–19

The eye of God is upon Job as the eye of the hunter is upon the wild beast; God "surrounds" him, God "spies on" him, he "encompasses him with his nets," he ravages his house and "exhausts his strength." Job goes so far as to suspect that it is that inquisitorial eye which makes man guilty: "Yes, I know that it is so; but how shall a man be just before God?" On the contrary, is not man too *weak* for God to require so much of him? "Will you frighten a leaf that is driven by the wind, or pursue a dry straw?" (13:25).

> Man born of woman,
> short-lived, but with more than enough troubles.
> Like a flower, he opens and then fades,
> he flees like a shadow without stopping.
> And you deign to open your eyes upon him,
> you bring him into judgment before you!
>
> Job 14:1-3

Then Job cursed the day of his birth: "Let the day perish wherein I was born, and the night in which it was said: A man child has been conceived! . . . Why did I not die from the womb? Why did I not perish as soon as I was born?" (3:3, 11).

> My hope is to inhabit Sheol,
> to make my bed in the darkness.
> I cry to the grave: "You are my father!"
> to the vermin: "You are my mother and my sister!"
>
> Job 17:13-14

Faced with the torturing absence of God (23:8; 30:20), the man dreams of his own absence and repose:

> Henceforth I shall be invisible to every eye;
> your eyes will be upon me and I shall have vanished.
>
> Job 7:8

Is it not the tragic God that Job discovers again? the inscrutable God of terror? What is tragic, too, is the dénouement. "Suffering for the purpose of understanding," the Greek chorus said. Job, in his turn, penetrates beyond any ethical vision to a new dimension of faith, the dimension of *unverifiable* faith.

We must never lose sight of the fact that Job's plaint, even when it seems to be destroying the basis of any dialogal relation between God and man, does not cease to move in the field of invocation. It is to God that Job appeals against God:

Oh! that you would hide me in Sheol,
  that you would shelter me there, until your anger passes,
that you would fix a time for me and remember me thereafter:
  —for, once dead, can a man come to life again?—
All the days of my service I would wait
  for my relief to come.

Job 14:13–14

"Even now I have a witness in heaven, and my defender is on high" (16:19). . . . "I know that my defender is living, and that at the end he will rise upon the earth. After my awakening, he will raise me up beside him and in my flesh I shall see God" (19:25–26).

This faith gets its veracity from the very defiance that argues against the vain science of retribution and renounces the wisdom that is inaccessible to man (Chap. 28). In his unknowing, Job alone has "spoken rightly" of God (42:7).

Shall we say that Job returns to the crushing silence of resignation, like the Babylonian Job? Yes, up to a certain point. The God who answers Job "out of the storm" reverses the relation of questioner and questioned: "Where were you when I laid the foundations of the earth? Speak, if your knowledge is enlightened" (38:4). "Gird up your loins like a man. I am going to question you, and you will give me the answers" (40:7). And Job gave this answer to Yahweh:

I know that you are all-powerful;
  what you plan, you can accomplish.
It was I who darkened your counsels
  by utterances without sense.
Therefore I have spoken without understanding,
  concerning things too wonderful for me, about which I know nothing.
(Listen, let me speak,
  I am going to question you and you will give me the answers.)
I did not know you except by hearsay,
  but now my eyes have seen you.
Therefore I take back my words,
  I repent in dust and ashes.

Job 42:2–6

And yet the silence of Job, once the question itself has been blasted by the lightning, is not altogether the seal of meaninglessness. Neither is it altogether the zero degree of speech. Certain words are addressed to Job in exchange for his silence. Those words are not an answer to his problem; they are not at all a solution of the problem of suffering; they are in no way a reconstruction, at a higher degree of subtlety, of the ethical vision of the world. The God who addresses Job out of the tempest shows him Behemoth and Leviathan, the hippopotamus and the crocodile, vestiges of the chaos that has been overcome, representing a brutality dominated and measured by the creative act. Through these symbols he gives him to understand that all is order, measure, and beauty—inscrutable order, measure beyond measure, terrible beauty. A way is marked out between agnosticism and the penal view of history and life—the way of unverifiable faith. There is nothing in that revelation that concerns him personally; but precisely because it is not a question of himself, Job is challenged. The oriental poet, like Anaximander and Heraclitus the Obscure, announces an order beyond order, a totality full of meaning, within which the individual must lay down his recrimination. Suffering is not explained, ethically or otherwise; but the contemplation of the whole initiates a movement which must be completed practically by the surrender of a claim, by the sacrifice of the demand that was at the beginning of the recrimination, namely, the claim to form by oneself a little island of meaning in the universe, an empire within an empire. It becomes suddenly apparent that the demand for retribution animated Job's recriminations no less than the moralizing homilies of his friends. That, perhaps, is why the innocent Job, the upright Job, repents. Of what can he repent, if not of his claim for compensation, which made his contention impure? Was it not still the law of retribution which drove him to demand an explanation in proportion to his existence, a private explanation, a finite explanation?

As in tragedy, the final theophany has explained nothing to him, but it has changed his view; he is ready to identify his freedom with inimical necessity; he is ready to convert freedom and necessity into fate. This conversion is the true "re-enactment"—no longer the material re-enactment which is still a kind of recompense and hence a sort of retribution, but the wholly internal re-enactment which is no longer restoration of an earlier happiness, but re-enactment of the present unhappiness.

I do not mean to say that all this is already in the book of Job. But that is how we can bring it to completion in ourselves, starting from the impulse that we receive from it. That impulse is given by a simple touch in the prologue: Satan has made a bet that Job, if he is confronted with misfortune, will not fear God "for nothing" (1:9). This is what is at stake: to renounce the law of retribution to the extent not only of ceasing to envy the prosperity of the wicked, but of enduring misfortune as one accepts good fortune—that is to say, as God-given (2:10). Such is the tragic wisdom of the "re-enactment" that triumphs over the ethical vision of the world.

If now we turn back from "faith in the hidden God" and the "re-enactment" of misfortune—which illuminates it with a sombre light—to the Adamic myth, we see what tragedy contributes to the understanding of that myth. It contributes two things: on the one hand, pity for human beings, who are nevertheless accused by the Prophet; on the other hand, fear and trembling before the divine abyss, before the God whose holiness is nevertheless proclaimed by the Prophet. Perhaps it is necessary that the possibility of the tragic God should never be abolished altogether, so that Biblical theology may be protected from the platitudes of ethical monotheism, with its Legislator and its Judge, confronting a moral subject who is endowed with complete and unfettered freedom, still intact after each act. Because the tragic theology is always possible, although not to be spoken, God is *Deus Absconditus*. And it is always possible, because suffering can no longer be understood as a chastisement.

Just as the tragic anthropology regroups the scattered signs of the ineluctable that are mingled with the growth of our concrete freedom, so the tragic theology regroups the signs of the apparent hostility of fate. Those signs appear when, for example, our vision of things becomes contracted. When wholeness is lost, we sink into the singularity of conclusions without premises. Only the "seer" of Greek tragedy and the "fool" of Shakespearian tragedy escape from the tragic; the seer and the fool have ascended from the tragic to the comic by their access to a comprehensive vision. Now, nothing is more likely to destroy that comprehensive vision than suffering. We are still close to the tragic theology when the contradiction seems to us not only unresolved but unresolvable. A non-dialectical contradiction; there we have the tragic. Thus Antigone and Creon destroy one another, and there is no third force that might mediate their opposition and embrace the good reasons of both. That a value cannot be realized without the destruction of another value, equally positive—there, again, is the tragic. It is perhaps at its height when it seems that the furthering of a value requires the destruction of its bearer.[6] It seems then that it is the very nature of things that makes such a thing happen; the very order of the world becomes a temptation to despair. "The object in the background of the tragic," says Max Scheler, "is always the world itself, thought of as a unity—the world in which such a thing is possible." The indifference of the course of events to human values, the *blind* character of necessity—of the sun that shines on the good and the bad—play the role of the Greek $\mu o \hat{\iota} \rho a$, which becomes a $\kappa a \kappa \grave{o} s$ $\delta a \acute{\iota} \mu \omega \nu$, as soon as value-relations and personal relations are confronted with relations of the causal order. The hero is the point of intersection, the "tragic knot," as Max Scheler also says, where the blindness of order is transformed into the enmity of fate; the tragic is always personal, but it makes manifest a sort of cosmic sadness which reflects the hostile transcendence to which the hero is a prey. And since the hero is the agent of that apparent enmity in the principle of things, since he "delays" the progress and "precipitates" the dénouement of the tragic action, blind necessity appears to be a hostile intention intertwined with the intention of the tragic hero.

That is why the tragic vision always remains possible, resisting any logical, moral, or esthetic reconciliation.

Shall we leave the Adamic myth and the tragic myth face to face, as two interpretations of existence between which we can only fluctuate endlessly? Not at all.

In the first place, the tragic myth saves the Biblical myth only

[6] Max Scheler, *Le phénomène du Tragique*.

insofar as the latter first resuscitates it. We must not grow weary of repeating that only he who confesses that he is the author of evil discovers the reverse of that confession, namely, the *non-posited* in the positing of evil, the always *already* there of evil, the *other* of temptation, and finally the incomprehensibility of God, who tests me and who can appear to me as my enemy. In this circular relation between the Adamic myth and the tragic myth, the Adamic myth is the right side and the tragic myth is the reverse side.

But, above all, the polarity of the two myths betokens the arrest of understanding at a certain stage. At that stage our vision remains dichotomous. On the one hand, the evil that is *committed* leads to a just exile; that is what the figure of Adam represents. On the other hand, the evil that is *suffered* leads to an unjust deprivation; that is what the figure of Job represents. The first figure calls for the second; the second corrects the first. Only a third figure could announce the transcending of the contradiction, and that would be the figure of the "Suffering Servant," who would make of suffering, of the evil that is undergone, an *action* capable of redeeming the evil that is committed. This enigmatic figure is the one celebrated by the Second Isaiah in the four "songs of the Servant of Yahweh" (Is. 42:1–9; 49:1–6; 50:4–11; 52:13–53:12), and it opens up a perspective radically different from that of "wisdom." It is not contemplation of creation and its immense measure that consoles; it is suffering itself. Suffering has become a gift that expiates the sins of the people.

> It was our sufferings that he bore
> and our griefs with which he was laden.
> And we thought of him as chastised,
> stricken by God, and humiliated.
> He was pierced for our sins,
> crushed for our crimes.
> The chastisement that brings us peace is upon him
> and it is owing to his wounds that we are healed.
> . . . .
> Yes, he was cut off from the land of the living
> for our sins, he was smitten to death.
>
> Is. 53:4–5, 8b

Whatever may be the meaning of this "Suffering Servant," whether he be a historical personage, individual or collective, or the figure of a Savior to come, he reveals an entirely new possibility —that suffering gives itself a meaning, by voluntary consent, in the meaninglessness of scandal. In the juridical and penal view of life, guilt had to provide the reason for suffering. But the suffering of the innocent broke the schema of retribution in pieces; sin and suffering are separated by an abyss of irrationality. It is then that the suffering of the "Suffering Servant" institutes a bond between suffering and sin, at another level than that of retribution. But the tragedy of the "Suffering Servant" is beyond the Greek tragedy of the hero.

Of course, there is no lack of "juridical theologies," which have understood substitutive suffering as a supreme way of salvaging the law of retribution. According to that schema, the suffering which is a gift would be the means by which mercy would give "satisfaction" to justice. In this mechanical balancing of the divine attributes, justice and mercy, the new quality of the offered suffering is swallowed up again in the quantitative law of retribution. In truth, the suffering that is a gift takes up into itself the suffering that is a scandal, and thus inverts the relation of guilt to suffering. According to the old law, guilt was supposed to produce suffering as a punishment; but now a suffering that is *outside* retribution, a senseless and scandalous suffering, anticipates human evil and takes upon itself the sins of the world. There had to appear a suffering which would free itself from the legal-mindedness of retribution and submit voluntarily to the iron law, in order to suppress it by fulfilling it. In short, a stage of absurd suffering, the stage of Job, was needed, to mediate the movement from punishment to generosity. But then guilt gets a new horizon: not that of Judgment, but that of Mercy.

What does the tragic vision signify with respect to this ultimate significance of suffering? The tragic vision always remains possible for all of us who have not attained the capacity for offered suffering. Short of this holiness of suffering, the question remains: Is not God wicked? Is it not that possibility that the believer evokes when he prays: "Lead us not into temptation"? Does not his request signify: "Do not come to meet me with the face of the tragic God"? There is a theology of temptation which is very close to the tragic theology of blinding. . . .

That is why tragedy has never finished dying. Killed twice, by the philosophical Logos and by the Judeo-Christian Kerygma, it survived its double death. The theme of the wrath of God, the ultimate motive of the tragic consciousness, is invincible to the arguments of the philosopher as well as of the theologian. For there is no rational vindication of the innocence of God; every explanation of the Stoic or Leibnizian type is wrecked, like the naïve arguments of Job's friends, on the suffering of the innocent. They leave intact the opacity of evil and the opacity of the world "in which such a thing is possible," as Max Scheler says in his essay on the "Phenomenon of the Tragic"; as soon as meaninglessness appears to swoop down intentionally on man, the schema of the wrath of God looms up and the tragic consciousnes is restored. Only a consciousness that had accepted suffering without reservation could also begin to absorb the Wrath of God into the Love of God; but even then the suffering of others, the suffering of children, of the lowly, would renew the mystery of iniquity in his eyes.[7] Only *timid* hope could anticipate in silence the end of the phantasm of the "wicked God."

3. The Appropriation of the Myth of Chaos

Meditation on the invincibility of the tragic myth gives an indication, in its turn, how the myth of chaos, too, can be reaffirmed up to a certain point at least. The question arises: Does the theogonic myth still speak to me, or is it radically dead? It must be admitted that this question cannot receive a complete answer at this stage in our meditation. Of course, in a way, the theogonic myth has been blasted by ethical monotheism, the connection of

[7] That the theology of love cannot become a systematic theology appears evident. Its powerlessness to integrate justice conceptually is nothing compared to its powerlessness to account for the position of evil in the world; the concept of "permission" (God "permits" evil, but does not "create" it) is the witness to this failure. We shall return to this point in the framework of the speculative symbols of evil.

which with the avowal of human evil we now know. That connection is very strong, for it is reciprocal: because God is holy, man alone is guilty; because man is guilty, God is innocent. And yet the last word has not been said. Reflection on the tragic gives rise to the thought that ethical monotheism itself must be transcended; it must be transcended insofar as it is ethical—perhaps also insofar as it is monotheism. Why this last doubt? For a reason of fact which is soon transcended in a reason of right. The fact is this: although the naïve theogony of Babylonia and archaic Greece is dead, more refined onto-theologies have not ceased to appear, according to which evil is an original element of being. The cosmological fragments of Heraclitus, the German mysticism of the fourteenth century, German idealism, propose philosophical and learned equivalents of theogony: evil has its roots in the pain of being, in a tragedy that is the tragedy of being itself. The fact that theogony revives under ever new forms gives cause for reflection.

This seductiveness of theogony can be understood on the basis of the tragic. On the one hand, as we have just said, the tragic is *invincible,* at least at a certain level of our experience of evil committed and evil suffered; on the other hand, the tragic theology is unavowable, *unthinkable.* The tragic is invincible at the level of man and unthinkable at the level of God. A learned theogony, then, is the only means of making tragedy invincible and intelligible at the same time; it consists, in the last resort, in assigning the tragic to the origin of things and making it coincide with a logic of being, by means of negativity.

As a consequence, everything that makes the tragic vision of the world ineluctable, makes the tragi-logic of being seductive, as the consecration and liquidation of the "wicked god." The "wicked god" of tragedy becomes a logical moment in the dialectics of being.

The tragi-logic of being is seductive, but is it true? We are not equipped to exorcize its spell, and so a complete answer to this problem will not be found either in this or in the following volume. The answer needs a *Poetics* of freedom and of the being of man which exceeds the possibilities of a philosophical anthropology. All that meditation on the symbols and myths lets us understand is that man's positing of evil discloses another side of evil, a non-posited factor, mingled with man's positing of evil. That non-posited factor points to an other than man, represented by the Serpent; but that non-posited factor, that Other, can only be at the frontier of an anthropology of evil. Any hypostatization of this non-human source of evil in an absolute dialectics goes beyond the resources of that anthropology. It must be said, then, that the pre-eminence of the Adamic myth gives rise to the thought that evil is not a category of being; but, because that myth has a reverse, or a residue, the other myths are invincible. Hence, an anthropology of evil can neither posit nor take away the right of an absolute genesis of being, to which evil would belong primordially.

For the purpose of stating, without any reserve, all the presuppositions of this investigation of finitude and evil, I will add this: the only thing that could dissolve the spell of that absolute genesis of being and that hypostatization of evil as a category of being would be a "Christology." By Christology I mean a doctrine capable of including in the life of God itself, in a dialectic of divine "persons," the figure of the suffering servant which we evoked above as the supreme possibility of human suffering.

According to "Christology," that suffering is a moment in divinity; that moment of abasement, of annihilation of the divine life, both completes and suppresses tragedy. Tragedy is consummated, for the evil is in God: "Do you not know that the Son of Man must be delivered up?" That "must" exalts fate and includes it in the divine life. But tragedy is suppressed because it is inverted. In theogony, Kronos mutilates his Father and Marduk cuts to pieces the monstrous power of Tiamat. On the contrary, it is as an absolute *Victim* that the Christ of the Gospels is glorified—that is to say, elevated in being. The "must," then, is unintelligible except in the light of the "gift." "No one takes my life from me, but I give it of myself," says Christ, according to John. That absolute Fate should also be absolute Gift—there is tragedy completed and suppressed.

But if this "Christology" is part of the prolongation of the meditation on the "Servant of Yahweh" which occupied us above, it is of another order. The figure of the servant of Yahweh still belongs to the symbolism of human existence; it discloses an extreme possibility of human suffering; the servant of Yahweh may be a man or a people, a prophet of the past, or a teacher to come; in short, that figure illuminates man's inner nature from the viewpoint of that which is an extreme limit for man; that is why a philosophical reflection on the symbols of human existence can learn something from the symbol of the servant of Yahweh. On the contrary, the doctrine that hypostatizes in God the suffering which is a scandal, itself having been taken up into the suffering which is a gift, does not belong to the symbolism of human existence, because it does not reveal a possibility, even an extreme one, in man. One can, of course, take the identity of "fate" and "gift," realized in Christ's sacrifice, as a model for our action and suffering, and thus enlist it in a symbolism within the confines of the human; but such a symbolism is not on the level of a Christology, and Christology is not of the same order as such a symbolism. Hence, tragedy as completed and suppressed in Christology is not within the power of a philosophical anthropology.

That is why theogony remains as a suspended question, even after the death of the archaic cosmogonies. The recognition of a non-human source of evil, included even in the confession of the human origin of evil, revives tragedy; and, since tragedy is unthinkable, theogony offers itself as the ultimate means of saving tragedy by converting it into logic. Everything that speaks in favor of the unavowable and unthinkable theology of the "wicked god" is also an appeal launched in the direction of a thinkable and avowable onto-theology, in which evil becomes mediation of being.

All the rest of our reflections will stay on this side of that ultimate *alternative:* either consolidation of the tragic in a logic of being, or its inversion in a Christology. The choice between those two possibilities depends on a *Poetics* of freedom that is not yet in our power. That is why the philosophical anthropology which we are going to elaborate under the guidance of the symbols and myths of human evil stands out from the background of an unresolved alternative. We are confronted by that alternative every time we skirt the enigma of a non-human, perhaps pre-human, evil; and we renew that enigma every time we manifest evil in ourselves and among ourselves.

4. The Struggle between the Adamic Myth and the Myth of Exile

The myth of the exiled soul, we have said, is separated from the others by a significant typological distance. Shall we say that it is accessible only to a re-enactment in sympathetic imagination and that it cannot be related to the Adamic myth except as an opposed myth?

The simple fact that the history of the use in Christianity of a Neo-Platonic mode of expression offers so many examples of contamination of the myth of the fall by the myth of the exiled soul lends itself to reflection. One may try to get rid of these mixed forms by denouncing them as simple misunderstandings. It may even be an important undertaking for the philosopher and the theologian to cut the knot of confusion forcibly. This contamination is responsible for the shift in Christianity to what Nietzsche called Platonism for the people; because of it, Christianity has seemed like the most considerable invention of afterworlds in history. We ourselves have already vigorously contrasted the dualism of soul and body, which makes evil a mixture, with the anthropological monism of the Adamic myth, to which corresponds the conception of evil as a deviation from a primordial state. The place of the Orphic myth, on the extreme periphery of the system gravitating around the Adamic myth, expresses, on the plane of dynamics, what the statics of the myths has already made apparent.

There still remains, however, the task of understanding the motivations that have governed the process of contamination. Now, it is only by discovering in each of these myths an affinity for the other that we shall be able to account for the possibility of their confusion; and in thus making the contamination intelligible through a play of underground affinities, we shall have stretched to the limit our endeavor to comprehend all the myths, including the most contrary ones, in the light of the dominant myth.

Let us begin with the Adamic myth, and see how it goes to meet the myth of the exiled soul.

Our starting-point must once again be the experience of evil as already there—that is to say, the other side of the Adamic myth, the side represented by Eve and the Serpent. But, while the tragic myth interprets passivity and seduction in terms of *divine* blinding and the theogonic myth interprets them in terms of a resurgence of *primordial* chaos, the Orphic myth develops the aspect of the apparent externality of the seduction and tries to make it coincide with the "body," understood as the unique root of all that is involuntary.

The passage from the theme of the serpent to the theme of the body-prison is not hard to understand. If we go back from mythical symbolism to the primary symbolism of the experience of evil, we find symbols which, although they belong to Hebrew literature, anticipate the transition to Orphic symbolism—for example, the captivity in Egypt and the departure from Egypt, the Exodus. Those symbols were re-enforced by the historical experience of the Babylonian Exile and by the vehement hope for a great Return, which animated the great Prophets of the Exile and which even today acts as a magnet for dispersed Judaism. Now this symbolism, directly connected with the Jewish theology of history, has its strictly mythical expression in the theme of banishment, inseparable from the story of the fall; the fall inaugurates a time of banishment, wandering, and perdition, symbolized successively by the expulsion of Adam and Eve from the garden of Paradise, the wandering of Cain, the dispersion of the builders of Babel, and the undoing of creation in the Flood. It cannot be said, then, that the theme of exile is alien to the theme of the fall; it is attached to it as a "curse." It may be said that captivity, in the Biblical sense, is to the exile of the soul what the Exodus of the Jews is to the odyssey of the soul according to the Orphics.

It is true that for the Orphics the exile and the return to the kingdom are an exile and return of the "soul," and that the "body" is the place of exile; but even that can be understood up to a certain point on the basis of Hebrew symbolism. The symbols of captivity and exodus, we have said, consecrate the aspect of externality in human evil. Now that externality was already expressed by the Prophets, particularly Ezekiel and Jeremiah, in a symbolism drawn from the body: heart of stone, the lewdness of the adulterer like the rut of beasts, etc. Moreover, it was the same experience of the externality of evil that made possible the survival of the symbolism of defilement in the symbolism of sin: "Cleanse me wholly from my iniquity and purify me of my sin! Purify me and I shall be without spot; wash me and I shall be whiter than snow!" the psalmist prays. From this renovated symbolism of defilement to the symbolism of the body, the distance is not insuperable; for the body itself is not only the literal body, so to speak, but also a symbolic body. It is the seat of everything that happens in me without my doing. Now seduction is also in me without my doing; and so it is not astonishing that the quasi-externality of the involuntary motions of the body could serve as a schema of externality, in order to convey an experience analogous to that which, in the Biblical story, was expressed in the encounter of Eve and the Serpent. It is enough for the notion of the body to retain a very great wealth of symbolic overtones and not to be reduced to a simple biological mechanism. This was the case before the birth of a science of the human body and outside the regions touched by the medical thinking of the Greeks.

A new stage in the process of contamination is represented by the type of religious experience found in St. Paul, St. Augustine, and Luther, which has very justly been called the type of the *twice-born*.[8] The ardent believers who belong to this type experience alternately the irresistibility of evil and the irresistibility of grace; their anthropology is as anti-voluntaristic as possible; man, at first a slave to sin, becomes by grace a "slave of Christ." The example of St. Paul is particularly striking. His language is sometimes so close to the language of Hellenistic and gnostic wisdom that it has lent itself to interpretation as the expression of an already active contamination of the Biblical tradition by the Neo-Orphism of the gnostics. He speaks of the "sin that dwells in me," of "another law in my members, warring against the law of my

[8] Cf. N. P. Williams, *Ideas of the Fall and of Original Sin* (New York and Toronto, 1927).

reason and bringing me into captivity to the law of sin which is in my members"; sometimes the body itself is called "body of death." But it is enough to extend the line that passes through the symbol of captivity and the expressions of Jeremiah and Ezekiel to reconstruct the Pauline theme. As we have already said, the Pauline concept of the "flesh" and the "body" designates not a substantial reality, but an existential category, which not only covers the whole field of the passions, but includes the moralizing will that boasts in the law. It is the alienated self as a whole, in opposition to the "desires of the Spirit," which constitute the inward man. The cleavage between me and myself and the projection into externality of this self that is alienated from itself is the key to the Pauline conception of the flesh. There is no need to dwell further on this genesis of St. Paul's symbolism of sin. What concerns us here is that that symbolism, although it can be explained in its essentials by the Hebrew tradition, gives significant pledges to the Hellenistic tradition of a soul exiled in a body that is evil from its origin, and prepares the way for all the subsequent contacts of Christianity with Neo-Platonism and for all the misunderstandings which result therefrom. Step by step, the Biblical theme of sin tends towards a quasi-dualism, accredited by the inner experience of cleavage and alienation.

As for St. Paul himself, far as he went in the direction of Hellenistic dualism, at least in his vocabulary,[9] it must be admitted

[9] We will consider some of those texts in which the equivocation is at its height: Rom. 8:1–12; Eph. 2:1–6; 4:22; II Cor. 4:16. All these texts can be interpreted according to the schema of externality proposed above; but, once the motivation is forgotten that leads to the concept of flesh, the bare expression becomes quasi-indistinguishable from the expressions of the Hellenistic conception. The equivocation becomes all the more inevitable because St. Paul himself perhaps conceded much to the language of his Hellenized surroundings in his description of a situation which owes nothing to the Hellenistic conception. Was St. Paul misled thereby? None of the texts, even the most suspect, convicts him openly of dualism. Thus, I Cor. 15 totally opposes the "psychic," "terrestrial," "corruptible," "mortal" body, that of the "first man," to the "spiritual," "celestial," "incorruptible," "immortal" body, that of the "second man"; but one cannot distinguish in that first man, sprung from the earth, terrestrial, an aspect created good and an aspect that became evil contingently. But perhaps it should be said that St. Paul had no need to make that distinction at that moment, since his problem is that of death and not that of sin, and since the series of

that he was kept from falling into gnosticism, first, by his acute sense of the incarnation of Christ in a flesh like ours; second, by his expectation of a redemption of our bodies; and finally, by the Adamic myth. This last point merits further attention; for, while it may have been disturbing to see St. Paul contributing to the Adamic mythology and congealing the Adamic symbol in literalism by regarding Adam as an individual situated at the beginning of history, it must now be granted that it is that mythology which keeps St. Paul from turning to dualism. The same pages that make the individual Adam the counterpart of Christ, called the second Adam ("as by one man . . ."), have a new ring when they are compared with the quasi-dualistic texts; they re-introduce contingency where there was a temptation to see a law of nature. The "one man" represents the divergence between the good creation and the actual state of man, which St. Paul calls elsewhere "the flesh," "the old man," "the world." Thus it is the Adamic mythology that strikes a counterblow in opposition to the drift towards gnosis.

The distance between the Adamic myth and the myth of the exiled soul, which is still very perceptible in St. Paul, will become smaller when, on the one hand, the peculiar traits of the Adamic myth become attenuated and, on the other hand, new traits of Christian experience make the myth of the exiled soul more seductive. On the one hand, Adam will be less and less the symbol of the humanity of man; his innocence will become a fantastic innocence, accompanied by knowledge, bliss, and immortality, whether by nature or as superadded gift; at the same time, his fault, instead of being a case of "going astray," will become truly a "fall," an existential downgrading, a descent from the height of a superior and actually superhuman status; consequently, Adam's fall will no longer be very different from the fall of the souls in

---

terms—psychic, terrestrial, corruptible, mortal—designates a creaturely state which is not necessarily evil. Moreover, 15:56 covertly connects this text with the theme of the inner struggle. Galatians 5:17 seems quite dualistic: "For the flesh lusteth against the Spirit, and the Spirit against the flesh: and these are contrary the one to the other: so that ye cannot do the things that ye would"; but the following verse allows us to link this dualism with the experience of the inner struggle under the regime of the law: "But if ye be led of the Spirit, ye are not under the law."

Plato's *Phaedrus,* where the soul, already incarnate, falls into an earthly body. Except for the image, the fall will tend to become confused with the exile of the soul far from its previous homeland.

At the same time as the Adamic myth is being altered, Christian experience will be transformed and, in order to account for its new qualities, it will, so to speak, breathe the air of the dualistic myth. In its ascetic form as well as in its mystical form, Platonizing Christianity adopts the opposition between contemplation and concupiscence, which, in its turn, introduces the opposition between the spiritual soul and the mortal and raving body; the old fear of defilement and the old fear of the body and sexuality are taken over by the new wisdom. Thus everything that leads the Christian experience of sin from pride towards concupiscence, also leads it towards the dualistic myths. It might be said that Christianity will tend towards the identification of evil and the body (without, it is true, ever reaching that limit), for the same reasons which impelled it to adopt the Greek theme of the immortality of the soul. Among the motives for that transformation we ought, no doubt, to give a special place to the experience of death, or rather, of dying;[10] with martyrdom, the experience of dying will reach a point of virulence and authenticity which has marked all later spirituality. Now martyrdom, accepted with joy and sometimes desired, inclines a man to regard death as the beginning of true life, the life with Christ; by contrast, the sojourn in this "valley of tears" seems to be no more than a time of trial and a figure of evil. The purest desire is to flee from here to the beyond, as it was for the Socrates of the *Gorgias.* Thus there will be assembled, within the Christian experience, the conditions for a fusion with Neo-Platonic spirituality, the remote heir of the myth of the exiled soul and the body-prison. We shall return later to this three-termed dialectic of Christianity, Neo-Platonism, and gnosis, which we are not yet equipped to understand rightly, because we have not yet brought to light all the factors involved. Moreover, it belongs to the plane of much more speculative symbols, such as "matter," "original sin," "fall of the eons." All of our analysis moves on a lower level. It is enough to have sketched, on the level of mythical symbols, the lines

[10] See Gargam, *L'amour et la mort* (Paris, 1959), pp. 281 ff.

of motivation which, beginning from the internal tensions of the Adamic myth, incline it toward the myth of the exiled soul and make possible their reciprocal influence on one another.

But this trend from the Adamic scheme toward the theme of the exiled soul would not have been possible if the latter, on its side, had not revealed an extraordinary potency for symbolic transposition. Several times we have alluded to the symbolic richness of the oldest of the symbols of evil, the symbol of defilement. Defilement is always more than a stain, and so it can signify analogically all the degrees of the experience of evil, even to the most elaborate concept of the servile will. Now the over-determination of the symbol of the body is not less than that of the symbol of defilement, for the two processes are inseparable. One can understand why. If the essence of the symbol of defilement is constituted by the themes of positiveness, externality, and non-destructive alteration, the body, in its turn, can serve as a symbol for the symbol; it, too, is brought into existence, it is on the border between the inner and the outer, it is essentially a producer of effects. That is why "explanation" of evil by the body always presupposes a degree of symbolic transposition of the body. Without this, the body would be simply an alibi for guilt, as it is when someone invokes character or heredity to excuse himself. The explanation of evil by the body is not an objective explanation, but an etiological myth; that is to say, it is ultimately a symbol of the second degree. But if that explanation aims at becoming scientific, as in modern times, then the ethical character of evil action disappears; man cannot impute evil to himself and at the same time refer it to the body, without treating the body as a symbol of certain aspects of the experience of the evil that he confesses. The symbolic transmutation of the body is a necessary condition for its belonging to the mythics of evil.

That is why it is not astonishing that history presents examples of the internalization of the Orphic symbol of the body-prison, corresponding to the externalization of the Biblical symbol of the fall. Just as St. Paul is on the road that goes from the image of the "fall" to the image of the "flesh," Plato illustrates the opposite movement, leading from the evil body to the unjust soul.

It would be inexact to see in Plato only the accusation against the body—"that evil thing with which our soul is mixed," says the *Phaedo*—and not to recognize the movement of review, rectification, and internalization of the previous symbolism of the body-prison. At the same time as he projects the Socratic analysis of the unjust soul into the body, he transmutes the body itself into a symbol of the passivity of the soul. On the one hand, the idea, which seems to be purely Socratic, of "tending" the soul, or "taking care" of the soul, calls for the symbolism of the body; "care" of the soul presupposes, in fact, that the soul is like a body threatened by disease, which must be cared for and saved; and so ethics and politics are comparable to a "medicine" of the soul (*Protagoras*, 311b–313a, 356c–357a). To this medical symbol of "care of the soul" corresponds the symbol of the "disease of injustice" (τὸ νόσημα τῆς ἀδικίας, *Gorgias*, 480b), and of the other discordances in the soul, conceived on the model of derangements of the humors of the body. The same symbolism governs the idea of expiation; it "relieves" the soul of its wickedness, as purgation "relieves" the body of its evil humors. That is why the soul that has been punished—purged of its ills by punishment—is happier than the unjust soul that has not made atonement; this function of punishment supposes that injustice is *like* a disease and that justice, which administers punishment, is *like* the art of healing. Hence, before the body is the *"cause"* of injustice, its own ills are the symbol of injustice. It was this medical metaphor of disease and cure, directly applied to the ills and the care of the soul, which made possible, in the other direction, the philosophical transposition of the Orphic myth of the body-prison and its transmutation into a cipher of the unjust soul. The Socratic soul was ready for Plato's resumption of the Orphic myths. That resumption marks both a re-immersion of philosophy in myth and an advance toward a symbolism of a higher degree, in which the literal meaning of the bodily symbol is increasingly muted.

The progressive transmutation of the symbol of the body is quite visible in a dialogue like the *Phaedo,* of which it has been said that it runs through the whole gamut of the degrees of knowledge. Now, just as the meaning of the soul changes, as one rises above

simple exhortation, which is itself close to mythical speech, the
meaning of the body changes also. At the first level, it is living in
its totality, and as such, that constitutes evil and forms the absolute
contrary of philosophizing; the body is the counterpole of thought;
apparently no innocence is left unsullied by contact with the world,
since it is the body that "troubles the soul and prevents it from
attaining truth and thought, every time we have dealings with it"
(66a); philosophy consists then in the death of the body, in order
to "behold things themselves with the soul itself" (66d); the body
appears to be pre-eminently the locus of evil: "our soul is mixed
with an evil thing" (66b), it is delivered up to the "dementia of
the body" (67a). But even at this lower degree of knowledge, the
evil influence of the body does not reside in what today we would
call its materiality, nor in its power to make contact with things;
rather, what is blamed in that contact is the "spell" that bewitches
it and thus rivets the soul to the body, making it captive to the
"contact": "The soul of every human being, when it is intensely
pleased or pained by something, thinks that the particular object
of its feeling is the clearest and truest thing in the world, although
it is not so at all" (83c). Hence, if the percept is not innocent,
that is because the feeling that clings to it is not innocent either;
and the feeling, in its turn, holds the soul captive because there is
in the soul a dizziness that transforms feeling and perception into
πάθος. It is this dizziness in the soul that precipitates the soul into
a body of desire (79c). Hence "passivity" is secretly an action of
the soul which makes itself a captive, which delivers itself up to
imprisonment: "And the astonishing thing about this prison, as
philosophy has seen, is that it is the work of desire and that he
who helps most to load the prisoner with his chains is perhaps the
prisoner himself" (82e). If this is so, it must be admitted that the
soul is "its own tormentor."

We are far from the myth of the evil body. Or, rather, the
ethical exegesis of the myth brings out the over-determination of
the expression "sôma" in the myth; this mythical "sôma" is already
more than body. Of course, the notion of reincarnation attracts
it toward a purely imaginative mode of representation, according
to which existence is a literal captivity in a series of corporeal

coverings which are put on and taken off like a garment; but the practice of purification already begins to attract the myth of the "body" in the direction of meanings that are symbolic, rather than literal.

That is why, when Plato goes farther up in the hierarchy of degrees of knowledge, the meaning of the body changes with the meaning of the soul. The soul is not only a fugitive that goes from body to body, wearing them out one after another; it is also—at least at a level which is not yet the level of dialectics—an existence characterized by its "likeness" to the Ideas (at a higher level it will be constituted by an Idea, the Idea of life). Now, if the soul is "that which is most like" the Ideas, which remain identical with themselves, the body is "that which is most like" that which perishes. Just as the soul is in labor with regard to being, so the body is less a thing than a direction of existence, a counterlikeness: "Then the soul is dragged by the body in the direction of those things that never preserve their identity; it wanders about, it is troubled, its head spins as if it were drunk, because it is in contact with things of that kind" (79c). Thus two existential movements are sketched, two movements governed by two "likenesses," by two "kinships," one with the perishable and one with the immutable. Just now we contrasted the Idea and the Body, in a naïve way, as two "worlds"; but the soul itself, which is between the two, is movement toward both—a movement by which it attempts to make itself immutable by means of geometry and dialectics, and a movement that consists in making itself perishable through the vertigo of desire.

That "something evil" which is the body is, then, less a thing than the direction of a vertigo, the counterpole of the likeness of the soul to the idea. The soul makes itself like the order of perishable things, instead of "seeking refuge" in the ideas.[11]

[11] The eschatological myth which separates the second and the third parts of the *Phaedo* itself bears the mark of this advance in reflection. The unjust soul, arrived in the underworld, bears the trace of its injustice, as blows that it has inflicted upon itself; it is by these traces in the naked soul that the judge recognizes the affinity of the soul for its body (τὸ σωματοειδές 81c). This affinity is represented in the myth by the wandering of the dead man, haunted by the desire for a new body appropriated to its

What is the principle of this counterlikeness?

The properly philosophical meaning of the myth of the body must be sought for in the direction of a meditation on "injustice."

That the dizziness of desire must be understood thus is already suggested by the *Cratylus*. There we find an allusion to an active-passive dizziness that escapes from a literal interpretation of the body-prison and already belongs to an interpretation of evil as a positive movement of the soul. Reflecting on the perversion of language, the *Cratylus* evokes the figure—still mythical—of a drunken legislator as the source of the aberrant meanings. If there is a language of becoming, if mobilism—itself a perversion of philosophy —finds words to express itself and finally to engender itself in expressing itself, that is because the initiators of that illusion "have themselves fallen into a sort of whirlpool where they are agitated and confused, and they have dragged us in after them" (439c).

This text is of great importance if one considers that Platonism is throughout a justification of language, laying the foundations of language first in the reality of meaning, then in the dialectical structure of meaning. If, then, man is essentially speech, the "passions" of speech are cardinal passions. Parmenides had already noted the bond connecting opinion, error, and confusion in naming. Now the "passions" of speech are not passive passions, so to speak. As political life shows, falsifications of language are active counterfeitings of true speech; they constitute a world of *para*—a paralogy—a world centered on the category of the *Pseudo;* they are "imitations" of discussion, of the restraint imposed by truth, and of the agreement of interlocutors in the same logos. We see how this theme of "falsehood" reacts on the theme of "desire," which seemed to throw the blame for evil on the body. Desire is evil only because it is no longer strictly corporeal; it must be seized by a frenzy of immoderation; and immoderation comes to desire only through "falsehood." The *tyrant* is the living proof of the madness that takes possession of desire. The tyrant, indeed, is for philosophy a magnitude that is more than political and is, properly speaking, metaphysical, because he is the symbol of the

---

care. The trace of the old body is like the *habitus* of the soul, its customary manner of being "chained and glued" (82c), "nailed" (83d) to its body.

man who has the power to satisfy all his desires; he is the myth of unlimited desire—unlimited because it is ministered to by a power that is itself not limited by law. Now the tyrant gives evidence that this body of desire undergoes a sort of mutation from the fact of the unjust soul which inhabits it, that desire is a creation of injustice and not vice versa.

"Injustice," then, and not the "body" as such, makes desire a disease of the soul.

We have now made the opposite journey of the one that led us from the Socratic idea of the unjust soul to the idea of an evil influence of the body, taken over from the myths of defilement. The dizziness that seemed to mount from the body toward the soul, in a first philosophical approximation that was still close to the language of myth, is really an evil of injustice, an evil of false discourse, which paralyzes the soul and delivers it up to the sorcery of its suffering. The body, then, is no longer the origin of evil, but only the "place" of the soul's captivity, while desire is "temptation," and injustice is the origin of the evil by which the soul makes itself like its body. Injustice begets the dizziness that disrupts the original community of the soul with truth, and produces the deceptive likeness of the soul to its body.

Is it possible to interpret the myth of the fall in the *Phaedrus* similarly? I think so. The opposition between the Biblical fall, construed as a deviation of the will, and the Platonic fall, construed as a fall into the body, should not be pushed too far. Otherwise, besides remaining a prisoner of the most literal interpretation of "body"—an interpretation encouraged, it is true, by those Platonic "revivals" which are closest to the myth,—one does not take account of the structure of the myth itself. We have had occasion to begin this exegesis in our phenomenology of fallibility and to note that the myth is a myth of "composition" before being a myth of a "fall." By the same token, evil is not exactly *outside,* in an alien and seductive body, but *inside,* in a discordance of self with self, the decisive philosophical interpretation of which belongs to the ethical order. The soul is composite and incarnate before the fall; that statement is so true that the proof of immortality in the *Phaedrus* rests on the hypothesis of a soul that moves itself in moving a body under its control. The combination of a "self-mover" and a "moved" is, then, prior to evil (245c–246a); it characterizes all the members of the great heavenly procession—gods, stars, and human souls: "How does it happen that mortal and immortal merit the name of living being? Let us try to explain this. Soul in all its species has charge of all that is soulless" (246b). Thus a god is "an immortal living being, possessing a soul and a body which are by nature united forever" (246d). As to the world-soul, that "perfect and ever-winged soul administers the whole cosmos" (246c). The *Timaeus* says the same thing (34c–36d): the whole of the corporeal is in the soul, not the soul in it (36d–e).

As the soul is from the beginning composite and corporeal, so it is from the beginning a mover: "As it goes around in the whole universe, it takes on different forms here and there" (246b). Thus, the business of administering the body and the world is a journey (μετεωροπορεῖ, 246b–c), and more precisely a desire to ascend, oriented in the opposite direction from heaviness, and to "lead upward that which is heavy" (246d). It is here, in the "composition" that precedes the fall, that the nascent disagreement between the rational and the emotional appears. This disagreement is not between the soul and the body, but is in the soul itself. Hence, it does not differ fundamentally from what we have called above the double likeness inscribed in the soul. That *double* likeness has only been enriched by a new trait that brings the "composition" of the soul in the *Phaedrus* closer to the *tripartite* division of the soul in the *Republic*, IV, where the frailty of the soul, its original ambivalence, is connected with an intermediate, "ambiguous" function, θυμός, which sums up in itself the double solicitaton of the soul. Thus the soul is originally a dramatic or polemic multiplicity, in which feeling does not play the role of a principle of evil, but rather of a principle of fallibility or temptation.

That is why the "fall" of the *Phaedrus* is not a fall into emotionality or into the body, but a fall into the "earthy." The "earthy" is in the opposite direction from the "heavenly"—that is to say, from the intelligible truth towards which Eros tends. The earthy is the contrary of philosophical Eros.

It can be said, however, that the human souls are the only ones

THE CYCLE OF THE MYTHS

in the procession which seem to be afflicted by a primordial grace-
lessness, while the gods have an "easy ascent" and the movement
of their contemplation is naturally perfect, the mixture in the
human souls prior to their fall is already a discordant union; the
soul is already distended between the heaviness of its Team and
the gracefulness of its Wings.

Thus the fall seems to be, by turns, a consequence of this primordial discord or a new cropping-up of the evil of injustice. As
in Kierkegaard's *Concept of Dread,* the "passage" from "composition" to "fall"—I would say: from fallibility to fault—is by turns,
or even at the same time, a subsequent misfortune or an unforeseeable "leap." But the Biblical myth of the fall also combined
the continuous progression from temptation to fault *and* the dis-
continuous outburst of the act itself. If the fall were only the
inevitable effect of a graceless constitution, evil would be entirely
reducible to the original indigence which, according to the *Sym-
posium,* attended the birth of Eros; it would be the Other of the
Word which the last dialogues evoke. Neo-Platonism understood
it thus, without, however, being able to eliminate the inner defection of the soul, which surrenders itself to that Other. But then
"conversion" would be incomprehensible, if it did not come from
the same source as corruption, as Kant rightly saw.

Everything leads to the conclusion that the philosophical point
of the myth is the suggestion that the "earthy" signifies the captivity imposed on the soul by itself, the "world" in St. John's sense,
the "flesh" (and the "body") in St. Paul's sense. In short, it is
"injustice" which predominates in the philosophical exegesis of the
earthy, just as it is the earthy "body" that mythically symbolizes
injustice.

The *Republic* resolves the ambiguity in favor of the philosophical
exegesis. The idea that injustice is the peculiar evil of the soul is
like the *basso continuo* of that collection of dialogues (I, 352c–
354a; IV, 434c–445b). Now, the evil of injustice is properly the
passage from original discord to civil war, while, inversely, justice
consists in "becoming one from many" (443e). Evil, then, is the
consecration of multiplicity in ourselves. Book X draws the most
radical consequences therefrom: this evil does not destroy the soul,

as corruption destroys the body, but, so to speak, consecrates and eternalizes its unhappiness; only the soul is an exception to the rule that evil destroys the thing of which it is the corruption (609a); the soul is that being which is not made to die by its evil. This evil, then, cannot be foreign to the soul, but must be its own; no longer the body, but injustice.

We have developed to considerable length the Platonic transposition of the Orphic myth.[12] For the reader instructed by the prophets of Israel and the Christian Kerygma, it represents an inflection of the symbolism of the "evil body" in the direction of the theme of "evil choice," and at the same time it helps to make intelligible the contamination by each other of the two mythical cycles, that which gravitates around the primordial "Anthropos" and that which begins with the mythology of the "body-prison." If we admit that, in St. Paul and St. John, the "flesh" is more than the physical body and the "world" more than the universe of things, it is fair to read Plato with the same understanding for the symbolism and the same irony. Consequently, the difference between the "flesh" according to St. Paul and the "body" according to Plato tends to vanish. We do not say, however, that there is no difference; for just as St. Paul is preserved from the gnosis of the evil body by his Adamic mythology, Plato is separated from the Biblical conception of evil by his attachment to the Greek concepton of Desire. τὸ λογιστικόν and τὸ ἐπιθυμητικόν constitute the fundamental polarity of existence according to Book IV of the *Republic;* the Rational and the Desirous form a pair of contraries in which the second term tends to take up into itself everything that blocks and resists thought. That is why the "concupiscible" in Plato cannot coincide exactly with the "flesh" according

[12] We have not carried this transposition beyond right opinion to the dialectical level, in order not to step out of the framework of hermeneutics that limits our present investigation. In Book III we shall return to the Platonic "metaphysics" and to the speculative ciphers it proposes: "necessity," "errant cause," the "inferior gods," the "other soul," the "unlimited," the "other," the "metempirical choice," etc. We shall see that that metaphysics erects symbols of a higher degree upon the phenomenology of desire and injustice which has found its expression in a resumption of the Orphic myth.

to St. Paul, for the latter includes, besides the passions in the Greek sense, morality and wisdom when they become "self-righteousness." The Socratics—the Cynics and the Cyrenaics, among others—inoculated Greek thought with a suspicious attitude toward pleasure which is altogether foreign to the morality of the Prophets; the latter is more sensible of pride than of concupiscence.

Hence the contribution of Aristotle, who restated the problem of pleasure and directed ethical reflection on pleasure toward the activity of which pleasure is only the bloom or the premium, is so much the more valuable; we shall come back to it. But Stoicism, in spite of Epicurus, led ethical reflection back into the old groove of the Cynics. Thus there is a line of force in Greek thought which goes from the Socratics through Plato to the Stoics, according to which evil is the passivity of desire, rather than active evil will. That is why this type of thought has a natural affinity to the Orphic myth, rather than to the Adamic myth. Through the Orphic myth, it prolongs the symbolism of defilement and the tradition of mystico-ritual purifications, rather than the Biblical symbolism of sin. The whole series of treatises on the "passions of the soul" is contained in germ in this old pact between Greek philosophy of the Platonizing type and the myth of the soul exiled in the prison of an evil body.

*

* *

Is this attempt to view all the myths in the perspective of a dominant myth entirely satisfactory? We do not pretend that it is. If it were, that would mean that the hermeneutics of myths can take the place of systematic philosophy, which is not the case. The universe of the myths remains a broken universe; not being able to unify the mythical universe on the basis of one of these myths alone, imaginative and sympathetic understanding, without personal appropriation, often remains as the thinker's only resource. Besides, alternatives which cannot be settled by a simple passage from the statics to the dynamics of the myths subsist at the flection of each of the pairs that we have constructed in order to get the dynamics going.

The failure of our undertaking challenges us to pose the more radical problem of the method of a philosophy which would learn from the symbols and yet be fully rational.

One thing that we have acquired, at the end of our exercise in hermeneutics, is a conviction that the three myths of chaos, of divine blinding, and of exile, reveal the hyper-ethical dimension of the myth of the fall and so indicate the limitations of any "philosophy of the will" which tries to remain an ethical vision of the world. The myth of the fall needs those other myths, so that the ethical God it presupposes may continue to be a *Deus Absconditus* and so that the guilty man it denounces may also appear as the victim of a mystery of iniquity which makes him deserving of Pity as well as of Wrath.

Conclusion: The Symbol
Gives Rise to Thought

AT THE END of our double approach—through the abstract description of *fallibility* and through the "re-enactment" of the religious consciousness of *fault*—the question arises: How shall we continue?

The hiatus between pure *reflection* on "fallibility" and the *confession* of "sins" is patent. Pure reflection makes no appeal to any myth or symbol; in this sense it is a direct exercise of rationality. But comprehension of evil is a sealed book for it; the reflection is pure, but it leaves everyday reality outside, insofar as man's everyday reality is "enslavement to the passions." On the other hand, the enigma of servile freedom is avowed by the religious consciousness, but at the price of a methodological rupture in the continuity of reflection. Not only does the confession of sins appeal to a different quality of experience, but it has recourse to a different language, which we have shown to be symbolic through and through. Is it possible, after this rupture, to come back to pure reflection and to enrich it with all that we have gained from the symbolic knowledge of evil?

The question is difficult, for we are required to advance between two hazards. On the one hand, it is not possible simply to *juxtapose* reflection and confession; it is not possible to interrupt philosophical discourse, as Plato does, by fanciful stories, and to say: here discourse ends, there myth begins. Lachelier is right: philosophy

347

must comprehend everything, even religion. Philosophy, in fact, cannot stop along the way; it has sworn at the start to be consistent; it must keep its promise right to the end. But neither is it possible to have a direct philosophical transcription of the religious symbolism of evil, for that would involve going back to an allegorizing interpretation of the symbols and the myths. We have already insisted that the symbol does not conceal any hidden teaching that only needs to be unmasked for the images in which it is clothed to become useless. Between these two impasses, we are going to explore a third way—a creative interpretation of meaning, faithful to the impulsion, to the gift of meaning from the symbol, and faithful also to the philosopher's oath to seek understanding. This is the road, requiring patience and rigor on our part, which is indicated by the aphorism inscribed at the head of this conclusion: "The symbol gives rise to thought."

That sentence, which enchants me, says two things: the symbol gives; but what it gives is occasion for thought, something to think about.

The symbol gives: a philosophy instructed by myths arises at a certain moment in reflection, and, beyond philosophical reflection, it wishes to answer to a certain situation of modern culture.

Recourse to the archaic, the nocturnal, the oneiric, which is also, as Bachelard says in his *Poétique de l'Espace,* a way of approaching the birthplace of language, represents an attempt to escape the difficulties of a radical beginning in philosophy. The beginning is not what one finds first; the point of departure must be reached, it must be won. Understanding of symbols can play a part in the movement towards the point of departure; for, if the beginning is to be reached, it is first necessary for thought to inhabit the fullness of language. We know the harassing backward flight of thought in search of the first truth and, more radically still, in search of a point of departure that might well not be a first truth. The illusion is not in looking for a point of departure, but in looking for it without presuppositions. There is no philosophy without presuppositions. A meditation on symbols starts from speech that has already taken place, and in which everything has already been said in some fashion; it wishes to be thought with its presuppositions. For it, the first task is not to begin but, from the midst of speech, to remember; to remember with a view to beginning.

Moreover, this task has a precise meaning *now,* at a certain stage in philosophical discussion, and, more broadly, in connection with certain traits of our "modernity." The historical moment of the philosophy of symbols is that of forgetfulness and restoration. Forgetfulness of hierophanies, forgetfulness of the signs of the sacred, loss of man himself insofar as he belongs to the sacred. The forgetfulness, we know, is the counterpart of the great task of nourishing men, of satisfying their needs by mastering nature through a planetary technique. It is in the age when our language has become more precise, more univocal, more technical in a word, more suited to those integral formalizations which are called precisely symbolic logic, it is in this very age of discourse that we want to recharge our language, that we want to start again from the fullness of language.

That also is a gift of our "modernity," for we moderns are the heirs of philology, of exegesis, of the phenomenology of religion, of the psychoanalysis of language. The same epoch holds in reserve both the possibility of emptying language by radically formalizing it and the possibility of filling it anew by reminding itself of the fullest meanings, the most pregnant ones, the ones which are most bound by the presence of the sacred to man.

It is not regret for the sunken Atlantides that animates us, but hope for a re-creation of language. Beyond the desert of criticism, we wish to be called again.

But what the symbol gives rise to is thinking. After the gift, positing. The aphorism suggests at the same time that everything has already been said enigmatically and yet that it is always necessary to begin everything and to begin it again in the dimension of thinking. It is this articulation of thought given to itself in the realm of symbols and of thought positing and thinking that constitutes the critical point of our whole enterprise.

How can we make the symbol the starting-point of our thinking, if it is not an allegory? How shall we disengage from the symbol an "other," if it is, as Schelling says, *tauté*-gorical? What we need is an interpretation that respects the original enigma of the symbols, that lets itself be taught by them, but that, beginning from there, promotes the meaning, forms the meaning in the full responsibility of autonomous thought.

Such is the problem: how can thought be bound and free at the same time? How can the immediacy of the symbol and the mediation of thought be held together?

The enterprise would be a hopeless one if symbols were radically alien to philosophical discourse. But symbols are already in the element of speech. We have said sufficiently that they rescue feeling and even fear from silence and confusion; they provide a language for avowal, for confession; in virtue of them, man remains language through and through. That is not the most important thing: there exists nowhere a symbolic language without hermeneutics; wherever a man dreams or raves, another man arises to give an interpretation; what was already discourse, even if incoherent, is brought into coherent discourse by hermeneutics. In this respect, the hermeneutics of modern men is continuous with the spontaneous interpretations that have never been lacking to symbols. On the other hand, what is peculiar to the modern hermeneutics is that it remains in the line of critical thought. But its critical function does not turn it away from its appropriative function; I should say, rather, that it makes it more authentic and more perfect. The dissolution of the myth as explanation is the necessary way to the restoration of the myth as symbol. Thus, the time of restoration is not a different time from that of criticism; we are in every way children of criticism, and we seek to go beyond criticism by means of criticism, by a criticism that is no longer reductive but restorative. That is the purpose which animated Schelling, Schleiermacher, Dilthey, and today, in various ways, Leenhardt, van der Leeuw, Éliade, Jung, Bultmann. Today we have a more acute awareness of the immensity of the wager of this hermeneutics. On the one hand, it represents the advanced point of criticism, as an awareness of the myth as myth. By that awareness it hastens the movement of demythologization, which is only the counterpart of an ever more rigorous decision about what is history according to the historical method; demythologization is the irreversible gain of truthfulness, intellectual honesty, objectivity. On the other hand, modern hermeneutics entertains the project of a revivification of philosophy through contact with the fundamental symbols of consciousness.

Does that mean that we could go back to a primitive naïveté? Not at all. In every way, something has been lost, irremediably lost: immediacy of belief. But if we can no longer live the great symbolisms of the sacred in accordance with the original belief in them, we can, we modern men, aim at a second naïveté in and through criticism. In short, it is by *interpreting* that we can *hear* again. Thus it is in hermeneutics that the symbol's gift of meaning and the endeavor to understand by deciphering are knotted together.

How does hermeneutics meet the problem?

What we have just called a knot—the knot where the symbol gives and criticism interprets—appears in hermeneutics as a circle. The circle can be stated bluntly: "We must understand in order to believe, but we must believe in order to understand." The circle is not a vicious circle, still less a mortal one; it is a living and stimulating circle. We must believe in order to understand: never, in fact, does the interpreter get near to what his text says unless he lives in the *aura* of the meaning he is inquiring after. As Bultmann very well says in his famous article on "the problem of hermeneutics" in *Glauben und Verstehen:* "All understanding, like all interpretation, is . . . continually oriented by the manner of posing the question and by what it aims at [by its *Woraufhin*]. Consequently, it is never without presuppositions; that is to say, it is always directed by a prior understanding of the thing about which it interrogates the text. It is only on the basis of that prior understanding that it can, in general, interrogate and interpret." And again: "The presupposition of all understanding is the vital relation of the interpreter to the thing about which the text speaks directly or indirectly." In insisting on this coincidence with the *Woraufhin,* with the thing about which the text speaks, Bultmann warns against a confusion which would consist in identifying this participation in the meaning with some psychological coincidence between the interpreter and the "particular expressions of life," according to Dilthey's expression. It is not a kinship of one life with another that hermeneutics requires, but a kinship of thought with what the life aims at—in short, of thought with the thing which is in question. It is in this sense that we must believe in order to understand. And yet, it is only by understanding that we can believe.

For the second immediacy that we seek and the second naïveté that we await are no longer accessible to us anywhere else than in a hermeneutics; we can believe only by interpreting. It is the "modern" mode of belief in symbols, an expression of the distress of modernity and a remedy for that distress.

Such is the circle: hermeneutics proceeds from a prior understanding of the very thing that it tries to understand by interpreting it. But thanks to that circle in hermeneutics, I can still today communicate with the sacred by making explicit the prior understanding that gives life to the interpretation. Thus hermeneutics, an acquisition of "modernity," is one of the modes by which that "modernity" transcends itself, insofar as it is forgetfulness of the sacred. I believe that being can still speak to me—no longer, of course, under the precritical form of immediate belief, but as the second immediacy aimed at by hermeneutics. This second naïveté aims to be the postcritical equivalent of the precritical hierophany.

The conjunction of belief and criticism furnishes, as a consequence, the second interpretation of the sentence we are meditating on: "The symbol gives rise to thought." And this conjunction is a circular relation between a believing and an understanding. We see, then, with what prudence one can speak of "demythologization"; it is legitimate to speak of "demythologizing" if demythologizing is distinguished carefully from "demythicizing." All criticism "demythologizes" insofar as it is criticism; that is to say, it always adds to the separation of the historical (according to the rules of the critical method) and the pseudo-historical. What criticism continually endeavors to exorcize is the *logos* of the *mythos* (for example, the representation of the universe as a series of places, one above the other, with the earth in the middle, the heavens above, and hell below). As an advance post of "modernity," criticism cannot help being a "demythologization"; that is an irreversible gain of truthfulness, of intellectual honesty, and therefore of objectivity.

But it is precisely because it accelerates the movement of "de-mythologization" that modern hermeneutics brings to light the dimension of the symbol, as a primordial sign of the sacred; it is thus that it participates in the revivification of philosophy through contact with symbols; it is one of the ways of rejuvenating philosophy. This paradox, in accordance with which "demythologization" is also a recharging of thought with the aid of symbols, is only a corollary of what we have called the circle of believing and understanding in hermeneutics.

These reflections on the "circle" in hermeneutics put us on the road to a *philosophical* hermeneutics, but they do not take its place. The awareness of that "circle" is only a necessary stage by which we pass from a simple "re-enactment" without belief to autonomous "thought."

There is, indeed, a way of understanding symbols which, in a sense, remains within the symbolic mode. This is the case of all purely comparative phenomenology that limits itself to understanding symbols through symbols. Such an understanding, within the symbols, is necessary for the purpose of breaking with explicative and reductive thinking, and indeed it is sufficient for a descriptive phenomenology, for it is already a way of understanding, insofar as it examines, retains, connects; for it, there is a "world" of symbols. To understand, for it, is to display the multiple and inexhaustible intentions of each symbol, to discover intentional analogies between myths and rites, to run through the levels of experience and representation that are unified by the symbol.

This mode of understanding, of which Éliade's works provide very good examples, tends to place the symbols in a whole which is homogeneous with the symbols, but vaster, and which forms a system on the plane of the symbols themselves. Our analysis of the symbols and myths of human evil belongs to that sort of understanding, insofar as it is a life of thought devoted to its symbols.

But it has not been possible to limit ourselves to such understanding *of* symbols in symbols. There the question of truth is unceasingly eluded. Although the phenomenologist may give the name of truth to the internal coherence, the systematicity, of the world of symbols, such truth is truth without belief, truth at a distance, reduced, from which one has expelled the question: do *I* believe that? what do *I* make of these symbolic meanings, these hierophanies? That question cannot be raised as long as one remains at the level of comparativism, running from one symbol to another, without oneself being anywhere. That level can only be an intermediate stage, the stage of understanding in extension, panoramic understanding, curious but not concerned. It has been necessary to enter into a passionate, though critical, relation with the truth-value of each symbol.

Thus, the transition to philosophical hermeneutics was begun when we passed from the statics to the dynamics of the mythical symbols. The world of symbols is not a tranquil and reconciled world; every symbol is iconoclastic in comparison with some other symbol, just as every symbol, left to itself, tends to thicken, to become solidified in an idolatry. It is necessary, then, to participate in the struggle, in the dynamics, in which the symbolism itself becomes a prey to a spontaneous hermeneutics that seeks to transcend it. It is only by participating in this dynamics that comprehension can reach the strictly critical dimension of exegesis and become a hermeneutic; but then one must abandon the position—or rather, the exile—of the remote and disinterested spectator, in order to appropriate in each case a particular symbolism.

Well, then, we have left the plane of truth without belief and come to the circle of hermeneutics, to the believing for the sake of understanding which is also understanding for the sake of believing. I entered that circle as soon as I admitted that I read the ensemble of the myths from a certain point of view, that the mythical space was for me an oriented space, and that my perspective angle was the pre-eminence of the Jewish confession of sins, its symbolism, and its mythology. By that adoption of one myth, the appropriation of all of them became possible, at least up to a certain point.

But that appropriation, in revealing its circular character, requires in its turn to be transcended. The exegete, as exegete, can live indefinitely within the circle, as the comparativist can practice endlessly the *epoché* of truth and live in neutralized belief. But the philosopher, who elsewhere practices rigorous consistency in reflection, cannot stop at this stage; awareness of the hermeneutic circle has torn him away from the conveniences of neutralized belief. But this is to instigate him to think with the symbols as a *starting-point,* and no longer *in* the symbols.

How shall we get beyond the "circle of hermeneutics"? By transforming it into a *wager.*

I wager that I shall have a better understanding of man and of the bond between the being of man and the being of all beings if I follow the *indication* of symbolic thought. That wager then becomes the task of *verifying* my wager and saturating it, so to speak, with intelligibility. In return, the task transforms my wager: in betting *on* the significance of the symbolic world, I bet at the same time *that* my wager will be restored to me in power of reflection, in the element of coherent discourse.

Then there opens before me the field of philosophical hermeneutics properly so called: no longer an allegorizing interpretation that pretends to find a disguised philosophy under the imaginative garments of the myth, but a philosophy that starts from the symbols and endeavors to promote the meaning, to form it, by a creative interpretation. I shall venture to call that endeavor, at least provisionally, a "transcendental deduction" of symbols. Transcendental deduction, in the Kantian sense, consists in justifying a concept by showing that it makes possible the construction of a domain of objectivity. Now, if I use the symbols of deviation, wandering, and captivity as a detector of reality, if I decipher man on the basis of the mythical symbols of chaos, mixture, and fall, in short, if I elaborate an empirics of the servile will under the guidance of a mythology of evil existence, then I can say that in return I have "deduced"—in the transcendental meaning of the word—the symbolism of human evil. In fact, the symbol, used as a means of detecting and deciphering human reality, will have been verified by its power to raise up, to illuminate, to give order to that region of human experience, that region of confession, which we were too ready to reduce to error, habit, emotion, passivity—in short, to one or another of the dimensions of finitude that have no need of the symbols of evil to open them up and discover them. But the expression, "transcendental deduction of symbols," is not absolutely satisfactory; it orients us toward the idea that the justification of the symbol by its power to reveal constitutes a simple augmentation of *self-awareness,* a simple extension of reflexive circumscription, whereas a philosophy instructed by the symbols has for its task a qualitative transformation of reflexive consciousness. Every symbol is finally a hierophany, a manifestation of the bond between man and the sacred. Now in treating the symbol as a simple revealer of self-awareness, we cut it off from its ontological function; we pretend to believe that "know thyself" is purely reflexive, whereas it is first of all an appeal by which each man is invited to situate himself better in being—in Greek terms, to "be wise." As the *Charmides* of Plato says: "The God [at Delphi], by way of salutation, says to them, in reality: *Be wise;* but, as a soothsayer, he says it in enigmatic form. *Be wise* and *Know thyself* are fundamentally the same thing, as appears from the text and as I maintain. But one may be deceived about it; and that is what happened to the authors of the following inscriptions: *Nothing too much* and *To stand surety for someone invites misfortune.* Regarding *Know thyself* as advice and not as a salutation of the god, they wished to contribute their share of good advice and so they made those dedicatory inscriptions" (165*a*).

Finally, then, it is as an index of the situation of man at the heart of the being in which he moves, exists, and wills, that the symbol speaks to us. Consequently, the task of the philosopher guided by symbols would be to break out of the enchanted enclosure of consciousness of oneself, to end the prerogative of self-reflection. The symbol gives reason to think that the *Cogito* is within being, and not vice versa. Thus the second naïveté would be a second Copernican revolution: the being which posits itself in the *Cogito* has still to discover that the very act by which it abstracts itself from the whole does not cease to share in the being that challenges it in every symbol. All the symbols of guilt—deviation, wandering, captivity,—all the myths—chaos, blinding, mixture, fall,—speak of the situation of the being of man in the being of the world. The task, then, is, starting from the symbols, to elaborate existential concepts—that is to say, not only structures of reflection but structures of existence, insofar as existence is the being of man. Then the problem will arise, how the quasi-being and the quasi-nothingness of human evil are articulated upon the being of man and upon the nothingness of his finitude.

If, then, we call the elaboration of an empirics of the servile will a transcendental deduction, the transcendental deduction itself must be inscribed in an ontology of finitude and evil that elevates the symbols to the rank of existential concepts.

Such is the *wager*. Only he can object to this mode of thought who thinks that philosophy, to begin from itself, must be a philosophy without presuppositions. A philosohy that starts from the fullness of language is a philosophy with presuppositions. To be honest, it must make its presuppositions explicit, state them as beliefs, wager on the beliefs, and try to make the wager pay off in understanding.

Such a wager is the contrary of an apologetics that pretends to lead reflection, without a break, from knowledge toward belief. A philosophy that begins with symbols proceeds in the opposite direction, in accordance with an essentially Anselmian schema. It finds man already settled, with a preliminary title, within its foundation. His being there may appear contingent and restricted. Why symbols? Why these symbols? But, beginning from this contingency and restrictedness of a culture that has hit upon these symbols rather than others, philosophy endeavors, through reflection and speculation, to disclose the rationality of its foundation.

Only a philosophy first nourished on the fullness of language can subsequently be indifferent to the modes of approach to its problems and to the conditions of its activity, and remain constantly concerned with thematizing the universal and rational structure of its adherence.

Epilogue:
Religious
Perspectives

Its Meaning and Purpose

THIS IS A REPRINT of Volume XVII of the RELIGIOUS PERSPECTIVES SERIES, which the present writer has planned and edited in collaboration with a Board of Editors consisting of W. H. AUDEN, KARL BARTH, MARTIN C. D'ARCY, CHRISTOPHER DAWSON, C. H. DODD, MIRCEA ELIADE, MUHAMMAD ZAFRULLA KHAN, ALEXANDRE KOYRÉ, JACQUES MARITAIN, JAMES MUILENBURG, SARVEPALLI RADHAKRISHNAN, GERSHOM SCHOLEM, D. T. SUZUKI, PAUL TILLICH.

RELIGIOUS PERSPECTIVES represents a quest for the rediscovery of man. It constitutes an effort to define man's search for the essence of being in order that he may have a knowledge of goals. It is an endeavor to show that there is no possibility of achieving an understanding of man's total nature on the basis of phenomena known by the analytical method alone. It hopes to point to the false antinomy between revelation and reason, faith and knowledge, grace and nature, courage and anxiety. Mathematics, physics, philosophy, biology and religion, in spite of their almost complete independence, have begun to sense their interrelatedness and to become aware of that mode of cognition which teaches that "the light is not without but within me, and I myself am the light."

Modern man is threatened by a world created by himself. He is faced with the conversion of mind to naturalism, a dogmatic secularism and an opposition to a belief in the transcendent. He begins to see, however, that the universe is given not as one existing and one perceived but as the unity of subject and object; that the barrier between them cannot be said to have been dissolved as the result of recent experience in the physical sciences, since this barrier has never existed. Confronted with the question of meaning, he is summoned to rediscover and scrutinize the immutable and the permanent which constitute the dynamic, unifying aspect of life as well as the principle of differentiation; to reconcile identity and diversity, immutability and unrest. He begins to recognize that just as every person descends by his particular path, so he is able to ascend, and this ascent aims at a return to the source of creation, an inward home from which he has become estranged.

It is the hope of RELIGIOUS PERSPECTIVES that the rediscovery of man will point the way to the rediscovery of God. To this end a rediscovery of first principles should constitute part of the quest. These principles, not to be superseded by new discoveries, are not those of historical worlds that come to be and perish. They are to be sought in the heart and spirit of man, and no interpretation of a merely historical or scientific universe can guide the search. RELIGIOUS PERSPECTIVES attempts not only to ask dispassionately what the nature of God is, but also to restore to human life at least the hypothesis of God and the symbols that relate to him. It endeavors to show that man is faced with the metaphysical question of the truth of religion while he encounters the empirical question of its effects on the life of humanity and its meaning for society. Religion is here distinguished from theology and its doctrinal forms and is intended to denote the feelings, aspirations and acts of men, as they relate to total reality.

RELIGIOUS PERSPECTIVES is nourished by the spiritual and intellectual energy of world thought, by those religious and ethical leaders who are not merely spectators but scholars deeply involved in the critical problems common to all religions. These thinkers recognize that human morality and human ideals thrive only when set in a context of a transcendent attitude toward religion and that by pointing to the ground of identity and the common nature of being in the religious experience of man, the essential nature of religion may be defined. Thus, they are committed to re-evaluate the meaning of everlastingness, an experience which has been lost and which is the content of that *visio Dei* constituting the structure of all religions. It is the many absorbed everlastingly into the ultimate unity, a unity subsuming what Whitehead calls the fluency of God and the everlastingness of passing experience.

These volumes will seek to show that the unity of which we speak consists in a certitude emanating from the nature of man who seeks God and the nature of God who seeks man. Such certitude bathes in an intuitive act of cognition, participating in the divine essence and is related to the natural spirituality of intelligence. This is not by any means to say that there is an equivalence of all faiths in the traditional religions of human history. It is, however, to emphasize the distinction between the spiritual and the temporal which all religions acknowledge. For duration of thought is composed of instants superior to time, and is an intuition of the permanence of existence and its metahistorical reality.

RELIGIOUS PERSPECTIVES is therefore an effort to explore the *meaning* of God, an exploration which constitutes an aspect of man's intrinsic nature, part of his ontological substance. The Series grows out of an abiding concern that in spite of the release of man's creative energy which science has in part accomplished, this very science has overturned the essential order of nature. Shrewd as man's calculations have become concerning his means, his choice of ends which was formerly correlated with belief in God, with absolute criteria of conduct, has become witless. God is not to be treated as an exception to metaphysical principles, invoked to prevent their collapse. He is rather their chief exemplification, the source of all potentiality. The personal reality of freedom and providence, of will and conscience, may demonstrate that "he who knows" commands a depth of consciousness inaccessible to the profane man, and is capable of that transfiguration which prevents the twisting of all good to ignominy. This religious content of experience is not within the province of science to bestow; it corrects the error of treating the scientific account as if it were itself metaphysical or religious; it challenges the tendency to make a religion of science—or a science of religion—a dogmatic act which destroys the moral dynamic of man. Indeed, many men of science are confronted with unexpected implications of their own thought and are beginning to accept, for instance, the trans-spatial nature of events within spatial matter.

RELIGIOUS PERSPECTIVES attempts to show the fallacy of the apparent irrelevance of God in history. The Series submits that no convincing image of man can arise, in spite of the many ways in which human thought has tried to reach it, without a philosophy of human nature and human freedom which does not exclude God. This image of *Homo cum Deo* implies the highest conceivable freedom, the freedom to step into the very fabric of the universe, a new formula for man's collaboration with the creative process and the only one which is able to protect man from the terror of existence. This image implies further that the mind and conscience are capable of making genuine discriminations and thereby may reconcile the serious tensions between the secular and religious, the profane and sacred. The idea of the sacred lies in what it *is*, timeless existence. By emphasizing timeless existence against reason as a reality, we are liberated, in our communion with the eternal, from the otherwise unbreakable rule of "before and after." Then we are able to admit that all forms, all symbols in religions, by their negation of error and their affirmation of the actuality of truth, make it possible to experience that *knowing* which is above knowledge, and that dynamic passage of the universe to unending unity.

The volumes in this Series will seek to challenge the crisis which separates, to make reasonable a religion that binds and to present the numinous reality within the experience of man. Insofar as the Series succeeds in this quest, it will direct mankind toward a reality that is eternal and away from a preoccupation with that which is illusory and ephemeral.

For man is now confronted with his burden and his greatness: "He calleth to me, Watchman, what of the night? Watchman, what of the night?"[1] Perhaps the anguish in the human soul may be assuaged by the answer, by the *assimilation* of the person in God: "The morning cometh, and also the night: if ye will inquire, inquire ye: return, come."[2]

RUTH NANDA ANSHEN

New York, 1960

[1] Isaiah 21 : 11.
[2] *Ibid.*, 21 : 12.

FLOR

INVEN